# Thresholds, Encounters

# SUNY SERIES
## LITERATURE...IN THEORY

SERIES EDITORS

David E. Johnson, *Comparative Literature, University at Buffalo*
Scott Michaelsen, *English, Michigan State University*

SERIES ADVISORY BOARD

Nahum Dimitri Chandler, *African American Studies, University of California, Irvine*
Rebecca Comay, *Philosophy and Comparative Literature, University of Toronto*
Marc Crépon, *Philosophy, École Normale Supérieure, Paris*
Jonathan Culler, *Comparative Literature, Cornell University*
Johanna Drucker, *Design Media Arts and Information Studies, University of California, Los Angeles*
Christopher Fynsk, *Modern Thought, Aberdeen University*
Rodolphe Gasché, *Comparative Literature, University at Buffalo*
Martin Hägglund, *Comparative Literature, Yale University*
Carol Jacobs, *German and Comparative Literature, Yale University*
Peggy Kamuf, *French and Comparative Literature, University of Southern California*
David Marriott, *History of Consciousness, University of California, Santa Cruz*
Steven Miller, *English, University at Buffalo*
Alberto Moreiras, *Hispanic Studies, Texas A&M University*
Patrick O'Donnell, *English, Michigan State University*
Pablo Oyarzun, *Teoría del Arte, Universidad de Chile*
Scott Cutler Shershow, *English, University of California, Davis*
Henry Sussman, *German and Comparative Literature, Yale University*
Samuel Weber, *Comparative Literature, Northwestern University*
Ewa Ziarek, *Comparative Literature, University at Buffalo*

# Thresholds, Encounters

Paul Celan and the Claim of Philology

Edited by
Kristina Mendicino
and
Dominik Zechner

Published by State University of New York Press, Albany

© 2023 State University of New York

All rights reserved

Printed in the United States of America

No part of this book may be used or reproduced in any manner whatsoever without written permission. No part of this book may be stored in a retrieval system or transmitted in any form or by any means including electronic, electrostatic, magnetic tape, mechanical, photocopying, recording, or otherwise without the prior permission in writing of the publisher.

For information, contact State University of New York Press, Albany, NY
www.sunypress.edu

### Library of Congress Cataloging-in-Publication Data

Names: Mendicino, Kristina, editor. | Zechner, Dominik, editor.
Title: Thresholds, encounters : Paul Celan and the claim of philology / Edited by Kristina Mendicino and Dominik Zechner.
Description: Albany : State University of New York Press, [2023] | Series: SUNY series Literature . . . in Theory | Includes bibliographical references and index.
Identifiers: ISBN 9781438494418 (hardcover : alk. paper) | ISBN 9781438494395 (ebook) | ISBN 9781438494401 (pbk. : alk. paper)
Further information is available at the Library of Congress.

10 9 8 7 6 5 4 3 2 1

# Contents

Acknowledgments     ix

Dis-positions: Introduction     1
    *Kristina Mendicino and Dominik Zechner*

## Part 1: Ex-posing the Poem

### History

Chapter 1
"In the Swell of Wandering Words": Celan's "Sprich auch du"     15
    *Michael G. Levine*

Chapter 2
A Different *Withness*: Bearing with the Past in Paul Celan's
"Engführung"     35
    *Simone Stirner*

### Ecology

Chapter 3
Flower Talk     61
    *Jan Mieszkowski*

Chapter 4
Poetic Involution: Adorno, Celan, Nature     83
    *Natalie Lozinski-Veach*

## Aurality

Chapter 5
Allophony: Celan's *Niemandsrosen-Lieder* — 109
   Michael Auer

Chapter 6
"A Chest Full of Cello Boughs": The Sonorous Force of Writing in Deconstructive Readings of Celan — 127
   Naomi Waltham-Smith

## Part 2: Language Dislodged

### Encounters

Chapter 7
*A limine* — 153
   Kristina Mendicino

Chapter 8
With—Paul Celan — 175
   Pasqual Solass

### Positions

Chapter 9
Occupiability — 199
   Sarah Stoll, trans. Aida Feng

Chapter 10
For Shame of Language — 231
   Dominik Zechner

### Translations

Chapter 11
Poetic Approach: Celan's Radio Essay "Die Dichtung Ossip Mandelstamms" — 259
   Irina Kogan

Chapter 12
The Mimetic Desire of Translation: Reading Celan and Derrida
with Girard 287
*Christine Frank*

List of Contributors 307

Index 309

# Acknowledgments

Thinking with and through Paul Celan presupposes the sense that whatever we are able to say is necessarily mediated and carried by others with whom we are in conversation and whose discourse grants us hospitality. That it's the language of the other that carries us—and carries us through—is something we have learned anew in the course of working on this volume whose realization is based on so many conversations and encounters—with friends and colleagues at our home institutions and beyond. In this respect, a published book is never to be understood as an end point but rather a testimony to a shared speech that is ongoing. We are grateful to the Department of German Studies at Brown University and the Department of German, Russian, and East European Languages and Literatures at Rutgers University for supporting our research as well as the Humanities Center at New York University for hosting a roundtable whose critical insights proved essential for the argumentative thrust of this volume. We would like to thank Farrar, Straus, and Giroux, Penguin Random House, Suhrkamp Verlag, and S. Fischer Verlag for generously granting us permission to reprint some of Celan's poems in full. Finally, we would like to acknowledge a philological debt—namely to the works and teachings of Werner Hamacher and Rainer Nägele, which continue to guide our writing and thinking as our inexhaustible antecedents.

# Dis-positions

## Introduction

KRISTINA MENDICINO AND DOMINIK ZECHNER

Paul Celan's works emerged as zones of intersection between the extremes of poetic expression and philosophical reflection. In this way, they dwell in the space of a threshold that harbors the possibility for speaking otherwise than in a manner that could pretend to occupy a position within presupposed "genres" or "fields." Not only have philosophers and theorists from Theodor W. Adorno via Peter Szondi to Philippe Lacoue-Labarthe engaged Celan's poems in profound and meaningful ways, drawing conceptual insight from the literary encounter—Celan's poems themselves mark critical turns in traditional philosophical aspirations, as recently shown by Werner Hamacher, who tracked the conceptual traces and import of Parmenides, Benjamin, and Heidegger within Celan's oeuvre.[1] The divergent poetic, philosophical, and critical idioms that have marked Celan's writing—and that Celan's writing has come to mark—thus solicit a philology that cannot be situated according to clearly demarcated areas of inquiry but instead explore the various ways in which the ambitions of poetic and philosophical writing meet in texts of and on Celan—pacing out his works as a borderland where the threshold between the literary and the philosophical is encountered, negotiated, unsettled, and *dis*-posed otherwise. This premise underpins and sustains the chapters gathered in *Thresholds, Encounters: Paul Celan and the Claim of Philology*, which all probe the consequences of Celan's poetry for thinking and writing, while inviting readers from diverse disciplinary directions to further the approaches that are traced through the liminal zones that Celan's oeuvre opens.

~

In articulating what is at stake in the polyvocal language of Paul Celan, as well as the philological attentiveness that his poems solicit, one would do well to begin by considering the fourteenth of Werner Hamacher's *95 Theses on Philology*, which reads: "Poetry is *prima philologia* [Dichtung ist *prima philologia*]."[2] Echoing the scholastic designation of metaphysics as *prima philosophia,* which was so called for its concern with first causes, the phrase not only alters what was—more than once—called "first," first with "poetry," and then with "philology"; it also poses no alternative. Rather, the notion of a "first" is here exposed—philologically—to radical indefinition through its parody or parallel, which at once renders it principally recognizable and remarkably unprincipled, an inchoate and anarchic alteration of "primacy," and thus one that fundamentally displaces the question of any first cause. Yet beside the unsettling consequences that the phrase "prima philologia" would entail for the thought of "first" principles, the formulation also—and perhaps before all else—raises the question of the place of poetry within and beyond the thinking on language that Hamacher traces in his text. Literally, "poetry" would seem to come first, but nearly as soon as it is said, the movement of the phrase troubles its apparent position as the "subject" of a "thetic" proposition. For the complexities of *prima philologia*—itself an instance of poetic *Verdichtung*, or "condensation"—render it impossible to determine, strictly speaking, which element of the syntagma should have priority; whether it should be understood as an assertion that "poetry is first philology," or whether "first philology" is instead said to be an instance of "poetry." Hamacher's minimal syntagm on poetry and philology does not *say*: it states no axiomatic premise, it forms no predicative proposition, and it pronounces no decision.

It is instead an exemplary instance of the threshold-language that philology will later be said to expose, as the comportment toward language that "emancipates the interval from its border phenomena and, going a step farther, opens up phenomena out of the interval between them," and it is in this way that philology might approach poetry, among other idioms, without confining the language that it addresses to a generic category or the object of a truth claim—and thereby falsifying what is at issue when it comes to language.[3] As Hamacher explicates in the following thesis, if poetry is "the factual ground for philology's gestures and operations," then the "*fundamentum in re*" for philology discloses itself as "an abyss," since neither the substantial *logos* of ontology nor the categorial forms of epistemology can be supposed as the basis for its speech: "Wherever there is no form of proposition, there is no ground of knowledge [Wo keine Form der Aussage, da kein Grund des Wissens]." Poetry and philology, that is to say, speak for language before every possible imposition of "firm contours," "constant form[s]," and "meanings fixed in advance."[4] They speak for language in its extreme possibilities and impossibilities, for language in and at its—abyssal—opening. This is why, when Hamacher returns to the affinity between poetry and philology in his essay, "For—Philology," it is an inclination toward the "openness of language" that they are said to share:

> Philology shares this *pathos* with everyone who speaks or writes, *a fortiori* with the poets, who speak of nothing other than this experience of the openness of language [*Sprachoffenheit*]: of the possibility of language under the conditions of its improbability, of the potency of language under the conditions of its impotence, of power in the horizon of its withdrawal. Poetry is the most unreserved philology, and only for this reason can it attract the privileged and arresting attention of philology.[5]

And it is also why the opening of Hamacher's essay is marked by a prepositional "for"-word, which returns in his commentary on a verse from Paul Celan: "Here, it unwords in the for [Hier, es entwortet im Für]." On that "first" word of his essay and this "unword" of Celan—and over the parodic-poetic displacement and condensation of yet another "first," namely, the prologue to the Gospel of John: "In the beginning was the Word"—"for" will be said to signify that "in the beginning was not the word. . . . Whenever it comes into language [zum Wort kommt], it does so in each case from and to a *Für-Wort*. And even when it is a word for a word, it is still a word for an *other* word, *in limine* a wordless 'word.'"[6]

Hamacher's exemplary philological performances offer a point of departure for *Thresholds, Encounters*, whose contributors seek to address the ways in which the poetry of Paul Celan uncloses unforeseen threshold-spaces for encounters with the idioms of nature, philosophy and literature, while opening those idioms, in turn, to possibilities for speaking otherwise. While many studies have sought to trace the intersections between Celan's poetry and the thought of Theodor W. Adorno,[7] Hans-Georg Gadamer,[8] Martin

Heidegger,[9] Edmund Husserl,[10] and Emmanuel Levinas,[11] among others, it is seldom that scholars have proceeded from the thought of language as the shared if abyssal grounding for both modes of writing, and still more seldom that the practice of philology remains true to that thought, by exposing its own thetic and propositional gestures to those movements of language that undermine them. The recent monograph of Denis Thouard, *Pourquoi ce poète? Le Celan des philosophes* (2016), for example, revolves around the interest that Celan's poetry has inspired among divergent philosophers of the twentieth century, but when the author suggests that this phenomenon can be explained along the lines of a certain philosophical tendency that had emerged in the wake of Heidegger's thinking to view poetry as "a pre-ontological document, apt to reveal originary traits of the experience of time [un document pré-ontologique, apte à révéler des traits originaires de l'expérience du temps],"[12] then ontology, temporality, and the philosophical hermeneutics that would address them are presumed to be stable terms, exempt from the permutations and contingencies of the very language that permits them to be stated in the "first" place.

In contrast to more recent scholarship that would presuppose the disciplinary and categorial formations that Celan's poetry troubles, the contributors to *Thresholds, Encounters* advocate for the possibility that the poetic reinscription of overdetermined "philosophical" terms—like Hamacher's evocation of "prima philosophia," and Celan's "unwording" of the *logos* in his "for"-word—may not only affect and alter but also comment on and expose their implications with more precision than "philosophical" writing often acknowledges. Using a term that designated the particular threshold-space shared by Adorno and Celan, we explore gestures, moments, movements, and occurrences of poetic "Entsetzen" rather than confirming preconceived notions and normative positions and positings. Once again, the point is to show that Celan's poetry—and perhaps poetry as such—does not rely on presuppositions, nor does it serve to presuppose. When Adorno claims that Celan's poems would speak the utmost "Entsetzen" through their silence, it is critical to refrain from embracing the term's more usual translation as "horror" and its assignation of a referential function so as to expose how Celan's language registers a much more unsettling undoing or "de-posing" (*Ent-setzung*) of linguistic forms than any reduction to the terms of experience and cognition would allow.[13] Celan's work consists of topoi that cannot sufficiently be located in one preestablished conceptual register or another, unfolding instead a site for encountering the "not" of language that cuts across various discursive genres and their hybrids. The chapters in this volume collectively explore this very *not* and corroborate our claim that the pathbreaking critical interventions, which were begun through readers such as Hamacher, Derrida, and Szondi, do not offer closure but open thresholds that Celan-philology—in all possible senses of that pairing—fundamentally broaches toward the unheard-of dimensions of language and thought, ever for the "first" time.

~

The scholarship carried out in the volume is characterized by a split attention toward working through tradition and breaking off toward new entry paths into the rich and inexhaustible poetic threshold-language that is the work of Paul Celan. Reading specific poems and anthologies of Celan through his musicality, his understanding of history, and the role that nature plays in his poetics, the contributors to part 1 of our volume offer critical interventions that speak to larger interdisciplinary conversations ranging from the philosophy of music to ecocriticism. Part 2 of the volume broaches broader questions concerning Celan's comportment toward language. By emphasizing Celan's rhetorical gestures, the linguistic structures and shifts at work in his poetics, its contributors seek to continue and provide with new impulses a tradition of critical close reading that will have unfolded from Szondi to Hamacher and beyond. The volume ends with two chapters addressing translation and multilingualism in Celan, which draw out further ways in which Celan's writing not only "crosses through the interval" marking the threshold-space between idioms but also "opens and extends" that interval, exposing language as a "form for the opening, withholding, and wresting of forms."[14] Each part is composed of three pairs of texts that entertain a close correspondence; these pairs depart from a shared conceptual interest, such that the volume can be divided into six concepts worked through and differently accentuated by our contributors: while part 1 ("Ex-posing the Poem") speaks to issues of history, ecology, and aurality, part 2 ("Language Dislodged") inquires into Celan's articulations of encounter, positionality, and translation.

Penned by Michael Levine, chapter 1 in our volume consists of a masterful reading of Celan's poem "Sprich auch du" (1955). Approaching the poem through Derrida's approaches to Celan, and situating it in the context of Celan's own engagement with Georg Büchner, Levine's contribution can be read as a meta-commentary on Derrida's *Shibboleth*. In particular, Levine seeks to explore the *temporal* dimension of Celan's concept of the *meridian* at which Derrida's commentary only hints, but which it does not exhaustively analyze. The moment of the meridian, Levine maintains, opens up time in such a way that an address between a "you" and an "other" becomes possible—a process Celan termed "Mitsprechen lassen" ("letting the Other speak," as Levine translates). Chapter 1 goes on to explore this type of *speaking-with* through a reading of "Sprich auch du."

Following Levine, chapter 2 presents an equally engaging close reading of a single poem, as Simone Stirner develops a careful reappraisal of Celan's "Engführung" (1958), a text that has attracted a vast number of important commentaries, including Peter Szondi's essay "Lecture de strette: Essai sur la poésie de Paul Celan." The latter convincingly demonstrates how the poem actively undermines its referential function such that, instead of representing a certain reality, it traces its own textual *Wirklichkeit* in terms of a path that the reader is called upon to follow. Stirner compellingly builds on this insight as she inquires into the poem's imperative ("Schau nicht mehr—geh!"): "What form of relation does this way of walking with a text and its history imply? What kind of attention does it entail?" The chapter proceeds to argue that the specific type of poetic attention demanded by Celan's "Engführung" allows for an engagement with history on the basis of what the author (borrowing from Anne Carson) calls "withness."

Chapter 3, written by Jan Mieszkowski, considers the relation between language, the organic, and the inorganic as it manifests in Paul Celan's oeuvre—a problem that connects the discourse of Celan scholarship with the larger conversation concerning the environmental humanities as it has taken shape over the past decades. Mieszkowski's intervention is all the more important as it emphasizes a dimension of Celan's poetry that has often been overlooked: while many readings of Celan have identified the stone as a privileged object and site of poetic inventiveness, Mieszkowski's argument zones in on the figure of the flower, asking, "Who can speak the language of flowers?" His impressive tour de force leads him from a discussion of Rousseau's reflections on his experiences with flora and Kant's idea of natural beauty in *The Critique of Judgment* to a meticulous reading of Celan's poem "Blume" (1959).

Closely corresponding to the concerns raised by Mieszkowski, chapter 4, written by Natalie Lozinski-Veach, too probes Celan's relation to the natural. Lozinski-Veach complicates Adorno's assertion that Celan's poetry imitates "a language underneath the helpless one of the human, indeed underneath all organic language,"[15] and thereby approaches a language of the dead matters of "stone and star [Stein und Stern]." Through careful readings of Celan's notes for the *Meridian*, as well as his prose text "Gespräch im Gebirg" and his poem "Sprachgitter," Lozinski-Veach suggests that the capacity of poetic language to involve others through mimesis allows for an affective relation to otherness that does not submit the other to the order of conceptual identity, such that even stones may come to speak.

Adding to Lozinski-Veach's consideration of Adorno's relationship with Celan, chapter 5, written by Michael Auer, also starts with a reference to Adorno. In particular, Auer is interested in Adorno's critique of songwriting, as he seeks to locate in the work of Paul Celan a certain, albeit "othered," continuation of the tradition of song. Defining the specific nature of Celan's *Lieder*, Auer explains that they are marked by a special "allophonic strategy of musicality." This strategy allows for a free variation of tonal elements beyond and before established semantic patterns. What ensues is a poetic play of assonance, paronomasia, alliteration, and slant rhymes, creating a type of song that particularly characterizes Celan's anthology *Die Niemandsrose* (1963).

Musicality is also the theme chapter 6, by Naomi Waltham-Smith, which explores the reception of Celan in the French intellectual context, especially by thinkers associated with deconstructive reading practices. Centering on the work of Hélène Cixous, this chapter also tracks Celan's impact on writers such as Jacques Derrida, Jean-Luc Nancy, and David Wills. Specifically, Waltham-Smith is interested in the way in which Cixous treats Celan's poem "Cello-Einsatz" in her *Jours de l'an*. Cixous's response to Celan's poem, Waltham-Smith suggests, should be understood in the context of the quasi-methodological remarks to be found throughout her writings that often put the sonorous at the heart of the birth of writing. Hence, the detour via Cixous allows us to appreciate Celan's *aurality* as an essential dimension of his poetic process.

Part 2 of the volume opens with a chapter by Kristina Mendicino, which retraces the liminal movements of language that Celan renders most pronounced in, among others, the collection of poems that he would call *From Threshold to Threshold* (*Von Schwelle zu Schwelle*). Already the title exposes each "threshold"-word to part from itself—"*from* threshold" toward the same "*to* threshold"—without coinciding with itself, collapsing into sameness, or coming to rest. Taking this minimal syntagm as her point of departure, Mendicino argues that Celan's poetry exposes the self-alteration to which language gives way, with every term. These remarks prepare for a reading of the poem "Mit wechselndem Schlüssel," whose title cites a central phrase from the *proemium* of Parmenides's poem on being, initiating a poetic exploration of those traits from Parmenides's threshold-scene, which show it to be no mere preliminary to a "steady way of being," but to mark a liminal site for alterity and alteration that there is no getting through with.

In chapter 8, Pasqual Solass builds on Celan's understanding of poetry as a site of encounter. Adding to Levine's meditation on Celan's "speaking with" and Stirner's emphasis on the "withness" invoked in Celan's poems, Solass's chapter offers a precise and rigorous investigation of the semantics and rhetoric of the preposition "with" ("mit"), locating in it a poetic principle that allows Celan to project the poem not only as the site of an encounter but as an encountering force itself. This reading opens up a new perspective into the poem, according to which it can be understood as an eventful polyphony, a contraction of multiplicities and voices that are put into relation; Solass calls it a "*con*versation/*Mitsprechen* . . . itself always already situated within a *com*plex of with-one-another/*Miteinander*."

With chapter 9, "Occupiability," Sarah Stoll explores a seemingly marginal term within Celan's poetics. In the notes to his famous *Meridian* speech, Celan claims that the poem is essentially "besetzbar." Translated as "occupiable" or "cathectable" (in the psychoanalytic sense), the term also partakes in the semantics of *Setzung*, which encompasses the ontological register of the creation and seizure of positions. Following Hamacher's seminal readings, Stoll argues that Celan's use of the term explicitly undermines this ontological mandate, arguing that, in Celan, "occupiability, even in its ostensible gesture towards occupation, . . . appears as dis-occupation." Stoll goes on to interrogate Celan's oeuvre looking closely at three examples (two poems and one passage from the *Meridian*) where the movement of occupiability is centrally at stake.

Intensifying Stoll's investigation of Celan's critique of the logic of positionality, chapter 10, by Dominik Zechner, adds to the discussion of *Setzung* and *Besetzung* the possibility of *Entsetzung*, that is, the undoing of all position, the sheer de-posing of what is posited. As his point of departure, Zechner picks a moment in Adorno's notes on Celan, where the latter's poems are described as a de-posing movement that takes place through deliberate silence ("to speak of the most extreme horror through silence [das äußerste Entsetzen durch Verschweigen sagen]").[16] According to Adorno, this collapse into silence is bound up with a certain *shame* that is carried by the artwork, elicited by the withdrawal of the experience it seeks to capture. Unfolding the concepts at stake in this assessment with precision and contextualizing them against the backdrop of Hamacher's recently published essay on Celan and Adorno ("Versäumnisse" [2008]), Zechner prepares a reading of Celan's poem "Vor Scham" (1966), demonstrating how shame, within Celan's poetics, is not reducible to the emotional function of an experiencing subject. Rather, it must be understood as a linguistic affect, detached from any kind of subject-centered psychology, that characterizes the expressive struggle of language itself.

The volume's concluding section is concerned with issues of translation. Chapter 11, written by Irina Kogan, develops a precise reading of Celan's radio lecture dedicated to the introduction of Russian poet Ossip Mandelstam to a German-speaking audience, while its wider argument branches out into a general reflection upon Celan's understanding of the relationship between poetry and translation. The central term around which Kogan's deliberations revolve is taken from a letter that Celan penned in 1959 where he speaks of translations as "Annäherungsversuche" (or "trials of approach," in Kogan's rendition). Unpacking Celan's essay in a remarkably attentive, slow-paced reading, Kogan argues that these "approaches," far from instantiating an accurately corresponding transmission, rely on modes of defamiliarization ("Befremden") and interference. This insistence on an irreducible foreignness further allows Kogan to conclude her chapter by shedding new light on Celan's complex relationship with Martin Heidegger, especially his critique of Heidegger's understanding of "Entsprechung" ("correspondence").

Seamlessly connecting to Kogan's analysis, chapter 12, by Christine Frank, also takes on the problem of translation. Adding to the vast array of philosophers this volume puts in conversation with the work of Celan, Frank invokes Derrida's engagements with the poet and puts a rare focus on French theorist René Girard. In particular, Frank proposes to recast Girard's narratological term "mimetic desire" (as developed in his *Deceit, Desire and the Novel* [1966]) as a concept to theorize translation. Completing the narrative arc we envision for this volume, Frank invokes and further complicates certain aspects also highlighted by Levine and Stoll, as she too advances an understanding of language "as always already occupied by the Other." For translation to be possible, Frank argues, the desire for language that becomes manifest in the speech of the Other has to be imitated. Such mimesis provides the basis for a poetic writing that unfolds as a translational process.

*Thresholds, Encounters* thus closes with another opening, true to the way in which it was composed from the outset. The volume itself marks the culmination of a series of events the co-editors dedicated to the work of Paul Celan over the past years: following a research seminar at the 2018 convention of the German Studies Association exploring "Celan and Philosophy," the conversation was continued in April 2019 at Brown University in the context of a conference titled "For—Paul Celan." The third event in the series took place at NYU's Center for the Humanities in October 2019, where we held a roundtable discussion devoted to Werner Hamacher's Celan studies. The collection of essays that took shape from these conversations brings together some of the most compelling interventions made at these colloquia in order to proffer a powerful and precise reflection of the readings that Celan made possible in the face of contemporary literary criticism, continental philosophy, and philological inquiry. But in speaking toward and for those possibilities, the editors and contributors to *Thresholds, Encounters: Paul Celan and the Claim of Philology* also speak for other conversations that may further the *dis*-positions toward language that Celan's writing will have marked, translated, and prepared thereafter: "From the outset, philology goes beyond to something other than that which it is; it is the way to that which it is not and thereby *is*—transitively—its not [Nicht] and its after [Nach]."[17]

## Notes

1. See Werner Hamacher, *Keinmaleins* (Frankfurt am Main: Klostermann, 2019).

2. Werner Hamacher, "95 Theses on Philology," trans. Catherine Diehl, in *Give the Word: Responses to Werner Hamacher's 95 Theses on Philology*, eds. Gerhard Richter and Ann Smock (Lincoln: University of Nebraska Press, 2019), xi–lvi, xvii.

3. Hamacher, "95 Theses on Philology," xxvi. In this sense, philology could be said to advance a sort of *Schwellenkunde*—a lore or science of the threshold—the way Walter Benjamin envisioned the term and Winfriend Menninghaus further unfolded it. See Winfried Menninghaus, *Schwellenkunde: Walter Benjamins Passage des Mythos* (Frankfurt am Main: Suhrkamp, 1986).

4. Werner Hamacher, "For—Philology," trans. Jason Groves, in *Minima Philologica* (New York: Fordham University Press, 2015), 110; trans. modified; see Werner Hamacher, *Für—die Philologie*, in *Was zu sagen bleibt* (Schupfart: Engeler, 2019), 10.

5. Hamacher, "For—Philology," 124; see Hamacher, *Für—die Philologie*, 22.

6. Hamacher, "For—Philology," 146; see Hamacher, *Für—die Philologie*, 40.

7. These readings largely seek to describe the ways in which Celan's oeuvre answers Adorno's famous dictum on the barbarism of poetry after Auschwitz. See, for example, Shira Wolosky, *Language Mysticism: The Negative Way of Language in Eliot, Beckett, and Celan* (Stanford: Stanford University Press, 1995).

8. See Denis Thouard, *Pourquoi ce poète? Le Celan des philosophes* (Paris: Seuil, 2016).

9. In addition to the bibliography on this relation that Denis Thouard offers in the monograph cited here, see James K. Lyon, *Paul Celan and Martin Heidegger: An Unresolved Conversation* (Baltimore: Johns Hopkins University Press, 2006). The concluding claims of this book—such as "Celan seems to have profited from his acquaintance with Heidegger more than the philosopher did from Celan's poetry . . . and could be counted among his most serious students"—do not allow for the possibility that poems such as "Todtnauberg" may mark a decisive critique of Heidegger's thinking, without being reducible to the "scathing judgment of Heidegger" that Lyon rightly criticizes in others' approaches to that poem (Lyon, *Paul Celan*, 215, 178).

10. See, for example, Jean Greisch, "*Zeitgehöft et Anwesen*: La dia-chronie du poème," in *Contre-jour: Études sur Paul Celan*, ed. Martine Broda (Paris: Éditions du Cerf, 1986), 167–83; Roland Reuss, *Im Zeithof: Celan-Provokationen* (Frankfurt am Main: Stroemfeld Verlag, 2001), 103–5; Sandro Zanetti, *zeitoffen': Zur Chronographie Paul Celans* (Munich: Fink Verlag, 2006), 143–48. Werner Hamacher's study, "Epoché. Gedicht. Celans *Reimklammer* um Husserls Klammern" in *Keinmaleins: Texte zu Celan* (Frankfurt am Main: Vittorio Klostermann, 2019), 143–79, offers the exception to readings that presume Husserl's thought to be unaffected by its evocation in Celan's poems. In his essay, Hamacher shows Celan to have extended the phenomenological *epoché* to the transcendental subject itself, with ruinous consequences for any egology or epistemology such as Husserl's.

11. Michael Eskin, *Ethics and Dialogue in the Works of Levinas, Bakhtin, Mandel'shtam, and Celan* (Oxford: Oxford University Press, 2000).

12. Denis Thouard, *Pourquoi ce poète? Le Celan des philosophes* (Paris: Seuil, 2016).

13. See Theodor W. Adorno, *Aesthetic Theory*, trans. Robert Hullot-Kentor (Minneapolis: University of Minnesota Press, 1997), 322; Theodor W. Adorno, *Ästhetische Theorie*, eds. Gretel Adorno and Rolf Tiedemann (Frankfurt am Main: Suhrkamp, 1973), 477.

14. Werner Hamacher, "Kontraduktionen," in *Transmission: Übersetzung—Übertragung—Vermittlung*, ed. Georg Mein (Vienna: Turia + Kant, 2010), 13–33, 13; our translation.

15. Adorno, *Aesthetic Theory*, 322; trans. modified.

16. Adorno, *Aesthetic Theory*, 322; Adorno, *Ästhetische Theorie*, 477.

17. Hamacher, "95 Theses on Philology," xlv.

Part 1

# Ex-posing the Poem

## History

Chapter 1

# "In the Swell of Wandering Words"
## Celan's "Sprich auch du"

MICHAEL G. LEVINE

Discussions of "Sprich auch du" ("Speak You Too"), one of Celan's better known and more frequently cited and commented on poems, are usually restricted to the first four of its five strophes. They are strophes dominated by an imperative voice that, depending on its tonality, commands, implores, or encourages "you" to speak, to give, to look around and to see:

> Speak, you too,
> speak as the last,
> have your say.
>
> Speak—
> But keep yes and no unsplit.
>
> And give your say this meaning:
> give it the shade.
>
> Give it shade enough
>
> Give it as much
> as you know has been dealt out between
> midnight and midday and midnight.

Look around:
see how alive it gets all around—
At death! Alive!
Speaks true, who speaks shadows.[1]

(Sprich auch du,
sprich als letzter,
sag deinen Spruch.

Sprich—
Doch scheide das Nein nicht vom Ja.

Gib deinem Spruch auch den Sinn:
gib ihm den Schatten.

Gib ihm Schatten genug

gib ihm so viel,
als du um dich verteilt weißt zwischen
Mittnacht und Mittag und Mittnacht.
Blicke umher:
sieh, wie's lebendig wird rings—
Beim Tode! Lebendig!
Wahr spricht, wer Schatten spricht.)

In a marked departure from these strophes couched in the second person, the fifth and last one begins in the third person with a description of the place where "you" are now said to stand. It is not just any place but one in which time itself comes to a momentary standstill. It is the moment of the midday meridian, a moment of shadowless illumination around which so many of Celan's poems, and above all his *Meridian* address, turn. Derrida was perhaps the first to hear in the title of this address a reference to time as well as to place. Of particular relevance to what follows is the way Derrida frames his own brief discussion of "Sprich auch du" with references to the figure of the meridian. On both occasions he takes pains to highlight its temporal dimension. While his explicit focus is on the question of the date, implicit in this questioning is the etymological derivation of the term "date" from the Latin *datus*, past participle of the verb *dare*, "to give." He turns to Celan's poem in part to develop this connection between dating and giving. Of particular interest to him is the relationship between time, certain times of the day, and giving. To further complicate the relationship, giving itself involves a certain way and a certain moment of speaking:

> Speak—
> But keep yes and no unsplit.
> And give your say this meaning:
> give it the shade.
> Give it shade enough
> Give it as much
> as you know has been dealt out between
> midnight and midday and midnight.
>
> (Sprich—
> Doch scheide das Nein nicht vom Ja.
> Gib deinem Spruch auch den Sinn:
> gib ihm den Schatten.
> Gib ihm Schatten genug,
> gib ihm so viel,
> als du um dich verteilt weißt zwischen
> Mittnacht und Mittag und Mittnacht.)

As Derrida emphasizes, shadows are to be dealt or parceled out *between* meridional moments—"between / midnight and midday and midnight." What happens *at* these extreme moments, at the moments of complete shade of midnight and the utter shadowlessness of midday, is another story. To approach these moments in general and that of the noontide meridian in "Sprich auch du" in particular, let us begin with the instant in Derrida's *Shibboleth* where questions of speaking, dating, and giving are posed together. Speaking himself in the imperative and italicizing what he says as though for emphasis, he asserts: "*What is dated must nonetheless not be dated* [*il faut bien que . . . ce qui est daté ne soit pas daté*]."[2] "The date," he adds, "yes and no Celan would say as he does a number of times."[3] As evidence of Celan's own affirmation of the yes *and* no he cites the following passage from "Sprich auch du": "Doch scheide das Nein nicht vom Ja [But keep Yes and No unsplit]."

Framed as an imperative, admonition, or dictate, the statement suggests that disobedience is at least possible, that the no can in principle be severed from the yes. Yet there are also imperatives like double binds that leave one with no choice, that force the "you" positioned by them to hover indecisively between the yes and the no. Such a situation is conjured in a scene from Georg Büchner's *Woyzeck*, a drama to which the Celan refers in his *Meridian*-address and in poems such as "Tübingen, Jänner." The scene opens with the title character engaged in a conversation about the weather:

> Nice weather we're having, sir. The sky has such a nice, solid, rough-cast look, it makes you want to bang a nail into it and hang yourself, just because of the tiny line between yes and no, d'you see, sir, yes and no? Is no to blame for yes, or yes for no? I must think it over.[4]

> (Wir haben schön Wetter Herr Hauptmann. Sehn Sie, so ein schön festen grauen Himmel, man könnte Lust bekomm, ein Klobe hineinzuschlage und sich daran zu hänge, nur wege des Gedankenstrichels zwischen ja und nein—ja und nein. Herr Hauptmann, ja und nein? Ist das Nein am Ja oder das Ja am Nein Schuld? Ich will drüber nachdenken.)[5]

So unusually firm does the gray sky appear that Woyzeck is tempted to bang a nail into it and hang himself from it. What apparently drives him to think about this form of suicide is a related mode of suspension: that associated with the tiny line between yes and no. "Is the No to blame for the Yes or the Yes for the No?" he wonders. Which one hangs from, is appended to, and dependent upon the other? Suspended between the yes and the no, Woyzeck thinks of death by hanging, a thought which is itself indefinitely prolonged by the reflection, "Ich will drüber nachdenken [I'll have to think it over]." The thought of the *Gedankenstrichel* may be Woyzeck's last, a consideration that not only leads him to contemplate suicide but leaves him indefinitely suspended on the brink of such an act. Thinking it over, thinking indecisively about the little thought stroke, about the *Strichel* in which he appears to perceive the specter of a *Strick* or rope, Woyzeck is effectively already hung from the nail he imagines knocking into the firm, gray sky. Suspended between life and death, he will perhaps already have pronounced his own death sentence, have already spoken his last words. Words uttered at the end of life and the beginning of death, they tie the one inconclusively to the other, linking them in turn—and with equal indecisiveness—to the question of whether the yes is suspended from the no or the other way around.

Reading Derrida's assertion, "*What is dated must nonetheless not be dated*," through the filter of *Woyzeck*, one comes to see how difficult it may be to sever the yes from the no. One also begins to get a sense of what it may mean to be positioned by a command that cannot simply be obeyed or refused, to find oneself suspended in the toils of a double bind. While Derrida's *il faut* may initially suggest a choice, the possibility in principle of severing the yes from the no, we are now made to think over a situation in which the yes and the no hang so indecisively from each other that both must be affirmed.

As though the matter admitted no easy development, Derrida lets it hang in suspense, leaving open the questions it poses regarding double binds and ineluctable ties—not only open in their lack of resolution but open to linger on in what follows. Rather than pursuing Derrida's discussion of the date, I would like at this point to remain with Celan's poem. As noted earlier, Derrida does not so much read the poem as cite it in support of a certain structure of double affirmation, one in which the yes and the no hang indecisively from each other. In staying with "Sprich auch du," my reading will nevertheless be guided by the way Derrida frames his citation of it with two references to *The Meridian*. The first introduces the entire question of dates and with it the related question of giving: of giving shade, giving meaning, and giving time. Rather than quote in my turn his lengthy citation of Celan's Büchner Prize speech, I reproduce only its last words: "I find something, like language, immaterial, yet earthly, terrestrial, something circular, which traverses both poles and returns to itself, thereby—I am happy to report—even crossing the tropics and tropes. I find . . . a *meridian*."[6] In his gloss of these famous lines, Derrida takes pains to shift from the more obvious—and much more frequently commented upon—spatial and tropical senses of the term "meridian" to its less apparent temporal dimension:

> Almost the last word of the text, near the signature. What Celan finds or discovers, on the spur of the moment, invents, if one may say so, more or less than a fiction, is not only a meridian, the Meridian, but the word and image, the trope *meridian*, which offers the example of the law, in its inexhaustible polytropy, . . . which *binds* . . . , and provokes in broad daylight, at noon, *at midday*, the encounter with the other in a single place, at a single point, that of the poem, of this poem.[7]

As though Celan's *Meridian* were itself the poem referred to here, "*this* poem," Derrida goes on to cite without comment the following very dense sentence:

"In the here and now of the poem—and the poem itself, after all, has only this one, unique, punctual present—even in this immediacy and proximity to itself it lets speak what the Other has that is most proper to it: its time."[8]

I return to this passage below, trying to unpack the complex ways in which questions of space, time, and speech—and, above all, what it might mean to let another speak—are posed together. Before doing so, let me begin by citing again the lines Derrida selectively quotes from "Sprich auch du":

> Speak—
> But keep yes and no unsplit.
> And give your say this meaning:
> give it the shade.
>
> Give it shade enough
> Give it as much
> as you know has been dealt out between
> midnight and midday and midnight.
>
> (Sprich—
> Doch scheide das Nein nicht vom Ja.
> Gib deinem Spruch auch den Sinn:
> gib ihm den Schatten.
>
> Gib ihm Schatten genug,
> gib ihm so viel,
> als du um dich verteilt weißt zwischen
> Mitternacht und Mittag und Mitternacht.)[9]

To this citation, Derrida immediately adds in the body of the text: "Again the meridian."[10] Framing the quote in this way, he emphasizes the temporal dimension of the highly overdetermined, "inexhaustibly polytropic" term "meridian," reminding us of the way it marks the moment when the sun, standing directly overhead, casts no shadows. Yet, between the passage cited and the comment, "again the meridian," there is an important footnote appended to the published version of what was initially delivered as an address:

> We will return below to the question of that which binds the word, and the word as decree, aphorism, sentence, verdict, judg-

ment (*Spruch*), to decision and circumcision, on the one hand, and to the date, and the hour, on the other. Here, the imparting or distribution (*Verteilung*), and the gift of shade, that which gives meaning to the *Spruch,* to the word as judgment (*Urteil*), spreads or distributes the origin of meaning, that is, the shade, *between the hours,* between complete shade and the absence of shade, midnight and midday and midnight. The shade is imparted, spread out, or apportioned (*verteilt*) among the hours. And this imparting of shade *gives the meaning.*[11]

As the footnote makes clear, the gift of meaning is dependent upon the gift of shade, of shade which is itself *verteilt*—that is, imparted, apportioned, or parceled out *between the hours*, between the complete shade of midnight and its total absence at midday.[12] Emphasizing the moment of the meridian in the passage immediately following the footnote, Derrida asks implicitly what happens not *between the hours* but *at* a certain hour, at a certain instant, in the punctuality of a unique moment. "The poem itself," we recall, "after all, has only this one, unique, punctual present" and it is precisely "in this immediacy and proximity to itself" that the poem "lets speak what the Other has that is most proper to it: its time."[13] In addition to inquiring into the nature of this present, into its uniqueness and punctuality, we might further ask what will have happened to the "you" at this instant. What is the relationship between the "you" called upon to speak and the Other that the poem is said to "*let* speak"? Will the "you" enjoined to speak, to speak as the last and to have its say, have somehow opened itself in the meantime, opened *in the very opening of time itself*, to another? Will it have given way to another "you," which it *lets speak* in the punctuality of this moment? In posing these questions I want to ask how the moment of the meridian might itself be viewed as an opening of time, a moment when the closing circle of the hour is made to stand open, if only for a shadowless and meaningless instant, before again taking up its appointed rounds.

To the extent that there are answers to these questions, I believe they are to be found in the fifth and final strophe of "Sprich auch du." Not only is it set off from the four previous ones by a blank space but, as was noted earlier, also by a shift from second-person imperatives to third-person description. In addition to the formal structure of the poem, one might locate something of a break in its critical reception. As a brief survey of the literature devoted to "Sprich auch du" demonstrates, readings of it tend to focus almost exclusively on its first part, leaving the final strophe more or less out of account.[14] One of the things that fascinates me about the poem is why this is the case—especially given the way the last part pointedly revises all that will have come before. It is as though something were stopping critics dead in their tracks, as though all there really was to say had already been said in the first four strophes, as though all the energy gathered into the series of imperatives voiced in rapid succession in the first four strophes had suddenly dissipated, as though the poem itself had had its say, had spoken its verdict, judgment, or *Spruch* when making its pronouncement: "Wahr spricht, wer Schatten spricht [Speaks true who speaks shadow]."[15] Having uttered this dictum, "Sprich auch du" itself seems to come to rest. What follows is language that appears to have lost its urgency and intensity. From this point on, imperious utterances give way gradually to descriptions of threads, stars, and maritime swells.

As noted earlier, Derrida reproduces only the second and third strophes of the poem, breaking off his citation at the moment when the noontide meridian is mentioned. By contrast, John Felstiner cites the poem in its entirety, focusing nonetheless primarily on the first strophe and paying particular attention to its famous first two lines, "Speak you too / speak as the last."[16] Felstiner reads the speech to "you" as a form of self-address, as an admonition to speak out against the kind of reception Celan's previous collection *Mohn und Gedächtnis* had received in the pages of *Merkur* in a critical review by Hans Egon Holthusen. As Felstiner writes, it is "as if the poet had been misheard and must tell himself to hold fast to the difficult way,"[17] adding that the line "speak as the last" should be read in the context of the poet's recent self-description as "one of the last who must live out to the end the destiny of the Jewish spirit in Europe."[18] To speak as the last, for Felstiner, is thus to speak "as the one on whom that destiny hangs."[19]

What it might mean to speak as the last is a question also taken up by the Italian philosopher Gianluca Solla.[20] Exploring a possible link to Paul's "First Epistle to the Corinthians," Solla concentrates in particular on a line that I cite in the King James version, "For I think that God has set forth us, the apostles, last, as appointed to death: for we are made a spectacle unto the world, and to angels, and to men" (1 Cor. 4.9). Whereas in Paul the last is the place of the witness, the place of the moribund, the one already on the verge of death, in Celan, according to Solla, to speak as the last is, more radically, no longer to be part of any series but instead to speak when all possibilities of speech have already been exhausted, to speak when there is no longer any place from which to speak, to speak as though no one were speaking or even existed any longer. Solla's rich and complex reflections, to which I cannot begin to do justice in this context, seem to point us in the direction of testimony that will have exceeded the speaker's capacity to impart, testimony that consigns the speaking subject to a position of subjection. "Speak as the last," he writes, is a "kind of demand: the witness speaks, his authority being derived as much from this demand as from the fact that he is its subject; at once subject *of* the law and subject *to* it. Speaking on the basis of this irreducible subjection, the witness speaks from a position of passivity."[21] Though Solla does not himself explicitly move in this direction, I would like to imagine that the passivity he has in mind is less that of utter subjection than the *active* passivity of the middle voice, or what Celan refers to in his *Meridian*-address as *Mitsprechen lassen*, or *letting* the Other speak. Had Solla developed his provocative reading of the poem beyond its first two lines, he would have had to grapple more extensively with the question of what "you" conceived of as a "last speaker" ultimately gives way to.

The critical literature devoted to "Sprich auch du" is extensive, and I have touched on only a few of the most important engagements with it. One text, however, that deserves special mention is Jan Mieszkowski's "*Ich, Ach, Auch*: Certain Also-Ran Languages of Jacques Derrida." One of the few to discuss the poem as a whole, it also provides a useful framework for approaching the shift from the first four strophes to the last. While Mieszkowski does not focus directly on this moment of transition, his remarks help us to understand the stakes and strategies of the poem. Thus, he writes, "setting out the precise demands that will define its specificity as a discourse that calls for the production of another discourse, Celan's text exposes itself to a movement it does not control and may never master."[22] In what follows, I trace the contours of this other discourse for which the poem calls and the movement to which it exposes itself.

In exploring this movement, I am guided in particular by Mieszkowski's discussion of the last lines of the poem—"in der Dünung / wandernder Worte": "If the last word of Celan's poem is 'words,' the concept of the word may not have the last word when it comes to describing what it is that the verses do."[23] At stake here is not only the general question of what the verses perform, but how they act in particular upon their own words. In the first four strophes linguistic performance involves primarily the use of imperatives addressed to a second-person "you," whether these imperatives are viewed as commands, implorations, appeals, or prayers. In the final strophe, such performatives come to be mixed with constative utterances, third-person descriptions and open-ended questions. Here the question of what the verses do and of what they do specifically and reflexively to the words of the poem itself is posed very differently.

The strophe opens punctually with the incipit *Nun*. While this "Now" may certainly be viewed as a positive moment in time, attention should also and above all be paid to the peculiar ways it lets time open, the ways, that is, it marks a gap, pause, or suspension of time:

> Now, however, the place where you stand shrinks:
> Whereto now, you, denuded of shadows, whereto?
> Ascend. Grope upward.
> Thinner you become, less knowable, finer!
> Finer: a thread
> on which it wants to come down, the star:
> so as to swim down below, below
> where it sees itself shimmering: in the swell
> of wandering words.[24]

> (Nun aber schrumpft der Ort, wo du stehst:
> Wohin jetzt, Schattenentblösster, wohin?
> Steige. Taste empor.
> Dünner wirst du, unkenntlicher, feiner!
> Feiner: ein Faden,
> an dem er herabwill, der Stern:
> um unten zu schwimmen, unten,
> wo er sich schimmern sieht: in der Dünung
> wandernder Worte.)

The word "Now" functions here less as a positive unit of time than as a stroke punctually marking and verbally incising the moment of midday. At this moment not only does the second-person repeatedly addressed in the first four strophes give way to another "you" whom it lets speak, but time itself is let open. At this moment not only do the shadows heretofore apportioned *between the hours* shrink but so too does the place where the "you" itself had heretofore stood. As they shrink, the tight weave of the text loosens. Apparent for the first time now are individual threads and the spaces between them.

In the midst of all this loosening, leaving open, and letting speak, the most dramatic shift is from the level of the signified to that of the signifier. In other words, the movements of shrinking, denuding, ascending, descending, groping, thinning, swimming, shimmering, and wandering are no longer performed or described in the signified content of the poem but are instead enacted on its linguistic surface. Of particular importance here is the way the second-person pronoun *Du* quite literally thins out in the phrase "Dünner wirst Du," doing so as the word "Dünner" becomes the very thread upon which a certain *er* ("he") may descend. In other words, located at opposite ends of the thread-word "Dünner," the slightly altered second-person pronoun *Du* becomes *Dü*, and the third-person pronoun *er* becomes a comparative ending, which are conjoined with the double *nn* between them to form a tenuous space of ascent and descent.

As Derrida notes, shadows are distributed, apportioned, and shared out in the first part of the poem, waxing and waning *between the hours* of midnight and midday and midnight. However, at the moment incised in the poem by the word "Nun," the instant of the noontide meridian, the *Du* is now stripped of its meaning-giving shadows. Laid bare in this way, its place not only shrinks but becomes the ever-finer, ever-more-tenuous line of the thread-word "Dünner," which itself now stands vertically like a thin shaft of light.

Dünner

And it is upon this luminous beam, this finely drawn out thread, that the "less knowable" *Du*, itself thinned out into an umlauted "Dü," ascends, groping its way upward toward the *er* at the other end. At once the far end of the thread-word "Dünner" and a pronoun standing in for the masculine noun, "der Stern," the *er* in its turn travels down the thread in order to make its way not only toward the *Du* as it once was but toward the thinned-out "Dü" it will, in the time lapse of the meridian, have become. What might have been initially conceived of as an encounter between second and third persons, between a *Du* and an *Er*, a *you* and a *he*, linked by the fine strand of the word "Dünner" will in the meantime have given place to something else. For the "Dü" toward which the *er* descends will have further thinned out into the word "Dünung," meaning "swell" in the maritime sense, a long drawn out movement of rolling waves. These waves are themselves perhaps to be seen as linguistic phenomena, as the fluid transition and gentle wavering back and forth between the verbs "schwimmen" and "schimmern," swimming and shimmering. In this way, words no longer shadowed by the command to have and give meaning, no longer standing in the shade of sense, may be said to wander. For, now, in lieu of any meaningful connection obtaining among them, words swim and shimmer, gliding fluidly on the undulating surface of the poem, passing swimmingly, shimmeringly, and above all errantly into one another.

How long, one might ask, does this meridional interval last? While certainly a positive moment of time, a brief instant to which the clock punctually returns once every twenty-four hours, it is also a moment let open by the swell of wandering words, a moment of indecision *held open* by an uncertain wavering back and forth, by a refusal or failure to sever the yes from the no. Not only does Derrida underscore the yes *and* no of the poem when articulating the double bind of the date, but he also connects the *Verteilung* of shadows, their imparting or distribution *between the hours* of midnight and midday and midnight, to the *Spruch* understood as a judgment or *Urteil*, a term he takes care to insert in German.[25] His point in linking the terms *Verteilung* and *Urteil*, imparting and judgment, is not only to draw attention to the root *teil* they share but, moreover, to underscore the indecisiveness of the moment when shadows—and the sense they may impart—vanish.

In the interval dilated by the swell of wandering words, shadows not only shrink up to nothing but, in doing so, also give place to the nothingness of other shadows—to shades of the dead—that now spectrally fill the air. Just as one sense of the word *Schatten* gives way here to another so too does the star associated in this moment with the sun standing directly overhead give way to another astral body, a star "of human making," as Celan refers to it in the Bremen prize address he would deliver three years later. Toward the end of that address he speaks of his own efforts as well as those of other lyric poets of a younger generation. They are, he says, the efforts of "someone . . . overarced by stars of human making [überflogen von Sternen, die Menschenwerk sind]."[26] These "stars" are often thought to refer to artificial satellites circling the globe such as the Sputnik, placed into orbit on October 4, 1957, just months before the Bremen address was delivered.²⁷ Yet they may also and perhaps above all refer to the unburied dead, the incinerated remains of those made to wear the star of David. Here one might recall the following famous lines from "Todesfuge": "Er ruft streicht dunkler die Geigen dann steigt ihr als Rauch in die Luft / dann habt ihr ein Grab in den Wolken da liegt man nicht eng [He calls out more darkly now stroke your strings then as smoke you will rise into air / then a grave you will have in the clouds there one lies unconfined]." These remains, Celan suggests, are still airborne, hovering overhead like stars in the firmament. Yet the evening sky, as he immediately goes on to note, has itself lost its firmness. Those flown over by stars of human making stand, as he says, "unsheltered even by the traditional tent of the sky, exposed in an unexpected and terrifying way [zeltlos auch in diesem bisher ungeahnten Sinne und damit auf das unheimlichste im Freien]."²⁸

The striking of the midday hour in "Sprich auch du" thus gives place to a kind of *Geisterstunde*, a time when the nothingness of another, more spectral kind of shade becomes uncannily palpable.²⁹ Given the presence of homonyms like "Du" and "Dü" in the poem, it is important to note how the shades of the dead never appear as such. Their spectrality has instead a distinctly linguistic cast with one sense of *Schatten* being shadowed homonymically by another. *Es gibt Schatten und es gibt Schatten*, one might say, bearing in mind what is said much more straightforwardly earlier in the poem about the necessity of giving shadows to your speech. In other words, there are shadows and there are shades and it is impossible to tell them apart. Only in the *Geisterstunde*, only in the moment when shadows shrink up to nothing does the nothingness of another kind of shadow, another more spectral shade, become apparent.

It should be recalled here the intensity with which the poem had heretofore focused on the second person *Du*. Now, however, it shifts into the third person, doing so at the very moment when the Jewish star, itself heretofore outshone by the shadowless illumination of the midday sun, seems shimmeringly to shine through. "A thread / on which it wants to come down, the star [Ein Faden / an dem **er** herabwill, de**r** Stern]." Couched in the third person, the line is also marked by the pointed repetition of the signifier *er*, which appears first as a pronoun standing in for the masculine noun "Stern," then in the adverb "herab," then again in the article "der," and finally in the word "Stern" itself. Like the manmade stars flying overhead in the Bremen address, like the airborne remains of those made to wear the *Davidstern*, the *er* scattered across this line never comes to rest, never stabilizes as any one particular part of speech. Excluded not only from the speech addressed in German to the second person but, more generally, from any I-thou relationship, this third-person *er* instead hovers spectrally at the limits of dialogic exchanges and scenes of mutual recognition. Suspended in this way, it is also left to hover at the edge of the poem itself, of a poem so exclusively focused on the second-person *you*, on the speech addressed to it, and on the ways it itself is supposed to speak, that readers have tended to focus on little else.

With the exception of Derrida, they have also tended to pay little attention to the temporal dimension of the poem, to the way shadows at a certain point give way suddenly to shades and suns uncannily shed light on stars of human making. That point is the moment of the meridian. At once a decisive turning point in a twenty-four-hour cycle, a recognizable moment of repetition and return, an annulus as closed as the anniversaries and wedding rings to which it is related, it is also a moment of suspense, an opening of time, and a way of holding it open to the coming of another. What comes in the meantime of the meridian never comes as itself, for at the moment marked and indeed opened by the Now with which the last strophe begins, the familiar *Du* of the poem, becoming less knowable, finer and threadlike, gives place to a certain "Dü." Less a free-standing pronoun or independent voice, less a shadow- and meaning-giving agent than a spectral presence, this "Dü" appears only in the guise of other words and even then only as their beginnings, only as the stammering insistence of "Dü," "Dü" in the terms "Dünner" and "Dünung," only as the onset of movements of thinning, wavering, and wandering. These movements have a way of loosening the weave of the text, exposing its individual signifying threads and the spaces between them. Yet the threads are themselves thread-words, connectives along which an attenuated *Du* might grope its way upwards, while an astral *er* beams its way down. If a thread-word is also a shaft of light, a thread sun or *Fadensonne*, as Celan will later call it, its verticality marks the moment when the sun stands directly overhead. Such moments of shadowless illumination are also ones when another kind of shade associated with another kind of star hovers palpably in the air.

All this is to say that the moment of the meridian is highly overdetermined both in this poem and in Celan's work more generally. It also plays a major role in the texts of Georg Büchner, structuring them in ways Celan, in his *Meridian* address, was the first to recognize. I owe my own sensitization to this moment to Derrida's *Shibboleth*. In approaching the poem "Sprich auch du," I have let myself be guided by the way he frames his own brief remarks on it with two references to the meridian, emphasizing both times its temporal dimension. For Derrida, the meridian is not merely a moment in or out of time but the locus of a chance meeting, *rencontre* or *Begegnung*. Thus, he writes of Celan's own roundabout encounter with the line, trope, and time of the meridian at the end of his address of the same name, "he finds or discovers, on the spur of the moment, invents, if one may say so, . . . *not only* a meridian, the Meridian," but also something that "provokes in broad daylight, at noon, *at midday*, the encounter [rencontre] with the other in a single place, at a single point, that of the poem, of this poem."[30]

In order to specify the singularity of this *place, time, and manner of encounter* Derrida immediately cites the following passage: "In the here and now of the poem—and the poem itself, after all, has only this one, unique punctual present—even in this immediacy and proximity to itself it lets speak what the Other has that is most proper to it: its time."[31]

While Derrida lets this passage speak for itself, I would like in conclusion to dwell a bit longer on it, thereby dilating in my turn the space and time of this dense and congested passage. It is a passage that brings together a present described as unique and punctual, an equally singular space of immediacy and proximity, and a certain way of speaking. Neither the speech of a poetic statement nor the voice of an I speaking in the poem, what concerns Celan here is a manner of speaking, a way of letting another or the Other speak. This *Mitsprechen* or *Mitsprechen-Lassen*, as he calls it,[32] emerges from a certain self-distancing of the proximity in question, a self-distance that lets speech open, *leaving* it open to that which might nevertheless speak with and through it. What speaks out of the dehiscence or gaping of this proximity, out of the inner hesitation and distension of this immediacy, never speaks on its own behalf or in its own voice. More than one speaks in this *Mitsprechen*, but it is a plurivocity that is more than a combination of voices—more than a mixture of one's own voice and that of another. The Other is instead carried by, carried within the host body of the speaking subject, carried by it without belonging to it. It is in this sense that the poetic voice, let open in this way, lets another, the very Otherness proper to it, speak.

This *Mitsprechen-Lassen*, this letting open of what will never have been fully one's own so that an Otherness within might speak is for Celan a form of hospitality—hospitality that only accommodates a certain alterity to the extent that it exposes, alienates, and literally alters itself. It is for this reason that the terms "Other" and "Most Proper"—"das ihm, dem Anderen, Eigenste"[33]—stand in the closest proximity to one another in this passage.

This othering of the most proper marks a threefold opening: a self-distancing of immediacy and proximity; a letting open of speech to that which speaks with and through it; and an opening of time. The *Mitsprechen* or "speaking with" that *leaves more time* in the sense of hesitation, vacillation, and indecision is also a relaxation, slackening and loosening of time itself. So loose is it that past, present, and future no longer follow lockstep on the heels of one another and are no longer to be thought either as modalities of presence or in terms of temporal sequence.

In "The Last One to Speak," a title that itself alludes to the second line of "Sprich auch du," Maurice Blanchot translates a number of Celan's poems into French, weaving these translations together with his own laconic glosses, with words that seem less to elucidate the poems he translates than to allow their stillness to carry, their fault lines and crevices to spread, and their "non-verbal rigor" to be unleashed.[34] As translator, Blanchot not only lends his voice to the other but lets it speak with and through him. For him, this *Mitsprechen* or *Mitsprechen-Lassen* is his own companionable way of abiding with Celan. "We always choose a companion," he writes at the outset. "Not for ourselves do we choose it, but for something inside us, away from us, that asks us to be absent from ourselves to cross the line we can never reach. The companion, lost in advance, is henceforth the loss in our place."[35]

## Notes

1. Paul Celan, "Sprich auch du," in *Die Gedichte: Neue kommentierte Gesamtausgabe in einem Band*, ed. Barbara Wiedemann (Berlin: Suhrkamp, 2018), 89. All subsequent references to passages from this poem refer to this edition. Paul Celan, "Speak You Also," *Poems of Paul Celan*, trans. Michael Hamburger (New York: Persea Books, 1988), 69; trans. modified. The modifications to Hamburger's translation are inspired in part by the translation offered by John Felstiner in *Selected Poems and Prose of Paul Celan* (New York: Norton, 2001), 77.

2. Jacques Derrida, "Shibboleth: For Paul Celan," trans. Joshua Wilner, revised by Thomas Dutoit, in *Sovereignties in Question: The Poetics of Paul Celan*, eds. Thomas Dutoit and Outi Pasanan (New York: Fordham University Press, 2005), 1–64, 14; emphasis in original; Jacques Derrida, *Schibboleth: Pour Paul Celan* (Paris: Galilée, 1986), 31. On Celan, Derrida, and the question of the date, see chapters 2–3 of my study *A Weak Messianic Power: Figures of a Time to Come in Benjamin, Derrida and Celan* (New York: Fordham University Press, 2013), esp. 17–21; 48–50. See also n. 11 below.

3. Derrida, "Shibboleth," 14.

4. Georg Büchner, *Complete Plays, Lenz and Other Writings,* trans. John Reddick (New York: Penguin Books, 1993), 124.

5. Georg Büchner, *Werke und Briefe Münchner Ausgabe,* eds. Karl Pörnbacher, Gerhard Schaub, Hans-Joachim Simm, and Emma Ziegler (Munich: Carl Hanser, 1988), 245.

6. Paul Celan, "The Meridian," qtd. in Derrida, "Shibboleth," 12.

7. Derrida, "Shibboleth," 12–13. In the passage that is marked with ellipses above, Derrida inserts the following parenthetical remark: "*Das Verbindende,* 'that which binds,' '*ce qui lie,*' as André du Bouchet translates; 'the intermediary,' '*l'intermédiare,*' as Jean Launay translates" (Derrida, "Shibboleth," 13).

8. Celan, "The Meridian," qtd. in Derrida, "Shibboleth," 13.

9. Celan, "Sprich auch du"; qtd. in Derrida, "Shibboleth," 14.

10. Derrida, "Shibboleth," 15.

11. Derrida, 194.

12. It is worth noting that the French word translated here as "apportioned" is *répartie* (Derrida, *Shibboleth,* 120). Using it, Derrida pointedly links its *part* to the *teil* words in the German, *Verteilung* and *Urteil,* which he goes out of his way to provide.

13. Celan, "The Meridian"; qtd. in Derrida, "Shibboleth," 13.

14. Jan Mieszkowski aptly summarizes the general state of Celan scholarship with regard to the poem when he writes: "'Speak, you also' is regarded as one of Celan's most direct comments on the nature of poetic speech after the Holocaust, an account of the imperative to bear witness to an event that in addition to forcing a reconceptualization of witnessing may have irrevocably transformed, or rendered obsolete, the very notion of speaking the truth." Jan Mieszkowski, "*Ich, Auch, Ach:* Certain Also-Ran Languages of Jacques Derrida," *Oxford Literary Review* 33.2 (2011): 207–30, 215. I might add that even readings attentive to the final strophe tend to focus on its imagery rather than on the level of the signifier, thereby missing the decisive, if momentary, shift that comes at this point. See, for example, Leslie Hill: "'Sprich auch du' concludes with an uncannily prophetic eschatological reference to a star, no doubt an image of the poem and the redemption it seems to promise, seeing its own reflection shimmering in the water, floating, says the poems, referring also to its own last dying words, 'in der Dünung / wandernder Worte,' 'dans le mouvement de houle / des mots qui toujours vont,' translates Blanchot: 'in the swell / of wandering words.'" Leslie Hill, "'Distrust of Poetry': Levinas, Blanchot, Celan," *Modern Language Notes* 120.5 (2005): 986–1008, 994.

15. The English translation of this verse follows the one that is offered in Felstiner, *Selected Poems and Prose,* 77.

16. John Felstiner, *Paul Celan: Poet, Survivor, Jew* (New Haven, CT: Yale University Press, 1995), 77–81.

17. Felstiner, 78.
18. Felstiner, 80.
19. Felstiner, 80.
20. Gianluca Solla, "'Sprich als letzter': Zeugenschaft—Ersetzung—Stellvertretung," trans. Judith Kasper, in *Singularitäten: Literatur, Wissenschaft, Verantwortung* (Rombach: Freiburg im Breisgau, 2001), 95–110. All translations from the German are my own.
21. Solla, 101.
22. Mieszkowski, "*Ich, Ach, Auch*," 218.
23. Mieszkowski, 219.
24. Again, while the English translation provided here is based to a great extent on that of Felstiner in *Selected Poems and Prose*, I have made certain small changes.
25. Derrida, "Shibboleth," 194.
26. Paul Celan, "Speech on the Occasion of Receiving the Literature Prize of the Free Hanseatic City of Bremen," trans. John Felstiner, in *Selected Poems and Prose*, 395–96, 396, trans. modified; Paul Celan, "Ansprache anlässlich der Entgegennahme des Literaturpreises der freien Hansestadt Bremen," in *Paul Celan: Der Meridian und andere Prosa*, eds. Beda Allemann and Stefan Reichert (Frankfurt am Main: Suhrkamp, 1988), 37–39, 39.
27. The address was delivered on January 20, 1958, a date that would return as a subject of extensive reflection in *The Meridian* delivered two years later. "Perhaps," Celan writes there, "we may say that every poem has its '20th of January' inscribed upon it? Perhaps what's new for poems written today is just this: that here the attempt is clearest to remain mindful of such dates?" Paul Celan, "The Meridian," in *Selected Poems and Prose*, 401–13, 408. In the context of the *Meridian* address, the date of the 20th of January refers at once to the beginning of Büchner's *Lenz* fragment, the 1942 Wannsee Conference, and perhaps even the eve of the execution of Louis XVI referred to in *Danton's Death*. Not only do dates, like anniversaries, repeatedly circle back in Celan but they are also encircled by—and made to orbit around—others. It is in this way that the date might be seen as being not only absolutely specific, a singular itinerary and a singularly ineluctable movement of (compulsive) return to and of the same, but also a movement that from the first will have been inhabited by and open to other returns—to those of the past as well as of the future ("And do we not all write ourselves from such dates? And what dates do we write toward and ascribe ourselves? [Und schreiben wir uns nicht alle von solchen Daten her? Und welchen Daten schreiben wir uns zu?])." Celan, "The Meridian," 408, trans. modified; Paul Celan, "Der Meridian," *Paul Celan: Der Meridian und andere Prosa*, 40–62, 53. As such, the date, while remaining singular and irreplaceable, will also at the same time never have been "one," never have been entirely identical with itself. "The date," as Derrida remarks, "yes and no." Derrida, "Shibboleth," 14.

28. Celan, "Speech on the Occasion," 396; Celan, "Ansprache anlässlich," 39.

29. Whereas the term *Geisterstunde* is usually associated with the midnight hour, it appears in conjunction with the noontide meridian in texts such as Wilhelm Jensen's *Gradiva*.

30. Derrida, "Shibboleth," 12–13, 28.

31. Derrida, 13.

32. Celan, "Der Meridian," 56.

33. Celan, 56.

34. Maurice Blanchot, "The Last One to Speak," trans. Joseph Simas, *Acts: A Journal of New Writing* 8–9 (1988–1989): 228–39, 228.

35. Blanchot, 228.

Chapter 2

# A Different *Withness*

Being with the Past in Paul Celan's "Engführung"

SIMONE STIRNER

What kind of *withness* is it?

—Anne Carson, *Economy of the Unlost:
Reading Simonides of Keos with Paul Celan*

"Displaced into / the terrain / with the unmistakable track: / Grass, written asunder. The stones, white / with the stalks' shadows [Verbracht ins / Gelände / Mit der untrüglichen Spur: / Gras, auseinandergeschrieben. Die Steine, weiß, / mit den Schatten der Halme]."[1] With these words begins Paul Celan's long poem "Engführung" ("Stretto") of 1958—a poem that will extend over 180 lines and several pages, frequently fragmented, moving through a poetic landscape marked by loss. The poem famously is in dialogue with Alain Resnais's film *Night and Fog* (*Nuit et brouillard*), the text of which—originally written by Jean Cayrol—Celan had translated.[2] The "terrain with the unmistakable track" evokes the landscape of the concentration camps that Resnais's film moves through. *Gras, auseinandergeschrieben*, in this line of thought, can be read as an evocation of the first long tracking shot that, carried by the calm and rhythmic voice of the speaker, pans over green grass "written asunder" by barbed wire fences.[3] At the same time, the "terrain" also seems to speak of the poem itself, its lines reaching across several pages like stalk shadows, a poetic terrain that is heavy with history.[4] The historical wounds of the concentration camps appear mirrored in the form of the poem.

With this wounded terrain—historical and textual—in view, two imperatives give reason to pause. Following the poem's turn toward a view onto "stones, white / with the stalks' shadows," we read:

Stop reading—look!
Stop looking—go!⁵

(Lies nicht mehr—schau!
Schau nicht mehr—geh!)⁶

What would it mean to "stop reading" and instead to "go" into this terrain, or to "walk" even; to read that one is to read no more and then to continue reading, but in a way that is also a form of walking, possibly perceiving or being with language otherwise? These imperatives seem suddenly to shift the reader toward an engagement with the poem that centers the body rather than the mind, one that experiences the poem's breaks and gaps and moments of silence not only as signs but also as something tangible.⁷ "Walking a poem" seems to guide us to the foot of its meter, its pace of breath. It indicates a mode of readerly relation that differs from the goal-oriented gesture of hermeneutics that so often accompanies interpretations of Celan.⁸ What, further, is at stake if we "stop reading" and "go," if the terrain is dense with the traces of history? What kind of relation between reading, text, and history does this establish? What practice of remembrance does it constitute? Or, to pick up a term that poet Anne Carson coins in her reading of Celan: "What kind of *withness* is it"?⁹

The centrality of "Engführung" within the larger context of Celan's work and poetics has been discussed extensively. Jean Daive, poet and friend of Celan, called the long poem his "*ars poetica* for the end of time."¹⁰ Taking the poem's own idiosyncratic instructions for reading (or *not* reading) as a point of departure (and bracketing Daive's "end of time"), my essay identifies "Engführung" as an *ars poetica* that posits poetry as the site of an intersubjective corporeality that opens to the depth of history. Rather than seeking to represent the past, I suggest, the poem compels a practice of reading—and with that of remembering—by which the past is experienced as implicated in the present of reading. This argument has to be understood in the context of a broader shift in Celan's work. Often, "Engführung" is seen as a direct comment on and departure from the aesthetics of Celan's "Todesfuge" ("Death Fugue"), with which it shares a commitment to testify, poetically, to the concentration camps. Like Celan's most famous poem, so Aris Fioretos, "Engführung" "tr[ies] to circumscribe the incomparable event of the Holocaust."[11] Stéfane Mosès, in a similar vein, argues that it "raises to the order of an allegory of absolute terror."[12] The Nazi genocide and the concentration camps in particular are one dimension of what we can, with Dominick LaCapra, call the poem's "aboutness," its historical referentiality.[13] Another comes to us through Celan's own comment on the text. In a letter to Erich Einhorn, Celan explains that the poem "evokes the devastation of the atomic bomb."[14] Throughout, the poem will hold space for these two historical referents—the concentration camps and the atomic bomb—as two histories of violence, alongside each other. While both "Todesfuge" and "Engführung," then, are concerned with the memory of the concentration camps, they differ significantly on the level of form. "Engführung" is often perceived as a turning point in Celan's aesthetics, away from what Pierre Joris has described as the "abundance of near-surrealistic imagery and sometimes labyrinthine metaphoricity" in his early poetry toward an aesthetic that is more obscure, in which the "syntax grew tighter and more spiny [and] his trademark neologisms and telescoping of words increased."[15] Indeed, neologisms abound in "Engführung," words cascade in ways that render language almost plastic.[16] The fragmented layout potentially interrupts the reading, disturbing attempts for goal-oriented meaning-making and cohesive understanding, seemingly complicating or even withdrawing access to what this poem is really "about." Celan's "obscurity" is frequently read in terms of a poetic withdrawal into hermeticism in the face of the "unspeakable" nature of the Nazi genocide. He famously denied the hermetic character of his work, but the sense persisted that something is not accessible in his writing, at the same time that it challenged (and continues to challenge) an excess of interpretations.[17]

Against this claim of the inaccessible nature of Celan's poetry, "Engführung" starts out by moving readers right *into* something. Without having asked for it, readers are granted access—not to cohesive "understanding" but to a "terrain" that is both textual and historical. In what might be the most famous interpretation of "Engführung" to date, Peter Szondi describes its peculiar status as follows: "Poetry is not mimesis, is no longer representation: it becomes reality."[18] The text therefore cannot be "read," nor can the images it describes be "looked" at, and "traditional methods of reading" are inadequate.[19] "Engführung," hence, requires us to read—and remember—otherwise. Like "Todesfuge," "Engführung" commits to the memory of the concentration camps, but—distancing itself from "Todesfuge"—"Engführung" insists that the past is not displaced through images and affirms instead a relation to the past that bears the porous, chiasmic parameters of touch and breath.

A crucial factor in understanding this dimension of "Engführung"—and Celan's poetics in general—is Celan's own engagement with phenomenology. Around the time when Celan writes "Engführung" and in the months leading up to his *Meridian* speech, Celan is increasingly concerned with matters of perception, attentiveness, and phenomenological orientedness. Frank König connects this to what he describes as Celan's "resistant attitude toward language as pure message."[20] Poems, as Celan writes in the notes to *The Meridian*, are not "messages," not "information"; they are rather, as he puts it, underway on routes "on which language becomes voice, . . . encounters, routes of a voice to a perceiving you [Wege auf denen Sprache stimmhaft wird, . . . Begegnungen, Wege einer Stimme zu einem wahrnehmenden Du]."[21]

In what follows, I trace a peculiar mode of perceptive orientation and encounter on different levels of "Engführung." I zero in on one passage that confronts us thematically with an attunement of breath, rhythmic touch, and a scene in which a finger reaches through time, all while withdrawing vision and foregrounding forms of tactile, instead of visual, perception. I recuperate this scene as a poetological reflection before tracing in a next step the breath-pattern of the poem itself. Breath, which has long been considered central to the poetics of Celan, reveals itself as the paradigmatic figure for a temporal and corporeal susceptibility. It is the site of an opening toward an other, a moment of vulnerability but also in this capacity a site of potentiality. In breathing with a poem, we might give life to the past, give air to traces that have been covered over. Beyond its semantic dimension, then, drawing on the resources of poetic form, "Engführung" reconfigures the relation between the text, the history that it carries with it, and the present of reading so that the question of how to be with this text—how to read it or look at it, breathe with it or possibly even walk with it—also becomes a question of how to be with its history—on and off the page. "Walking" the terrain with the unmistakable trace—instead of reading it or looking at it—readers experience its historic weight as entwined with their own present, turning reading into a practice of "withness," of being with the past in the present. This withness constitutes its own form of witnessing, *ein Zugegen-sein, das auch Zeugenschaft ist.*

## Blind Palpations

"Engführung" does not extend an imperative to stop reading and "go" right away. Interjected, briefly, is also a call to "look." Let me hence begin by looking at the text. In the edition of Celan's *Collected Works* (*Gesammelte Werke*) edited by Beda Allemann and Stefan Reichert, the poem spans over ten pages.[22] It stands out, not only because of its length but also due to the peculiar organization on the page: the sequence of stanzas on the left side of the pages is repeatedly interrupted by brief visual echoes on the right side. An asterisk marks the beginning of the poem and precedes each of the nine sections on the right.[23] The typographic layout appears fragmented because of its unusual semi-rhythmic dispersal across the page and at the same time highly formalized. In the poem's shape, we might see the fingers of a hand or an electrocardiographic image rotated by ninety degrees.

Returning to a more "conventional" form of reading, we find that the poem speaks of not seeing while increasingly withdrawing images from its language. Following the opening lines that move into the "terrain with the unmistakable track" or "trace" (*Spur*) and the imperative to "stop reading . . . go," the subsequent passage follows the movement of a wheel whose "spokes climb, climb on a blackish field," through night that "needs no stars."[24] At this point, the layout opens up for the first time. The words "nirgends / fragt es nach dir [nowhere / are you asked after]" conclude the first section and then reappear and repeat like an echo on the right end of the page.[25] Between the stanzas and the single words on the right, the white page is at once a visual negative to the "blackish field" and an echo to the absence of vision and the darkness that are thematized in the poem. The next stanza continues with a series of displacements of certainty:

> The place where they lay, it has
> a name—it has
> none. They didn't lie there. Something
> lay between them. They
> didn't see through it.
>
> Didn't see, no,
> talked of
> words. None
> woke up,

> sleep
> came over them.
>
> (Der Ort, wo sie lagen, er hat
> einen Namen—er hat
> keinen. Sie lagen nicht dort. Etwas
> lag zwischen ihnen. Sie
> sahn nicht hindurch
>
> Sahn nicht, nein,
> redeten von
> Worten. Keines
> erwachte, der
> Schlaf
> kam über sie.)

A place is first announced as having a name and then none. Someone is identified as lying "there" before the poem withdraws this statement again: "Sie lagen nicht dort [They didn't lie there]." Something came between "them" and intercepts vision ("They didn't see through it") before the fall of sleep reaffirms the closure of eyes. Someone "talked of words," but in reading, we as readers do not learn what this speaking-of-words is about, just as we might not fully understand the poem itself. And yet we stay with it, continue to walk through this scene, feel our way through the unknown, until we hear of "sleep" that "came over them." Then the layout opens up once more, and the poem signals toward a question that remains open:

> Came, came. Nowhere
>             asked after—[26]
>
> (Kam, kam. Nirgends
>           fragt es—)[27]

At this point in the poem, vision has been suspended ("Didn't see, no") but something (the word?) pushes forward. The next stanza draws a strange scene of intimacy and precarious encounter into focus:

> It's me, me,
> I lay between you, I was

open, was
audible, I ticked toward you, your breath
obeyed, I
am still the one, as
you're asleep.
\*

                                    Am still the one—

Years.
Years, years, a finger
feels down and up, feels
around:
seams, palpable, here
they gape wide open, here
it grew together again—who
covered it up?[28]

(Ich bins, ich,
ich lag zwischen euch, ich war
offen, war
hörbar, ich tickte euch zu, euer Atem
gehorchte, ich
bin es noch immer, ihr
schlaft ja.
\*

                                  Bin es noch immer—

Jahre.
Jahre, Jahre, ein Finger
tastet hinab und hinan, tastet
umher:
Nahtstellen, fühlbar, hier
klafft es weit auseinander, hier
wuchs es wieder zusammen—wer
deckte es zu?)[29]

An "I" announces itself, is audible, ticks toward an other—a plural "you"—whose breath, then, falls in step with the speaker. As if in affirmation of the previous section that suspended vision, readers also have to endure a striking reduction of imagery and figurative language at the very moment that these lines thematically carry over into different perceptive registers, first to listening and then to touch.³⁰ There is a ticking sound, the response of "breath," and then a finger that slowly feels its way downward, a blind palpation of covered-over seams or sutures (*Nahtstellen*).

Curiously, the language in this passage of "Engführung" in which touch and breath take over vision resonates with a central passage in Celan's *Meridian* speech in which Celan speaks of the attentiveness of the poem:³¹

> The attention the poem tries to pay to everything it encounters, its sharper sense of detail, outline, structure, color, but also of the "tremors" and "hints," all that is not, I believe, the achievement of an eye competing with (or emulating) ever more precise instruments, but is rather a concentration that remains mindful of all our dates.

> (Die Aufmerksamkeit, die das Gedicht allem ihm Begegnenden zu widmen versucht, sein schärferer Sinn für das Detail, für Umriß, für Struktur, für Farbe, aber auch für die "Zuckungen" und die "Andeutungen," das alles ist, glaube ich, keine Errungenschaft des mit den täglich perfekteren Apparaten wetteifernden (oder miteifernden) Auges, es ist vielmehr eine aller unserer Daten eingedenk bleibende Konzentration.)³²

Two years after "Engführung," Celan hence describes an attention that is not "the achievement of an eye" but the manifestation of a sense for detail, for "tremors" and "hints." The critique of the "eye" competing with the ever more "precise instruments" links up with the suspension of "looking" in "Engführung." The sense for "Zuckungen" ("tremors") suggests a form of perceptive encounter that seems closer to corporeal touch, attentive to the unexpected movements of a body. In characterizing the attention of the poem as concentration "mindful of all our dates," the above segment from Celan's speech also echoes the temporal depth present in "Engführung," when a voice speaks of the past, and a finger feels its way downward through "years. / years, years," before it hits upon sutures, traces of a past covered over. Touch, here, seeks to bridge not only between an "I" and a "you" but also between different times. The most striking site of a crossing between touch and time, however, might be the verb "ticken" in "I ticked toward you [Ich tickte euch zu]." Most immediately, "ticken" indicates the sound of a clock—and, with it, metonymically evokes the passing of time. As Szondi has pointed out, the word "ticken" in this verse "means both what it signifies today and 'touching'; the word imparts both meanings simultaneously, because both at this point become one."³³ "Ticken" momentarily holds the sense of hearing and the sense of touch in one, before the next stanza draws the reader further into a scene in which the connection between time and touch now unfolds to convey a sense of fingers touching, reaching through "years," tracing downward toward sutures: "Here / they gape wide open, here / it grew together again." The word "Nahtstellen" ("seams" or "sutures"), seems to indicate stitches, potentially of a wounded body, but the consequent line, "it grew together again," also suggests that this sutured scar might be a *Grasnarbe*, which translates directly as "grass-scar," returning us to the images of the grown-over landscape of the concentration camps from *Nuit et brouillard*. In the midst of this movement, Celan's own comments on what the poem is about return: "Engführung" is also a poem that speaks of the devastations of the atomic bomb. And according to Dietlind Meinecke, Celan emphasized specifically that there are "bombs ticking in this poem," that something "announces itself."³⁴ As the poem's speaker "ticks," as breath obeys, and as a finger runs over a surface for palpable traces, the "terrain" that this blind palpation attends to is thick with historical reality: bombs ticking, the wounds of the concentration camps resisting to be covered over.

In a long poem that marks Celan's shift toward a more "obscure" aesthetic, the passage that intercepts vision and foregrounds a sense of physical touch as well as an encounter through breath, reads like a meta-poetic statement. This idea that "Engführung" tells us something about poetry is confirmed in other instances. For one, in its focus on a breathing encounter, "Engführung" appears to prefigure a moment from the *Meridian*, in which Celan famously states: "Poetry: that can mean an *Atemwende*, a breathturn [Dichtung, das kann eine *Atemwende* bedeuten]."³⁵ There is a turn of breath happening at this moment in the poem, a turning toward an other through breath, suggesting that this scene, in which we do not truly see what we are reading and attending to, brings us to the heart of poetry. Lesser known, but equally relevant, Celan once noted: "Poetry, that is not 'word art'; it is a matter of listening and obeying—[Dichtung ist nicht 'Wortkunst'; sie ist ein Horchen und Gehorchen—]."³⁶ The German "gehorchen" that the English translation of "Engführung" renders as "obeyed" in the line "your breath obeyed," contains in the original the term "horchen," "listening," drawing together the two dimensions that constitute poetry for Celan. The speaker is "audible [hörbar]," and when the breath of an addressed "you" "obeys," this response is hence a form of "listening [horchen]." It is a peculiar form of attunement and encounter that this scene describes and enacts through a thickening of language, an *Engführung*, or "leading into closeness" of sorts, *ein Verdichten*.

We can see now how this scene that confronts us with an embodied, rhythmic witness projects poetry as the site of a corporeal susceptibility toward the past. If "Engführung" is an *ars poetica*, as Daive suggested, it tells us—similarly to *The Meridian* two years later—that poetry is a breath-turn, that it bears a sense of direction, feeling its way toward an other, a movement of attentive directionality that is also "mindful of all its dates," reaching through years and years.[37]

## Breathing with "Engführung"

Celan's statement that poetry "can mean an *Atemwende*, a breathturn," is only one among many instances in his *Meridian* speech and the preparatory notes to it that turn on the figure of breath.[38] For instance, one of them reads: "On breathroutes, it comes, the poem, it is there, pneumatic: for everyone [Auf Atemwegen kommt es, das Gedicht, pneumatisch ist es da, für jeden]."[39] Another one remarks: "Breath: The poem remains . . . pneumatically touchable [Atem: Das Gedicht bleibt . . . pneumatisch berührbar]."[40] The poem is "the trace of our breath in language," and the "aura [Hauch] of our mortality."[41] At yet another moment, Celan writes "the poem = breath = creature."[42] Breath operates semantically in Celan's poetry and poetics—as a term, trope, metaphor, or figure. If we conjoin the English "breath" and the German "Atem" with the Greek "*pneuma*" and the Hebrew "*ruah*" and "*neshima*," then the term opens up to notions of inspiration and animation, unsettles the boundary between the spiritual and the corporeal, and reminds us of the threshold between life and death.[43] It describes a form of temporalized experience that is both momentary (the individual moment of inhalation and exhalation) and ongoing (the rhythmic interchange between both across time). In this sense, breath is a ticking and touching of its own. Crucially, in the context of poetry that is marked by the concrete historical reality of the concentration camps, to think about breath is to think about the gas chambers—inscribing the historical dimension into the semantic dimensions of breath.

With this in mind, what would it look like if the readers' breath "obeyed" the claim of "Engführung" and what is at stake in such a form of encounter? Celan himself emphasizes the importance of attending to breath as a somatic operation. Picking up on a German idiom, his notes to *The Meridian* give remarkable instructions for reading:[44]

> "What's on the lung, put on the tongue," my mother used to say. Which has to do with breath. One should finally learn how to also read this breath, this breath-unit in the poem; in the cola meaning is often more truthfully joined and fugued than in the rhyme; shape of the poem: that is the presence of the single, breathing one.
>
> ("Was auf der Lunge, das auf der Zunge," pflegte meine Mutter zu sagen. Das hat mit dem Atem zu tun. Man sollte endlich lernen, im Gedicht diesen Atem, diese Atemeinheit mitzulesen; in den Kolen ist der Sinn oft wahrer gefügt und gefugt als im Reim; Gestalt des Gedichts: das ist Gegenwart des Einzelnen, Atmenden.)[45]

In emphasizing the importance of reading the "breath-units" of a poem, Celan draws on Martin Buber and Franz Rosenzweig's practice of Bible translation, which highlighted the importance of recuperating the breath rhythm of the Hebrew original in the German version.[46] In her discussion of Celan and the Buber-Rosenzweig translation, Maya Barzilai has shown that "reading Celan's poetry in view of the breath-unit implies heeding both the literal and thematized breaks and pauses of which the poems consist."[47] In "Engführung," breath is not only a figure for the specific relational structure of poetry but can also take a concrete shape through the act of reading the breath-rhythm, giving over one's body to the rhythm of the text, letting it come to bear upon one's breath, if only for the limited time of reading a poem. Breath, in other words, is not only a trope for a particular relationality, but also a somatic practice exercised in reading. From here, I want to follow Celan's instructions, focusing on the very passage that introduced breath as the relating moment between an "I" and a "you" to see how the poem itself attunes the reader to its rhythm, and what happens if the reader's breath obeys the ticking/touching of the poem.

Once more, we might begin by observing the fragmentariness of the poem as a whole, its layout on the page that breaks apart the stanzas, setting them to different sides of the pages. The shorter, single lines to the right of the longer stanzas give off the impression of a response, maybe an echo. Between both "sides," the wide gaps create an occasion for breath, they allow for the reader to inhale and pick up the reading again after a pause—potentially at least.[48] These empty spaces seem like visualizations or indeed materializations of the "Atemhöfe," "breath-steads," whose importance Celan would emphasize elsewhere.[49] But the breath rhythm is not only produced through the pauses between words. Breath is carried and guided by individual words, as some demand aspiration, others expiration. Remarkably, one of the texts that Celan read around the time of preparing *The Meridian*, Gaston Bachelard's *Air and Dreams*, (*L'Air et les songes*) points us to the nuances of breathing with poetry—down to the level of the single word and syllable.[50] In the French word for soul, "*âme*," for instance, Bachelard suggests that "the broad 'â' is a vowel that is pronounced with a sigh—the word *âme* gives a bit of sonority to the aspirated vowel"; with the word "*âme*," we exhale.[51] Paying attention to the phonetic patterns in the sections of "Engführung" that follow upon the moment that addresses breath directly, one can detect a remarkable pattern of words that all place the accent on a short "a" that is exhaled in a repetitive sequence. Consider these stanzas again:

> Jahre.
> Jahre, Jahre, ein Finger
> tastet hinab und hinan, tastet
> . . .
> Kam, kam.
> Kam ein Wort, kam,
> kam durch die Nacht,
> wollt leuchten, wollt leuchten.
>
> Asche.
> Asche, Asche.
> Nacht.
> Nacht-und-Nacht. . . .[52]
>
> (Years.
> Years, years, a finger
> feels down and up, feels
> . . .
> Came, came.
> Came a word, came,

came through the night,
wanted to shine, wanted to shine.

Ashes.
Ashes, ashes.
Night.
Night-and-night. . . .)[53]

Voicing the poem in the original, following the series of *a*'s, breath narrows down, tightens, as the poem demands exhalation upon exhalation. A sequence like "kam, kam. / Kam" minimizes the opportunity to draw in air. The plosive phoneme "k," formed further back in the oral passage than other consonants, obstructs the air where vocal chords are vibrating against each other.[54] Voicing the poem, the reader is drawn into a nearness with the rhythm of the poem, into an "Engführung" of sorts. If we breathe with "Engführung," we have to endure a tightening and restriction of breath. This narrowing of breath occurs at the very moment that the poem speaks of the coming of the word through the night, before subsequently passing into darkness, encountering ashes—a scene that evokes the memory of the concentration camps and the atomic bomb. The readers accompany the poem into this darkness precisely as their own breath narrows. In a text, which is marked by the memory of toxic, lethal air, the realization that the readers run out of breath profoundly affects our understanding of this text's relation to remembrance.[55] What kind of withness is this?

The fact that "Engführung" takes its readers with it, guiding their breath, is of course not unique to this one poem. Presuming that we do indeed vocalize poetry—as Celan asks us to do—then any poem shapes the reader's breath-rhythm through its rhythm. What is unique in "Engführung," however, is that it allows for an awareness of this pattern in the very moment that the poem's implicit theorization of poetry as a corporeal, pneumatic encounter allows us to see the connection between such a form of withness and history. Being "with" the poem, we are also "with" its dates and the historical reality to which it testifies.

## Reaching through Time

In order to understand the stakes of breathing with the poem but also thinking of a practice of reading and remembrance that is akin to breath,

Celan's engagement with phenomenology proves helpful. As bibliographical notes confirm, Celan reads Husserl, including *On the Phenomenology of the Consciousness of Internal Time* (*Vorlesungen zur Phänomenologie des inneren Zeitbewusstseins*) and the *Logical Investigations* (*Logische Untersuchungen*); he takes notes on Franz Brentanos's notion of "intentionality," as well as on Bachelard's *Air and Dreams*.[56] Axel Gellhaus recalls that, in 1958, Celan expressed intent to write a study on the "phenomenology of the poetic [eine Phänomenologie des Poetischen]."[57] An emphasis on poetry as an encounter that involves forms of corporeal presence and attention returns, in different iterations, all throughout his notes to *The Meridian*. "On the hands . . . the poem comes to you, puts itself into your hand [Auf den Händen . . . kommt das Gedicht zu dir, gibt es sich dir in die Hand],"[58] states another note, which also recalls a moment from a letter Celan sent to Hans Bender that speaks of the poem as a "handshake."[59] These notes point us to the corporeal dimension of reading.[60] However, they also alert us, importantly, to understanding the practice of reading and relating to the poem and the past *like* a physical activity, as bearing the characteristics of physical touch—an understanding that carries temporal implications. When Celan uses the term "*Atemeinheit*," "breath-unit," the most immediate reference is Buber's use of the term in the context of his and Rosenzweig's Bible translation. There is, however, another term that recurs throughout the notes to *The Meridian*, and that is "breathstead," or "Atemhof," which in turn invokes that of "timestead," or "Zeithof."[61] In one of the preparatory fragments, Celan notes: "Timesteads, breathed through, breathed around [Zeithöfe, durchatmet, umatmet]," affirming the intimate connection between the two terms—and between time and breath.[62] "Zeithof" is a term used by Edmund Husserl to describe the "halo" of "retentions" and "protentions" belonging to each moment in time.[63] This temporal structure in Husserl seems to lack the corporeal dimension of Celan's "Atemhof," but there is a moment in his *On the Phenomenology of the Consciousness of Internal Time* that offers a helpful example for the experience of temporal "halos." In it, Husserl likens their structure of temporal retentions and protentions to the physical experience of music:

> Like the violin tone (thought of as something physical), the appearance of the tone has its duration; and in this duration it changes or remains constant. I can focus my attention on one phase or another of this appearance: appearance here is

the immanent tone or the immanent tonal movement, apart from its "signifying." But this is not the ultimate consciousness. This immanent tone becomes "constituted"; namely, together with the tone-now of the moment we also continuously have tone-adumbrations, and in these adumbrations the extent of tone-pasts that belong to this now presents itself. . . . In the case of a melody, for example, we can bring a moment to a halt, so to speak, and find in it the memorial adumbrations of the preceding tones. Obviously the same thing also applies to each individual tone. We then have the immanent tone-now and the immanent tone-pasts in their succession. But, in addition, we are supposed to have the following continuity: perception of the now and memory of the past; and this whole continuity is itself supposed to be a now.[64]

Husserl's "Zeithof"—the temporal "halo" that thinks the present "now" as drawing together layers of pasts and futures, retentions and protentions of the "now," into an intimate belonging—resonates with the temporal structure implied in the image of breath ticking and touching toward an other through "years, years, years" in "Engführung."[65] Where Husserl uses the physical experience of music as an example to describe the structure of time as a form of temporal belonging, Celan's "Engführung" projects poetry as the privileged site for such a temporal experience. "Engführung," this long poem that draws together the history of the concentration camps with the ticking of the atomic bomb in the present of reading, provides a figure for the experience of a temporal intertwining of different times. At the same time, as readers breathe with the poem reading becomes the site of a "timestead, breathed through," in which the past realizes itself as entwined with the present.

As Pajari Räsänen has noted, one of the first mentions of the Husserlian "Zeithof" in Celan occurs in the poet's engagement with Osip Mandelstam when Celan suggests that the latter's poems "stand" in a "timestead."[66] In 1959, in an introductory text to his Mandelstam translations, Celan describes this as follows:

For Mandelstam, the poem is a place where all we can perceive and attain through language is gathered around a center which provides form and truth: around the being of an individual,

> challenging the hour, its own and that of the world, the heartbeat and the aeon. This is to show to what extent Mandelstam's poems . . . concern us today.[67]
>
> ([Bei] Mandelstam [ist] das Gedicht der Ort, wo das über die Sprache Wahrnehmbare und Erreichbare um jene Mitte versammelt wird, von der her es Gestalt und Wahrheit gewinnt: um das die Stunde, die eigene und die der Welt, den Herzschlag und den Äon befragende Dasein dieses Einzelnen. Damit ist gesagt, in welchem Maße das Mandelstamsche Gedicht . . . uns Heutige angeht.)[68]

For Celan, the possibility of thinking Mandelstam's poem as "concerning" the present depends on understanding language as the site of what König describes as an "intersubjective corporeality with spatio-temporal implications [intersubjektive Leiblichkeit mit raumzeitlichen Implikationen]."[69] The poem concerns us today because of its peculiar relationality that implies the body. As König has emphasized in his reading of the passage cited above, it is through one's being and one's body ("den Herzschlag") that the individual is connected to the Eon, to the infinite, the world—and then to us in our embodied being ("mit unserem jeweiligen Leib")—today.[70] In this description, Celan comes close to Maurice Merleau-Ponty who, in a section of the *Phenomenology of Perception* that discusses the spatiality of the body, writes:

> Insofar as I have a body and insofar as I act in the world through it, space and time are not for me a mere summation of juxtaposed points, and no more are they, for that matter, an infinity of relations synthesized by my consciousness in which my body would be implicated. I am not in space and in time, nor do I think space and time; rather, I am of space and of time; my body fits itself to them and embraces them.[71]

In the language of "Engführung" as well as through his writing on Mandelstam, Celan approximates the thought of Husserl and Merleau-Ponty. If it is through our body that we reach into the world of perception, then poetry—which, for Celan, holds a corporeal dimension—allows for this opening toward the past and a different form of being with it. The poem with its breathed-through timesteads is a site where the past "concerns us today." The reader—corporeally present to the poem—is entwined with its history. There is, then, in Celan, an implicit argument that posits poetry as an interface between the past and the present, relying specifically on its corporeal dimensions. The past is neither something to be seen nor something to be decoded. Rather, in reading, we experience our enmeshment with it and are rendered susceptible to it.

The practice of breathing with a poem might be the most concrete form of this intersubjective corporeality. Ultimately, however, the relation spanning poem, reader, and history does not rely on the poem being voiced. Celan's "Engführung" posits this entwinement as constitutive of poetry as such. In "Engführung," it is foregrounded through the embodied attention both figured in and invited by the text. "Engführung" teaches us to experience the intertwining of past and present in a way that emphasizes that the past is inextricably bound up with the present while also retaining its otherness. That is to say, in reading, this other time—of the camps, of the atomic bomb—is not only irretrievable, and in this sense, definitively other to our own, but also at once part of it. For Celan, it is crucial to think of the past and present as sharing the same time—if not breath. Even if the past is unseen and cannot be represented, poetically or otherwise, it forms part of the now.

In the final moments of Resnais's *Nuit et brouillard*, as the camera moves once more over the "terrain" and the physical remainders of the former concentration camp, the voice-over extends a warning:

> *And here we are, earnestly looking at these ruins as though the old monster of the camps lay dead beneath the rubble,*
> *we who pretend to regain hope before this image that recedes into the distance, as if one could ever be cured of the plague of the camps,*
> *we who pretend to believe that it is all confined to a single epoch and a single country, and who don't think of looking around ourselves,*
> *and who don't hear that people are crying out without end.*[72]

Looking at the rubble as if the old monster of the camps lay dead beneath it: these words remind us that looking is no guarantee for seeing and acting upon persistent danger. Witnessing can harden and become inattentive. In "Engführung," something resists being covered over; sutures are still palpable as a finger reaches through years; something is audible and someone listens. Past violence is not confined to a single epoch; the memory of the Nazi camps and that of the atomic bomb form part of the same halo of the poem's present. This restructuring of the relation between past and present into an embodied withness is not just a model provided through the poem's images or figures; it is also realized in the process of reading as a pneumatic susceptibility toward the past in the present, concerning us today.

## Notes

1. Paul Celan, "Engführung," in *Gesammelte Werke*, vol. 1, *Gedichte I*, eds. Beda Allemann and Stefan Reichert (Frankfurt am Main: Suhrkamp Verlag, 1983) 195–204, 197; Paul Celan, "Stretto," in *Memory Rose into Threshold Speech: The Collected Earlier Poetry: A Bilingual Edition*, trans. Pierre Joris (New York: Farrar, Straus, and Giroux, 2020), 227–39, 227. All subsequent citations of passages from this poem refer to these pages.

2. Jean Cayrol, "Nacht und Nebel: Kommentar zum Film von Alain Resnais," trans. Paul Celan, in *Gesammelte Werke*, vol. 4, *Übertragungen I*, eds. Beda Allemann and Stefan Reichert (Frankfurt am Main: Suhrkamp Verlag, 1983), 76–99. For discussions of the relation between the film and the poem, see, for instance, Otto Lorenz, *Schweigen in der Dichtung: Hölderlin, Rilke, Celan* (Göttingen: Vandenhoeck and Rupprecht, 1989), 207. On Celan's translation itself, David N. Coury writes: "Celan's translation of the script is at once an exact, thoughtful translation from the French, as well as a poetic work in and of itself, echoing and utilizing many of the themes and images that reverberate throughout his poetry." In "Engführung," we encounter such reverberations frequently. David N. Coury, "'Auch ruhiges Land': Remembrance and Testimony in Paul Celan's *Nuit et Brouillard* Translation," *Prooftexts* 22.1/2 (Winter/Spring 2002): 59.

3. Coury, "'Auch ruhiges Land,'" 66; Eric Kligerman, "Celan's Cinematic: Anxiety of the Gaze in *Night and Fog* and 'Engführung,'" in *Visualizing the Holocaust*, eds. David Bathrick, Brad Prager, and Michael D. Richardson (Rochester: Camden House, 2008), 185–210, 205.

4. As Peter Szondi states in his substantial engagement with the poem: "The blades of grass are also letters, and the landscape is text. Only because the 'terrain / with the infallible trace' is (also) text can the reader be 'driven' into its interior." Peter Szondi, "Reading 'Engführung': An Essay on the Poetry of Paul Celan," trans. D. Caldwell and S. Esh, *Boundary* 2 no. 11.3 (1983): 231–64.

5. Celan, "Stretto," 227.

6. Celan, "Engführung," 197.

7. For another discussion of the opening of "Engführung" that negotiates the poem's transition from "reading" to "walking" see also Aris Fioretos, "Nothing: History and Materiality in Paul Celan," in *Word Traces* (Baltimore: Johns Hopkins University Press, 1994), 295–344. Fioretos suggests that the act of reading a poem, which extends the imperative to "stop reading," causes readers to "exert violence

in each step of its process" (323). I see this continuation of reading less as a form of violence and rather as an expansion of our understanding of what constitutes reading in the first place and as a challenge to be and bear with a text despite what is irresolvable in it. In that sense, both these approaches might ultimately hold true.

      8. In the words of Sidra de Koven Ezrahi, for instance, there is an entire school of interpretation that has treated "Celan's encoded, private, opaque poetry" as a "buried text that can be deciphered and materialized by a laborious unearthing of every shard of biographical, empirical, and intertextual material." Sidra de Koven Ezrahi, *Booking Passage: Exile and Homecoming in the Modern Jewish Imagination* (Berkeley: University of California Press, 2000).

      9. Anne Carson, *Economy of the Unlost: (Reading Simonides of Keos with Paul Celan)* (Princeton, NJ: Princeton University Press, 2001), viii. As Andre Furlani notes, "The question invites us to rethink notions of literary propinquity," considering forms of "approaching, engaging, touching, replying to, respecting, and accompanying Celan's work." It is with these modes of relationality in mind that I use the term "withness" throughout my chapter. See Andre Furlani, "Reading Paul Celan with Anne Carson: 'What Kind of Withness Would That Be?,'" *Canadian Literature* 176 (2003): 84–104, 88.

      10. Jean Daive, *Under the Dome: Walks with Paul Celan*, trans. Rosmarie Waldrop (Providence, RI: Burning Deck Press, 2009), 29.

      11. Aris Fioretos, "Nothing: Reading Paul Celan's 'Engführung,'" *Comparative Literature Studies* 27.2 (1990): 158–68, 159.

      12. Stéphane Mosès, "'Wege, auf denen Sprache stimmhaft wird': Paul Celan's 'Gespräch um Gebirg,'" in *Argumentum e Silentio*, ed. Amy D. Colin (Berlin: de Gruyter, 1987), 43–57, 54.

      13. Dominick LaCapra, *Writing History, Writing Trauma* (Baltimore: Johns Hopkins University Press, 2014), 188.

      14. Paul Celan to Erich Einhorn, 10 August 1962, *Einhorn: Du weißt um die Steine . . . Briefwechsel*, ed. Marina Dmitrieva-Einhorn (Berlin: Friedenauer Presse, 2001), 7. See Paul Celan, *Die Gedichte*, 669.

      15. Pierre Joris, introduction to *Breathturn into Timestead: The Collected Later Poetry of Paul Celan* (New York: Farrar, Straus, and Giroux, 2014), xl.

      16. In one moment, for instance, the poem moves through a long series of adjectives that create a felt sense of material surfaces, foregrounding the plasticity of organic matter: "Gritty and stringy. Stalky / dense; / clustery and raying; knobbly / level and / clumpy [körnig und faserig, stengeling, / dicht; traubig und strahlig; nierig, / plattig und / klump:g]." Readers do not know what these terms describe, that is, what *is* gritty and stalky in the first place. Celan, "Engführung," 201; Celan, "Stretto," 234–35. Joel Golb offers an excellent interpretation of this passage and what he calls Celan's "adjectival clump[s]." Joel Golb, "Reading Celan: The Allegory of 'Hohles Lebensgehöft' and 'Engführung,'" in *Word Traces*, ed. Aris Fioretos (Baltimore: Johns Hopkins University Press, 1994), 185–218, 202–3.

17. See James K. Lyon, "'Ganz und gar nicht hermetisch': Überlegungen zum 'richtigen' Lesen von Paul Celans Lyrik," in *Psalm und Hawdalah*, ed. Joseph Strelka (Bern: Lang, 1987), 171–91. For an overview of the early critical responses to Celan's poetry, see Bianca Rosenthal, *Pathways to Paul Celan: A History of Critical Responses as a Chorus of Discordant Voices* (New York: Peter Lang, 1995).

18. Szondi, "Reading 'Engführung,'" 231.

19. Szondi, 231.

20. König speaks of Celan's "Verweigerungshaltung gegenüber der Sprache als reine Form der Mitteilung" in Frank König, *Vertieftes Sein: Wahrnehmung und Körperlichkeit bei Paul Celan und Maurice Merleau-Ponty* (Heidelberg: Universitätsverlag Winter, 2014), 21; my translation.

21. Paul Celan, *Der Meridian: Endfassung—Entwürfe—Materialien*, eds. Bernhard Böschenstein and Heino Schmull (Frankfurt am Main: Suhrkamp Verlag, 1999), 11; Paul Celan, *The Meridian: Final Version—Drafts—Materials*, trans. Pierre Joris (Stanford: Stanford University Press, 2011), 11. All citations from the English version of *The Meridian* refer to this edition but will not be noted separately since the pagination is the same in both editions.

22. In Barbara Wiedemann's edition with commentary, the poem takes up six pages. See Paul Celan, "Engführung," in *Die Gedichte: Neue kommentierte Gesamtausgabe in einem Band*, ed. Barbara Wiedemann (Berlin: Suhrkamp, 2018), 117–22.

23. For more on the asterisk in "Engführung," see Fioretos, "Nothing."

24. Celan, "Stretto," 227.

25. Celan, 227.

26. Celan, 229.

27. Celan, "Engführung," 198.

28. Celan, "Stretto," 229, 231.

29. Celan, "Engführung," 198–99.

30. Of course, this reduction of imagery finds itself counterbalanced on another level by the graphic and visual presence of the poem on the page.

31. For an extended discussion of the notion of attention in *The Meridian*, see Werner Hamacher, "Bogengebete," in *Aufmerksamkeit*, eds. Norbert Haas, Rainer Nägele, and Hans-Jörg Rheinberger (Eggingen: Edition Klaus Isele, 1998), 11–44.

32. Celan, *Der Meridian*, 9.

33. Szondi, "Reading 'Engführung,'" 240. See also Fioretos, "Nothing," 325. In dialogue with Szondi, Fioretos notes that "temporality becomes 'listenable' . . . and the listenability refers to an act of touching." My reading aims to expand this understanding to highlight the import of this touchable/touching temporality for remembrance.

34. Dietlind Meinecke, *Wort und Name bei Paul Celan* (Bad Homburg: Koch, 1970), 177; see also n. 37 in Celan, *Die Gedichte*, 688.

35. Celan, *Der Meridian*, 7.

36. Celan, 147.
37. Daive, *Under the Dome*, 29.
38. Celan, *Der Meridian*, 7.
39. Celan, 108.
40. Celan, 108.
41. Celan, 115.
42. Celan, 117. This list goes on and extends to the poems in which Celan introduces compound words such as "breath crystal" (*Atemkristall*) or "breath-rope" (*Atemseil*). Of course, his collection of poems from 1967 is called *Atemwende* (*Breathturn*).
43. For discussions of the role of breath in the context of Celan's work, see, for instance, Antti Salminen, "On Breathroutes: Paul Celan's Poetics of Breathing," *Partial Answers: Journal of Literature and the History of Ideas* 12.1 (2014): 107–26; Lydia Koelle, *Paul Celans pneumatisches Judentum: Gott-Rede und menschliche Existenz nach der Shoah* (Mainz: Matthias-Grünewald, 1997). During the review process of this chapter, Maya Barzilai published a major article on the relation between Paul Celan's poetics and the Buber-Rosenzweig translation that offers a significant contribution to the relevance of the "breath-unit" for Celan, the status of Hebrew in his writing, and the intersection of poetry, breath, and remembrance. See Maya Barzilai, "'One Should Finally Learn How to Read This Breath': Paul Celan and the Buber-Rosenzweig Bible," *Comparative Literature* 71, no. 4 (2019): 436–54.
44. Both Salminen's "On Breathroutes" and Barzilai's "'One Should Finally Learn How to Read This Breath'" further expand on the significance of Celan's remark.
45. Celan, *Der Meridian*, 109.
46. In the preparatory notes to *The Meridian*, a comment on the term "Atemeinheiten," or "breath-units," is followed by "Buber" in parentheses—most likely with reference to Martin Buber's Bible translation (Celan, *Der Meridian*, 109). On Buber and Rosenzweig's Bible translation, see Leora Batnitzky, "Translation as Transcendence: A Glimpse into the Workshop of the Buber-Rosenzweig Bible Translation," *New German Critique* 70 (1997): 87–116. Against the background of Celan's engagement with the Buber-Rosenzweig Bible, Barzilai has shown that the poem's cola "are sites of remembrance" and that Celan "emphasized the breaks that punctuate the spoken word in order to claim a place for the silence of remembrance within the structure of the cola." Barzilai, "'One Should Finally Learn,'" 444. From this perspective, "Engführung," with its heavily segmented layout, is filled with sites of remembrance.
47. Barzilai, "'One Should Finally Learn,'" 445.
48. With each pause comes the risk that the breath might not pick up again. Barzilai notes in this sense: "For Celan . . . poetic pauses are desacralized sites of remembrance and painful recognition of the dead. As such, these silences between one exhalation and a following inhalation point to the difficulties of resuming poetic writing and recitation." Barzilai, "'One Should Finally Learn,'" 438.

49. See Celan, *The Meridian*, 107. Remarkably, in a recording of Celan reading the poem, the wide gaps on the page between the lines on the right and those on the left do not result in a pause of breath; Celan reads the poem in an almost breathless manner.

50. Gaston Bachelard, *Air and Dreams: An Essay On the Imagination of Movement*, trans. Edith R. Farrell and C. Frederick Farrell (Dallas: Dallas Institute Publications,1988), 239–42; Gaston Bachelard, *L'air et les songes: Essai sur l'imagination du mouvement* (Paris: José Corti, 1994), 273–74.

51. Bachelard, *Air and Dreams*, 241.

52. Celan, "Stretto," 231.

53. Celan, "Engführung," 199.

54. The pronunciation of the plosive "*k*" resembles that of the glottal stop. Pierre Joris has written an insightful comment on his translation of Celan's poem "Frankfurt, September," where he reflects on the figure of the "Kehlkopfverschlusslaut," or the glottal stop, which similarly doubles as a topos and a textual principle that engages the reader. See Pierre Joris, "Celan, Kafka & the Glottal Stop," January 30, 2009, http://www.pierrejoris.com/blog/?p=725.

55. In her reading of the passage that arrives at a similar conclusion, Oriana Schällibaum has shown how this pattern of assonances shifts in the following stanzas, affirming thereby that the word that wants to shine is not entirely suffocated. Her discussion of "Zeithöfe" or "timesteads" in Celan offers an intriguing complementary reading of this passage. Schällibaum focuses on the temporal implications of the recurring structure "x-and-x" in Celan's poetry. The hyphenated "Nacht-und-Nacht" in "Engführung," Schällibaum shows, embraces both temporal progress and cyclical time and visualizes the "timestead." (My chapter will turn to the "timestead" in the final section.) I do not see my reading as a competing interpretation. Rather, it strikes me that Celan negotiates a certain temporal density and porosity on various levels of his poetry—and in "Engführung" in particular. I associate this temporal structure with a corporeal, pneumatic relation, seeking to recover its poetological implications for the question of remembrance. Oriana Schällibaum, "Atem und Intervall: Zeithöfe bei Paul Celan," *Wirkendes Wort* 66.1 (2016): 67–92, 75.

56. Celan, *Der Meridian*, 210. See also Pajari Räsänen, "Counter-Figures: An Essay on Antimetaphoric Resistance; Paul Celan's Poetry and Poetics at the Limits of Figurality" (PhD diss., University of Helsinki, 2007), 209. For a recent study of Celan's poetry in relation to Husserl's time consciousness, see Yi Chen and Boris Steipe, "Phenomenological Comparison: Pursuing Husserl's 'Time Consciousness' in Poems by Wang Wei, Paul Celan and Santoka Taneda," *Comparative and Continental Philosophy* 9.3 (2017), 241–59.

57. Axel Gellhaus, *"Fremde Nähe": Celan als Übersetzer: Eine Ausstellung des Deutschen Literaturarchivs in Verbindung mit dem Präsidialdepartement der Stadt Zürich im Schiller-Nationalmuseum Marbach am Neckar und im Stadthaus Zürich*, eds. Axel Gellhaus et al. (Marbach am Necker: Deutsche Schillergesellschaft, 1997), 389–90.

58. Celan, *Der Meridian*, 139.

59. Paul Celan, "Letter to Hans Bender," *Collected Prose*, trans. Rosmarie Waldrop (Riverdale-on-Hudson, NY: Sheep Meadow Press, 1986), 25–26; Paul Celan, "Brief an Hans Bender," in *Mein Gedicht ist Mein Messer*, ed. Hans Bender (Munich: List, 1961), 86–88.

60. Emmanuel Lévinas comments on Celan's statement on the poem as handshake as follows: "It thus comes about that, for Paul Celan, the poem situates itself precisely at that level which is pre-syntactic and pre-logical . . . at the moment of pure touch, of pure contact, of that grasping, that pressing which is, perhaps, a way of giving even to the hand that gives." Emmanuel Lévinas, "Being and the Other: On Paul Celan," trans. Stephen Melville, *Chicago Review* 29.3 (1978): 16–22, 17.

61. Celan, *The Meridian*, 107.

62. Celan, 110.

63. Edmund Husserl, *Collected Works, Vol. 4: On the Phenomenology of the Consciousness of Internal Time (1893–1917)*, trans. John Barnett Brough (Dordrecht: Kluwer Academic Publishers, 1991), 111. I do not understand these two points of reference for Celan's own thinking about the "Atemeinheit" / "Atemhof"—the translational (Buber and Rosenzweig) and the phenomenological (Husserl)—as standing in opposition to each other. Both inform Celan's poetics. Future studies might interrogate their relatedness.

64. Husserl, *Collected Works, Vol. 4*, 117. See also Räsänen, "Counter-Figures," 212.

65. Husserl's description of the temporal "halo" can also be seen in relation to the very title of the poem: "Engführung" takes its name from a musical principle, the "stretto," which designates the overlapping of different subjects in a fugue.

66. "In einem solchen Zeithof stehen die Gedichte Ossip Mandelstamms." Celan, *The Meridian*, 71. Räsänen, "Counter-Figures," 209. See also Schällibaum, "Atem und Intervall," 88–90. I thank Irina Kogan for alerting me to the relevance of Celan's writing on Mandelstam for my argument.

67. Paul Celan, *Collected Prose*, 63; trans. modified.

68. Paul Celan, *Gesammelte Werke*, vol. 5, *Übertragungen II*, eds. Beda Allemann and Stefan Reichert (Frankfurt am Main: Suhrkamp Verlag, 1983), 623.

69. König, *Vertieftes Sein*, 176. König's *Vertieftes Sein* offers the most substantial study of the phenomenological dimensions of Celan's poetics in relation to the philosophy of Merleau-Ponty to date.

70. See König, *Vertieftes Sein*, 175.

71. Maurice Merleau-Ponty, *Phenomenology of Perception*, trans. Donald A. Landes (New York: Routledge, 2012), 141. See also König, *Vertieftes Sein*, 176.

72. See Cayrol and Celan, "Nacht und Nebel," 97–98. The English translation is taken from Richard Raskin's foreword to *Concentrationary Cinema: Aesthetics as Political Resistance in Alain Resnais's "Night and Fog" (1955)*, eds. Griselda Pollock and Max Silverman (New York: Berghahn, 2011), xi.

# Ecology

Chapter 3

# Flower Talk

JAN MIESZKOWSKI

Flowers, only flowers, too many flowers . . .

—Jacques Derrida, *Glas*

Je dis: une fleur!

—Stephane Mallarmé, *Divagations*

Who can speak the language of flowers? Perhaps the real question is: Is there any other language to speak, especially if one is a poet? In virtually every literary tradition, the flower enjoys a pedigree of such length and richness that its prominence almost appears to be coextensive with written culture itself. Alternately an ornament or an emblem, a symbol or a cipher, the flower is also one of the most venerable figures of figuration. While the Attic Greek corpus has no instance of "anthea rhetorika" ("the flowers of rhetoric"), terms such as "flower," "blossom," and "garland" are routinely used in classical texts as synonyms for "poem," and when Cicero and Quintilian describe specific instances of language as being overly or insufficiently "flowery," they are relying on a trope that was already more than half a millennium old. Whether it is the flower's naturalness, autochthony, or beauty that is at issue, it unfailingly presents itself as exemplary or paradigmatic, which is why any reference to or description of a flower is apt to become a claim—at least minimally—about the possibility of referentiality or representability as such.

There is an irony in appealing to the primordiality of floral motifs as evidence of their systemic import insofar as plants have always been implicated in attempts to manufacture "originals" through grafting. From this perspective, Friedrich Hölderlin's well-known reference to words originating like flowers is an indirect acknowledgment that neither words nor flowers are easily understood genealogically, a problem highlighted by Jacques Derrida when he wryly declares that those metaphors that "are primarily encountered in nature demand only to be picked, like flowers."[1] In a strange clash of identity and difference, the very fact that no one would ever confuse words and flowers somehow ensures that the latter are routinely invoked as what words *must* be like, even as such a gesture seems to say far more about the power of language to posit than it says about onto- or phylogenesis in the plant kingdom. Ubiquitous though it may be, the flower's seemingly inexhaustible pretension to signify is hard to localize within a given system or order, be it aesthetic, linguistic, or scientific. "The flower," writes Derrida, "is nothing, never takes place because it is never natural or artificial. It has no assignable border, no fixed perianth, no being-wreathed."[2] In this respect, the flowers of rhetoric are a name for the absence as much as the presence of a stable conceptual vocabulary with which to characterize linguistic dynamics, and to claim to speak the language of flowers is necessarily to challenge as well as trumpet language's powers.

Can we conceive of a new language of flowers, one not governed by these venerable floral forms? The following chapter considers several attempts to do just this. I begin by looking at an article by Elaine Scarry, then test its idiosyncratic argument in readings of Jean-Jacques Rousseau, Immanuel Kant, and finally Paul Celan, an author whose work ruthlessly exposes the flower as both a cornerstone of and a stumbling block for any conception of poetic praxis.

For Scarry, the central question is why colorful buds and blossoms have routinely been identified by both philosophers and poets as the representative objects of the imagination. Her deceptively simple answer is that flowers play this role because they are just the right size and shape, that is, they constitute a localized phenomenon that neatly aligns with the perceptual and cognitive powers of human beings. In a nutshell, flowers are easy for us to imagine.[3] "People and flowers," proclaims Scarry, "were made for one another."[4] "When a poet describes a flower, even," she adds, "when a poet merely names a flower, it is always being offered up as something that after a brief stop in front of the face can immediately pass through the resisting bone and lodge itself and light up the inside of the brain."[5] Going even further, Scarry suggests that when a poet makes a reference to a flower, its petals in effect become surfaces on which less easily envisioned images can take shape, the one imagined object facilitating the mental composition of others.

Scarry takes some care to avoid grounding her account of the poetic faculties in claims about the workings of language, choosing instead to focus on the nature of perception and cognition and on the empirical qualities of our blossoming friends. In the process, however, she cannot avoid raising questions about how difficult it is to formulate stable propositions about the denizens of the floral realm. As Anne-Lise François has observed, Scarry's statements about flowers are invariably accompanied by a qualifying "almost" that threatens to undermine what is being said, as if just talking about flowers were tantamount to letting negation run amok.[6] Understood in terms of the paradigmatic status of the floral, the imagination is thus "the *almost* percipient, the *not yet* percipient."[7] Flowers may kick the imagination into high gear, but they also reveal it to be defined by a potentially permanent delay between perception and understanding, as if the comprehension promised by the imagination's products were forever just around the corner. Suspending the mind between determinations of possibility and actuality, flowers simulate the prospect of insights that they may never deliver and as such are exercises in, to use a term Scarry does not, virtuality.

At a number of points in her essay, Scarry invokes the work of Rousseau, Kant, and Friedrich Schiller, as if to suggest that her line of thought sheds light on the tradition of philosophical aesthetics they helped shape. As one of the best-known plant enthusiasts of the eighteenth century, Rousseau would appear to be good ally to enlist. During the last fifteen years of his life, he wrote extensively about botany and the many natural specimens he gathered on various expeditions. Indeed, in the decades after his death, Rousseau's claim to fame arguably rested as much on his promotion of this particular branch of the natural sciences as on his literary or political writings.

When we look more closely at Rousseau's reflections on his experiences with flora, the figure of the avid plant collector quickly gives way to something less familiar. In the final book of his *Confessions*, Rousseau is singing the praises of true idleness (*l'oisiveté*), which he likens to the activities of a child "who is always in motion and always doing nothing [ne rien faire]," or to the activities of the driveller (*radoteur*), "who rambles on endlessly while never stirring from his seat."[8] For Rousseau, idleness means giving in fully to "the caprice of the moment," but not in order to allow the imagination to run wild.[9] To the contrary, this idleness is desirable precisely because it keeps the imagination in check, and here plants play an important role:

> Botany, as I have always considered it and in the form in which I was beginning to conceive a passion for it, was just such an idle study, one that filled the void of my leisure-time without leaving room for the fevered workings of the imagination or the boredom of total inactivity. Wandering carelessly through the woods and the fields, gathering mechanically, here and there, now a flower, now a branch; browsing almost at random in my hayfield, examining again and again a thousand times the same things, and always with the same interest, because I had always forgotten them, these things were enough to last me an eternity without my being bored for a moment.[10]

Anything but a straightforward embrace of natural beauty, Rousseau's botanical praxis has equally little to do with clichés about the classificatory imperialism of Enlightenment systems of knowledge. In his relationship to the plant world, Rousseau is scarcely more directed than a malfunctioning robot, his browsing just this side of random. No instant of activity relates to the next because the moment something is registered, it is forgotten. As objects of reflection, plants are distinctive not because they are ideally suited to the mind's compositional powers, but because they arrest the eye only long enough to be cursorily registered before any memory of them fades away. Hardly a scientific inquiry or even a parody thereof, this is an investigative nightmare based in a model of consciousness that borders on madness. In his *Reveries of a Solitary Walker*, Rousseau describes his ambition to write a book about a single blade of grass; here, in contrast, he lauds the blades of grass because there is nothing to say about them, and even if he were to start writing a sentence about one, he would presumably forget what he was doing before he finished.

If identifying flowers and their ilk temporarily turns Rousseau into an automaton, this is evidently an acceptable price to pay for sparing himself both the exhaustion that comes with exercising one's imagination and the boredom that comes from inactively rather than actively doing nothing. This uniquely impractical practice of energetic idleness may sound like something out of Samuel Beckett more than a proto-romantic impulse, and it certainly has not made it into the standard picture of Rousseau the gentleman botanist. In any case, the crucial point is that for Rousseau flowers do the opposite of what Scarry says they should do, that is, rather than helping the presentational powers of the imagination come into their own, flowers keep the mind from having to think about, much less create, anything.

Does Scarry's argument have more affinity with Kant's *Critique of the Power of Judgment*, where roses and tulips are the main examples of free natural beauty? In a passage whose full implications have rarely been appreciated, Kant writes: "In order to find something good, I must always know what sort of thing the object is supposed to be, i.e., I must have a concept of it. I do not need that in order to find beauty in something. Flowers, free designs, [and] lines aimlessly intertwined in each other under the name of foliage: they signify nothing, do not depend on any determinate concept, and yet please [Blumen, freie Zeichnungen, ohne Absicht in einander geschlungene Züge, unter dem Namen des Laubwerks, bedeuten nichts, hängen von keinem bestimmten Begriffe ab, und gefallen doch]."[11] With surprising ease, Kant passes from objects in a garden to abstract pictures and decorative frills. Far from idealizing the colorful denizens of the natural realm, he includes flowers here only as one example of visual phenomena that are free precisely because they are not part of a representational logic that exceeds them. The aimless marks with which he finishes his list are not signifiers, but Kant insists that they do not mimetically represent anything either: "Thus designs à *la grecque*, foliage for borders or on wallpaper, etc., signify [bedeuten] nothing by themselves: they do not represent anything [sie stellen nichts vor], no object under a determinate concept, and are free beauties."[12] Perched on the border between representational and nonrepresentational art, these squiggles and whirls are the visual equivalent of the language of Rousseau's idle driveller.

For Kant, to engage with the beauty of flowers is not to react to what they look like but to register the palpable absence of any concept of what they should be. Flowers are beautiful because they appear purposive even as it is equally apparent that they have no purpose. In judging them to be beautiful, then, what one sees is their freedom from any plan or design, that is, one sees what is not there to be seen at all. As depictions of a spontaneity that can never be part of the picture, even pretty paintings of roses and tulips are just this side of something thoroughly haphazard and therefore not fundamentally different from aimlessly intertwined lines.

Kant and Rousseau offer glimpses of what it would mean to unsettle the hegemony of the flower as an archetypal emblem or a foundational spark for the imagination. Something similar happens in the poetry of Paul Celan, where the flower is at least as much an enemy as an ally of reference and signification. While no reader of Celan would dispute that natural motifs are a central feature of his work, he is not necessarily the first modern author who comes to mind when one thinks about poetry as a sustained engagement with the powers—and dangers—of plants. When flowers do appear in his writing, they seem to confirm Scarry's insight that to discourse about the floral is inevitably to give negation free rein. At the opening of a short piece from *Mohn und Gedächtnis* (1952), we read: "Der Tauben weißeste flog auf: ich darf dich lieben! [The whitest dove flies off: I can love you!]"[13] The speaker's expression of love initially takes place as a celebration of the fact that his feelings have a right to exist, a permission authorized by an event that is overdeterminately symbolic—only in a poem can "the whitest" dove fly off. We are in Charles Baudelaire's forest of symbols rather than on a bird-watching trip, and the dove's departure is a linguistic event that occurs with the opening of the text, not an empirical event being described in verse.

The ensuing interaction between the lovers heightens the sense that in this poem connections are predicated on determinations that may have no analog in the natural world:

> From my hand, you take the great flower:
> it is not white, not red, not blue—yet
>     [you take it.
> Where it never was, it will always remain.
> We never were, so we remain with it.[14]
>
> (Aus meiner Hand nimmst du die große Blume:
> sie ist nicht weiß, nicht rot, nicht blau—doch
>     [nimmst du sie.
> Wo sie nie war, da wird sie immer bleiben.
> Wir waren nie, so bleiben wir bei ihr.)[15]

This introduction to indeterminate negation is an exercise in negative theological botany. In principle, the enumeration of the traits that "the great flower" does not have should be open-ended, even endless—by definition, a flower is not every imaginable color save one. The bond of love between "us" therefore has to be articulated by a leap of faith, or rather a leap of dash, as the punctuation mark and the word "doch" team up to interrupt the unbounded string of not-this-color, not-this-color, and so forth. The integrity of the individual formulations is thereby pitted against a more abstract interplay of identity and difference. Logically the line should continue ad nauseum, but grammatically, metrically, and/or rhetorically it must be interrupted. "The great flower" is nothing but not x, not y, and not z—"yet, you take it," and you take it precisely in all its *Nicht-heit*; you take everything the flower is not with it, certain only that it is not not a flower, even as it is unquestionably a flower of nots. Far from a symbol or metaphor of love, the flower in this poem represents the retreat of representability, the fact that whatever such a "notting" flower is, a mere reference to it can never "light up the inside of the brain" with any sort of image, as Scarry would have it.[16]

In an earlier version of this poem, the penultimate line reads: "Wo sie nie war, da trug sie einen Namen [Where it never was, there it bore a name]."[17] In Celan, "flower" is an impossibly burdensome appellation, as the unstable forces of negation it brings with it threaten to turn anyone who adopts it into a no-name or a nothing.[18] This sense of denominative dissonance is the central concern of the poem "Psalm," which opens by ambiguously restaging and yet not restaging the creation story at the start of Genesis: "NoOne [Niemand] kneads us again of earth and clay, / noOne conjures our dust. / Noone."[19] Confronted with a nobody (*ein Niemand*) that may just be nobody (*keiner*), we may well fear that, like the cyclops confronting the intruding Odysseus, we will be unable to hear the difference between "No Man" and "no man." In short order, the existential status of this figure appears to be at least provisionally resolved, for we are said to praise this "NoOne" the way we would praise God, the One:

> Praise be thou, NoOne.
> For your sake we
> want to flower.
> Toward
> you.
>
> A Nothing
> we were, we are, we will
> remain, flowering:
> the Nothing-, the
> NoOnesRose.[20]
>
> (Gelobt seist du, Niemand.
> Dir zulieb wollen
> wir blühn.
> Dir
> entgegen.

> Ein Nichts
> waren wir, sind wir, werden
> wir bleiben, blühend:
> die Nichts-, die
> Niemandsrose.)²¹

Some plants are hydrotropic and others are heliotropic, but we claim to be No One–tropic as we bloom toward or against our addressee, and in doing so, we designate ourselves "a Nothing," "the Nothing[Rose]," and "the NoOnesRose." In the earlier poem, we were told: "Wo sie nie war, da wird sie immer bleiben. / Wir waren nie, so bleiben wir bei ihr"; in "Psalm," this is rewritten as: "Ein Nichts / waren wir, sind wir, werden / wir bleiben." On this basis, "Psalm" arguably stabilizes the vertiginous not-identity of the earlier text insofar as it appears more confident about our status as *a* nothing, as something positive that can be presented in language, whereas in the first poem we are defined by a *not* that has to be conceived of as prior to any proposition that it might help affirm or negate, a *not* that leaves us suspended between non-determinations of the rose that is not one: the rose of no one, of *no* one, and of no *one*. Ultimately, however, "Psalm," a discourse of turns from *not* to *not* and from *nothing* to *nothing*, has to turn against the turns of language as well. Rejecting the claim of metaphor to produce meaning by giving one thing the name of another, it substitutes the no-name of one no-thing for the no-name of another no-thing.²²

In taking us through a floral review of what was, is, and will be, both poems suggest that flower time is a kind of no-time, or better, a time of lingering with *not*. This uncertain temporality is further explored in another poem in the *Niemandsrose*-volume, "Die Silbe Schmerz" ("The Syllable Pain"), in which, as the title hints, the very integrity of words begins to erode under the burden of flower names. In one crucial section, we read:

> . . . Columbus,
> autumn
> crocus in his sight, the mother-
> flower,
> murdered masts and sails. Everything set forth,
>
> free,
> discovery-eager,
> the wind rose wilted, ex-
> foliated . . .²³

(. . . Kolumbus,
die Zeit-
lose im Aug, die Mutter-
Blume,
mordete Masten und Segel. Alles fuhr aus,

frei,
entdeckerisch,
blühte die Windrose ab, blätterte
ab . . .)²⁴

A reminder that modern botany emerged as an appendage of colonialism, this Columbus figure is seeking out a very special plant, the *Colchicum autumnalea*—in French, "le colchique," in English the "autumn crocus" or "meadow saffron," and in German "die Herbstzeitlose." In hunting this particular—highly poisonous—specimen, Columbus is following in some hallowed adventurers' footsteps. Celan explained that this poem was prompted by a letter from a friend who was going to spend his holidays in the Georgian town of Colchis on the Black Sea.²⁵ Colchis is famous as the home of Medea, hence the destination of the Argonauts, where they hoped to find the Golden Fleece; "Les Colchiques" is also the title of a poem by Apollinaire translated by Celan as "Die Herbstzeitlosen."²⁶

In a letter to his wife, Celan relates that a few days after having written "Die Silbe Schmerz," he went out on a walk and "suddenly a flower appeared: *un colchique*!"²⁷ If Rousseau savored his strolls in the meadows because they helped deaden his imagination, here it is almost as if Celan's imaginative text has refashioned the world in its image. For Scarry, part of the power of flowers lies in the fact that we can easily see them even when they are not there—say the word "tulip," and we all immediately picture a tulip without any further ado. What happens, however, if one thinks one sees a tulip, but it is actually something else? As if to foreground the potential gap between name and image, "Die Silbe Schmerz" presents the reader with flowers that definitely do not look like anything Celan, Rousseau, or anyone else has ever seen while out on a walk, as the plants' names are broken up by hyphens and line breaks: "die Zeit- / lose"; "die Mutter- / Blume." With the appearance of "wind rose" a few lines later, we finally have a flower word that is not typographically fractured, but in this line of verse, "rose" appears only secondarily in its capacity as a flower, since in a nautical context, the term "wind rose" refers to the graphic on a map that shows wind speed and direction; composed of a circle of pointed parts, the graphic gets its name because it resembles a flower.[28] At one moment, the typography of the poem underscores its power to disarticulate words and with them any simple correspondence between grapheme and imago; in the next moment, we are reminded of the ways in which names can bring the verbal and visual orders together. Complicating things further, the verbs that immediately follow the noun "wind rose" treat it as if it were a vegetal being. Having faded (*abblühen*) like a flower, it then flakes away or exfoliates itself (*sie blätterte ab*), with the separable prefix *ab* (*ex*) appearing alone on the next line. *Die Sprache blättert ab*—the syllables themselves flake away. At the same time, this scattering of linguistic units does not become a stable representation of the dissemination of petals or seeds. A wind rose should help orient sailors, yet here it marks the breakdown of the language of flowers, since nothing tells us how to coordinate *die Windrose* with its brethren, *die Zeitlose* and *die Mutterblume*. "We never were, so we remain with [the flower]"—in this poem, the uncertain interplay of never and forever sees the timeless, *die Zeit-lose*, broken up by the timely yet irregular spacing of verbal elements, one following semi-haphazardly after another. Susan Sontag said of Walter Benjamin that his "major essays seem to end just in time, before they self-destruct."[29] In contrast, Celan's poems begin just in time, which is to say right after they have begun flaking out into a timeless time out, flaking out into an out-time that is never entirely out of time.

In the poem "Psalm," floral self-determination, identifying ourselves as "the No-One's-Rose," becomes an act of anti-self-appellation whereby no-thing would be given the no-name of another no-thing. At first glance, something very different appears to take place in "Flower," a poem Celan published four years earlier in his 1959 *Sprachgitter* (*Speech-Grille* or *Language Mesh*). Far from revealing the language of flowers to be constitutively disruptive of any effort to ground one's self-identity, this text boldly puts the word "flower" at the center of the process by which one comes into one's own as a linguistic being, for the composition of the poem was purportedly prompted by the momentous event of Celan's twenty-month-old son Eric speaking his first word, the French noun "fleur."[30] In its final version, the text comprises four short stanzas:

FLOWER

The stone.
The stone in the air that I followed.
Your eye, as blind as the stone.

We were
hands,
we scooped the darkness empty, we found
the word that came up the summer:
flower.

Flower—a blindman's word.
Your eye and my eye:
they ensure
water.

Growth.
Heartwall by heartwall
refoliates.

One more word, like this one, and the hammers
will swing free.[31]

(BLUME

Der Stein.
Der Stein in der Luft, dem ich folgte.
Dein Aug, so blind wie der Stein.

Wir waren
Hände,
wir schöpften die Finsternis leer, wir fanden
das Wort, das den Sommer heraufkam:
Blume.

Blume—ein Blindenwort.
Dein Aug und mein Aug:
sie sorgen
für Wasser.

Wachstum.
Herzwand um Herzwand
blättert hinzu.

Ein Wort noch, wie dies, und die Hämmer
schwingen im Freien.)[32]

A host of drafts of this poem exist, and in the first two, the body of the text is written in German while the title is in French ("Fleur"), whereas in the subsequent drafts as well as the final copy, the title is also in German ("Blume").[33] Although *Blume, fleur,* and *flower* are all thought to be derived from the same Indo-European root, *bhel-* ("to thrive, to bloom"), the multilingual staging of the title unsettles the attribution of any given word to a specific tongue, as if every time one said "Blume," "flower," or "fleur," one could not be sure precisely what language one was speaking.

In his remarks about the poem "Flower," Hans-Georg Gadamer argues that one should not make the mistake of trying to reduce Celan's text to a personal dawn of language narrative, not least given Celan's own oft-referenced notion that true poetry is anti-biographical.[34] Gadamer is confident that "Flower" can be seen to trace a tale of origination and development irrespective of the information about Celan's life that the reader has at her disposal. At the very least, one can read and interpret the text without knowing that it is a father and son in particular who are tending to the word "flower" and watching it grow. At the same time, once one has been told that the poem was supposedly inspired by Celan's son's first word, the story is hard to forget, especially given how far-fetched it is. After all, who has ever heard of a child's first word being "flower"? Skepticism on this point is compounded by the fact that any child's first word is almost certainly the product of an eager parent's imagination, a mother or father straining to discern some trace of the articulate in the midst of infantile babble.[35]

As it happens, the poem's early drafts are quite explicit that the word "flower" is emerging from babble: "Ein Mund . . . lallt / Blume [A mouth . . . gurgles / flower]"; "Lippen . . . lallend: / Blume [Lips . . . gurgling: / flower]."[36] The insistent repetition of the letter *L* hints that the text's own language may not be free of infantile gurgling, and this is hardly the only evidence that the phonic may hold sway in this discourse. In his notes on the poem, Peter Szondi emphasizes the repetition of the two-letter consonant blend *bl* (blind, Blume, Blinden, blättert), and he calls attention to the string of words that begin with *W*: Wort, Wasser, Wachstum, and Wand (as well as *wir* and *wie*).[37] Regardless of whether the poem "Flower" ever confirms itself to be babble-free, we should not underestimate the potential violence inherent in the notion of a child's first utterance. As a radically proto-linguistic act, such an exclamation may well have no pretension to signify or refer, despite the fact that whoever overhears the putative utterance will strive to bring it back into the verbal fold, typically by understanding what the child has quote/unquote "said" as a reference to someone present: "He called me 'flower'!"[38]

If the poem "Flower" appears to dwell on a primal speech act ("In the beginning was the word, and the word was flower"), the word "Finsternis" in the second stanza ups the theological ante by taking us back to the beginning of Genesis and God's first act of denomination: "Da schied Gott das Licht von der Finsternis und nannte das Licht Tag und die Finsternis Nacht [And God divided the light from the darkness, and God called the light day and the darkness he called night]."[39] Viewed in this light, or darkness, virtually every phrase in the poem acquires a potentially ultra-paradigmatic quality as a foundational utterance on the basis of which all subsequent verbal acts must be measured. Crucially, the result is not a hymn to the hegemony of the word "flower." To the contrary, there is no indication that this poem called "Flower" is at a loss for non-floral vocabulary, not least because it opens in an eminently lapidary fashion with: "Der Stein [The stone]." Like many of the other short words in this text, including "eye," "blind," "heart," and the word "word" itself, the noun "stone" recurs throughout the *Sprachgitter* collection, whereas instances of "flower" are much less common. As is well known, stones and language, particularly writing, have an intimate relationship throughout Celan's oeuvre. Scholars often observe, for example, that the letters of the Hebrew alphabet are traditionally said to be put together to form words in the same way that stones are put together to form houses. The opening of "Flower," however, is far removed from any sense of construction—there is no indication that "der Stein" will become some sort of cornerstone or building block. Nor is the word "stone" being apostrophized, as if the language of the poem could win power by interpolating the geological, something that happens in other texts by Celan. The first line of "Flower" appears to be entirely comfortable with its own verbal minimalism, betraying no anxiety about the absence of a verb or any other part of speech that would give it some pretension to being at least proto-propositional, and in this respect, the verse may well recall a child's first stabs at speech—perhaps young Eric's first word was not "fleur" but "pierre" (French for "stone").

Read in the context of the poem's title, the word "stone" stands out because whatever it is, it is not "flower." Recalling "Psalm," the first line could even be read as "the not-flower." The second line of the poem begins as if it were repeating the first line but quickly adds a prepositional phrase and a relative clause, and with these additions comes the alignment of a first-person pronoun with a finite verb: "Der Stein in der Luft, dem ich folgte [The stone in the air that I followed]." With this relatively complex sentence, we ostensibly move beyond any rendition of a child's first word, although one could still read the poem's opening lines as a series of increasingly intricate verbal forms, a simulation of language acquisition over time. In any case, if we were tempted to gloss the first appearance of the word "stone" as "not-flower," we will want to read the "stone" of the second line as "not-star," because the more common expression in both English and German would be "to follow a star" ("dem Stern folgen"), and in an earlier draft of the poem, this is exactly what Celan wrote: "So blind wie der Stern in der Luft, dem ich folgte [As blind as the star in the sky that I followed]."[40]

Following the word "stone" across the lines of the poem as we might follow a bouncing ball, we find its trajectory to be rather brief insofar as its last overt appearance is in the third line of the first stanza, which would appear to differ from the first line in that a verb, while not written out, is clearly implicit: "Your eye [is] as blind as the stone." Equally important is the minimal introduction of rhetoric: Is "your eye" literally as blind as "the stone"? As rhetorical figures go, this is far from ornate, but it is nonetheless significant that the grammatical and lexical parameters of the text no longer enjoy full control over the relationships between its words. In this vein, if the word "as" ostensibly clarifies the relationship between "your eye" and "the stone," it does not clarify the relationship between lines two and three. "I track the stone in the air," but it is not what "I" do with the stone but rather something about the stone itself that becomes the basis for the comparison with "your eye," and possibly for an implicit contrast between your eye and my eye.

As with most Celan texts, we need only dip our toe in the first stanza to begin feeling uncertain about precisely what we should be taking note of from line to line. What kinds of repetition need to be identified? What sequences or developments must be traced? Should we primarily be reading at the level of the clause, the word, or the letter, or should we be focusing on the tensions between these different registers? These questions are anything but rhetorical—in a sense, any commentary on a poem by Celan is nothing more or less than a sustained reflection on them. In his analysis of the text, Szondi attempts to show that the patterns of letters and words in "Flower" are not at odds with one another. Having identified the insistent repetition of *bl* and *W*, he notes that the arc of the poem sees these two sound chains come together in a single term in the middle, "**Bl**inden**w**ort," which is the complement to the word whose discovery stands at the very center of the text, "das Wort, das den Sommer heraufkam: / Blume [the word that came up the summer: / flower]." The event of this word's advent almost feels as if it could be the end of the poem since we have managed to look around or through the stones and follow the travels of the word "flower" all the way from the title to the last line of the second stanza. Far from bringing the text to a close, however, the discovery of this wondrous noun is presented as the beginning of a lifetime of existence as a linguistic being, or at least its halting first step. Articulated with some fanfare, the word "flower" is immediately repeated, which might be taken as evidence that it is the only word one has, except that this happens in order that "flower" may, in a very adult gesture, be outed as a particular kind of word, "a blind man's word."

Of course, to maintain that the poem identifies the word "Blume" as a "Blindenwort" may be to assume too much because what stands between the two nouns is not a comma but a dash: "Blume—ein Blindenwort." First and foremost, the punctuation mark functions to highlight a word or symbol that is not there, whether this is the copula *is*, an equal sign, or the preposition or conjunction *as* (*wie*). In this fashion, the poem asserts a relationship between these two *Bl* nouns precisely by not clarifying the nature of their connection. The dash may also bring a broader asymmetry into relief, accentuating the imbalance of a latent chiasmus, with "Wort" and "Blume" on one side, "Blume" and "Blinden-Wort" on the other.

Immediately following the dash, the poem shifts from the preterite to the present tense. This adds to the sense that this punctuation mark—whether it ultimately serves to unite or divide—is a hinge between the two halves of the text. Having learned that the power of the word "Blume" does not rest in what can be seen, we are not surprised to see our eyes watering the word, and evidently with some success, since growth ensues. An eye may be as blind as a stone, but apparently we can squeeze water from such an eye-stone nonetheless, even if this just means shedding tears in an odd exchange of an eye for an eye, if not an instance of the blind leading the blind. In case our word "flower" does not already feel well cared for, it now receives further assistance in the form of additional petals: "Herzwand um Herzwand / blättert hinzu [Heartwall by heartwall / refoliates]." In an earlier version of the poem, Celan wrote "Herzblatt um Herzblatt / tauchen [dive] hinzu."[41] "Herzblatt" is a term for a heart-shaped leaf, and this shift from one *Herz*-word to another would appear to be a perfect example of the way in which Scarry claims flowers facilitate imagination, since the leaves or the petals of the poetically fashioned flower are a surface onto which other images or words can be fashioned, that is, the "Herz-Blatt" (literally "a heart-shaped leaf," figuratively "a heart-shaped sheet of paper") becomes the place on which the poet can write the word "Herzwand."[42]

The problem with this line of analysis is that these petals or sheets of paper are not so much facilitators of signification or representation as sites of disarticulation. In another poem in the same collection entitled "Niedrigwasser" ("Low Tide"), Celan writes: "Niemand schnitt uns das Wort von der Herzwand [No one cut us the word from the heart wall]."[43] Apparently, what is at issue in this line is a heart of words rather than a heart of stone, or at least a heart wall on which words grow, and somewhere in the background one might hear the expression "Mir fällt ein Stein vom Herzen" ("It's a load off my mind"—literally: "A stone falls from my heart"), or perhaps "Mir fällt ein Wort vom Herzen" ("A word falls from my heart"—one assumes the word is "flower"). A couple of lines later in "Niedrigwasser," Celan offers an odd parenthetical insertion, in italics, an intervention into the poem that threatens to rip its language out of it: "(*niemand / schnitt uns das Wort von der – –*) [(no one / cut us the word from the – –)]."[44] If previously we were told that no one cut the word "von der Herzwand," the word "Herzwand" is nevertheless here cut out of the poem, presumably by "no one" or perhaps by the "NoOne" of "Psalm," and this occurs in a gesture that the text associates with closed eyes that can still follow things, like stones in the sky. "Herzwand," the word from which no one would cut "the word," is itself cut out just as one, or no one, might slice up a piece of paper or a leaf ("ein Herzblatt"). That this can only happen in a section of text whose status as a part of the poem proper is very much in doubt suggests that the first step in writing a lyric is to cut up some words; that is, one must compromise the integrity of one's text before it exists, making it impossible to know which verbal elements belong to it, much less whether the incisions and excisions of which it is composed are the work of a someone or a no one. In this context, one necessarily thinks of the role played by the figure of circumcision in Celan's poetry, yet precisely what the verbal operations in this poem are questioning is the existence of a stable textual body from which one could tidily detach a discrete piece.[45] For Scarry, every verbal flower is a field on which the imagination may create something new. For Celan, every verbal flower is a word that may have been chopped up to the point of unrecognizability, meaning that we cannot know whether it is a whole or a part, be that a part of something or a part of nothing, a part of someone's text or a part of No One's text.

In order for the word "Herzwand" to appear in the poem "Blume," the word "Herzblatt" has to be cut out of or away from the *Blatt*. Scarry maintains that when "a poet merely names a flower, it is always being offered up as something that can . . . light up the inside of the brain."[46] In Celan, when a poet names a flower, it is a sign that the language of their poem has already started to carve up its own words, be those words "flower," "stone," or "eye," and this happens because each word is nothing more or less than an incision that divides as much as it unites withdrawing as much as supporting the integrity of any presentational gambit.

Turning finally to the last sentence of Celan's "Blume," we read: "Ein Wort noch, wie dies." If the formulation recalls the comparison of the text's third line ("so blind *wie* der Stein"), this particular alignment—"one more word like this one"—seems to posit something impossible, since no word can ever truly be like the first word, the primal word, which of course in this text, if not in all texts, is "Blume." When one consults the manuscript drafts, it would appear that it was no easy matter for Celan to find the right word for what would ultimately prove to be the word "word." In the place of "Ein Wort noch," earlier versions included "ein Regen noch [one more downpour]," "ein Blatt noch [one more leaf/sheet of paper]," and "Ein Kelchblatt noch [one more sepal]" (sepals, the outermost layer of a flower, enclose the developing bud).[47] When the word for this "one more thing" finally becomes the word "word," we cannot be sure whether this is cause for celebration or consternation, for what assurance do we have that there is any word that is like this "Blindenwort"? Etymologically, blinding has the sense of both radical illumination and darkness or confusion, for instance, the darkness or confusion that follows an explosion of light—an antonymic quality that is nicely preserved by the presence of *S-t-e-r-n* in *Finsternis*. "Ein Blindenwort," one—or no one—might say, drowns all other words in light, making it impossible to see any of them clearly. Following Scarry, this blinding word does light up something inside the brain, but the result is not a perfect image of a flower but a chaos of characters that may or may not spell "star," "stone," or "flower." This is why we can never be sure that what we are seeing on the page when we read the poem "Blume" is an orderly string of codified lexical elements rather than a confusing mess of syllables, and this is why we can never be sure whether embracing the language of flowers means generating strings of elegant formulations or confounding our interlocutors with scribbles and babble.

## Notes

1. See Friedrich Hölderlin, "Brod und Wein," in *Sämtliche Werke, Frankfurter Ausgabe: Historisch-kritische Ausgabe*, vol. 6, *Elegien und Epigramme*, eds. D. E. Sattler and Wolfram Groddeck (Frankfurt am Main: Stroemfeld/Roter Stern, 1976), 250; Jacques Derrida, "White Mythology: Metaphor in the Text of Philosophy," in *Margins of Philosophy*, trans. Alan Bass (Chicago: University of Chicago Press, 1982), 220 n.21. Derrida famously explores these dynamics at length in *Glas*, trans. John P. Leavey Jr. and Richard Rand (Lincoln: University of Nebraska Press, 1986). For an effort to broaden Derrida's analyses of the floral into a full-fledged theory of literature, see Claudette Sartiliot, *Herbarium Verbarium: The Discourse of Flowers* (Lincoln: University of Nebraska Press, 1993).

2. Derrida, *Glas*, 86.

3. Scarry elaborates: "That ease [with which we can imagine flowers] is in turn attributable to *their* size and the size of our heads, *their* shape and the shape of our eyes, *their* intense localization and the radius of our compositional powers, *their* rarity that lets them rise and enter our brains and our willingness to receive them as the template for the production of other, more resistant compositions." Elaine Scarry, "Imagining Flowers: Perceptual Mimesis (Particularly Delphinium)," *Representations* 57 (1997): 90–115, 105.

4. Scarry, 105.

5. Scarry, 94. Scarry is hardly the first to have maintained that simply referring to "flowers" is enough to cause the mind to light up. In a discussion of Stéphane Mallarmé, Virginia A. La Charité writes:

> *Fleur* is not only a phenomenon which relates man directly to his world, it is also a picture word, a term which conjures up a visual image in space. In this sense, *fleur* always suggests a plant or a part of a plant, and the very evocation (enunciation) of the word casts a spell of immediacy, for it is a familiar substance within the grasp of everyone. The very tactility of *fleur* betrays its sensory power and leads intellectually to an unending range of associations. In Western literature, there is perhaps no other term which has been used as frequently as *flower* to form a basic poetic image. In artistic terms, it is truly catholic.

Virginia A. La Charité, "Mallarmé: 'Je dis: une fleur!'" *Nineteenth-Century French Studies* 10.1–2 (1981–1982): 96–106, 99.

6. See Anne-Lise François, "Flower Fisting," *Postmodern Culture* 22.1 (2011): n.p.

7. Scarry, "Imagining Flowers," 106; my emphasis.

8. Jean-Jacques Rousseau, *The Confessions*, trans. Angela Scholar (New York: Oxford University Press, 2008), 627.

9. Rousseau, 627.

10. Rousseau, 627–28.

11. Immanuel Kant, *Critique of the Power of Judgment*, trans. Paul Guyer (New York: Cambridge University Press, 2000), 93; Immanuel Kant, *Kritik der Urteilskraft, Werkausgabe*, vol. 10, ed. Wilhelm Weischedel (Frankfurt am Main: Suhrkamp, 1974), 120.

12. Kant, 114; Kant, *Kritik der Urteilskraft*, 146.

13. Paul Celan, *Werke, Historisch-kritische Ausgabe, I. Abteilung: Lyrik und Prosa*, vol. 2/3.1: *Mohn und Gedächtnis*, ed. Andreas Lohr (Frankfurt am Main: Suhrkamp, 2003), 121; the English translation is cited in Werner Hamacher, "The Second of Inversion: Movements of a Figure Through Celan's Poetry," in *Premises: Essays on Philosophy and Literature from Kant to Celan*, trans. Peter Fenves (Cambridge, MA: Harvard University Press, 1996), 346.

14. Cited in Hamacher, *Premises*, 346.

15. Celan, *Werke*, 2/3.1:121.

16. The result is that in this poem love is nothing other than an unconditioned embrace of *not*. The logical consequences of this insight are drawn in the next two lines of the stanza through a twisted inversion of Yahweh's "I will be who I will be," which here becomes, "we will remain where [the flower] never was because we never were." In his well-known essay on inversion in Celan, Werner Hamacher writes of these lines: "In the language of this flower, which is indeed not metaphorical in the traditional sense but meta-metaphorical, laying bare the carrying-over mechanism of imagistic language at its extreme, thus trope, turn, and reversal *par excellence*—: in the language of this flower, separated things have been brought together and what never was has turned into ever-remaining existence, for this very language came from a nothing and became something that remains." Hamacher, *Premises*, 347.

17. Celan, *Werke*, 2/3.2:237; my translation.

18. This is why there is arguably no end to the exegetical glosses one can make on the flowers that appear in Celan's texts, although in seeming to name everything, they may name precisely nothing. On the lengthy list of associations that Celan's flowers have inspired in his interpreters, see Winfried Menninghaus, *Paul Celan: Magie der Form* (Frankfurt am Main: Suhrkamp, 1980), 126.

19. Paul Celan, "Psalm," in *Memory Rose into Threshold Speech*, trans. Pierre Joris (New York: Farrar, Straus, and Giroux, 2020), 263. For a fascinating study of unnamable no ones, see Daniel Heller-Roazen, *No One's Ways: An Essay on Infinite Naming* (New York: Zone Books, 2017).

20. Celan, "Psalm," *Memory Rose*, 263/265.

21. Paul Celan, *Werke, Historisch-kritische Ausgabe, I. Abteilung: Lyrik und Prosa*, vol. 6.1: *Die Niemandsrose*, ed. Axel Gellhaus (Frankfurt am Main: Suhrkamp, 2001), 27.

22. In the final stanza of "Psalm," "we" move to put a new spin on the flowers of rhetoric, parodying classical taxonomies of tropes and figures with a detailed review of the sexual organs of the rose:

With
pistil soul-bright,
stamen heaven-desolate,
the corona red
from the scarlet-word, that we sang
above, O above
the thorn. (Celan, *Memory Rose*, 265)

Mit
dem Griffel seelenhell,
dem Staubfaden himmelswüst,
der Krone rot
vom Purpurwort, das wir sangen
über, o über
dem Dorn. (Celan, *Werke* 6.1:27)

23. Celan, *Memory Rose*, 343; trans. modified. For a superb book-length study of "Die Silbe Schmerz," see Michael Levine, *Atomzertrümmerung: Zu einem Gedicht von Paul Celan* (Vienna: Turia + Kant, 2018).

24. Celan, *Werke*, 6.1:82–83.

25. Celan, 83.

26. See Paul Celan, *Gesammelte Werke*, vol. 4, *Übertragungen I*, eds. Beda Allemann and Stefan Reichert (Frankfurt am Main: Suhrkamp, 2000), 792–93. On the semantic and symbolic complexity of the word "Colchis," see Katja Garloff, *Words from Abroad: Trauma and Displacement in Postwar German Jewish Writers* (Detroit, MI: Wayne State University Press, 2005), 154–55.

27. Paul Celan and Gisèle Celan-Lestrange, *Briefwechsel*, vol. 1, ed. Bertrand Badiou (Frankfurt am Main: Suhrkamp, 2001), 126; my translation.

28. The wind rose was the predecessor to the compass rose (in German, "Kompassrose"), which displays the orientation of the cardinal directions and their intermediate points. Visually, the two graphics can be virtually indistinguishable, and their names are sometimes used interchangeably.

29. Susan Sontag, *A Susan Sontag Reader* (New York: Farrar, Straus, and Giroux, 1982), 398.

30. On these biographical details, see John Felstiner, *Paul Celan: Poet, Survivor, Jew* (New Haven, CT: Yale University Press, 1995), 105ff.

31. Paul Celan, "Flower," *Memory Rose*, 187.

32. Paul Celan, "Blume," in *Werke, Historisch-kritische Ausgabe, I. Abteilung: Lyrik und Prosa*, vol. 5.1, ed. Holger Gehle (Frankfurt am Main: Suhrkamp, 2002), 29.

33. Celan, *Werke*, 5.2:157–59.

34. See Hans-Georg Gadamer, *Gadamer on Celan: "Who Am I and Who Are You?" and Other Essays*, trans. Richard Heinemann and Bruce Krajewski (Albany: State University of New York Press, 1997), 133–35.

35. This tale about Celan's son may suggest that Scarry is right about the primacy of flowers where the imagination is concerned, but for the wrong reason. Rather than the image of the flower forming the basis for envisioning anything and everything, the word *flower* here becomes the basis for imagining an entire language that has yet to be acquired.

36. Celan, *Werke*, 5.2:158, 162. *Lallen* means "to gurgle" (as of a baby) or "to babble."

37. Peter Szondi, *Celan Studies*, trans. Susan Bernofsky (Stanford: Stanford University Press, 2003), 109–13. Following Szondi's stress on the insistence of *bl*, Fritz Breithaupt has noted that "blättert hinzu" in the final stanza can be read "B lettert hinzu." Fritz Breithaupt, "Echo: Zur neueren Celan-Philologie," *Modern Language Notes* 110.3 (1995): 531–57, 639.

38. In *Allegories of Reading*, Paul de Man offers a detailed interpretation of a passage in Rousseau's *Essay on the Origin of Languages* in which "a primitive man" ("un homme sauvage") meets another man for the first time and in fear exclaims: "Giant!" Following Celan, one wonders how this primal scene might have been different if the man had instead called out: "Flower!" See Paul de Man, *Allegories of Reading* (New Haven, CT: Yale University Press, 1979), 149–55.

39. *Die Bibel*, trans. Martin Luther (1522); *The King James Bible* (1611), Genesis 1:4–5.

40. Celan, *Werke*, 5.2:159. The word *Stern* lurks in the poem's final version, appearing in the third line of the second stanza in the middle of the word *Finsternis*, and when one removes the *s-t-e-r-n* of *Finsternis* (or when those letters flake away on their own), what is left is *f-i-n-i-s*, *finis*, the first-person indicative of the French *finir* ("to finish"). This point has been made by Aris Fioretos, "Finsternis," trans. Arnd Wedemeyer, in *Lesarten. Beiträge zum Werk Paul Celans*, eds. Axel Gellhaus and Andreas Lohr (Cologne: Böhlau, 1996), 153–76, 164; and Breithaupt, "Echo," 639. Fioretos also observes that the Latin word for light, "lumen," can be read in "Blume" (Fioretos, "Finsternis," 175).

41. Celan, *Werke*, 5.2:157.

42. "Herzblatt" is also a term for grass of Parnassus, a genus of wildflower.

43. Celan, *Werke*, 5.1:57; my translation.

44. Celan, 57.

45. On circumcision in Celan, see Jacques Derrida, "Shibboleth: For Paul Celan," trans. Joshua Wilner, rev. Thomas Dutoit, in *Sovereignties in Question: The*

*Poetics of Paul Celan*, eds. Thomas Dutoit and Outi Pasanen (New York: Fordham University Press, 2005), 1–64.

46. Scarry, "Imagining Flowers," 94.

47. Celan, *Werke*, 5.2:159, 163. On this series of substitutions, see Kim Su Rasmussen, "The Inconclusive Text: On Paul Celan's 'Blume,'" *seminar* 51.3 (2015): 213–24, 220–21.

Chapter 4

# Poetic Involution
## Adorno, Celan, Nature

NATALIE LOZINSKI-VEACH

To say that poetry involves language is to say nothing of substance. In the case of Paul Celan, however, all linguistic preconceptions fall away so that not even the most obvious remark can be taken for granted. When Celan writes, "The poem involves language: it folds itself," in his notes to *The Meridian*, his assertion demands careful parsing.[1] Language constitutes the poem, so much is true. At the same time, the verb *involvieren* also inverts this expected poetic structure. If the poem "involves" language, it also envelops it, like a caterpillar spinning a cocoon. As the poem "folds itself [sich faltet]," Celan's words evoke a moth (*Falter*) in the process of a strange metamorphosis that will invariably change the language that comprises it. Such a transmutation is, of course, an essential aspect of Celan's poetry, which emerges from the chasm between *Muttersprache* and *Mördersprache* as a new, uncanny idiom, a spectral German, both haunting and haunted. Yet in folding itself in this way, the poem not only engages in the linguistic self-reflexivity that has been so well established in Celan scholarship; it also acquires a sense of density. Coming together, the edges of a fold create depth and texture, just as the many meanings of a word multiply its referents. There is substance here, then, after all; with each fold, each denotation, language becomes more poetic, *dichter*, and as such, more material.

This involutive movement marks Celan's late poetry, in which words coil in on themselves like tendrils. From "Speech-Grille" on, his poems display an increasing tendency toward sparseness, without ever giving up the complexities of his earlier work. The term involution itself, however, appears not only in the notes to *The Meridian* but also in Celan's communications with Theodor W. Adorno, composed around the same time. In a letter sent to Adorno along with "Conversation in the Mountains" (1959), the prose text written after their (perhaps not unintentionally) missed encounter in Sils Maria, Celan notes: "It is, in the title already, 'Jewish German.' . . . Is it anything else? An acquired and to-be-acquired atavism perhaps, a hoped-for unfolding via involution."[2] In this chapter, I wish to explore Celan's notion of involution in the light of Adorno's philosophy. Involution forms a point of connection between Celan's poetry and Adorno's aesthetics that is, among other things, crucial to understanding the philosopher's much contested remarks about the purported inorganicity of Celan's language in *Aesthetic Theory*. Adorno's reading of Celan hinges, as I will show, on his own notion of mimesis, an affinity with the other that resists objectification and that can arise only through art. In posing a noninstrumental relationship to the world, mimesis imbues aesthetics with an ethical aspect that extends beyond the human. Involution contains a similar ethical core, one that has as of yet been overlooked in Celan scholarship.[3] As the opposite of evolution, involution rejects the kind of biological and historical progressivism that underpins the social Darwinist ideologies of the National Socialists. At the same time, poetic involution is not merely an inversion of such hierarchies—rather, it breaks them apart in order to forge strange, new entanglements that call into question all binary notions.

Reading Celan together with Adorno highlights the disruption of one such binary in particular: the sharp separation between human and nature. For Adorno, our domination of nature is humanity's original sin—it is integral to our worst tendencies, from capitalist exploitation to anti-Semitism. Only in the mimetic aspect of aesthetic experience does it briefly disintegrate to leave us with the afterimage of a nonhierarchical relation to the world. Celan's poetic involution expresses such mimetic potential. With Adorno, I read the affinity for more-than-human life that makes itself felt in involution as a seminal aspect of Celan's poetic practice of commemoration; instances of mourning, the involutive moments in Celan's work, are also connective tissue—synapses between language and individual histories, not all of which are human. Knots of endlessly multiplied meaning, these involutive instances are at the same time palpably concrete, even literal, infusing each other with significance through juxtaposition. Embedded with and among these other histories—natural, literary, biographical, evolutionary—unspeakable human experience finds expression. In folding language like the wings of a moth, involution brings together what is otherwise kept apart, without erasing the difference that is necessary for otherness to linger.

## Adorno, Speaking of Stones and Stars

Despite his frequently cited intentions to write about Celan's poetry, "Speech-Grille" in particular, Adorno leaves us with only sparse commentaries on the poet's work.[4] His most sustained engagement with Celan appeared posthumously in the paralipomena to *Aesthetic Theory*, where Adorno calls Celan the "most significant representative of hermetic poetry of the contemporary German lyric."[5] He continues: "Celan's poems want to speak the most extreme horror through silence. Their truth content itself becomes negative. They imitate a language underneath the helpless one of the human, indeed underneath all organic language, that of the dead material of stones and stars. Eliminated are the last rudiments of the organic."[6] Often read in conjunction with Adorno's so-called dictum about poetry after Auschwitz, this short passage has evoked much critical opposition.[7] It is easy to see why: in all its complexity, Celan's poetry remains a medium of encounter, written by a poet "who does not forget that he speaks under the angle of inclination of his . . . creatureliness."[8] Adorno, by contrast, seems to align the poet's work with the kind of hermetic impenetrability that Celan himself strongly resisted, imbuing Celan's poems with an inhuman silence that situates them closer to the calcified concept of art embodied in Büchner's Medusa's head than to the living conversation of *Dichtung*.

Yet considered in the context of Adorno's philosophy, it is precisely this turn toward the inorganic that permits an interpretation of these enigmatic statements that does not reject the poem's affinity toward the other. While the notion of inorganicity is at the core of Adorno's notes on Celan, the language of stones and stars does not simply equal inhuman muteness. After all, having read *The Meridian*, we know that an inclination toward silence does not negate expression; we know that, at times, such an inclination can provide the refuge that is necessary for creaturely speech to take root where there is no ground.[9] Adorno, too, knew this: Celan's description of poetry's inclination toward silence is a direct quotation from Adorno's essay on Arnold Schönberg, whose music bears this tendency without ceasing to resonate.[10] Adorno notes a similar capacity in Celan's work, a dissonant musicality that dances on the edge of language and cannot be reduced to the soothing cadences attributed to the lyric.[11]

Neither, however, is Celan's poetry mute—quite the opposite. The strange relation between the inorganic language of inanimate nature and Celan's work speaks to the seminal task of art according to Adorno: "to give a voice to mutilated nature, meaning nature in the respective form in which it exists through its historical mediations at a particular stage in history."[12] Nature plays a complex role in Adorno's aesthetics, where art longs to give expression to nature as it has never existed, a nature beyond instrumentalization and exploitation. To give voice to such nature cannot simply mean the aesthetic rendering of idealized landscapes nor that of ravaged ones; both make themselves complicit in violence toward nature, the former by obscuring the status quo, the latter by reinforcing it. Instead, art speaks to the suffering of nature in a different way: beyond, or rather in-between, words, images, and melodies, in a language that can hardly be called a language at all. This expression is one of dissonance (*Dissonanz*), as art emulates what *is not* by rejecting what *is*. For Adorno, the desire of art to give voice to repressed nature manifests as a disruptive force that shakes us, shattering the impression that the conditions under which we exist are normal and unchangeable. By fragmenting the illusion of its own cohesion in plain sight, such aesthetic expression reveals its artifice and so draws attention to the discrepancy between the world as it could be and the world as it is. If organicity implies harmonious relations between all parts of a whole, such an aesthetic language would indeed have to be *in*organic, inherently disjointed—perhaps even creased.

This aesthetic expression cuts to the core of Adorno's philosophy, which is, from his very first writings on, concerned with the noxious effects of identity thinking and the domination of nature. These two notions cannot be thought apart—intertwined, they form a central nerve that runs through Adorno's work. Both originate with the emergence of consciousness out of "the terror of the blind nexus of nature."[13] Only through the rupture between subject and object, between self and other, does the human break away from this state of indistinction, which is marked above all else by helpless compulsion.[14] The engine of this separation is reason; its tool, the concept: "In thought, human beings distance themselves from nature in order to arrange it in such a way that it can be mastered."[15] This subjugation of nature relies on the abstraction inherent in identity thinking, which identifies multifaceted objects with their concepts as if these were one and the same. In abstraction, objects become expendable—turned into timber, one tree is like any other, regardless of the singular networks of life that it sustains.

In this paradigm, everything that is nonidentical, everything that exceeds and resists conceptual definitions and thus indicates the limits of systematic thought, is eradicated or repressed. In this manner, one form of violence replaces another as subjection to nature gives way to subjection to reason, which is itself a part of nature, "unreconciled and self-estranged."[16] These repressive tendencies, therefore, also turn inward, against those aspects of human being that we tend to see as "natural" or irrational.[17] Affects, bodies, other people—all of these are incarnations of repressed nature, forcefully integrated into a system of thought that does not allow for singularity. Nor can the eradication of difference that occurs in identity thinking be separated from its physical manifestations. Epistemic abstraction leads to reification; its ultimate consequence is genocide, a frantic attempt to force an absolute correspondence between concept and object that confirms "the philosopheme of pure identity as death."[18] In Adorno, then, the question of nature and its domination is no mere sentimentalism; its implications run deep, affecting every fiber of his philosophy, particularly after the Shoah.

While identity thinking determines every aspect of the world as it currently is, its spell can be broken. Reason may be the medium of oppression, but it can also be that of liberation, if only thought could recognize its kinship with nature without, in the process, regressing into a state of indistinction. In such a reconciled condition, binaries would be canceled without absolute fusion so that the particular and the general, object and subject, nature and culture would no longer be at odds with each other: "Utopia would be above identity and above contradiction; it would be a togetherness of diversity."[19] Dependent on reason's ability to perform critical self-reflection, this idea can be approached only incrementally through determinate negation. In order to hold open any possibility of reconciliation, thought must be willing to linger on the incongruities of the nonidentical without attempting to absorb them into its own logical structures.

In its effort to make space for the radical particularity of nonidentity, therefore, philosophy depends on the affinity of art for the nonconceptual, for as false as the equation between objects and their concepts is, thinking inevitably proceeds by identification.[20] Art, in contrast, speaks differently, in a "languageless [sprachlos(e)]" language, which "takes priority over poetry's significative element."[21] Adorno's phrasing is as strange as it is appropriate, for this language is not merely without words; it is, indeed, a language *without* language, an absolute negation of the communicative element of everyday speech. Inarticulate, and thus inorganic, it is the other of language, but also, in its nonidentity, the language of the other, perhaps that of the "wholly other" on behalf of whom Celan's poems attempt to speak.[22] Freed from conceptual frameworks, the affective dimension of language, its capacity to assimilate "itself completely into subjective impulses," finds expression in art.[23] While in human language, this capability is always tempered by conceptuality, artworks, even those composed of words, have a different expressive faculty, a similarity to language that "touches most closely on a *Here I am* or *This is what I am*, a selfhood not first excised by identificatory thought from the interdependence of being [die nicht erst durchs identifizierende Denken aus der Interdependenz des Seienden herausgeschnitten ward]."[24] From the vantage point of rational thought, such selfhood seems absurd, for it would have to be both absolutely autonomous and, simultaneously, embedded in a network of relations. In fact, these two aspects would be mutually constitutive: the radical singularity of the self would emerge *from* its particular interconnections with its others, to whose own particularity it would contribute. In a language that is not a language at all, artworks whisper of such interrelation, indicating a reciprocity between subject and object that is—for now—as impossible as it is radical.

Yet Adorno's wording complicates the simple attribution of this state to a utopian future. By replacing the common verb *wurde* (*werden*, "to become") with its poetic and antiquated counterpart "ward," Adorno situates the expression of the artwork in an altogether different, liminal time. Neither strictly subjunctive nor entirely indicative, "ward" differs from *werden* in that it does not simply connote a process at work in the past; its temporality is strangely elusive, indicating something that has already been completed and, at the same time, not yet begun. The poetic form of the verb suggests that the possibility of such a state arises only in the realm of the aesthetic. The artwork's semblance of the "interdependence of being" is not a return to the indistinct state before the separation of subject and object, but rather its memory, considered from the vantage point of critical thought as it turns to its own shortcomings with the help of art. It is, in other words, an instance of "remembrance of nature within the subject," a recognition of self as other that is a precondition for an end to the autocracy of subjectivity.[25]

Such anamnesis, which simultaneously occurs as recollection and dream, resonates in the artwork's similarity to language, which itself only barely touches on this utopian state. Twice removed, ungraspable, this memory brings the past into resonance with an unwritten future, folding time: "The object of art's longing—the reality of what is not—is metamorphosed in art as remembrance. In remembrance what is, qua what was, combines with the nonexisting because what was no longer is."²⁶ The memory of the artwork, then, perhaps like any act of recollection, brings the past together with its extinction to outline something entirely different. In its proximity to "a selfhood not first excised by identificatory thought from the interdependence of being," the artwork recalls a condition before the schism between subject and object, not as it was but as it might be. By placing the past in a new constellation with a possible future, the artwork remembers: it puts what was broken apart back together, albeit in an entirely different constellation, and only for a moment.

The suggestion that such memory may arise in something akin to language is fitting, since even conceptual language, the organ of identity thinking, contains an echo of reconciliation in Adorno. Language always expresses more than it says: each word that indicates multiple objects at once also implies their kinship, an entwinement that exceeds conceptuality even as it is restrained by it.²⁷ In this way, language anticipates a state of reconciliation, an essential component of which would be "the communication of what is differentiated."²⁸ Communication as it is now, writes Adorno, "is so shameful because it betrays what is best—the potential for agreement between human beings and things—to the idea of imparting information between subjects according to the exigencies of subjective reason."²⁹ What subjective reason demands above all else is the abstraction necessary for reification, an instrumental application of language that reinforces the domination of subject over object. A condition of peace, by contrast, would involve a form of communication closer to its etymology, one based on a recognition of commonalities "between human beings as well as between them and their Other [ihrem Anderem]."³⁰ Yet even as it is now, language contains the seeds of such a relation, for, as Adorno notes, only in language can "like recognize like."³¹ Such recognition necessarily precedes reconciliation; in it, the mimetic aspect of language makes itself felt.

This involved path through Adorno's philosophy brings us back to the beginning, to the inorganic language of stones and stars, and to the improbable likeness between Adorno's passage and Celan's poems. For when Adorno makes his claim about the affinity between Celan's poetry and the language "of the dead material of stones and stars," his words pivot on an unassuming verb: *nachahmen* ("to imitate").³² Overshadowed by the enigmatic imagery of speaking stones, the term is nevertheless central to Adorno's interpretation, as it marks the relationship between Celan's poetry and the inorganic as an instance of mimesis as it appears in Adorno's work. Adorno's notion of mimesis is—quite intentionally—too disparate to be deemed a concept; instead, Adorno refers to it as an impulse or a behavior (*Verhalten*). Both terms imbue mimesis with a corporeal aspect that serves as a reminder of its ritual roots in sacraments, which intended to placate or interpret nature through bodily imitation. Their physicality, however, also acknowledges the objectivity of our embodied being, the fact that each subject is also an object. This sensibility renders mimetic comportment deeply empathetic. An antidote to reification, the mimetic instinct is "the plenipotentiary of an undamaged life in the midst of the damaged one";[33] if identity thinking eradicates difference through subsumption, mimesis is radical openness in the hope of an encounter, with all of the vulnerability that such a position entails. A true mimetic relation between subject and object would be one of noncoercive affinity; a challenge to existing epistemic frameworks, it would indicate similarity while maintaining difference.

While in most areas of modern life, identity thinking has supplanted such mimetic comportment, its remnants persist in art. In dialectical tension with art's own implication in the hegemony of reason, its mimetic element suggests an alternative, nonconceptual form of cognition, rational precisely in its rejection of the domination of *ratio*. Art, then, harbors not only the possibility of a more ethical relation to others but also the promise of an entirely new form of thinking, one spacious enough to accommodate the nonidentity of the object. The nonconceptual cognitive value of art challenges the classificatory structures by which logic abides, calling on reason to examine its own presuppositions. Such artistic mimesis must be nonrepresentational; instead of imitating *something*, it is "an attempt to restore . . . a state in which . . . a relationship of similarity and thus kinship prevailed between subject and object."[34] While reason's incessant compulsion to dominate nature renders such a reinstitution impossible as long as identity thinking holds sway, the artwork's very existence indicates an alternative relation to the other by its negation of the current conditions.

It is such ethical potential that Adorno's words locate in the imitation that they attribute to Celan's poems, which shelter the possibility of a non-binary relation between subject and object that cannot, as of yet, exist in damaged life. In their mimesis of "a language beneath the helpless one of human beings, indeed beneath all organic language,"[35] Celan's poems engage in a linguistic catabasis that places them on uncertain ground. By positing not one but two mimetic objects for Celan's poems, Adorno's text seems to suggest that there is, underneath it all, something that is being imitated, at least grammatically. Yet Adorno's own words belie their syntax, for the objects remain ungraspable—*ungreifbar*—*unbegrifflich*. In their reference to these dense materials, stones and stars, Adorno's words disperse into thin air and so make palpable the dissimilarities between concept and thing, carving out space for nonidentity. Critique must maintain its difference from poetry, but both take shape in language, allowing Adorno's words to approach Celan's in a display of mimetic kinship.

For they themselves perform the imitation that they attribute to Celan's language by reiterating two of the most salient paronomastic terms from the poet's oeuvre, "stone and star [Stein und Stern],"[36] words that are almost repetitions, all the more unlike for their resemblance. By referring back to Celan's poems in this manner, Adorno implies their radical mimetic potential: profoundly self-referential, the poet's language approximates an iteration that displaces its own origin. By speaking only on its own terms, the poem also speaks with the accord of the other. Art's mimetic capability dwells in its resistance to the imposition of external functions, which means that it expresses its dissonant kinship with the other most incisively in its moments of radical selfhood: "Through expression art closes itself off to being-for-another, which always threatens to engulf it, and becomes eloquent in itself: this is art's mimetic consummation. Its expression is the antithesis of expressing something."[37] The mimetic element of Celan's poetry, then, lies in its aporetic quality. In Adorno's reading, the language that the poems imitate is not external to them but arises from within their own margins; the poems distinguish themselves from themselves—they crease.

By using Celan's own words to make a claim about the mimetic capacity of his poems, Adorno highlights their radical singularity, their ability to undermine conceptuality from within language. The subversive force of Celan's poems arises from their ability to forge wordscapes that turn inward, unfolding a vast poetic space within each single term and thus rendering it nonidentical with itself. In this way, Celan's poems alter the words that constitute them, instantly creating a new language within the old, a language that is incessantly diverging from itself. Part of this capacity emanates from Celan's dedication to the utmost historical specificity, in the face of which "all tropes and metaphors want to be carried ad absurdum."[38] The language of stones and stars poses no exception to this precision, however unfathomable its inorganic rhythms may be. Underwritten by their historical and biographical connotations, stones and stars speak of the memories indelibly etched between their letters the *Cariera de Piatra*, the stone quarry in which

Celan's parents were forced to work before their deportation to the labor camp in Michailowka, where they eventually died; the *Judenstern* that they, and Celan, wore like so many others.

In the dense weft of Celan's language, these connotations flash up without becoming overdetermined; a precarious balancing act that demands, as Adorno notes, "infinite discretion."[39] Discretion, however gentle, is a form of separation, a gesture of negativity; in focusing absolutely on a single and singular date, on a specific event or encounter, the poem and its words also cease to signify generally, undermining conceptual logic, and with it, identity thinking. At the same time, Celan's poems remain aware of their linguistic substance and therefore of the limits by which their radical particularity must inevitably be curtailed. The fact that the experience of suffering eludes direct representation as much as it seeks expression is a both a truism and true after the Shoah; in Adorno's framework, human language is helpless in this regard, for it not only falls short of this bipolar demand, but is inherently implicated in the conceptual violence at its root.[40] The mimetic, languageless aspect of art, however, finds expression where there are no words.

Adorno's observation that "the truth content [of Celan's poems] itself becomes negative [ein Negatives],"[41] is therefore not a negation of their expressive force but its acknowledgment. Both substantive and ungraspable, the nominalized adjective is a contradiction, an impossibility made manifest in poetry. Aesthetic expression is, for Adorno, that of suffering; it is the always futile "imitation of an objective expression, remote from psychology, of which the sensorium was perhaps once conscious [innewardxs] in the world and which now subsists only in artworks."[42] Such objective expression is nothing but the language of nature, of "the dead material of stones and stars," a language that has never existed; to situate it outside of time, Adorno once more resorts to the poetic form of *werden* ("to become"). *Innewerden* ("to become conscious") literally means to internalize but also to turn inward, to involve, perhaps in inadvertent anticipation of recollection, *Erinnerung*. By opening up a space between that which is and that which could be—a space that has to remain indeterminate and, as such, negative—the artwork becomes a form of the "unconscious writing of history, [an] anamnesis of the vanquished, of the repressed, and perhaps of what is possible."[43]

Such future-oriented memory takes root in the crevasses of the poem, where poetic topoi turn inward, demanding to be read, as Celan writes in *The Meridian*, "in light of u-topia."[44] Hyphenated, and thus fragmented, Celan's utopia is no reconciliation but a turning point. Read "in light of u-topia," poetic images are "to be perceived once and always again once, and only here and now"; that is, in their utmost particularity with every reading.[45] Illuminated by the nowhere of their own negation, and thus inverted, Celan's tropes upend the directionality of metaphorical language, infusing it with an acute specificity that suspends the conceptual mechanics of identity thinking. In this way, speaking neither for the dead nor for inanimate nature, Celan's poems give voice to both. Rendering rhetorical language "ad absurdum," out of tune, and thus dissonant, these poems imitate a condition of reconciliation in reverse. Inorganic material does not speak; stones are, as Martin Heidegger insists, without world, yet Celan's poems express solidarity with their muteness.[46] In opening toward something that does not exist, they bring its semblance to life, without pretense to actuality. In their negative mimetic capability, Celan's poems remember what happened in light of what never was, in and through a lapidary language whose "inclination toward silence" gives expression to the possibility of justice.

## Celan, Involving Poetry

Read in the context of his philosophy, then, Adorno's comments on Celan are anything but counterintuitive: in their affinity for the inorganic, Celan's poems reveal their capacity to crease language so that it folds in on itself, challenging normative conceptual structures in the process. Here, language, the philosophical medium, releases itself from a strictly identificatory structure and so offers a paradigm for a form of thought that would attend to the nonidentical.

What, however, if we attempt to trace such mimetic affinity in inverse, not through philosophy but from within poetry? To do so, we must return to *The Meridian* and its many notes, where the affinity for the inorganic that Adorno senses in Celan's poetry finds its reflection in the process of poetic involution: '. . . Büchner's last words on his deathbed, Lenz's words (Moscow) have not come down to us—it is the return into the just still voiced, as in Woyzeck—it is language as involution, the unfolding of sense [Sinnentfaltung] in the one, word-estranged syllable—: it is the 'root-syllable' recognizable in the ⌊death-rattled⌋stuttering, ~~the~~ ⌊language as⌋ what has returned to the germ—the morpheme is the {mou} mortal mouth, whose lips no longer grow round."[47] This passage beckons to be read together with the quotation with which we began: "The poem involves language: it folds itself."[48] In its connection between involution and the moment of death, the longer note reminds us that such a folding is both a doubling over *and* a doubling down, both a moment of vulnerability and, at the same time, one of resilience. The expression of the poem, on the most extreme margins of language, finds a new origin in the stammer (*Stammeln*) of the death rattle: here, a root-syllable (*Stammsilbe*) emerges that can also be thought of as a stem cell (*Stammzelle*)—involution contains the seed of its own inversion as the final moments of death turn into the genesis of poetry: "the poem persists at the edge of its own self."[49]

This emergence of poetry provides no consolation but it is a form of commemoration. An inflection point, the involutive moment binds the poem to the mortal body on which it depends; their connection is so intimate that even morphemes become corporeal. In this moment, the poem remembers, but it also anticipates. If in Adorno's aesthetic theory the artwork is the anamnesis of a utopian state, in Celan the poem's focus on singular experience also radiates from and into multiple temporalities: the memory of mortality permeates these poems, driving them toward an encounter. In involution, language evolves, unfolding into the sense (*Sinnentfaltung*) that emerges from a rupture of linguistic organicity—"in the one, word-estranged syllable."[50] In withdrawing into itself in this manner, the poem links words and their many denotations in tightly wound knots of signification and so reaches out beyond itself in its moments of most radical sparsity. At the same time, such unfolding *into* sense is also an unfolding *of* sense, of a sensory awareness of that which may otherwise go unnoticed, an attention that may well be "the natural prayer of the soul."[51] Read with Adorno, this too is a mode of future-directed memory, an attunement to the "objective expression" of what has been subjugated that can only be approached within the aesthetic.[52]

It is fitting that poetic involution would emerge in relation to such an awareness of the corporeality of language, since as a term "involution" belongs to the language of bodies. In the medical idiom, it denotes the shrinking of organs, primarily that of the uterus (*Gebärmutter*) after birth, a physical manifestation of maternal loss, which Celan, a former student of medicine, would have known. In the language of biology, the word has a darker resonance; here, it implies the reversal of evolutionary processes. According to the National Socialist doctrine of "racial hygiene," involution is the consequence of the genetic degeneration of a people, and it was cited as a pseudoscientific argument against "interbreeding."[53] Celan, however, inscribes the term with a radically different valence. For him, involution is something to be yearned for, something to be worked toward: "a hoped-for unfolding via involution," as he writes in his letter to Adorno.⁵⁴ If to involve means to regress in Nazi ideology, poetic involution undermines the structural foundations of such a belief. The social Darwinist concept of progress depends on an arbitrary and historically contingent notion of advancement that is inherently hierarchical: what—or rather *who*—is deemed to be more developed is also seen as better, more valuable, superior. Such a justification of supremacy depends on a linear perception of the importance of life; a counter word, Celan's poetic involution bends this line, not once, but again and again. In this way, it not only collapses such hierarchies but renders them impossible through careful attention to the intricate connections between different forms of life that arise in the poem.

The poetic iteration of involution inscribes the term with an altered meaning but without erasing that which came before. Only by incorporating the historical connotation of the concept can Celan's version reject it. The word "involution" itself participates in the gesture it denotes: creased, it means in more than one register, forging a new language, dissonant with itself. Perhaps we can read Adorno's remark that Celan's poems want to "speak of the most extreme horror through silence" along these lines, with reference to Celan's Bremen speech, where language is said to go "through terrifying silence."⁵⁵ Read against themselves, Adorno's lines may be understood to attribute a disintegrating force to Celan's poems, which does not proceed by silence but shatters it. To trace the intricate meanings of and in Celan's words means to enter into the depths of the fold, to become involved with language and its material histories, and, above all, to develop a keen sense for even the smallest instance of suffering.

It is clear that such an unfolding of sense cannot take place within the structures of historical and evolutionary progressivism on which National Socialist ideologies are based; instead, it has to follow a much more intricate path, one that moves into multiple directions and temporalities at once, a "u-topian" path, full of twists and turns.⁵⁶ Indicating an affinity between the notion of involution and Adorno's thought, such a path makes itself felt in the letter that Celan sent to the philosopher along with "Conversation in the Mountains": "It is, in the title already, 'Jewish German.' . . . It is . . . something thoroughly hooknosed . . . by means of which the Third (and probably also the silent) can perhaps become straight again. Is it anything else? An acquired and to-be-acquired atavism perhaps, a hoped-for unfolding via involution [auf dem Weg über die Involution erhoffte Entfaltung]."⁵⁷ Atavism, another biological term, denotes the arbitrary reemergence of an ancestral trait. Celan, however, transforms this passive process into a task, one that has both already been achieved and is yet to come. Its temporal disjunction indicates that such atavism must be incessantly cultivated, for its past existence does not guarantee future continuity. What this transformation might look like remains vague in the letter, but in his notes for his Büchner Prize speech, written around the same time, Celan specifies it as "a second degree hooknosed-ness, an acquired atavism."[58] Such poetic atavism, then, is related to the process to which Celan elsewhere refers as "to jewify [verjuden]."[59] This anti-Semitic term, whose origins lie in the nineteenth century, referred to an overwhelming Jewish influence on culture and society and became so common in Nazi Germany that it even appeared in the *Duden* dictionary between 1929 and 1947.[60] "Jewification" can be understood as the sociocultural iteration of the social Darwinist interpretation of involution, and it too is given a different valence in Celan: "It is finally only a word for recognizing-oneself-in-the-other, it is communion [Einkehr] with the other as with the self, it is a turning back [Umkehr]."[61] Here, the affinity between self and other emerges through a turn inward that is simultaneously a turn back, an inversion that is also an involution. "Jewification" is, in other words, a form of mimetic capacity.

The mimetic affinity that lingers in art is not a form of representation; if anything, it is a depression, a negative space deepened by the unrelenting weight of history. After National Socialism's deadly euphemisms and propagandist word games, the German language has been "angereichert," as Celan writes in his Bremen speech.[62] This enrichment continues to resonate in and beyond the German language even today, even in English, every time there is mention of the Third Reich. In having been strained in this manner, language has been hollowed out, always in danger of collapsing in on itself. Celan's rejection of simple metaphor is also a refusal of merely bridging such perilous ground. Instead of forging fragile semantic bonds between words and their meanings, poetic involution folds language, both revealing and deepening its cavities, and in the process, strengthening it.

Such involutive potential emerges in the "Jewish German" of the title, "Conversation in the Mountains" ("Gespräch im Gebirg"), in the negative shape of an omission. *Gebirg* descends from *Hochdeutsch* into dialect by dropping a single vowel, as if the word were in the process of curling in on itself. In its clamorous absence, the letter conveys the devastation of an entire culture as well as Celan's private loss. "Language as involution . . . the rhyme-sound as self-sound [der Reimlaut als Selbstlaut],"[63] posits Celan in the fragment on death and involution cited above, situating normative poetic harmony just beyond possibility, for a rhyme depends on a difference that cannot arise out of sameness. In its omission, however, the vowel or *Selbstlaut*, "e," echoes indefinitely, fundamentally unlike itself. It is a gyre dense with implications, coil upon coil of unsaid, but spoken, meaning. Inhabiting the no-man's-land between word and body, this dropped vowel links the organic to its opposite, a negative mimesis of ineffable experience. In drawing into itself, language unfolds its expressive capabilities, "a hoped-for unfolding via involution." Innumerable connotations orbit the blank space that distinguishes the German of Celan's past from that of his present, none of which settle into the kind of conceptual certainty that facilitates identification and, with it, a sense of closure. In this instance of poetic involution, the nonidentical speaks in silence, delineating our inability to think it in all its complexity.

The question of nonidentical expression in "Conversation in the Mountains," which Celan calls a "prehistory" to *Der Meridian*, takes us back to Adorno's comments in *Aesthetic Theory*, for Celan's text does, in fact, speak to the language of stones:

> ". . . and the stone—who does it talk to?"
> "Who should it talk to, cousin? It doesn't talk, it speaks, and whoever speaks, cousin, talks to no one, he speaks, because no one hears him, no one and No One, and then he says, he and not his mouth and not his tongue, says he and only he: Do you hear?"[64]

In contrast to "Jud Groß" and "Jud Klein," avatars for Adorno and Celan, the stone does not talk ("redet"); it speaks ("spricht").[65] In Celan's Büchner Prize speech, the difference is crucial, for while the former is the kind of empty discourse that leads nowhere, the latter refers to poetic expression. In "Conversation," however, "talk" seems to have a slightly different cadence to it. Even though their conversation is really a soliloquy full of repetitions and breaks, talk, in all its ineptness—when "the tongue bumps dumbly against the teeth and the lip does not grow round [die Lippe sich nicht rundet]"—nevertheless expresses a deep-seated bodily need to be heard.[66] A repetition with a difference, these lines return us to the quotation above; to language as involution and to "the mortal mouth whose lips no longer grow round [dessen Lippen sich nicht mehr ründen]."[67] Here, talk, in all its clumsiness, touches on the involution of poetic language, as both are linked by the mortality of the bodies that originate them.

There is, then, a corporeal, and thus organic, dimension to the conversation that undermines one of the central claims of the text: "Because the Jew [der Jud] and nature, that is two different things [das ist zweierlei], still, even today, even here."[68] Their irreconcilability, so the narrative suggests, lies in the garrulousness of Jews, a stereotype that encounters another one in its contrast with the silence of nature. The separation, however, is undone as soon as it is stated, for Celan's "Jewish German" brings the two together in a single word in the very instance in which their difference is announced. The "Jew and nature, *that* [das] is two different things," posits the text, and thus joins two ostensibly separate terms in a single pronoun. Only if we dismiss the grammar of the dialect—which here is also the grammar of a dialectic—as irrelevant can the claim of the content of the text stand. Read otherwise, however, language forges a connection between them that suspends the power of the stereotypes for an instance that speaks despite itself, against proper claims.

In contrast to the two men, the stone speaks inorganically; its expression is entirely itself, aligned with the radical selfhood that Adorno attributes to authentic art. It is, therefore, neither aimed at anyone, nor can it be heard; it speaks in dissonant silence. At the same time, it forms the necessary counterpoint to living speech: "The stone, the inorganic, the mineral, is the older, that which stands toward and opposite the human from the deepest time-layer ⌊, from prehistory—that is also the prehistory of the human, ⌋ . . . with its silence it gives direction and space to the one who speaks."[69] The linguistic atavism of involution brings language closer to this prehistoric other, negatively indicating an incongruous kinship that connects opposites. The language of stones and stars, then, may be radically alien to the living expression of the poem without, ultimately, being discordant with it. The taciturn soundscape of the inorganic, is, as Celan writes, "determined from the direction of death," yet it also opens up a realm "of the most essential turning-toward the one speaking in the poem [des im Gedicht Sprechenden]."[70] Such is the impact of the inaudible language of the stone in "Conversation in the Mountains," for only after it finds its voice does the empty talk of the two protagonists, who are really only one, gain substance enough to mourn the dead. "The most essential turning-toward [Zuwendung]," this affectionate turn toward the human other, relies on the poem's mimetic affinity with nonidentity beyond organicity, a nature that is *not* and that can therefore be given voice only negatively.

Celan leaves us with a hint at what a specific instance of such involution might look like: "the language of the poem: involutive → by the light sense (*Lichtsinn*) <you> divine the soul: the creaturely as the poem's horizon—."[71] Citing a line from "Speech-Grille," this note connects the poem to the hope that is inherent in involution, a hope that is always also infused with a sense of vulnerability, for the ultimate culmination of involution is death. Celan's note, however, also indicates the living potential in involutive language. The "creaturely [das Kreatürliche]' that is the horizon of the poem remains indeterminate, nonconceptual: the word's suffix, -*lich*, so close to *Licht*, light, indicates similarity with a difference. Both a limit and a destination, the horizon, like the dash that both continues and concludes the note, leads nowhere, at least not in a straight line. The poem takes us on "detours," "re-routings," "creaturely routes," and perhaps, just perhaps, it moves us closer to utopia.[72]

The first step on such a twisted path is the poem's precise attention to even the slightest sign of life. "Light sense," an organism's ability to respond to light, can manifest in a variety of ways, from the complexity of the human eye to the reaction of protozoa that occurs entirely without organs. Eyes may be the windows to the soul, but to look for spirit in such a base instinct would indicate a heretical confusion of physical reflex and metaphysical significance. Dissonant, this proposition is also one of radical empathy, one reflected in the strange image of the eye that opens Celan's poem:

> Eye round between the bars.
> Flitterbug lid
> rows upward,
> frees a gaze.[73]

> (Augenrund zwischen den Stäben.
> Flimmertier Lid
> rudert nach oben,
> gibt einen Blick frei.)[74]

Pierre Joris's striking translation of "Flimmertier" emphasizes the creatureliness of Celan's words, preserving an image that is evocative of ciliates—in German, *Wimpertierchen* ("lash-animals")—or unicellular organisms whose bodies are surrounded by countless hairlike protrusions. Ciliates do not see in the traditional sense of the word, but some of them do have a sense for light. They seek it out, displaying what Adorno, along with Max Horkheimer, describes in *Dialectic of Enlightenment* as "the tender, never-extinguished impulse of creaturely life toward expression and light."[75] The involutive capacity of the poetic links the light sensitivity of the human eye with that of the ciliates from within the space between two words, grammatically disjointed but profoundly intertwined. The ciliate is only alluded to, its presence in the line emerging out of the nowhere of language, only to be intuited. If we fold the sense for light, *Lichtsinn*, along the line that forms its meridian, the result is the word *sinnlich* ("sensory"). Like moths to a flame, we are drawn to such language games in poetry, whose conceptual stakes are, as Adorno's philosophy shows, inescapably real, for such games unfold our sense for what may be possible.[76]

In its link between the protozoon and human sight, the poem connects our evolutionary roots with an unspoken future for a brief moment before its mimetic longing interrupts itself:

(Were I like you. Were you like me.
Didn't we stand
under *one* trade wind?
We are strangers.)[77]

([Wär ich wie du. Wärst du wie ich.
Standen wir nicht
unter *einem* Passat?
Wir sind Fremde.])[78]

As the parentheses separate this stanza from the others, they fragment the flow of the lyric to express the hopelessness of its desire for unity. Wrapped in parentheses, the stanza both sinks deeper into the poem and becomes external to it, a duality that also applies to its content, for formally, the curved lines gather together what is otherwise kept apart. Involution, a mimetic regression toward affinity, is only possible in poetry, and even here it can take shape only through negation. "Light sense," this corporeal awareness of the inorganic, is a guessing game, the enigmatic capacity of poetic language to reach out toward something that is not, and may never be, there, something that Adorno might call nature. In order to approach this other, poetry has to traverse, and incorporate, the petrified realm of art, remaining open to its own undoing, for only in its discordant moments, on the brink of silence, can it give voice to nonidentity.

## Notes

1. Paul Celan, *The Meridian: Final Version—Drafts—Materials*, eds. Bernhard Böschenstein and Heino Schmull, trans. Pierre Joris (Stanford: Stanford University

Press, 1999), 102. Cf. Paul Celan, *Der Meridian: Endfassung—Entwürfe—Materialien*, eds. Bernhard Böschenstein and Heino Schmull (Frankfurt am Main: Suhrkamp Verlag, 1999), 102. All citations from the English version of *The Meridian* refer to this edition but will not be noted separately in the following because the pagination is the same in both editions.

    2. Theodor W. Adorno and Paul Celan, *Briefwechset 1960–1968*, ed. Joachim Seng, in *Frankfurter Adorno Blätter VIII*, ed. Rolf Tiedemann (Frankfurt am Main: Suhrkamp, 2003), 179; my translation.

    3. Although critics acknowledge the ethical force of involution, they consider its sphere to remain that of the human. Marlies Janz interprets Celan's involution as a turn to the inorganic whose resistance to normative aesthetics after the Shoah is a precondition for the retrieval of a lost humanity. Marlies Janz, "'Judendeutsch': Paul Celans 'Gespräch im Gebirg' im Kontext der Atemwende," *Celan-Jahrbuch* 9 (2005): 75–102, 93. Like Janz, Mirjam Sieber's reading relates the term to "Conversation in the Mountains," focusing on involution as a turn to the other, specifically the Jewish other, that facilitates humanity. Mirjam Sieber, *Paul Celans "Gespräch im Gebirg": Erinnerung an eine versäumte Begegnung* (Tübingen: Max Niemeyer, 2007). While both Sieber and Janz offer valuable insights, this chapter aims to take involution into a different direction through a focus on the entanglement with nature that emerges in the process.

    4. For a thorough account of the relationship between Adorno and Celan, see Joachim Seng, "'Die wahre Flaschenpost': Zur Beziehung zwischen Theodor W. Adorno und Paul Celan," in *Frankfurter Adorno Blätter VIII*, ed. Rolf Tiedemann (Frankfurt am Main: Suhrkamp, 2003), 178–76. Janz, who was present for Adorno's presentation on Celan in Peter Szondi's seminar on hermeticism, notes that the philosopher's remarks were disappointingly vague, focusing on the relationship between language and music in his own methodology rather than on Celan. Janz, "Judendeutsch," 90 n.52. In her monograph, Janz also quotes letters from Adorno that express his intention to write about Celan. Marlies Janz, *Vom Engagement absoluter Poesie: Zur Lyrik und Ästhetik Paul Celans* (Frankfurt am Main: Athenäum, 1984), 222 n.83.

    5. Adorno, *Aesthetic Theory*, trans. Robert Hullot-Kentor (Minneapolis: University of Minnesota Press, 1997), 322; trans. modified.

    6. Adorno, 322; trans. modified.

    7. See, among others, Otto Pöggeler, who argues that Adorno not only misunderstands Celan but completely inverts the poet's intentions. Otto Pöggeler, *Spur des Worts: Zur Lyrik Paut Celans* (Freiburg: Karl Aber, 1986), 155. Kim Teubner offers a book-length study of what she sees as the discrepancies between Celan's poetry and Adorno's philosophy in *Celans Gedichte wollen das äusserste Entsetzen durch Verschweigen sagen: zu Paul Celan und Theodor W. Adorno* (Würzburg: Königshausen and Neumann, 2014). Beau Shaw focuses on, and rejects, Adorno's claim of the hermeticism of Celan's poetry in "The Image that Was in the Blood: Adorno and Celan's 'Tenebrae,'" *Philosophy Today* 61.1 (2017): 233–48.

8. Celan, *The Meridian*, 9.

9. Celan, 59.

10. Theodor W. Adorno, "Arnold Schoenberg, 1874–1951," in *Prisms*, trans. Samuel and Shierry Weber (London: Spearman, 1967), 147–72, 168.

11. See Adorno's letter to Celan from 13 June 1960. Adorno and Celan, *Briefwechsel*, 181.

12. Theodor W. Adorno, *Aesthetics: 1958/59*, ed. Eberhard Ortland, trans. Wieland Hoban (Medford, MA: Polity Press, 2018), 77.

13. Theodor W. Adorno, "On Subject and Object," in *Critical Models: Interventions and Catchwords*, trans. Henry W. Pickford (New York: Columbia University Press, 1998), 245–58, 246.

14. Adorno, 246.

15. Max Horkheimer and Theodor W. Adorno, *Dialectic of Enlightenment: Philosophical Fragments*, ed. Gunzelin Schmid Noerr, trans. Edmund Jephcott (Stanford: Stanford University Press, 2002), 31.

16. Horkheimer and Adorno, 31.

17. Horkheimer and Adorno, 31.

18. Theodor W. Adorno, *Negative Dialectics*, trans. E. B. Ashton (New York: Routledge, 2004), 362. See also section 68 of *Minima Moralia*, where Adorno describes the process of reification through murder in a passage on the structural connections between violence toward animals and violence toward humans: "What is not seen as a human being and yet is a human being, is turned into a thing, so that it can no longer rebut the manic gaze through any sort of impulse." Theodor W. Adorno, *Minima Moralia: Reflections from Damaged Life*, trans. E. F. N. Jephcott (New York: Verso Books, 2005), 104.

19. Adorno, *Negative Dialectics*, 150.

20. Adorno, 5.

21. Adorno, *Aesthetic Theory*, 112; trans. modified; cf. Theodor W. Adorno, *Ästhetische Theorie*, eds. Gretel Adorno and Rolf Tiedemann (Frankfurt am Main: Suhrkamp, 1970), 171.

22. Celan, *The Meridian*, 8.

23. Theodor W. Adorno, "On Lyric Poetry and Society," in *Notes to Literature: Volume 1*, ed. Rolf Tiedemann, trans. Shierry Weber Nicholson (New York: Columbia University Press, 1991), 37–54, 43.

24. Adorno, *Aesthetic Theory*, 112; Adorno, *Ästhetische Theorie*, 171.

25. Horkheimer and Adorno, *Dialectic of Enlightenment*, 32.

26. Adorno, *Aesthetic Theory*, 132.

27. Adorno, *Negative Dialectics*, 111.

28. Adorno, "Subject and Object," 247.

29. Adorno, 247.

30. Adorno, 247.

31. Adorno, *Negative Dialectics*, 56; trans. modified.

32. Adorno, *Aesthetic Theory*, 322.

33. Adorno, 117. For a detailed discussion of Adorno's mimesis, see Ruth Sonderegger, "Ästhetische Theorie," in *Adorno Handbuch: Leben—Werk—Wirkung*, eds. Richard Klein, Johann Kreuzer, and Stefan Müller-Doohm (Stuttgart: J. B. Metzler, 2011), 414–27.

34. Adorno, *Aesthetics*, 42.

35. Adorno, *Aesthetic Theory*, 322.

36. Adorno, 322; Adorno, *Ästhetische Theorie*, 477.

37. Adorno, *Aesthetic Theory*, 112.

38. Celan, *The Meridian*, 10.

39. Adorno, *Aesthetic Theory*, 322.

40. These limitations of human language in the face of catastrophe also enter Adorno's revision of his statement about poetry after Auschwitz. In *Negative Dialectics*, he writes: "Perennial suffering has as much right to expression as a tortured man has to scream [brüllen]; hence it may have been wrong to say that after Auschwitz you could no longer write poems." Adorno, *Negative Dialectics*, 362; cf. Theodor W. Adorno, *Negative Dialektik* (Frankfurt am Main: Suhrkamp, 1966), 353. The German verb *brüllen* denotes an animalistic howl, stripped of any articulation, and therefore resistant to the conceptual aspect of language.

41. Adorno, *Aesthetic Theory*, 322; Adorno, *Ästhetische Theorie*, 477.

42. Adorno, *Aesthetic Theory*, 112; Adorno, *Ästhetische Theorie*, 171.

43. Adorno, *Aesthetic Theory*, 259.

44. Celan, *The Meridian*, 10.

45. Celan, 10.

46. Martin Heidegger, *The Fundamental Concepts of Metaphysics: World, Finitude, Solitude*, trans. William McNeill and Nicholas Walker (Bloomington: Indiana University Press, 1995), 196–97.

47. Celan, *The Meridian*, 182.

48. Celan, 102.

49. Celan, 8.

50. Celan, 182.

51. Celan, 9.

52. The proximity of language to material in the moment of involution bears a resemblance to the notion of literalness ("Buchstäblichkeit") that Adorno sees as the primary quality of Kafka's writing, and without which, as he notes, the ambiguities of Kafka's texts would overwhelm them. Celan's copy of Adorno's "Notes on Kafka" bears the signs of heavy annotation on this subject. A similar notion makes its way into Celan's "Reply to a Questionnaire from the Flinker Bookstore," where Celan describes the "greyer language" that is called for in German poetry after the Shoah: "This language, notwithstanding the inalienable multiplicity of expression, is concerned with precision." Paul Celan, *The Collected Prose*, trans. Rosmarie Waldrop (New York: Sheep Meadow Press, 1986), 16; trans. modified. Such precision,

dangerously sharp, is also a form of involution; in Celan, it emerges not in spite of, but through the "inalienable multiplicity of expression" (16).

53. See, for instance, the work of Nobel Prize laureate Konrad Lorenz, "Die angeborenen Formen möglicher Erfahrung," *Zeitschrift für Tierpsychologie* 5 (1943): 235–409. For a contextualization of Lorenz in National Socialist ideology, see Daniel S. Lehrman, "A Critique of Konrad Lorenz's Theory of Instinctive Behavior," *Quarterly Review of Biology* 28.4 (1953): 337–63; and Richard W. Burkhardt, Jr., *Patterns of Behavior: Konrad Lorenz, Niko Tinbergen, and the Founding of Ethology* (Chicago: University of Chicago Press, 2005), esp. 231–80.

54. Adorno and Celan, *Briefwechsel*, 179; my translation.

55. Celan, *The Collected Prose*, 34.

56. Celan, *The Meridian*, 10.

57. Adorno and Celan, *Briefwechsel*, 179.

58. Celan, *The Meridian*, 129.

59. Celan, 199.

60. Jeffrey Herf, *The Jewish Enemy: Nazi Propaganda during World War II and the Holocaust* (Cambridge, MA: Harvard University Press, 2009), 313 n.54.

61. Celan, *The Meridian*, 199.

62. Paul Celan, "Ansprache anlässlich der Entgegennahme des Literaturpreises der freien Hansestadt Bremen," in *Der Meridian und andere Prosa*, eds. Beda Allemann and Stefan Reichert (Frankfurt am Main: Suhrkamp, 1988), 37–39, 38.

63. Celan, *The Meridian*, 182.

64. Celan, *The Collected Prose*, 20; trans. modified.

65. Celan, *Der Meridian und andere Prosa*, 26.

66. Celan, *The Collected Prose*, 19; trans. modified; Celan, *Der Meridian und andere Prosa*, 25.

67. Celan, *The Meridian*, 182.

68. Celan, *The Collected Prose*, 18; trans. modified; Celan, *Der Meridian und andere Prosa*, 24.

69. Celan, *The Meridian*, 98; trans. modified.

70. The English translation obscures the ambiguity in Celan's phrasing, for in German, the "one speaking" could also be "that which is speaking," perhaps in a language beyond itself.

71. Celan, *The Meridian*, 124.

72. Celan, 11.

73. Paul Celan, *Memory Rose into Threshold Speech: The Collected Earlier Poetry; A Bilingual Edition*, trans. Pierre Joris (New York: Farrar, Straus, and Giroux, 2020), 191.

74. Paul Celan, "Sprachgitter," in *Die Gedichte: Kommentierte Gesamtausgabe*, ed. Barbara Wiedemann (Frankfurt am Main: Suhrkamp, 2012), 100.

75. Horkheimer and Adorno, *Dialectic of Enlightenment*, 186.

76. In his reply to the questionnaire of the Flinker Bookstore, Celan posits that poetry "tries to measure the area of the given and the possible." Celan, *The Collected Prose*, 16. Here, too, his poetology and Adorno's aesthetics approach each other. Adorno, as cited above, sees the artwork as the "unconscious writing of history, [an] anamnesis of the vanquished, of the repressed, and perhaps of what is possible." Adorno, *Aesthetic Theory*, 259.

77. Celan, *Memory Rose*, 191.

78. Celan, *Die Gedichte*, 100.

# Aurality

Chapter 5

# Allophony

## Celan's *Niemandsrosen-Lieder*

MICHAEL AUER

And some of us who know quite well what the
bell has tolled cannot give up song-writing.

Und manche von uns, die recht wohl wissen,
was die Stunde geschlagen hat, können sich
das Liederschreiben nicht abgewöhnen.

—Adorno, "Situation des Liedes"

In his response to a survey from the Librairie Flinker initiated in 1958, Paul Celan stated that lyric poetry in postwar Germany is distinguished by a radically new kind of "musicality," one that he sees "settled at a place where it has nothing in common any more with that 'harmony' that still—more or less blithely—chimed in with, and accompanied, the most terrible things [an einem Ort angesiedelt . . . , wo sie nichts mehr mit jenem 'Wohlklang' gemein hat, der noch mit und neben dem Furchtbarsten mehr oder minder unbekümmert einhertönte]."[1]

Celan had already put this critique of the traditional musicality of lyric poetry to practice in his famous "Todesfuge," which was published in 1952. The poem intertwines the "appalling" and the "blithely harmonic" so densely, they virtually become inextricable. And *Sprachgitter*, published one year after the Librairie Flinker survey, also brings distinctly musical structures to bear upon the poems. The volume that opens with a polyphonous cue of singing voices closes with the equally well-known "Engführung," which is German for "stretto."[2] Despite these and other unmistakably musical accents of Celan's poetry—and although he belongs to the poets of the latter half of the twentieth century most often set to music—the specific musicality of his works has rarely awakened much scholarly interest.[3] The fact that texts such as "Deathfugue" or "Stretto" have not suffered from this disregard may be due, at least in part, to the sophisticated early modern musical forms the titles of these two poems evoke.[4] Others, however, have suffered. And this is poignantly true for a group of poems whose seemingly unprepossessing form has led to an undue marginalization: the *Lieder* Celan wrote right after publishing *Sprachgitter* and collected in *Die Niemandsrose* in 1963.

Instead of focusing on the specific sonorous and rhythmic features of poems such as "Selbdritt, Selbviert," "Eis, Eden," "Nachmittag mit Zirkus und Zitadelle," "Kermorvan," or "Was geschah," scholars working on *The No-One's-Rose* have predominantly explored the complex intertextual play in which the long poems (particularly the ones that are found in the final, fourth cycle) engage with the literary, religious, philosophical, and political traditions of Western and Eastern Europe.[5] As the ongoing developments of scholarship evidence forcefully, the efforts at contextualizing these poems can go on and on, leading to an ever greater overdetermination. But such an approach tends to turn a deaf ear to the specifically lyrical qualities of Celan's poems—and, apparently, for Celan this still means their specifically musical qualities.[6] To exemplify the shift in perspective that a stronger consideration of Celan's "musicality" would exact, I find it very promising to turn to the above-mentioned *Niemandsrosen-Lieder* for two reasons: first, these poems hauntingly articulate a "Singable Remnant" ("Singbarer Rest") that characterizes many of Celan's works until the very last,[7] and second, the *Niemandsrosen-Lieder* are texts that put an immense strain on the relation that the specific sound and rhythm of Celan's poetry entertains to its engagement with the literary, religious, philosophical, and political traditions of Western and Eastern Europe.

The *Lied* figures prominently in *Die Niemandsrose*. Its opening poem speaks of an undefined plurality of humans that "invented no song."[8] And yet, this does not mean that singing simply goes silent. What happens is that it separates itself from this indistinct multitude as "the singing [das Singende]," thus also gaining a deictically indicated distance: "there."[9] In the volume's closing poem, a "Junebug's song [Maikäferlied]" is mentioned that—in spite of all that occurred—has "remained motherly," "on the edge" of the "syllables."[10] This is to say that what enters the cycles of *Die Niemandsrose* in terms of song continues to bear a promise, a promise so deeply ambivalent, however, that it can only appear in a differed or marginalized mode instead of ever being fulfilled. Hence, the "Maikäferlied" gives a last echo of the nursery rhyme that "rauchst der Brunnen" says it will sing but then doesn't. The simple future of "Wir werden das Kinderlied singen" ("We will sing the nursery rhyme"; literally, "the children's song"), thus never comes true.[11] This framing lets the entire volume pivot back and forth uneasily between a faded, and yet remembered, song on the one hand and a completely new song on the other, a song that will have to be voiced in the future but that, for now, remains external: "there."[12] This suspense haunts all the *Lieder* that Celan collected in *Die Niemandsrose*. Their rhythms and their rhymes literally explore the "edges" of the "syllables" in order to yield new potentials of phonation and resonance.[13]

Numerous cross-references show that the *Niemandsrosen-Lieder* form a kind of network. Just to point out one telling example, the poem "Eis, Eden," written in an alternating rhyme scheme, begins with the words: "Es ist ein Land Verloren, / da wächst ein Mond in Ried [There is a land called Lost / where the moon grows in the reeds],"[14] making it a kind of contrafactum of the Protestant Christmas hymn "Es ist ein Ros entsprungen."[15] Two poems that are vaguely reminiscent of German *Volkslieder* respond to these opening words. The penultimate line of "Nachmittag mit Zirkus und Zitadelle"—from the third cycle—reads: "Verloren war Unverloren [Lost was Unlost]."[16] And "Was geschah"—the first poem of the closing, fourth cycle—shifts into a musical register by replacing "Unverloren" with "Unverklungen [Unfaded]."[17] It is remarkable that Celan chose this short song written in a singularly plain, alternating rhyme scheme to open the cycle that features the lengthier, grand philosophical poems:

WAS GESCHAH? Der Stein trat aus dem Berge.
Wer erwachte? Du und ich.
Sprache, Sprache. Mit-Stern. Neben-Erde.
Ärmer. Offen. Heimatlich.

Wohin gings? Gen Unverklungen.
Mit dem Stein gings, mit uns zwein.
Herz und Herz. Zu schwer befunden.
Schwerer werden. Leichter sein.[18]

> (WHAT HAPPENED? The stone stepped out of the mountain.
> Who woke up? You and I.
> Language, language. Co-star. By-earth.
> Poorer. Open. At home.
>
> Where did it lead? Toward unfaded.
> With the stone it went, with us two.
> Heart and heart. Judged too heavy.
> Become heavier. Be lighter.)[19]

This simple ditty speaks of a movement "toward unfaded" that, despite mention of a home or "Heimat," never leads to closure or to a successful homecoming.[20] Here, as elsewhere in Celan, the references to the *Volkslied* and to German Romanticism are deeply vexed and vexing. What the poem articulates on the level of themes and motifs also has a meta-poetic dimension. The imperfect tense of stepping ("trat"), awaking ("erwachte"), and going ("gings") recurs in the unfulfilled, self-contradictory movement of seesawing in the final line. The fact that the paradoxical comparative ("Schwerer" / "Leichter") pivots uneasily between a fulfilled state ("sein") and an unfulfilled development ("werden") literally sets the "Language, language" of the first stanza free. It can unfold in and as an articulate, accentuated series of sonic elements that repeat and differentiate themselves in such a way as to form the complex of meter and rhyme that "is" the song itself. Because of the poem's irregular meter and slant rhyme scheme, the multiple inversions informing the final line's movement apply to the form of the text as a whole. The verses oscillate between a trochaic pattern of four and of five stresses, and the extremely rich (but impure) rhyme scheme plays with assonance, paronomasia, and the repetition of the consonants *g* and *d*: "aus dem Berge" / "Nebenerde"; "Unverklungen" / "schwer befunden."

This conspicuous play with repetitions of sound that simultaneously introduce variance is at work in many of Celan's texts. In terms borrowed from phonology, one could characterize the sound patterns that thus emerge as allophones, in contradistinction to phonemes. As an element of *langue* (the structure of a given language), a phoneme cannot be uttered. And since every spoken sound is unique, any realization of a phoneme could also only articulate one possible variant belonging to an infinite number of infinitesimally small variations. And this is because, as an instance of *parole*, all phonation belongs to an analogous continuum. Therefore, any vocalization can be said to be an allophone, as the free variation of allophones does not result in a change of meaning.

The fact that the differences of *g* and *d* in Celan's poem do not follow a differential logic (*Berge / Berbe* and *Erde / Erge* are not minimal pairs, nor are *verklungen / verklunden* or *befunden / befungen*) points to a special, one might say, allophonic strategy of musicality at play (not only) in *The No-One's-Rose-Lieder*. Their use of assonance, paronomasia, alliteration, and slant rhymes engages in a free variation of tonal elements beyond—or better yet before—established phonetic or semantic structures. And it is this free variation that grants the opening of "You and I" as "Heart and heart" by means of "Language, language."[21] This is to say that the repetition of the words "heart" and "language" should not be understood as identical rhymes in the common sense. Much rather, they need to be read as allophones belonging to the infinite—and thus never self-identical—soundscape (*parole*) between "You and I." That is borne out by the sonic as well as the rhythmic figures of repetition that feature so prominently in the songs of *The No-One's-Rose*. They help to access a dimension that, strictly speaking, always remains outside the text: the singular event of phonation, an act that Celan famously calls "breath."

Hence, the choice of the *Lied*-form does not signify a neo-Romantic internalization. On the contrary: the simplicity of "Was geschah" escapes the psychological depth of the Romantic *Lied*, a musical form that eminently belonged to what "more or less blithely—chimed in with, and accompanied, the most terrible things [noch mit und neben dem Furchtbarsten mehr oder minder unbekümmert einhertönte]."[22] Instead, the "Heart and heart" are involved in impersonal movements (the "[e]s" in "gings") that do not give access to any form of interiority. It is in this impersonal sense only that the split and shared "Language, language" between "You and I" can be said to be "Open."[23]

Such a deliberate impoverishment—"Ärmer [Poorer]," writes Celan[24]—of the tradition of the Romantic *Lied* is reminiscent of a critique that the early Theodor W. Adorno formulated in a short text entitled "Situation des Liedes."[25] The *Lied* should—and in this respect the Celan of 1963 concurs with the Adorno of 1929—lend itself to a completely novel musical "idiom" that succeeds in subverting the influential notion of lyric poetry as an act of foundation and endowment (*Stiftung*) by means of naming. And it should do this in spite of Celan's and Adorno's shared interest in, and engagement with, philosophy and theory. For Adorno (and it would seem also for Celan), the notion of lyric poetry as an act of foundation is associated less with Friedrich Hölderlin—with whom the perennial failure of poetic attempts at such an onomastic act becomes the most fundamental problem[26]—than with Stefan George, who even believed himself to have founded a new "Reich" using elements and strategies taken from, among others, the Romantic *Lied*. In order to subvert precisely this model, Adorno lets "the word go under in the tone [untergeh(en) im Ton]."[27] This passage refers to Arnold Schönberg's musical settings of poems from George's *Buch der hängenden Gärten*. Disintegrating ("Zersetzung") and breaking up ("zerschlagen") George's semantic structures allow Schönberg's *Lieder* to begin with the "smallest particles [kleinsten Partikeln]" and, thus, to reestablish an "ontological relation" to an "outside [auswendigen]" dimension of truth.[28] In other words, Adorno has his Schönberg already engage in what Michael Levine recently called "Atomzertrümmerung."[29]

It is rather unlikely that Celan read this early article. It not mentioned in the *Bibliothèque philosophique*, and it was originally published in a fairly remote journal. But, as we know, Celan did very carefully study a later text of Adorno's that deals with Schönberg: the essay "Arnold Schönberg," which was published in 1960.[30] And Celan was also familiar with the text by Schönberg that had initially inspired Adorno's argument that, in Schönberg, the word—far from being a "founder"—is supposed to "founder" (*untergehen*) in a soundscape. In this essay, "Das Verhältnis zum Text," which was published in *Der Blaue Reiter*, Schönberg claims that his settings are only inspired by "the initial sound of the first words of the text [Anfangsklang der ersten Textworte],"[31] and that he therefore does not know what the actual meaning of such a poem is: "Thus, I fully heard the Schubert-Lieder and their poetry only from out of the music and Stefan George's poems only from out of the sound [So hatte ich die Schubert-Lieder samt der Dichtung nur aus der Musik, Stefan Georges Gedichte nur aus dem Klang heraus vollständig vernommen]."[32] This form of adaptation casts the text as a purely "external occasion [äußerer Anlaß]," as Schönberg readily concedes.[33]

Adorno's essay from 1960 on Schönberg does not explicitly refer to the earlier idea of a "submersion of the word in the tone," although it obviously refers to the musical practice that Schönberg speaks of in "Das Verhältnis zum Text." What it does discuss, though, is Schönberg's "Gestus des Zerschlagens," his "gesture of shattering,"[34] as well as the way in which this gesture establishes what Adorno calls the "primacy of breathing [Primat des Atems]."[35] This fundamental idea of Adorno recurs in the *Philosophie der neuen Musik* (1948), which Celan also must have browsed through, at the very least.[36] Here, the only reason that music can successfully assert itself as an "antipode of verbal language [Gegenpart der Wortsprache]" is because "it is able to speak with no precise obligation towards meaning," which is also why "the rebellion of music against its own meaning" culminates in "the destruction of 'meaning'" tout court.[37]

These musical and music-philosophical contexts are decisive for Celan's engagement with the lyrical form of the *Lied*. In a certain sense, he wants to anticipate the submersion of the word in the tone—which, for Adorno, is the achievement of setting texts to music—in his own lyric poetry. And to do this, he lets the differential logic that phonology and *langue* are based on founder upon the infinite continuum of an allophonic *parole*. Thus, the clues that I have gathered from Celan's readings of Adorno and Schönberg are (as always in Celan) much less important than the ways in which he positions his own works in the intertextual space that such readings provide, that is, the ways in which his texts orient themselves, and move, within this space. And in this specific case, that means the ways in which *The No-One's-Rose-Lieder* perform the *Untergang des Worts im Ton* and the *Untergang* of phonemics in allophony.

The very first song in *Die Niemandsrose* is inscribed not only in the triad George-Schönberg-Adorno; it also introduces further inter-texts:

THREESOME, FOURSOME

Curly mint, mint, curly,
before the house here, before the house.

This hour, your hour,
in conversation with my mouth.

With the mouth, with its silence,
with the words that refuse themselves.

With the wide, with the narrow stations,
with the nearby devastations.

With me alone, with us three,
half-bound, half-free.

Curly mint, mint, curly,
before the house here, before the house.[38]

(SELBDRITT, SELBVIERT

Krauseminze, Minze, krause,
vor dem Haus hier, vor dem Hause.

Diese Stunde, deine Stunde,
ihr Gespräch mit meinem Munde.

Mit dem Mund, mit seinem Schweigen,
mit den Worten, die sich weigern.

Mit den Weiten, mit den Engen,
mit den nahen Untergängen.

Mit mir einem, mit uns dreien,
halb gebunden, halb im Freien.

Krauseminze, Minze, krause,
vor dem Haus hier, vor dem Hause.)[39]

As is well documented, the occasion of the poem is a meeting of the Celans with Nelly Sachs. In its choice of words, the text alludes to this encounter and to the poems of Sachs.[40] But the intertextual play already sets in with the choice of the stanza. Andrea Bánffi-Benedek has shown that the pair rhymes of this very simple stanzaic pattern, as well as the plant mentioned in the first line, evoke elements of a Romanian folksong genre called the Doina.[41] And this is not the only context implied by the mere form of the poem. Instead, the allusions proliferate in a way that is as striking as it is common in Celan. For the pair rhymes of the stanza also bring to mind the poem from George's *hängende Gärten* that immediately precedes the eight poems Schönberg set to music. Besides adopting the stanza of this poem, Celan also employs its key word "untergänge,"[42] which suggests the *Untergang* of the word in the tone that Schönberg achieves according to Adorno. Analogously, the text of "Selbdritt, Selbviert" lets the artistic and artificial text-"gärten" of George (which sovereignly hang over entire "unterworfenen welten" in sublime suspense) sink into the soundscape of a (forged) Doina.[43] This is certainly one reason the word "Untergänge" here does not rhyme with George's "festgepränge"[44] but with the "Engen" that occur so frequently in the *Niemandsrose* and that, moreover, play such a central role in the Büchner Prize speech that Celan also wrote in the early sixties.

But Stefan George is not the only poet to which the form of the song alludes. Osip Mandelstam chose a similar pair rhyme scheme for a poem published in *Stone* that presents an artificial world. Thanks to a seemingly slight tonal shift, however, Mandelstam can turn the self-contained garden landscapes of George's late romanticism into a prison of glass: *tepliza* ("greenhouse") becomes *temniza* ("dungeon").[45] All that human "breath" can effect on the glass walls of this diaphanous jail is an ephemeral obfuscation (in his translation, Celan writes of "Trübung") that vanishes almost instantaneously.[46] What remains inscribed on the glass is an eternal, unreadable "writing" that resists all efforts of live reading breath.[47] In other words, the semiosphere consumes the atmosphere here. And this is why the poem, which begins with the Lenin quotation "čto delat [what is there to do?],"[48] has to end with the evanescence of the human voice and its warmth, an evanescence that can only articulate itself in the jarring dissonance that turns the greenhouse into a dungeon.

The contexts of literary history that I have briefly indicated here were already brought to bear upon the poem in the choice of the rhyme scheme. Such formal dimensions certainly also have a far-reaching and hitherto hardly ever studied significance for the much more complex soundscapes of Celan's unrhymed poetry. This also holds true for metrical details such as the trochees of "Selbdritt, Selbviert" that rhythmically strike a countertone to George's iambic poem "Friedensabend." Such formal features fit exceptionally well to a poem that is set "vor dem Haus hier, vor dem Hause," and thus outside of the artificial world of claustrophobic greenhouses and hanging gardens. At this distinctly different place, a novel—almost infantile—musicality is given voice. And it is certainly not a coincidence that the poem's trochees are inspired by the counting-out rhymes of children's games.[49] In this "here" that pivots between the allophone variants of the dative "Haus [house]" and "Hause [house]," the text can orient itself toward a—highly precarious because only half-successful—liberation. Although the "Gespräch [conversation]" hardly becomes vocal (the mouth is silent, and the words refuse themselves), the lyrical voice is only "half-bound" and thus stands in an intimate relation not only with the "Engen [narrow stations]" (that rhyme with "Untergängen [devastations]") but also with the "Weiten [wide . . . stations]" (and their assonance "Freien [free]"). Thus, markedly unlike traditional counting-out rhymes, which serve to perform an act of exclusion and selection, Celan's poem stages itself as a kind of counting-*in* rhyme that—just as the title "Threesome, Foursome" announces—includes by adding. This does not simply translate Stefan George's verse "Strengstes maaß ist zugleich höchste freiheit [The strictest standard is also the supreme freedom]" that Adorno claims for Schönberg's techniques as a composer in a much more laconic idiom.[50] It also gives it a vastly different sense. Instead of identifying law and freedom, as George does, Celan's poem positions itself on the border of "Engen" and "Weiten," which is why it can be said to be "halb gebunden, halb im Freien [half-bound, half-free]." It is the poem's pair rhymes that grant access to this liminal locus. They half-tie the rhyme words together while letting them half-stand for themselves. And the cyclical arrangement of the poem, which ends by repeating the first stanza, leads this rhyme scheme into a kind of "foursome" of words: each of the words "Minze [mint]," "krause [curly]," and "Haus(e) [house]" occurs four times in the poem.

It is hard not to think of *The Meridian* speech here, which Celan, as I mentioned before, wrote around the same time. For, indeed, "Selbdritt, Selbviert" performs what Celan's speech calls for: "Go with art into your innermost narrows. And set yourself free [Geh mit der Kunst in deine allereigenste Enge. Und setze dich frei]"[51] by allowing the "time" of the "other" to join in.[52] The repetition of the word "hour" ("Diese Stunde, deine Stunde") lets the hour of someone else join in as an allophone. As in "Was geschah," the doubled "Language, language" of "Selbdritt, Selbviert" is "Open," except that here the perspective is broadened to include more others than just "You and I."[53] And it is the submersion of the word in the tone that allows for such an opening. Only because the "words" in "Selbdritt, Selbviert" "refuse themselves" can they grant an expanse, since the transition from "Worten [words]" to "weigern [refuse]" and then to "Weiten [wide . . . stations]" does not establish a semantic or associative series but one based on similarities in sound. Even to characterize such a paronomastic series as a chain of signifiers would be misleading. Here, sound moves away from phonology in order to expose itself to the "primacy of breathing [Primat des Atems]."[54]

To be sure, this submersion of sense does not mean that everything merges in a harmony of pure sounds. On the contrary, Celans's *Lieder* deliberately engage the tension and discord of "Worten" and "Weiten." Thus, the rich and yet impure rhyme of "Schweigen [silence]" and "weigern [refuse]" in "Selbdritt, Selbviert" takes on a programmatic dimension in the following poems: "Kermorvan," "Nachmittag mit Zirkus und Zitadelle," and "Was geschah" (the alternating rhyme schemes of these three poems are reminiscent of German folksongs). With a central word of Celan's Bremen speech, one might say that the sounds of these *Lieder* are always already "angereichert": "enriched."[55] And this enrichment is the principle at work in Celan's allophonic poetry. The second poem that I just mentioned is exceptionally well suited to show the consequences that such an allophony has for semantic structures. That this text also plays a key role for the volume as a whole is intimated by the fact that it is the first poem in which the word "Mandelstamm" occurs:

AFTERNOON, WITH CIRCUS AND CITADEL

In Brest, before the flaming rings,
in the tent, where the tiger sprung,
there I heard how you, Finitude, sung,
there I saw you, Mandelstam.

The sky hung over the roadstead,
the gull hung over the crane.
The Finite sung, the Steady,—
you, gunboat, are named "Baobab."

I greeted the tricolor
with a Russian word—
Lost was Unlost,
the heart an anchored place.[56]

(NACHMITTAG MIT ZIRKUS UND ZITADELLE

In Brest, vor den Flammenringen,
im Zelt, wo der Tiger sprang,
da hört ich dich, Endlichkeit, singen,
da sah ich dich, Mandelstamm.

Der Himmel hing über der Reede,
die Möwe hing über dem Kran.
Das Endliche sang, das Stete,—
du, Kanonenboot, heißt "Baobab."

Ich grüßte die Trikolore
Mit einem russischen Wort—

Verloren war Unverloren,
das Herz ein befestigter Ort.)[57]

None of these three stanzas is purely rhymed, and the deviances are always introduced when a word is used that cannot be clearly attributed to a specific language. "Mandelstamm" could be a Russian name or a German compound noun; "Trikolore" could be a German version of the French *tricolore*, but it also sounds close to the Italian *tricolore*; and "Baobab" (besides being the name of a military vessel) is also the name of a tree, and, moreover, its sound is reminiscent of children's games with nonsensical words.

The poem "Kermorvan" offers a comparably subtle and ambivalent play with rhyming words. Although the mysterious Breton (and not French) title is given an extremely rich—and extremely impure—rhyme in the final phrase, "fort aus Kannitverstan [away from 'Dontunderstand'],"[58] this does not lead to a satisfactory semantic solution to the enigmatic language of the poem and therefore cannot afford understanding ("Verstehen") in any emphatic sense.[59]

Many scholars have pointed out the significance that translation and (foreign language) quotations have for Celan.[60] In the specific case of "Nachmittag mit Zirkus und Zitadelle," the work on the margins of the syllables also probes and transgresses the margins of languages as such. This rhyming strategy is supposed to help Celan's polyglot intertextual play with the traditions of Western and Eastern Europe to "go under" in a play of sound that enriches the alternate rhyme scheme of the Romantic *Volkslied* with new and impure sound qualities literally lying between languages. In this way, the "Finitude" of the allophonic breath can burst into a translinguistic "singing." And, bearing in mind that the phrase "Verloren war Unverloren [Lost was Unlost]" gestures both back to the "land called Lost" in "Eis, Eden"[61] and forward to the "gen Unverklungen [Toward unfaded]" in "Was geschah,"[62] one may begin to fathom the promissory potential that such *Lieder*—which escape differential structures within, and between, languages—harbored for Celan. Hence, the fact that the song's new tone emerges in a realm between French, German, and Russian also has a decidedly political import. Once semantics are submerged in a soundscape, Celan's "Zitadelle" ("citadel") is stripped of its military function and is free to enter into an alliterative play with "Zirkus" ("circus") and "Zelt" ("tent"). And this is equally true for the word "Baobab," which escapes naming by means of baptism as well as a poetry of onomastic endowment. Only insofar as the word can liberate itself from sense can the looming threat of a confrontation between a navy artillery and an army fortification turn into an asemantic yet impure soundscape resonating between languages.

The metrical divergence in the last line of the middle stanza grants this new realm of sound a rhythm of its own. In order to follow the iambic trimeter of the rest of the poem, the verse would have to end with the word "Kanonenboot" ("gunboat"). But it is a trochaic pentameter. The naming of the boat "Baobab" (which can be read as a satire of attempts at an onomastic foundation) thus opens not only a new tonal field between languages but also a new rhythmic field lying between the literary traditions of Western and Eastern Europe. In German literature, the trochaic pentameter is called the "Serbian trochee" because it was borrowed from southern Slavic poetry, where it is very common. Again, it is tempting to think of the title of the counting-in rhyme, "Selbdritt, Selbviert": thanks to Serbian, the "threesome" of German, French, and Russian becomes a "foursome."

Thus, the role that the *Niemandsrosen-Lieder* play should have become somewhat clearer. Just like the nursery rhymes that Adorno wrote about in 1929, they stand "daringly askew to what is [gewagt und schief zu dem, was ist]."[63] And this is due to their sound and their rhythm, in particular. If one wanted to put it in such terms, one could say that this also points to the most fundamental "philosophical" dimension of Celan's poetry. His poems try to establish an ontological relation to an exterior realm of truth in the sense that Adorno had in mind when speaking of the submersion of words in tone. This is a realm where the phonation of breath structurally escapes semantics and phonology. As a consequence, the linguistic material of Celan's poems is not established in a differential play of minimal pairs. It consists of accentuated, impure sounds that are deliberately "enriched."

Politically speaking, such allophonic poetics undermine the possibility of drawing a border along a shibboleth, which—although it is not a minimal pair in the phonological sense—follows an analogous differential logic. In this case, the sonic difference of /s/ and /ʃ/ even decides over life and death. When the poem "In Eins" (which immediately follows upon "Was geschah") says, "In the heart's mouth / awakened shibboleth [im Herzmund / erwachtes Schibboleth],"[64] the "heart and heart" from "Was geschah" and the "mouth with its silence" in "Selbdritt, Selbviert" are condensed into one figure.[65] But the title of the poem is not supposed to suggest there is a closed front unifying itself against an Other. Instead, the "One" of "In Eins" itself is enriched with a whole series of foreign language elements (taken from Spanish, French, and Russian), as well as slogans from different revolutions (from the Paris Commune to the Spanish Civil War). This lets "In Eins" ("In One") perform yet another counting-in game of allophonic politics.[66]

## Notes

1. Paul Celan, *Gesammelte Werke in sieben Bänden*, 7 vols., eds. Beda Allemann and Stefan Reichert (Frankfurt am Main: Suhrkamp, 1983), 3:167.

2. Apparently, Adorno planned a longer study on *Sprachgitter* that was to focus on musical aspects in particular. At least, this is what he communicated to Celan in a letter from 1968. Cf. Rolf Tiedemann, ed., *Frankfurter Adorno Blätter VIII* (Frankfurt am Main: Suhrkamp, 2003), 197–98.

3. See, for example, Jerry Glenn, "Paul Celan: Eine Liste der veröffentlichten Vertonungen," in *Stundenwechsel: Neue Perspektiven zu Alfred Margul-Sperber, Rose Ausländer, Paul Celan, Immanuel Weissglas*, eds. Andrea Corbei-Hoisie, George Gutu, and Martin A. Hainz (Bucharest: Hartung-Gorre, 2002), 455–60; and Hartmut Lück, "Celan," in *Die Musik in Geschichte und Gegenwart: Allgemeine Enzyklopädie der Musik*, ed. Ludwig Finscher, vol. 4 (Kassel: Bärenreiter/Metzler, 1989), sp. 518–24. For a recent exception, see Axel Englund, "Modes of Musicality in Paul Celan's *Die Niemandsrose*," *Seminar: A Journal of Germanic Studies* 45.2 (2009): 138–58.

4. See, for example, the two recent studies by Andrea Bánffi-Benedek and Marik Froidfond: Andrea Bánffi-Benedek, "Intermediale Systemreferenzen zur Musik bei Paul Celan in den Gedichten *Todesfuge* und *Engführung*," in *Globale und lokale Denkmuster: Festschrift für Elena Viorel zum 70. Geburtstag*, ed. Szabolcs János-Szatmári (Oradea: EME-Partium, 2010), 129–45; Marik Froidfond, "Agencement et dégagement des voix dans *Todesfuge* et *Sprachgitter*: L'art de la fugue selon Paul Celan," in *Paul Celan, la poésie, la musique: Avec une clé changeante*, eds. Antoine Bonnet and Frédéric Marteau (Paris: Hermann, 2015), 109–28.

5. For a monument dedicated to the results of these pursuits, see Jürgen Lehmann, ed., *Kommentar zu Paul Celans "Die Niemandsrose"* (Heidelberg: Winter, 1997).

6. Following up on reflections of Peter Szondi, Winfried Menninghaus pointed out the difficult relation of commentary and interpretation in Celan studies. The "citations of a movement of pure language [Zitate reiner sprachlicher Bewegung]" to which he alludes in this context furnish an important insight from which a future investigation of musicality in Celan might profit. Winfried Menninghaus, "Zum Problem des Zitats bei Celan und in der Celan-Philologie," in *Paul Celan*, eds. Werner Hamacher and Winfried Menninghaus (Frankfurt am Main: Suhrkamp, 1988), 170–90, 176.

7. See the poem of this title in Celan, *Gesammelte Werke*, 2:36; and Paul Celan, *Breathturn into Timestead: The Collected Later Poetry*, trans. Pierre Joris (New York: Farrar, Strauss, and Giroux, 2014), 20–23.

8. Paul Celan, *The No-One's-Rose*, trans. David Young (Grosse Pointe Farms: Marick, 2014), 21.

9. Celan, 21; Celan, *Gesammelte Werke*, 1:211. For a reading of the sonoric and musical structures of this poem, see Englund, "Modes of Musicality."

10. Celan, *The No-One's-Rose*, 159; Celan, *Gesammelte Werke*, 1:290.

11. Celan, *Gesammelte Werke*, 1:237.

12. Celan, *The No-One's-Rose*, 21.

13. Celan, 159. Celan's decision to use a rhyme scheme is quite surprising, given his critique of rhyming in *The Meridian* speech. But even in the drafts for this speech, rhyme plays a key performative role: "'What's on the lung, put on the tongue,' my mother used to say ['Was auf der Lunge, das auf der Zunge,' pflegte meine Mutter zu sagen]" is used thrice as the introduction to a note. One of these instances continues as follows: "Which has to do with breath. One should finally learn how to also read this breath, this breath-unit in the poem; in the cola meaning is often more truthfully joined and fugued than in the rhyme. [Das hat mit dem Atem zu tun. Man sollte es endlich lernen, im Gedicht diesen Atem, diese Atemeinheit mitzulesen; in den Kolen ist der Sinn oft wahrer gefügt und gefugt als im Reim]." Paul Celan, *Der Meridian: Endfassung—Entwürfe—Materialien*, eds. Bernhard Böschenstein and Heino Schmull (Frankfurt am Main: Suhrkamp Verlag, 1999), 108; Paul Celan, *The Meridian: Final Version—Drafts—Materials*, trans. Pierre Joris (Stanford: Stanford University Press, 2011), 108. All citations from the English version of *The Meridian* refer to this edition but will not be noted separately in the following because the pagination is the same in both editions.

14. Celan, *Gesammelte Werke*, 1:224; Celan, *The No-One's-Rose*, 45.

15. See Winfried Menninghaus, "Anti Christ: Paul Celans zitierende Revision christlicher Kirchenlieder," *Kaspar: Zeitschrift über den Umgang mit Literatur* 1 (1978): 13–23. "Eis, Eden" is prominently placed as well: it immediately precedes the unofficial title poem of the volume, "Psalm," which is the only text that mentions the "No One's Rose" explicitly.

16. Celan, *Gesammelte Werke*, 1:261; my translation.

17. Celan, *Gesammelte Werke*, 1:239; Celan, *The No-One's-Rose*, 119. The "Unfaded" in Young's translation refers to the fading of a sound.

18. Paul Celan, *Memory Rose into Threshold Speech: The Collected Earlier Poetry: A Bilingual Edition*, trans. Pierre Joris (New York: Farrar, Straus, and Giroux, 2020), 325.

19. Celan, *Gesammelte Werke*, 1:269.

20. Celan, *The No-One's-Rose*, 119.

21. Celan, *Memory Rose*, 325.

22. Celan, *Gesammelte Werke*, 3:176. In his article on the "Situation des Liedes" (from which I have also chosen the motto for this chapter) Adorno mockingly writes that, after Schubert's *Winterreise*, the "interiority" and "psychology" of Romanticism "took possession of the *Lied* as if it were a piece of furniture, cancelling every rela-

tion to a real outside [das Lied gleich einem Möbel in Besitz genommen . . . jeden Bezug aufs wirkliche Außen getilgt]." Theodor W. Adorno, "Situation des Liedes," in *Gesammelte Schriften*, ed. Rolf Tiedemann, vol. 18 (Frankfurt am Main: Suhrkamp, 1984), 345–53, 345.

23. Celan, *Memory Rose*, 325.

24. Celan, 324–25.

25. Joachim Seng was able to show that Adorno's influence on Celan's poetics was particularly due to his work on *Neue Musik*. See Joachim Seng, "'Die wahre Flaschenpost': Zur Beziehung zwischen Theodor W. Adorno und Paul Celan," in *Frankfurter Adorno Blätter VIII*, ed. Rolf Tiedemann (Frankfurt am Main: Suhrkamp, 2003), 151–76, 158, 164–68.

26. Here, Werner Hamacher's claim that, in Hölderlin, the "language material's finitude resists a universalization of its semantic energy [Bedeutungsresistenz des endlichen sprachlichen Materials . . . der Universalisierung seiner semantischen Energie entgegensetzt]" remains authoritative. Werner Hamacher, "Die Sekunde der Inversion: Bewegungen einer Figur durch Celans Gedichte," in *Paul Celan*, eds. Werner Hamacher and Winfried Menninghaus (Frankfurt am Main: Suhrkamp, 1988), 81–126, 85.

27. Adorno, "Situation des Liedes," 349. In fact, Adorno also seems to have attributed a completely new kind of musicality to Celan's works. In a letter from 13 June 1960, he writes Celan: "Es will mir scheinen, als wäre damit wirklich in die Lyrik ein Element aus der Musik hereingekommen, das es in dieser Weise zuvor nicht gegeben hat, und das mit dem Klischee des musikalischen Wesens der Lyrik nicht das mindeste zu tun hat." Tiedemann, *Frankfurter Adorno Blätter VIII*, 181. Here, Adorno is simultaneously referring to Gustav Mahler and to "Das Gespräch im Gebirg."

28. Adorno, "Situation des Liedes," 347, 348, 350.

29. See Michael Levine, *Atomzertrümmerung: Zu einem Gedicht Paul Celans* (Vienna: Turia + Kant, 2018).

30. See Alexandra Richter, Patrik Alac, and Betrand Badiou, eds., *Paul Celan: La bibliothèque philosophique* (Paris: Éditions Rue d'Ulm, 2004), 241–42. Joachim Seng has already investigated Celan's engagement with this text of Adorno. However, he focused on the consequences that it had for "Engführung." See Joachim Seng, "Von der Musikalität einer 'graueren' Sprache: Zu Celans Auseinandersetzung mit Adorno," *Germanisch-Romanische Monatsschrift* 45 (1995): 419–30.

31. Arnold Schönberg, "Das Verhältnis zum Text," in *Der Blaue Reiter*, eds. Wassily Kandinsky and Franz Marc (Munich: Piper, 1965), 60–75, 60.

32. Schönberg, "Das Verhältnis zum Text," 74.

33. Schönberg, 75.

34. Theodor W. Adorno, "Arnold Schönberg, 1874–1951," in *Gesammelte Schriften*, ed. Rolf Tiedemann, vol. 10.1 (Frankfurt am Main: Suhrkamp, 1977), 152–80, 167. For Celan's notes to this passage, see Richter et al., *Paul Celan: La bibliothèque philosophique*, 241.

35. Theodor W. Adorno, "Arnold Schoenberg, 1874–1951," in *Prisms*, trans. Samuel and Shierry Weber (Cambridge, MA: MIT Press, 1983), 147–72, 152; Adorno, "Arnold Schönberg, 1874–1951," 155. For the question of breath in Celan and Adorno, see Andréa Lauterwein, "Au-delà des humains: De Schoenberg à Celan via Adorno," in *Paul Celan, la poésie, la musique,* 143–52, 151–52.

36. See Richter et al., *Paul Celan*, 264.

37. Theodor W. Adorno, *Philosophy of Modern Music*, trans. Anne G. Mitchell and Wesley V. Blomster (London: Bloomsbury, 2007), 90; cf. Theodor W. Adorno, *Philosophie der neuen Musik*, ed. Rolf Tiedemann (Frankfurt am Main: Suhrkamp, 1975), 121.

38. Celan, *Memory Rose*, 249–51; trans. modified.

39. Celan, *Gesammelte Werke*, 1:216.

40. See Gisela Bezzel-Dischner, *Poetik des modernen Gedichts: Zur Lyrik von Nelly Sachs* (Bad Homburg: Gehlen, 1970), 124; and Matthias Loewen, "Gespräch mit dem Schweigen: Zu Paul Celans Gedicht 'SELBDRITT, SELBVIERT,'" *Deutsche Vierteljahresschrift für Literaturwissenschaft und Geistesgeschichte* 61 (1987): 163–82, 172–75.

41. Andrea Bánffi-Benedek, "Medien der Klage: Intermediale Überlegungen zu den Gedichten *Espenlaub* und *Selbdritt, Selbviert* von Paul Celan," *Temeswarer Beiträge zur Germanistik* 11 (2014): 269–81, 273.

42. Stefan George, "Friedensabend," in *Sämtliche Werke in 18 Bänden*, vol. 3 (Stuttgart: Klett-Cotta, 1991), 81. Schönberg set to music the poems that immediately follow, from "Unter schutz von dichten blättergründen" to "Wir bevölkerten die abend-düstern / Lauben." The fact that the word "Untergänge" also alludes to one of Nelly Sachs's poems shows just how overdetermined individual words often become in Celan. See Loewen, "Gespräch mit dem Schweigen," 175; and Lehmann, *Kommentar*, 72. This overdetermination can be seen as a consequence of Celan's strategy of allophonic "enrichment" discussed in the following.

43. George, "Friedensabend," 81.

44. George, 81.

45. I would like to thank Susanne Strätling for pointing out the phonetic proximity of *temniza* and *tepliza*. Celan translated Mandelstam's poem into German and rendered *temniza* as "Kerker Welt." Celan, *Gesammelte Werke*, 5:52–53.

46. Celan, 53.

47. Celan, 53.

48. Celan, 5:52. Celan does not translate these words literally. For this famous Lenin quotation, see Jacques Derrida, *Was tun—mit der Frage "Was tun"?* trans. Oliver Precht and Johannes Kleinbeck (Vienna: Turia + Kant, 2018).

49. In 1958, Celan wrote a poem entitled "Abzählreime" that he never published in a volume of poetry (Celan, *Gesammelte Werke*, 3:133); for a facsimile of the manuscript, see the cover of the paperback edition of Paul Celan, *Die Gedichte: Kommentierte Gesamtausgabe in einem Band*, ed. Barbara Wiedemann (Frankfurt am Main: Suhrkamp, 2005). In 1969, Wilhelm Höck already noted the proximity of

"Selbdritt, Selbviert" to counting-out rhymes (see Wilhelm Höck, *Formen heutiger Lyrik: Verse am Rande des Verstummens* [Munich: List, 1969], 57–58). For the influence of children's poetry on Celan, see Ruth Lorbe, "Außerdem und Innerdem, Polykarp und Polyphem: Elemente der Kinderlyrik in der Dichtung Paul Celans," in *Psalm und Hawdalah: Zur Werk Paul Celans: Akten des Internationalen Paul Celan-Colloquiums New York 1985*, ed. Joseph P. Strekla (Bern: Lang, 1987), 79–111.

50. Adorno, "Arnold Schönberg, 1874–1951," 165; Adorno, "Arnold Schoenberg, 1874–1951," 160.

51. Celan, *Der Meridian*, 11.

52. Celan, 9.

53. Celan, *Memory Rose*, 325.

54. Adorno, "Arnold Schoenberg, 1874–1951," 152; Adorno, "Arnold Schönberg, 1874–1951," 155.

55. Celan, *Gesammelte Werke*, 3:186; cf. Paul Celan, *Selected Poems and Prose of Paul Celan*, trans. John Felstiner (New York: Norton, 2001), 395.

56. Celan, *Memory Rose*, 315.

57. Celan, *Gesammelte Werke*, 1:261.

58. Celan, 263; Celan, *The No-One's-Rose*, 111.

59. Perhaps, the Breton words in Celan's title are directed against Marcel's reflections on Merovingian-Germanic words that figure so prominently at the beginning of Proust's *Recherche*. The use of the word "Kannitverstan" in Johann Peter Hebel is understood as a means of undermining linguistic differences in Thomas Schestag, *Para-. Titus Lucretius Carus, Johann Peter Hebel, Francis Ponge—zur literarischen Hermeneutik* (Munich: Klaus Boer, 1991), 207–15.

60. See Menninghaus, "Zum Problem."

61. Celan, *The No-One's-Rose*, 45.

62. Celan, *Gesammelte Werke*, 1:269.

63. Adorno, "Situation des Liedes," 345. For the fundamental relevance of childhood in Adorno, see Lars Bullmann, *Spielräume der Kindheit: Adorno-Konstellationen* (PhD diss., Ludwig Maximilian University, Munich, 2016).

64. Celan, *Memory Rose*, 325; Celan, *Gesammelte Werke*, 1:270.

65. Celan, 216, 269.

66. A German version of this text has already been published as "Allophonie: Musikalität in den *Niemandsrosen*-Liedern," *Celan-Perspektiven* 1 (2019): 85–96.

Chapter 6

# "A Chest Full of Cello Boughs"
## The Sonorous Force of Writing in Deconstructive Readings of Celan

Naomi Waltham-Smith

The concept of frontier is aporetic. The more sharply the frontier tries to delimit itself, the fuzzier it becomes, threatening to dissolve. If a concept is to be clearly delimited—if it is to have sharp boundaries, as Frege would say—then we must know its frontiers, what its limits are, what goes beyond its threshold, what happens outside its confines. But to know where it starts and ends, we must also presuppose the concept of frontier and thus know *its* limits, that is, the limits of the concept of frontier, the frontier of *frontier*, so to speak.[1] And so it is that when philosophy attempts to delimit itself in relation to something that is always an experience of the outside, that opens itself to an experience of the new and unexpected, that lives life on the edge—in this attempt to delimit itself by way of the frontier, philosophy finds itself unraveling, always already passing over into this thing that, for want of better words, we call literature or poetry. As Jacques Derrida says in the fifth session of the recently published seminar, *Théorie et pratique* (1976–1977), there is nothing more philosophical than philosophy's overflowing itself. He notes first that

> the overflowing of a philosophy by another, the overflowing of philosophy by a "thinking" that is no longer simply *philosophical*, such an overflowing is the essential trait (but how can an

overflowing be a drawn line?) of every discourse (but is discourse theory or practice?) on the "theory/practice" relation.²

(le débordement d'une philosophie par une autre, le débordement de la philosophie par une "pensée" qui n'est plus simplement *philosophique*, ce débordement est le trait essentiel [mais comment le débordement peut-il être un trait ?] de tout discours [mais le discours est-il théorie ou pratique ?] sur le rapport "théorie/ pratique.")

Shortly thereafter he continues the thought: "Philosophie débordée, donc. Mais il a toujours appartenu au philosophique de déborder, de se déborder soi-même, de se comprendre lui-même et le reste. [Philosophy overflowed, then. But overflowing, philosophy's overflowing itself, comprising itself and the rest, has always belonged to the philosophical.]"³

This possibility of drawing a line between philosophy on one side and literature and poetry on the other returns a decade later in the essay *Schibboleth*, devoted to the poetry of Paul Celan, in which Derrida suggests that the limit of the philosophical as such is blurred precisely there where "la philosophie se trouve, se retrouve alors dans les parages du poétique, voire de la littérature [philosophy finds itself, finds itself again in the vicinity of poetics, indeed, of literature]."⁴ Again, however, emphasizing that philosophy's place is on this fuzzy edge, Derrida goes on to question the very possibility of keeping within limits.

It finds itself again there, it does not necessarily lose itself there, as some believe, those who, in their tranquil credulity, believe they know where this limit runs and timorously keep within it, ingenuously, albeit without innocence, stripped of what one must call the philosophical experience: a certain questioning traversal of limits, uncertainty as to the border of the philosophical field—and above all the experience of language, always just as poetic, or literary, as it is philosophical.⁵

(Elle s'y retrouve car l'indécision de cette limite est peut-être ce qui la provoque le plus à penser. Elle s'y retrouve, elle ne s'y perd pas nécessairement comme le croient, dans leur tranquille crédulité, ceux qui croient savoir où passe cette limite et s'y tiennent peureusement, ingénument, quoique sans innocence, dénués de ce qu'on doit appeler *l'expérience philosophique* : une certaine traversée questionnante des limites, l'insécurité quant à la frontière du champ philosophique—et surtout l'expérience de la langue, toujours aussi poétique, ou littéraire, que philosophique.)

Far from an external opposition, the frontier of literature—literature as frontier, as the albeit indiscernible limit by which philosophy seeks to shore up its boundaries—is the trace of this poetic force of overflowing. That is, this frontier holds back the experience of frontier that is said to belong to literature and against which philosophy seeks to protect itself. Literature, then, is not what lies *beyond* philosophy's frontiers. Rather, the frontier that joins and separates them is the retroactive effect of a constitutive poetic force—an irreducible and incalculable dissemination—by which philosophy is instituted and which at the same time threatens the security of its conceptuality and rationality. The frontier through which philosophy seeks to banish poetry from the *logos* is thus an attempt to protect itself not from the other outside but from an immanent self-de(con)structive tendency or, in more Derridean parlance, against its autoimmunity. This means that, far from being an obstacle to be overcome, the frontier is what makes philosophy possible through the delimitation of literature or poetry and at the same time what ruins it from the outset and, by virtue of delimiting it, makes any absolute philosophy purified of the poetic impossible.

If philosophy's poetic institution is thus not without a certain violence, this destructive impulse is then retroactively figured as the penetration of a limit or the forceful expulsion through a constricted passage. There emerges a dialectics of containment and expulsion, of appropriation and abandonment. Celan's poetry both makes acutely palpable and destabilizes one of the traits via which the poetic is said to overspill the philosophical. Closely aligned with a certain bodily figuration that locates the frontier of literature at the cuttable membrane of the skin or the openings of bodily orifices, there is also the tangential attempt to distinguish between sense and sound and thus to situate the literary in an oral or aural breach—a nexus that Jean-Luc Nancy, for instance, has explored in detail in such texts as *Ego Sum* and *Corpus*.[6] Further, in the analysis of someone like Giorgio Agamben, the line between *phonē* and *logos*, which metaphysics has mapped onto the distinction between life and death in the guise of the living breath in contrast with the inanimate letter, continues to inform the notion of an incalculable poetic inspiration in excess of conceptual deduction, as if sound were the trait that traced the limits of articulate rational language.

One of the lessons of deconstruction has been to complicate these distinctions. *Phonē* and *logos* cannot simply be opposed because the phonocentric "hegemony accorded to vocal speech and phonetic writing" is, in Derrida's reading, in "essential and immediate proximity" with logocentrism without coinciding with it.[7] This proximity touches upon a common misconception about Derrida's interest in writing: namely, that this comes at the expense of the voice or of sound. It is undoubtedly the case that Derrida, especially when first setting out the stakes of deconstruction by focusing on subordinate terms, is suspicious of any appeal to the voice that would uphold the metaphysical opposition. But just as the work of deconstruction has been to show that the supposedly pure articulate, rational *logos* is in fact always already compromised from the outset by cunningly deceptive rhetoric, alluring poetry, or wordless sound, it equally demonstrates that voice and writing cannot be so cleanly divided. Close reading of Derrida's work reveals that, far from consisting in the hierarchy of sounding, living breath over inanimate writing, logocentrism is in fact the very structure of opposition as such. It is the gathering that thereby creates the fiction of a frontier beyond which lies the other. What this opposition attempts to contain and thereby exclude is nothing other than what I am here calling a poetic force—another name or non-synonymous substitution for what Derrida calls *archi-écriture* to describe writing in an enlarged sense beyond its narrow vulgar concept.

I figure this disseminating, overflowing force as expressly poetic because this has the advantage of suggesting that it has a sonorous character and, moreover, because it is in Celan's poetry in particular that deconstruction—in readings by Derrida and Hélène Cixous that I will discuss below and also in Werner Hamacher's work—finds this sonorous or even musical poetic force. Due to the intense suspicion toward the sounding voice exhibited by the texts of the late 1960s in particular, there remains an assumption that this generalized writing, like the more narrowly defined category of writing, would necessarily be silent—and Derrida himself does give support to this view on multiple occasions. The two essays on Antonin Artaud in *L'écriture et la différence*, for instance, are deeply ambivalent about the raw cry, ever wary of a metaphysical pneumatics even as they give some credit for a deconstructive impulse in the theater of cruelty. And yet in a late interview alongside Cixous, Derrida insists that it was never his intention to replace the voice with writing or to reject orality, and by extension, aurality, outright: "Those who do not read me reproach me at times for playing writing against the voice, as if to reduce it to silence. In truth, I proposed a reelaboration and a generalization of the concept of writing, of text or of trace. Orality is also the inscription [frayage] of a trace."[8] Even if Derrida himself did not go so far as to thematize this, thinking of a dispersive, self-disseminating sonic force as a part of this generalized notion of writing can be situated as an extension of Derrida's evolving project. As Geoffrey Bennington observes, the later Derrida (perhaps now less concerned with establishing the "clean-break" of deconstruction) turns his attention away from the secondary terms of metaphysics and instead toward the primary ones of justice, dignity, sovereignty, and so forth in order to show their autoimmunity from the outset.[9] I want to suggest that doing something similar with the poetic voice means engaging with its sonorous dimension—or rather, that the poetic voice becomes noisy to the extent that it divides and defers itself into what it is not, into sound and sense, rational and inarticulate, human and nonhuman, and so forth. And it is Celan who is mobilized by Derrida and Cixous not so much to interrupt or turn away from a poetics of breath as to tease out another thinking of the sonorous, its reinscription and paleonymy outside—or, more precisely, since the point is that this is impossible, at the frontier of—a metaphysics of life.

To this end I want to explore a nexus of deconstructive readings of Celan: Cixous's reimagining of "Cello-Einsatz" in *Jours de l'an*, Derrida's remarks on the same poem in *Schibboleth*, and his repeated return not only in *Béliers* but also in the second year of his final seminar on *La bête et le souverain* to the line that ends another of the poems in the 1967 collection, *Atemwende*: "Die Welt ist fort, ich muß dich tragen [The world is gone, I must carry you]."[10] While there is no direct link between these readings, I am interested in the points of contact between their various edges. One of these comes to the fore, for example, in Derrida's extended essay on Cixous, *H. C. pour la vie*, in which he confronts her on the nature of this living poetic force as it variously appears in her writings.[11] Another emerges in "L'Oreille de Heidegger: Philopolémologie (*Geschlecht* IV)," which anticipates the association of a key word in Celan's line, *tragen*, with the force of *Walten* that we find in Derrida's final seminar and also expressly ties it to the question of aurality.[12] My interest lies in the frontiers between these texts—in what passes between them.

I am by no means the first to highlight either the musicality of Celan's poetry or its reflexive thematization of poetic breath. The entwinement of critical thought and poetic language in Celan suggests that philosophy's encounter with "its" frontier is, as it is for Derrida and Cixous, a matter of orality, of what passes by way of the mouth as an outer edge of the body, of what traverses its frontier—of digestion, of gobbling up, of wolfing down and of vomiting, of spluttering and sputtering, of an animal vociferation, but also of the breath, of the rhythmic inhalation and exhalation that regulates the dialectic between sound and silence in the poem. While the readings of Celan to which I am about to turn situate poetic breath at the limit of language—at the threshold between *logos* and *phonē*—they also map the boundary between sound and writing onto another, arguably more decisive frontier between life and death. The frontier between poetry and philosophy, no less than the one traced and disrupted by *la vie la mort*—the life-death or spectral life more than life, living on (*survivre*) that exceeds the opposition between life and death—thus appears, moreover, as a question of aurality, of taking in, incorporating the other via the ear, and also of what escapes the ear. In the first instance, poetry asserts the possibility of sound beyond sense—of, for instance, the animal or female cry, the rabble-rousing mob, the rhythm and resonance of poetry liberated from the syntactic constraints and semantic ends of prose, even as literature unfettered by the concept— and in this way, it traces the limit of the philosophical. It thus follows that philosophy's relation to its outside comes to be figured as a kind of listening in the history of philosophy.

This is why Derrida speaks in "Tympan" of philosophy's "*entente*" with its nonphilosophical outside according to the model of hearing-oneself-speak (*s'entendre parler*) that was deconstructed in *La voix et le phénomène*:

> If philosophy has always intended, from its point of view, to maintain its relation with the nonphilosophical . . . if it has constituted itself according to this purposive *entente* with its outside, if it has always intended to hear itself speak, in the same language, of itself and of something else, can one, strictly speaking, determine a nonphilosophical place, a place of exteriority or alterity from which one might still treat *of philosophy*? Is there any ruse not belonging to reason to prevent philosophy from still speaking of itself, from lending its categories to the logos of the other, by affecting itself without delay, on the domestic page of its own tympanum (still the muffled drum, the *tympanon*, the cloth stretched taut in order to take its beating, to amortize impressions, to make the *types* (*typoi*) resonate, to balance the striking pressure of the *typtein*, between the inside and the outside), with heterogeneous percussion? Can one violently penetrate philosophy's field of listening without its

immediately . . . making the penetration resonate within itself, appropriating the emission for itself, familiarly communicating it to itself between the inner and middle ear . . . ? In other words, can one puncture the tympanum of a philosopher and still be heard and understood by him?[13]

(Si la philosophie a toujours entendu, de son côté, se tenir en rapport avec le nonphilosophique . . . si elle s'est constituée selon cette entente réfléchie avec son dehors, si elle s'est toujours entendue à parler, dans la même langue, d'elle-même et d'autre chose, peut-on, en toute rigueur, assigner un lieu non philosophique, un lieu d'extériorité ou d'altérité depuis lequel on puisse encore traiter *de la philosophie*? Ce lieu, toujours, n'aura-t-il pas été d'avance occupé de philosophie? Est-il une ruse qui ne soit pas de la raison pour empêcher la philosophie de parler encore d'elle-même, de prêter ses catégories au logos de l'autre, en s'affectant sans retard, sur la page domestique de son propre tympan [toujours le tambour assourdi, *tympanon*, toile tendue, tenue à recevoir les coups, à amortir les impressions, à faire résonner les *types* (*typoi*), à équilibrer les pressions frappantes du *typtein*, entre le dedans et le dehors] de la percussion hétérogène? Peut-on pénétrer violemment son champ d'écoute sans qu'aussitôt . . . le fasse résonner en elle, s'en approprie l'émission, se le communique familièrement entre l'oreille interne et l'oreille moyenne . . . ? Autrement dit, peut-on crever le tympan d'un philosophe et continuer à se faire entendre de lui?)

There is, then, a nonphilosophical battering of philosophy's eardrum, the permeability of which membrane is at stake in this passage. But it is not simply a question of philosophy's overflowing its borders and thus appropriating its outside to itself but, moreover, of philosophy's containing the force of overflowing, penetrating, punctuating itself as its own tune. As the final question hints, however, this penetrating of philosophy's eardrum is its condition of (im)possibility or, in another Derridean phrase: *more* (*plus de*) philosophy—its excessive overflowing and expansion beyond its purported borders—leads to *no more* (*plus de*) philosophy.

I want to connect this aporetic character of philosophy's auto-hetero-percussion to the ways in which the sonorous comes to be figured as the lifeforce of the poem in Celan and deconstructive readings of his poetry:

that is, as a power to survive beyond (the poet's) death or even to bring the dead back to life. Celan's "Cello-Einsatz" is one of a cycle of short of poems published under the title *Atemwende* ("breathturn" or "turn-of-the-breath"). It would then be possible to imagine its sonic entry as an apostrophe whose turn toward the addressee summons the inanimate to life or recalls the recently dead to turn back. But I also aim to open up some space—to trace a frontier, if you like, knowing that it will vibrate and tremble—between on the one hand this spiritual, pneumatic sense of breath, which is founded in a metaphysics of life and is so often thematized and questioned by Celan, and on the other an altogether more technological force of turning from one to the other, of tropology, metaphoricity, of survival as substitution and prostheticity, that is, nonetheless I shall argue, not without sound.

In short, I want to situate the sonorous at the threshold between the interruption of the breath (subjective genitive: inhalation interrupting words) and the interruption *of* the breath (objective genitive: always already interrupting itself). Among readings of Celan there is a tendency, on the one hand, to note a poetics of the breath, the musicality of his poetry, the tendency to drift away from the semantic in the direction of the purely sonorous with its sharp condensations, multilingual wordplays, a predilection for idiomaticity, and so on. On the other hand, deconstructive readings have tended to emphasize the alienation of authorship and estrangement of linguistic expression with a turn toward silence ("two mouthfuls of silence"[14]), ellipsis, spacing, punctuation, white space, black holes, interruption, the cut of the breath (*couper le souffle*), and the circumcision of the word. There is, however, no clean frontier between the two. Rather, what Celan's poetry illustrates is that there is also contamination between the interruption and what is interrupted and in turn between the interruptions. There is at once a gathering *and* a dispersion of the breath, stricture *and* destricturation.

"Cello-Einsatz," which supposedly refers to the solo entry in Antonín Dvořák's concerto, thematizes the breath less as free-flowing inspiration than as somehow constricted specifically insofar as it connects the poetic breath to the memory of the Holocaust:

> the
> scaled evening
> stands full of lungbranches,
>
> two
> blaze-clouds of breath

dig in the book
which the temple-din opened,[15]

(der
erklommene Abend
steht voller Lungengeäst,

zwei
Brandwolken Atem
graben im Buch,
das der Schläfenlärm aufschlug,)

This prompts Cixous, in what is a hybrid between a reading and a creative rewriting of Celan's poem at the beginning of *Jours de l'an*, to remark:

> Just as the cello had been created to moan the animal music of our entrails and the oboe to give wings to the triumphal moods of our adolescences, so a Celan had been created for singing, his mouth full of earth, under the century's cleaver, under the pickax, the unique little slip of fleshy paper that will have succeeded in escaping the shovel of the Apocalypse. . . . and behold him standing on the silent soil, his chest full of cello boughs. Only thus are we able to advance, by beginning at the end, death first, life next, teetering life next, so teetering, so chancy, so cela(n)tive.[16]

> (De même que le violoncelle a été créé pour mugir la musique animale de nos entrailles ; de même le hautbois pour ailer les humeurs triomphales de nos adolescences, de même un Celan a été créé pour chanter, avec la bouche pleine de terre, sous le hachoir du siècle, sous la pioche, l'unique petit morceau de papier de chair qui aura réussi à échapper à la pelle de l'Apocalypse. . . . et le voilà debout sur le sol silencieux, la poitrine pleine de branches de violoncelle. C'est seulement ainsi que l'on peut s'avancer, en commençant par la fin, la mort la première, la vie ensuite, ensuite la vie chancelante, si chancelante, si chance, si celante.)

I want to consider in some detail the musical character of Cixous's prose in its response to hearing Celan and specifically to the remarkable conclusion of this passage, but first I want to consider the interpretation of Celan's *Atemwende* and of Cixous's reading offered by Derrida scholar and translator David Wills. The crux of his argument is that "it would also be necessary . . . to relate the particularities of Celan's poetic singing with a mouth full of earth to what has just been developed concerning a poetry divorced from its orality."[17] Wills focuses not on the sonic and musical metaphors employed by Celan and Cixous but on punctuation and especially its withholding, and in particular on the white spaces between words and the idiosyncratic, quasi-poetic spaces Cixous inserts following paragraphs that break off with ellipses, commas, or dashes (such as after "celante"). True to the deconstruction of metaphysical subordination of the *grammē* to the *phonē* in the guise of phonetic writing and taking inspiration from Derrida's reading of the Mallarméan *blanc*, Wills calls for radically severing written from oral language such that these various marks of "silence" be understood not as transcriptions of living breath, specifically of inhalation, but as a machinic, inanimate life. If the early Derrida was keen to point out the subordination of writing as a secondary, derivative term—as the mere transcription of speech and breath—Wills accordingly insists on liberating writing from orality, discovering in Cixous's reading of Celan "a new writing of a new silence" and in Celan's *Atemwende* "a diverting or detouring of the breath into silence," "a turning of the breath out of the breath [that] occurs to inanimate the life that breathing sustains."[18]

Wills even argues that the homonymy that runs rampant in Cixous's writing and that lends it its poetic character should be thought "beyond aural signification."[19] This untethering of literary textuality from breathing does not simply arise from the incommensurability between text and speech. It reflects a materiality in which the silence that makes it possible to distinguish between different sounds also makes such distinctions impossible, for this silence is itself disseminated into an array of homonymic substitutions—marks and blanks, black and white. The result is to destabilize the dialectic of black and white on the page from which the economy of literary representation emerges, with its relations between poetry and breathing, text and life. It is an elegant, inventive, rigorous argument, which captures well the role of substitution and prosthesis in Cixous's writing and their tendency to overwrite any appeal to living breath. And Wills already anticipates the counterargument that homonymy and homophony are functions of sound:

> Now it might be countered, throughout what I have been advancing here, that homonymy is in the first instance a fact

of spoken language, a confusion deriving from a single sound's being required to perform double duty, a confusion heard rather than seen, especially because, in the case of impurely phonetic languages, the same sound may be written differently. But in calling attention here to a poetic graphemization of the word that divorces it from its oral form, and in emphasizing in particular the radical divorce of written from oral language that takes place by means of punctuation, more radically still by means of an absence of punctuation, I am arguing for something, as it were, beyond the fact of the incommensurate relation of spoken to written and beyond the difficulty, if not impossibility, of representing silence in graphic form.[20]

Whilst embracing much of what is set out here I cannot help but wonder, with Derrida's reflections on abolitionist arguments in *La peine de mort* in mind: Is it not a risk that this rigor become too rigorous, so rigorous as to become brittle, almost to the point of *rigor mortis*, hence the sudden, radical break between sound and writing?[21] If Derrida's thought has shown that there can be no sounding voice that is not always already compromised by the spacing, technicity, and supplementarity of writing—and no life worthy of the name that is not exposed to the chance of death—it is surely also the case that there can be no pure writing without or beyond sound. And it is Cixous who constantly reminds Derrida of this.

Cixous's prose is notoriously recalcitrant in the face of translation, not least because it is riddled with homonymic and homophonic effects such as those that conclude the passage just quoted from the opening of *Jours de l'an* where the poet's proper name morphs into a participle emerging out of hearing the participle of *chanceler* as a portmanteau of "chance" and *celante*, the latter to be heard as both the participle of *celer* and the neologism "Celaning"—which homonym can only shatter upon translation into English into multiple words, pointing to the untranslatable singularity of the idiom. Such effects are, of course, much more commonly found in poetry, and indeed Cixous herself suggests the name "poem" for the unwritten force of writing that impels the first pages of this text, a "generative" force that scatters generic classification as much as any teleological conception of literary genesis or genealogy, as Derrida observes in *Genèses* with a flurry of virtuosic play on the root shared by those terms.[22]

Cixous's response to "Cello-Einsatz" should be understood in the context of the quasi-methodological remarks to be found throughout her writings that often put the sonorous at the heart of the birth of writing. As one of her translators into English, Peggy Kamuf puts it, "I am both listening and reading, hearing and seeing."[23] The play between the read and the heard in Cixous's prose pushes at the boundaries of language's representational or mimetic functions, leading not simply to a polysemia across written and sounding senses but, moreover, to a dispersal and shattering of signification itself. Cixous's "many-voiced speech" with its multilayered dialogues is, Kamuf argues, a "sensation, in the eyes and the ears, on the tongue and the skin . . . of a writing that burns *through* its fuel, language, without consuming it yet without leaving it intact."[24] But whereas Kamuf's metaphor of afterburn emphasizes the visual aspects of this effect, Cixous immediately associates the metaphor of the flame's extinction and rekindling with what she dubs "le cri de la littérature" or "l'é-*cri*-ture." Writing in "Le manuscrit volant" about Derrida's "Le ver à soie," which also makes extensive use of homonymic and quasi-homophonic effects to play on Cixous's word "voiles," she says:

> He cries toward *Vers*, in verse, he cries vermiformally, like a worm, inaudible cry, the silky cry of a self. . . . He cries, and he sends me this cry enveloped in some paper, from Buenos Aires advising me not to receive it before it/he has been extinguished, the cry. I read it therefore only extinguished. Cryore. To tell the truth: I read it not. I so much read it not that it is upon this rainy April that I read it, "for the first time," that I listen to it absolutely, this cry-sigh, kept vibrant, and perfectly audible, for a cry starts up again like a flame, as soon as it is kindled with a loving gaze.[25]

The notions of the cry and of listening as metaphors for writing and reading literature are always bound up in Cixous's thought with the question of extinction, of teetering on the brink between life and death, and with the idea of writing as mourning and as the possibility of (re)calling the dead back to life. In *Jours de l'an*, the discovery of both the poet's old and new names—Ancel and its anagram Celan—in the word *chancelante* leads to the wordplay on "chance" and *celante*, the invented participle, "Celaning," coming to mean something like life's trembling with the chance of death or what, with Derrida, I want to call *la vie la mort*.

Like many of Cixous's texts, *Jours de l'an* is both in part autobiographical and in part a philosophical meditation on the event of writing as creation and loss. The title of the book, which itself can be heard in multiple senses as "Days of the Year" and "New Year's Days" with a portmanteau effect similar to that of *chancelante*, announces that this is a book about the birth pangs of writing. It would be easy to read this opening, in which a third-person author hesitates to write a book that has remained unwritten for thirty years, as being on the side of life—as Derrida will characterize Cixous's position more generally in *H. C. pour la vie*. The musical and the sonorous here at first blush appear to be associated with the very living presence of speech deconstructed in Derrida's *La voix et le phénomène*, as if the force of writing were the breath of (authorial) inspiration, the magic of an animist pneumatology, initially held back and then released in rhythmic sobs. The book begins:

> Writing had returned, the stream, the slender silent stream with its singing arms, the blood flow in the veins between the bodies, the wordless dialogue from blood to blood, with no sense of the distances, the magic flux full of silent words flowing from one community to the other, from one life to the other, the strange legend, inaudible except to the heart of the one or the other, the narrative weaving itself on high, who will decipher it, the throbbing weave of clandestinity,
>
> Writing, that link, that growth, that orientation had returned,
>
> Space is full of voices again, the whole body is heart. It was land that was missing, the port, the other shore, and, over there, the unknown house, the sister who might receive the letter and adopt it.[26]

(L'écriture était revenue, le fleuve, le mince fleuve meut aux bras chantants, le cours du sang dans les veines entre les corps, le dialogue sans mots de sang à sang, sans aucun sens des distances, le cours magique plein des mots muets qui coule d'une commune à l'autre, d'une vie à l'autre, l'étrange légende inaudible sinon par le cœur de l'un ou de l'autre, le récit se tissant là-haut, qui déchiffrera, le tissu palpitant de la clandestinité.

L'écriture, ce lien, cette croissance, cette orientation, était revenue,

A nouveau l'espace est plein de voix, le corps entier est cœur. C'était le pays qui manquait, le port, l'autre rive, et là-bas la maison inconnue, la sœur qui recevrait la lettre et qui l'adopterait.)

And the idea of a living, breathing, *singing* source of inspiration returns at various points later in the book.

One ought not, however, rush to conclude that a metaphysics of presence lies behind Cixous's appeal to the sonorousness of the voice, for it turns out that the singing arms do not sing aloud but only silently, inaudibly. Moreover, Cixous shows the structure of the Derridean trace already at work in this silent speech. This voice comes from the other—from multiple others whose voices are stronger than the author's (a theme that recurs in the exchanges between Derrida and Cixous)—and this address is itself susceptible to *destinnerance*: it might not arrive at the ears of the author. Further, as we have already heard, the singing Celan, whose poem "sprouts" behind the unsung pain ("derrière la douleur, pousse le poème"),[27] is described—in what may be read as a creative fusion of Celan's verses "zwei / Brandwolken Atem / graben im Buch," and the later lines "die Schwarz- / blütige trinkt / des Schwarzblütigen Samen"—as "aux poumons à demi asphyxiés de terre et de sang [half-asphyxiated with earth and blood]," "la bouche pleine de terre [the mouth full of earth]"; the phrase "sur le sol silencieux, la poitrine pleine de branches de violoncelle [the chest full of cello boughs]" meanwhile reads as a creative translation of "der / erklommene Abend / steht voller Lungengeäst," from which "Atem" is generated associatively in the poem.[28] Cixous has pointed out in an interview that "the book that [she] is not writing," referred to here and elsewhere, is not simply a not-yet-written book but a writing that resists all possibilization, a not-to-be-written whose power (*puissance*) is that of the impossible.[29] Thus the power of writing as such, rather than what is written or what is capable of being written, is not a full-throated song but the voice choking on itself, muting itself. The reference to the Holocaust, omnipresent throughout Celan's poems, is thus inscribed via the interplay of cry and silence in Cixous's characterization of the force of writing teetering between life and death.

Wills is careful to argue, though, that the silence cannot be reduced to one that signifies asphyxiation or unspeakable horror (although it is also that) but is, moreover, a matter of survival beyond organic life. What makes commemoration of the lives lost possible is the inanimate life of writing, evidenced in the homophonic replacement and iterability of blanks whose substitution of life *for* life makes possible life's violent termination *and* its continuation in memory. If this is not simply an interruption of the breath but its self-interruption—the interruption of interruption—would not this silence interrupt itself and hence give itself to sing? In *Schibboleth*, Derrida likens "Cello-Einsatz," which "sets into musical play something indecipherable or unsignifying (*Undeutbares*)," to Celan's "*singbarer Rest*," which "*remains without being, by force of music, remains for song.*"[30] It is a muted speech (*lautlos*) or, in Cixous's words, a "forlorn, far-off song' from "a native land not found on any map," which does not remain silent but will have "made a clear sound."[31] For Derrida, the singable remnant is bound up with that which remains "by force of music" and which opens up the possibility of song to come:

> [The date] is not an effect of being, of some meaning of being; it is on this condition that its mad incantation becomes music. It remains without being, by force of music, remains for song; "Singbarer Rest" is the incipit or title of a poem that *begins* by saying the remainder. It begins with the remainder—which is not and which is not being—leaving a song without words (*lautlos*) be heard therein, a song perhaps inaudible or inarticulate, yet a song whose turn and whose line, whose outline, whose contour (*Umriß*) no doubt stems from the cutting, sharpened, concise, but also rounded, circumvenient form of a sickle, of yet another writing, of a sickle-script (*Sichelschrift*). . . . Another turning, another trope. . . . Shall one say that it circumcises words in silence, when speech is muted (*lautlos*), so that song may come: *singbarer Rest*[32]

> (Elle ne relève pas de l'être, de quelque sens de l'être, voilà à quelle condition sa folle incantation devient musique. Elle *reste* sans être, à force de musique, reste pour le chant. *Singbarer Rest*, c'est l'*incipit* ou le titre d'un poème qui *commence* par dire le reste. Il commence par le reste—qui n'est pas et qui n'est pas l'être—, en y laissant entendre un chant sans mot (*lautlos*), un chant peut-être inaudible ou inarticulé, un chant pourtant dont le tour et le trait, l'esquisse, le trait de contour (*Umriss*) tiennent sans doute à la forme coupante, aiguisée, concise, mais aussi arrondie, circonvenante d'une faucille, d'une écriture encore, d'une écriture de faucille (*Sichelschrift*). . . . Autre tournure,

un autre. . . . Dira-t-on qu'elle circoncit des mots en silence, quand le discours se tait (*lautlos*) pour laisser venir le chant: *singbarer Rest?*)

Far from a writing that turns into silence, then, Celan opens up the possibility for Derrida of thinking another kind of writing that interrupts muted speech. If poetry is the turn-of-breath, as Celan wonders—if it is a kind of theft, the *parole soufflée* of which Derrida speaks in *L'écriture et la différence* apropos of Artaud—at the same time this cutting off and spiriting (away) is also an interruption of the interruption of sound such that it gives way to another song. This songful quality of *écriture* is associated with its survival beyond the poet that signs and indeed beyond any specific reader or listener. Derrida returns to this affinity between writing, survival, and song in *Béliers* again via a reading of another poem from Celan's *Atemwende* and specifically of its final line: "Die Welt is fort, ich muß dich tragen."[33] Far from speaking for itself, the poem addresses and entrusts itself to the other.[34] It gives itself to the other to bear (*tragen*). Derrida here understands this *tragen/porter* both in the sense of mourning as carrying the other within me after the end of the world and also in the sense of bearing a child to term. The poem is thus addressed to a survivor or ghost as well as the living yet to come. Engaging with Gadamer's interpretation of Celan, Derrida qualifies this *tragen* as reading, making a distinction between a formal-hermeneutic and a disseminal reading-writing that directs itself to an excess, to the *singbarer Rest*, and is the condition of possibility of all reading:

> This hermeneutic is made necessary, and also possible, by the excess. Likewise, excess here makes possible, among other things, the trace of the poetic work, its abandonment or its survival, beyond any signatory and any specific reader. Without this remainder, there wouldn't even be the *Anspruch*, the injunction, the call, the provocation that sings or makes one sing in any poem, in what one could, with Celan, name "Singbarer Rest," "Singable Remnant," the title or the incipit of another poem from *Atemwende*.[35]

> (Cette herméneutique, il la rend nécessaire, il la rend aussi possible, comme il rend ici possible, entre autres choses, la trace de l'œuvre poétique, son abandon ou sa survie, au-delà de tel signataire et de tout lecteur déterminé. Sans ce reste, il n'y aurait

même pas l'*Anspruch*, l'injonction, l'appel, ni la provocation qui chante ou fait chanter dans tout poème, dans ce qu'on pourrait surnommer, avec Celan, selon le titre ou l'incipit d'un autre poème de *Atemwende*, *Singbarer Rest*.)

What sings or makes one sing in any poem, then, is this life-death, this teetering undecidability between life and death that is the very chance of life captured elegantly by Cixous's portmanteau of "chance" and *celante*. Her play on the homophone *celante* folds its standard meaning of concealing into its novel sense as a participle of a neologism, to Celan—which means something like an unheard-of singing-as-survival, not singing after or beyond the frontier of life but a living on that restrains itself and inoculates itself with death and hence a half-asphyxiated singing with a mouth full of earth and lungs full of cello boughs.[36]

It is this singing *Anspruch* that impels Cixous's author to write the book she has not ceased to write in thirty years. The poem—first understood abstractly and then specifically identified as "Cello-Einsatz"—quenches her heart's thirst, giving her the tears that she has lost, but it also exerts a certain violence or force as Cixous, reconfiguring a privileged figure in her work of writing as a taking flight reworks the militaristic image of Celan's poem where the cello enters like aircraft in formation, the powers (*Gewalten*) arranged into echelons. Writing is described as "the promise, the force, the source that knows only pulsation, return" with a "superhuman élan."[37] This force makes a clear sound; it is a voice stronger than her own that sprouts or pushes up (*pousse*) *hinter dem Schmerz* such that it will lift and carry her. She is "*portée par l'écriture*." But Cixous's cello-Celan sortie is also shot through with impossibility like its half-asphyxiated song: "Je suis comme celle qui essaie de faire rouler dans un hangar d'aviation la carcasse du violoncelle. Abri du vol brisé. [I am like she who attempts to have the cello's carcass rolled into an aviation hangar. Shelter for a broken flight.]"[38]

One would want to investigate this impossible sonorous force of writing along several trajectories or flight paths. In one direction, one would turn to Derrida's various reflections on force besides *Force de loi*, in particular to the essay on Roger Laporte's *Fugue Supplément* entitled "Ce qui reste à force de musique" in *Psyché: Inventions de l'autre*, where Derrida finds an affinity between writing-as-dissemination and music as a quasi-performative force ("fugue *musics*") or, more precisely, the rhythm of writing's blanks.[39] In another, one would look to the reading of Cixous's mighty *puisse* as *impuissance* and displacement in *H. C. pour la vie*, where this power of writing, which recalls back to life, is expressed through monosyllabic interjections, telegraphic injunctions, and what Derrida dubs a "differential econohomonymy."[40] The more circuitous path, though, is the one that passes through Celan, discerning there a certain constellation of sound or music and uncontainable poetic force. This flightpath connects this force to everything Derrida will have said about *Trieb/pulsion* and *Walten*, and in particular, the ways in which *walten* and Celan's *tragen* are found to be intertwined in both the second year of Derrida's final seminar and also years earlier in *Geschlecht IV*, where the point of departure is expressly the possibility of carrying the voice of the friend by ear, following Heidegger's phrase, "als Hören der Stimme des Freundes, den jedes Dasein bei sich trägt."[41]

These themes find a destination of sorts in Cixous's *Insister: à Jacques Derrida*, where she weaves together the themes of living, voice, and listening: the question of the multiplicity of voices that make themselves heard in their texts is thought alongside a partial rebuttal of Derrida's contention in *H. C. pour la vie* that she is on the side of life and he on that of death. If there is one voice that resonates in these reflections, especially in the second and third essays, it is Celan's. Cixous muses on the conjunction of *tragen* and *mögen*, of *porter* and *pouvoir*, in Derrida's thought, but she moves, via Celan's "ich muß dich tragen," to suggest that the carrying of the other, including the other that is in me, takes place by "*force de l'ouïe* [force of hearing]."[42] Here, the musical instrument is neither the cello nor Celan himself, but the shofar of Celan's "Große, glühende Wölbung," which is echoed in Derrida's *Béliers*. "Le shofar qui ressuscite," writes Cixous, "c'est la voix du là, la voix qui jaillit du chasme, ouverture des lèvres de ce monde-ci à ce monde [The shofar that resuscitates . . . is voice from the there, the voice that leaps out of the chasm, the opening of the lips of this world to that world after the end of the world]."[43] Linking the shofar that summons the dead back to life to the umbilical telephone line, she struggles to fathom "comment faire pour vivre sans fil, sans cor, sans voix [how is one supposed to live cordlessly, without *cor*, without horn, without voice]."[44] With the death of her father when she was ten, Cixous ventures that she has lived in reality Derrida's "*asif*"; the world had ended, and she confronts something similar with the loss of her friend, whom she *must* now carry.

The heartrending joy of the survivor's song is thus always poised between connection and cutoff, between "*penser comment* la coupure peut nouer un lien ou *comment la liaison* peut être *l'interruption même* [thinking how *the cut can tie a link or* how the liaison *can be* the interruption itself]."[45] What moves all Derrida's "forces," she speculates, is "la nécessité de faire passer la pensée dans les strictures qui coupent le souffle . . . ce faufilement par un étranglement [the necessity of making thought pass through strictures that squeeze the breath out (literally, "cut the breath") . . . this slipping through a strangulation]."⁴⁶ Thus we find ourselves again resonating with the voices of the half-asphyxiated Celan. Cixous ends the essay with the memory of a dream in which she finds herself struggling with the breath, the flight of her writing-mourning blown off course pilotless, and hearing a certain "Freuderridian" analysis from the lips of Celan:

*Dream J. D. May 2002*

*I had a dream. My father played the saxophone very well. After him I tried myself. Not the least sound. I didn't even understand how it was possible. While telling you this, I associated with the shofar. It's difficult to blow into a reckless driver, that is, chauffard, this horn*

*My uncle [NB: Uncle Freud] was blowing/whispering a message: longs, shorts, breves, images of power.*

\*

*That May I had no voice. He says to me: Stay on the right (voice) track.*⁴⁷

*(Rêve J. D. mai 2002*

*J'ai fait un rêve. Mon père jouait très bien du saxophone. Après lui j'essayais moi-même. Pas le moindre son. Je ne compensais même pas comment c'était possible. En te racontant la chose, j'associais au shofar. C'est difficile de souffler dans un chauffard, cette corne*

*Mon oncle [NB: Freud] soufflait un message : longues, courtes, brèves, images de puissance.*

\*

*Ce mai-là j'étais aphone. Il me dit : Reste sur la bonne voie.)*

We might then imagine that whatever track that is, she carries this breathless voice *by force of Celan.*

## Notes

1. This aporetic condition of the frontier is precisely set out by Geoffrey Bennington in *Kant on the Frontier: Philosophy, Politics, and the Ends of the Earth* (New York: Fordham University Press, 2017).

2. Jacques Derrida, *Théorie et pratique*, ed. Alexander García Düttmann (Paris: Éditions Galilée, 2017), 104; Jacques Derrida, *Theory and Practice*, eds. Geoffrey Bennington and Peggy Kamuf, trans. David Wills (Chicago: University of Chicago Press, 2019), 71. Note that the English translation is based on the typescript held at the Critical Theory Archive at the University of California Irvine and not on the French edition, which contains significant silent editorial interventions beyond the editorial policies and practices established as part of the seminar publication project.

3. Derrida, *Théorie et pratique*, 104; Derrida, *Theory and Practice*, 71.

4. Jacques Derrida, *Schibboleth: Pour Paul Celan* (Paris: Éditions Galilée, 1986), 88; Jacques Derrida, "Shibboleth: For Paul Celan," trans. Joshua Wilner and Thomas Dutoit, in *Sovereignties in Question: The Poetics of Paul Celan*, eds. Thomas Dutoit and Outi Pasanen (New York: Fordham University Press, 2005), 44.

5. Derrida, *Schibboleth*, 88; Derrida, "Shibboleth," 44.

6. See Jean-Luc Nancy, *Ego Sum* (Paris: Flammarion, 1979); Jean-Luc Nancy, *Ego Sum: Corpus, Anima, Fabula*, trans. Marie-Eve Morin (New York: Fordham University Press, 2016). See also the bilingual edition of *Corpus*, trans. Richard A. Rand (New York: Fordham University Press, 2008).

7. See the remark Derrida makes on this distinction in his final seminar, *Séminaire: La bête et le souverain I (2001–2002)*, eds. Michael Lisse, Marie-Louise Mallet, and Ginette Michaud (Paris: Galilée, 2008), 461; Jacques Derrida, *The Beast and the Sovereign, Volume I*, trans. Geoffrey Bennington (Chicago: University of Chicago Press, 2009), 347–48. In this seminar, Derrida refers to the much earlier analysis from *Of Grammatology* that is quoted here: Jacques Derrida, *De la grammatologie* (Paris: Minuit, 1967) 21–24; Jacques Derrida, *Of Grammatology*, trans. Gayatri Chakravorty Spivak (Baltimore, MD: John Hopkins University Press, 1974), 11–14.

8. Jacques Derrida and Hélène Cixous, "From the Word to Life: A Dialogue Between Jacques Derrida and Hélène Cixous with Aliette Armel," trans. Ashley Thompson, *New Literary History* 37.1 (2005): 1–13, 1.

9. Geoffrey Bennington, *Scatter 1: The Politics of Politics in Foucault, Heidegger, and Derrida* (New York: Fordham University Press, 2016), 272.

10. Hélène Cixous, *Jours de l'an* (Paris: Éditions des femmes, 1990); Hélène Cixous, *FirstDays of the Year*, trans. Catherine A. F. MacGillivray (Minneapolis: University of Minnesota Press, 1998); Jacques Derrida, *Béliers: Le dialogue ininterrompu: Entre deux infinis, le poème* (Paris: Éditions Galilée, 2003); Jacques Derrida, "Rams: Uninterrupted Dialogue—Between Two Infinities, the Poem," trans. Thomas Dutoit

and Philippe Romanski, in *Sovereignties in Question: The Poetics of Paul Celan*, eds. Thomas Dutoit and Outi Pasanen (New York: Fordham University Press, 2005), 135–63; Jacques Derrida, *Séminaire: La bête et le souverain II (2002–2003)*, eds. Michael Lisse, Marie-Louise Mallet, and Ginette Michaud (Paris: Galilée, 2010); Jacques Derrida, *The Beast and the Sovereign*, vol. 2, trans. Geoffrey Bennington (Chicago: University of Chicago Press, 2011); Paul Celan *From Breathturn into Timestead: The Collected Later Poetry of Paul Celan*, trans. Pierre Joris (New York: Farrar, Straus, and Giroux, 2014), 96–97.

    11. Jacques Derrida, *H. C. pour la vie, c'est-a-dire . . .* (Paris: Éditions Galilée, 2002); Jacques Derrida, *H. C. for Life, That Is to Say . . .* , trans. Laurent Milesi and Stefan Herbrechter (Stanford: Stanford University Press, 2006).

    12. Jacques Derrida, "L'Oreille de Heidegger: Philopolémologie (*Geschlecht* IV)," in *Politiques de l'amitié* (Paris: Galilée, 1994), 341–419; Jacques Derrida, "Heidegger's Ear: Philopolemology (*Geschlecht* IV)," trans. John P. Leavey, in *Reading Heidegger: Commemorations*, ed. John Sallis (Bloomington: Indiana University Press, 1993), 163–218.

    13. Jacques Derrida, *Marges de la philosophie* (Paris: Minuit, 1972), III; Jacques Derrida, *Margins of Philosophy*, trans. Alan Bass (Chicago: University of Chicago Press, 1990), xii; trans. slightly modified.

    14. See Paul Celan, "Speech-Grille," in *Selected Poems and Prose of Paul Celan*, trans. John Felstiner (New York: Norton, 2001), 107.

    15. Both the German and English versions of Celan's "Cello-Einsatz" ("Cello Entry") are cited according to the bilingual edition, Celan, *From Breathturn into Timestead*, 66–69.

    16. Cixous, *Jours de l'an*, 13–14; Cixous, *FirstDays of the Year*, 9.

    17. David Wills, "Living Punctuations," in *Inanimation: Theories of Inorganic Life* (Minneapolis: University of Minnesota Press, 2016), 118.

    18. Wills, 133, 143, 113.

    19. Wills, 129.

    20. Wills, 128–29.

    21. Jacques Derrida, *Séminaire: La peine de mort I (1999–2000)*, eds. Geoffrey Bennington, Marc Crépon, and Thomas Dutoit (Paris: Galilée, 2012), 82; Jacques Derrida, *The Death Penalty, Volume I*, trans. Peggy Kamuf (Chicago: University of Chicago Press, 2014), 48. On this point, see also Geoffrey Bennington, "Rigor or, Stupid Uselessness," *Southern Journal of Philosophy* 50.2 (2012), 20–38.

    22. See Jacques Derrida, *Genèses, généalogies, genres et le génie: Les secrets de l'archive* (Paris: Galilée, 2003); Jacques Derrida, *Geneses, Genealogies, Genres, and Genius: The Secrets of the Archive*, trans. Beverley Bie Brahic (New York: Columbia University Press, 2006).

    23. Peggy Kamuf, "Afterburn: An Afterword to 'The Flying Manuscript,'" *New Literary History* 37.1 (2006): 47–55, 47.

24. Kamuf, 47.
25. Hélène Cixous, *Insister: à Jacques Derrida* (Paris: Galilée, 2006), 73–74; Hélène Cixous, *Insister of Jacques Derrida*, trans. Peggy Kamuf (Stanford: Stanford University Press, 2007), 101–2.
26. Cixous, *Jours de l'an*, 5; Cixous, *FirstDays of the Year*, 3.
27. Celan's poem begins: "Cello-Einsatz / von hinter dem Schmerz: / die Gewalten." Celan, "Cello-Einsatz," in *From Breathturn into Timestead*, 66.
28. Celan, 66–68.
29. Héléne Cixous with Frédéric-Yves Jeannet, "The Book that You Will Not Write: An Interview with Hélène Cixous," trans. Thomas Dutoit, *New Literary History* 37.1 (2006): 249–61, 249.
30. Derrida, "Shibboleth," 38; Celan, "Cello-Einsatz," in *From Breathturn into Timestead*, 66–69.
31. Cixous, *Jours de l'an*, 9–10; Cixous, *FirstDays of the Year*, 6.
32. Derrida, *Schibboleth*, 68–69; Derrida, "Shibboleth," 38–39.
33. See Celan, *From Breathturn into Timestead*, 96–97.
34. Derrida, *Béliers*, 69–72; Derrida, "Rams," 158–59.
35. Derrida, 47–48, 149.
36. Cixous, *Jours de l'an*, 13–14; *FirstDays of the Year*, 9. Further, the word *chancelant*, meaning teetering or wavering, has an interesting etymological derivation, coming from the Latin *cancello*, meaning to cross out, criss-cross, or make a lattice, from which we get chancel, the part of a church separated by a grille, and chancellor, originally a court official stationed at the grating dividing the judiciary from the public—whence a staggering or teetering on folded limbs. This etymology, though, also gestures toward the *texture anagrammatique* with which Derrida describes *écriture* in "La pharmacie de Platon," *La dissemination* (Paris: Seuil, 1972), 183; see Jacques Derrida, *Dissemination*, trans. Barbara Johnson (Chicago: University of Chicago Press, 1981), 158.
37. Cixous, *Jours de l'an*, 6–8; Cixous, *FirstDays of the Year*, 4–6.
38. Cixous, 13, 8.
39. Jacques Derrida, "Ce qui reste à force de musique," in *Psyché: Inventions de l'autre* (Paris: Galilée, 1998 [1987]), 95–103; Jacques Derrida, "What Remains by Force of Music," trans. Peggy Kamuf, in *Psyche: Inventions of the Other*, vol. 1, eds. Peggy Kamuf and Elizabeth Rottenberg (Stanford: Stanford University Press, 2007), 81–89.
40. Derrida, *H. C. pour la vie*, 68; Derrida, *H. C. for Life, That Is to Say . . .* , 74.
41. Derrida, "L'Oreille de Heidegger," 341; Derrida, "Heidegger's Ear," 164; see Martin Heidegger, *Sein und Zeit* (Tübingen: Niemeyer, 2001), 163.
42. Cixous, *Insister: à Jacques Derrida*, 24.
43. Cixous, 98, 148.

44. Cixous, 99, 150.
45. Cixous, 105, 160.
46. Cixous, 105, 160.
47. Cixous, 111, 168.

Part 2

# Language Dislodged

**Encounters**

Chapter 7

# *A limine*

### Kristina Mendicino

Neither before nor beyond any limit that would define its location or orientation, whatever might be characterized as "liminary" could not itself be placed. Belonging to (*-aris*) the threshold (*limen*), the liminary could only move to and from the threshold whence it comes. Hence, it also could neither "belong" nor "be" in any way but for this longing, this restless hedging and edging toward that which ever again escapes all settings, grounds, or ways.

Restlessly on edge—and therefore indefinitely in suspense—these are the traits that Hesiod draws out in the *Theogony* in the passage that introduces the area at the "limits" or "outermost-edge" of the earth (ἔσχατα γαίης),[1] which also marks the juncture where night and day alternately pass. This area, that is, delineates nothing less than the threshold of space and the threshold of time. But if it would therefore seem to be a singular *origo*, there are also no limits to these limits: beyond space and time per se, there will also be talk of Tartarus (725); then the walled-in enclosure of the Titans (733); then a "great chasm [χάσμα μέγ(α)]" (740); and then again, the "frightful house [οἰκία δεινά] of Night the obscure" (744), whose gates are said to gape such that "one would not reach the ground [οὖδας ἵκοιτ'] as a year bears to its end, if one were once to come there within [ἔντοσθε] [them], but blast for troubling blast of wind would bear one there and there [κεν ἔνθα καὶ ἔνθα]" (740–43).

The justice of Zeus as well as the order of the cosmos all rest upon this critical area, where the lines are drawn for the Titans, the dead, and the night, but also the very time of day. Yet the terms for this threshold (οὐδός) not only multiply but also blur, as it is alternately characterized as domestic *and* chasmic, as with *and* without ground (οὖδας), shifting from threshold to threshold without transition: shifting from "there within [ἔντοσθε]" to a bottomless "there and there [ἔνθα καὶ ἔνθα]" within it. In all of these ways and more, Hesiod's verses thus chart an expanse closer to the unimaginable topography of Roman history that Sigmund Freud would describe at the outset of *Civilization and Its Discontents*,[2] than to the more recognizable descriptions of thresholds as transitional zones or rites that mediate between certain states, areas, ages, or orders.[3] Here, it is utterly over- and unde*term*ined where the threshold begins and ends, what it opens "between," and whether "there" *is* a "between" at all, as the space itself is altered, term for term, and never seems to be what it was said to be before. As Eric Havelock has written on this passage: "Different spatial arrangements are superimposed one upon another. . . . Eye and ear are invited to jump around, from Earth to Tartarus to Night to Hades to Ocean. There is a prison somewhere, required by the myth of the Titans, sometimes in empty space, sometimes with borders."[4] Yet before all else, the permutations of space and time that take place through Hesiod's verses are borne out through the language of the poem: from the differential repetitions of the same ("there and there," "blast for . . . blast"), through to the rearrangements of letters that let the "ground" (οὖδας) and "threshold" (οὐδός) cross through one another as well. Hesiod's language for this threshold is itself a threshold-language, whose movements, on the same grounds, do not and could not stop "there."

Hence, Hesiod's restlessly shifting lines on the limits of the cosmos will be further transposed in the proem of Parmenides's poem on being: a poem that will call for speaking, thinking, and being as *the same*, but only after its speaker will have been conducted by daughters of the sun to "the gates of the ways of night and day [πύλαι Νυκτός τε καὶ Ἥματός εἰσι κελεύθων]" (Fr. 1).[5] But also at an apparent remove from the lineage that can be traced from archaic Greek poetry to early Greek philosophy, the moving thresholds of Hesiod's and Parmenides's lines will be carried further still with, among others, the language of Paul Celan's collection of poems *From Threshold to Threshold* (1955), whose title alone should indicate the liminal character of poetic speech. As Celan emphasizes in a letter to Jürgen Rausch from February 22, 1954:

> With that, it is suggested, or so at least I believe and hope, besides a not inessential trait of the poetic, namely, its <u>liminary</u>

character, also the never-coming-to-rest of the poetic, and therewith too the—straight-out unfulfillable—infinite claim [or: claim to infinitude] of every utterance in this area.⁶

(Damit ist, so glaube und hoffe ich zumindest, ausser einem gewiss nicht unwesentlichen Zug des Dichterischen, seinem <u>liminaren</u> Charakter nämlich, auch das Nie-zur-Ruhe-Kommen des Poetischen angedeutet und mithin wohl auch der—schlechthin unerfüllbare—Unendlichkeitsanspruch jeglicher Aussage in diesem Bereich.)

With these remarks, Celan makes clear that the syntagma "from threshold to threshold" does not describe a trajectory between two determinate locations, marked off by two instances of the same substantive. Rather, he elucidates how the phrase signifies a "trait of the poetic," which, as such, would traverse and exceed the limits of every single poem, as well as any "utterance" that should occur in the area from and to which poetic language speaks.

Before any cosmic, juridical, or architectural limit that one may come across, as well as any metaphor besides this very transport—this "over-stepping and carry-over [Übertritt und Übertragung]" of the threshold "itself"⁷—Celan's formulation thus addresses the through-movement of language that will have been ongoing since, at the latest, Hesiod, and that could never be over and through with. Celan addresses a linguistic movement that could also be called, with Werner Hamacher, a "transcending without transcendence."⁸ It is along these lines that the phrase "from threshold to threshold" both invites further commentary and already implies the "never-coming-to-rest" of which Celan goes on to speak, as it exposes each word of a threshold to part from itself ("*from* threshold") toward itself ("*to* threshold"), tracing a restless, interminable passage not unlike the one that took place within Hesiod's threshold from "there within [ἔντοσθε]" to "there and there [ἔνθα καὶ ἔνθα]," or the unpausing approach (and thus ongoing deferral) to the same that will turn out to mark the trajectory that is traced in Parmenides's poem. And it is along the same lines that, whether one should speak of cosmic limits or poetic thresholds, no single word could contain the passage of which it speaks. The liminary character of poetic language is uncontainable, as is further indicated by the fact that *From Threshold to Threshold* names only one among several alternative titles that Celan had considered for the collection, each of which describes a similarly "self"-altering movement and returns to name a cycle and/or poem in the volume, marking shifting thresholds and changing keys to the movements that are drawn throughout. For instance, the cycle, poem, and word "Islandward [Inselhin]," which appears on the title page of the manuscript Celan initially delivered to his publisher in Stuttgart,[9] describes an indefinite trajectory because it is at once insular and outbound—both "insel-" and "-hin"—and therefore beyond all bounded regions. No less indefinite, however, is the elucidation from out of silence evoked in "Argumentum e silentio,"[10] which names the poem that Celan dedicates to René Char and speaks to not only the questionable evidence of omissions but also the nocturnal withdrawal of language as one speaks.[11] And in the meantime, the third possibility Celan entertained—namely, the phrase that he had encountered in Parmenides and adopted for the cycle and the poem "With a Changing Key" ("Mit wechselndem Schlüssel")— metonymically evokes thresholds, but in such a way that the restless altering of key surpasses and thereby suspends any opposition between opening and closure, while spelling an "alteration" or "w-e-c-h-s-e-l" of the "threshold" ("s-c-h-w-e-l-[l]-e") itself.[12]

All of these movements "from threshold to threshold" speak to how the liminary "trait of the poetic" also entails that poetic language in no way keeps to itself but restlessly gives way to word of others: hence the dedications that are inscribed in *From Threshold to Threshold* more frequently than in any previous or subsequent collection Celan would publish;[13] hence the poems set under the signs of not only the memorial and the epitaph but also the cenotaph—"In Memoriam Paul Eluard," "Epitaph for François," "Cenotaph." But beyond every single explicit or implicit addressee, the endless and wayless, aporetic motion of this porous volume also allows each passage to be crossed through by traces and variations of "key" phrases and words from the oeuvres of Parmenides and Anaximander, Martin Heidegger and René Char, among others, whose more- and less-marked occurrences expose each iteration as variable from the outset. Hence, in the commentary that Celan offers Jürgen Rausch on his title *From Threshold to Threshold*—itself drawn from his previous collection, *Poppy and Memory* (*Mohn und Gedächtnis*)[14]—he adds a remark upon those repetitions of "the same," which expands upon the "threshold" in yet another way: "And in addition to this, there comes perhaps as well, albeit at another level, the fact that the same 'main word' steps twice before the reader's (more or less awake) eye [Hinzu kommt auch noch, auf anderer Ebene freilich, dass dem Leser dasselbe 'Hauptwort' zweimal vors (mehr oder minder wache) Auge tritt]."[15] Another "level" of the liminary emerges, in other words, as the word "threshold" "steps" twice before one's eyes and thus not only insists upon itself but also refuses to stay in place, ever getting away with each approach and thus deferring the "threshold" that it is said to be, all the same. And with that, *From Threshold to Threshold* also reiterates in advance what may be said of those echoes that traverse it, and what may also be said of "the same [das Selbe]" in the later poem "On Both Hands" ("Zu beiden Händen"): "This 'same' cannot once have been the same with itself; it cannot *be* and is not to be *thought* of as the same that it is nonetheless named [Dieses Selbe kann nicht einmal mit sich selbst das Selbe gewesen sein, es kann nicht sein und ist nicht zu denken als das Selbe, als das es doch benannt wird]."¹⁶

∽

Again, what is said through *From Threshold to Threshold*—but also "Islandward," "Argumentum e silentio," "With a Changing Key," and so forth—could not be limited by the bounds of Celan's book or bound to his signature alone. Already the fragment from Parmenides's proemium that "With a Changing Key" translates, transports, and transforms—without ever coming past it or leaving it behind—traces a threshold-movement that, as such, could not but cross through the more definitive distinctions that Parmenides will seem to draw between the ways of being, non-being, and semblance. If truth claims concerning being should turn out to be uncertain, however, the threshold to Parmenides's text places being on the line in ways that remain unsurpassed and thus extend the "infinite claim" of poetic speech, whose utterance Celan sets forth "from threshold to threshold."¹⁷

The verses of Parmenides's first fragment read:

> The mares that carry me [φέρουσιν] kept conveying me [πέμπον] as far as ever my spirit reached [ἱκάνοι], once they had taken and set me on the goddess's way of much discourse, which carries over all towns a man who knows. On this I was carried [φερόμην], for on this the sagacious mares were carrying me [φέρον], straining at the chariot and guided by the maidens along the way. The axle in the naves kept blazing and uttering the pipe's loud note, driven onwards at both ends by its two metalled wheels, whenever the daughters of the sun made haste to convey me, having thrust with their hands their veils from their heads and deserted the home of night for the light. There stand the gates of the ways of night and day, enclosed at top and bottom by a lintel and threshold of stone, and they them-

selves fitting closely to a great architrave in the aether. Justice of much-recompense [πολύποινος] holds the alternating keys [κληῖδας ἀμοιβούς], whom the maidens, speaking to sway her with soft words, persuaded cunningly to thrust the locked bar for them in a moment from the gates, which, flying open, made a gaping chasm [χάσμ' ἀχανὲς] of the gateway, turning alternately in their sockets the bronze-fitted posts fixed to them with pegs and nails. Whereupon the maidens drove the chariot and mares straight on through the gates along the road. And the goddess received me warmly, and taking my right hand in hers spoke as follows and addressed me: "Welcome, O youth, reaching [ἱκάνων] our home as consort of immortal charioteers and mares that carry you [ταί σε φέρουσιν]; no ill lot [μοῖρα] sent you forth [προὔπεμπε] to arrive upon this way [τήνδ' ὁδόν], which is removed indeed from the step of men, but right and justice [did so]. You must be informed of everything, both of the untrembling heart of persuasive reality and of the beliefs of mortals, which comprise no genuine conviction; nevertheless you shall learn these also, how the things that are believed had to be in a valid / credible way, ranging through all things."[18]

With these preliminary words, Parmenides imparts a journey to the same limits of the earth that Hesiod had broached (731) but that no longer seem take any time to reach and no longer seem to be the abyssal space where "blast for troubling blast of wind would bear one there and there [ἔνθα καὶ ἔνθα]" (740–43). Still, the seemingly more accessible and steady frame that is constructed in this passage for the "gates of the ways of night and day" reveals nothing, at bottom, but an opening—"a gaping chasm [χάσμ' ἀχανὲς]"—and that means: nothing that could be seen and known, nothing that could be experienced, and therefore nothing that could or could not be. It is in this way, then, that the area of Parmenides's opening resembles the gap that precedes it—he arrives without a point of departure—just as it recalls the "great chasm" that Hesiod disclosed (740). Coming and continuing from out of nowhere, the trajectory of the poem is as abrupt as the rupture to which it leads—the rupture of the threshold—which may be all that was ever "there [ἔνθα]."[19]

Over all of the shifts that are suggested in the course of Parmenides's lines, then, the poem remains moving upon a threshold that is itself no place to go or pass, which becomes only more and not less pronounced, when the "home" of a goddess is invoked in lieu of the opening chasm. For the place that the goddess calls "home" is itself sheer passageway: upon receiving Parmenides, she says he is "reaching [ἱκάνων]" her home with the mares that "are carrying [φέρουσιν]" him;[20] she speaks of him as still being on "this way [τήνδ' ὁδόν]," and in speaking in this way, the goddess thereby indicates that her guest comes merely to go on as he was going from the outset: "The mares that carry me kept conveying me as far as ever my spirit reached [ἱκάνοι], once they had taken and set me on the goddess's way [ὁδὸν] of much discourse." And what goes for the speaker goes for the maidens who "made haste to convey" him: for insofar as they will have departed from the "home of night" in order to approach the "gates of the ways of night and day [πύλαι Νυκτός τε καὶ Ἤματος κελεύθων]," their departure was also their arrival; they too will have changed places in no time, and they will have similarly had nowhere to stay in the first place because their "home" is situated at the non-place and non-time where differences like day and night first open and where the keys themselves are changing (κληῖδας ἀμοιβούς).[21]

From the outset, then, nothing could seem farther from the stable and solid truth that the goddess promises to tell this "man" who "knows [εἰδότα]," if the truth to be told were solely the "myth [μῦθος]" of "how it-is [ὡς ἔστιν]"[22] and if that were all there is to it. But as "it is" is explicated, it turns out that this myth of the only "way [ὁδοῖο]" to go recycles key motifs from the wayless way that was initially described. The sheer indetermination of the speaker's opening conveyance, as well as the indefinite reaching that persists past his welcome, corresponds precisely to the way in which being will be said to be steadily reaching itself: "For there is no not-being that could pause it from *reaching* the same [οὔτε γὰρ οὐκ ἐὸν ἔστι, τό κεν παύοι μιν ἱκνεῖσθαι / εἰς ὁμόν]" (Fr. 8).[23] "Reaching" [ἱκνεῖσθαι]: this was the word that had verbalized Parmenides's arrival; it signifies a striving and attaining but therefore too the distance of a certain stretch, with an ambivalence that can be further traced through the ways in which the root of the verb branches off into words such as "suppliant" (ἱκέτης) and "sufficient" (ἱκανός) in Ancient Greek. Its use in Parmenides's passage thus suggests that being keeps from itself as it keeps coming to itself, perhaps as a sort of supplicant for its self-sufficiency, over a "pauseless [ἄπαυστον]" (Fr. 8)—and only therefore "motionless [ἀκίνητον]"—movement that stays on the threshold of being. Hence, if being can also be called "motionless [ἀκίνητον]"—"motionless" being one among the many the "non"-determinations that the goddess will name as "signs [σήματα]" of being: "non-generated and non-perishable, for it is whole-of-limb and non-trembling [ἀγένητον ἐὸν καὶ ἀνώλεθρόν ἐστιν, / ἔστι γὰρ οὐλομελές τε καὶ ἀτρεμὲς]" (Fr. 8)²⁴—then its motionlessness could not refer to a dead standstill but could only signify the incessant character of its striving, as it reaches for, and therefore past, itself. Ever behind itself in advance, being therefore not only invites the comparison to a perfect circle that the goddess later draws—like a "well-rounded sphere [εὐκύκλου σφαίρης]," being is never more or less here or there (Fr. 8)—but it also describes a restless movement from threshold to threshold that never comes to itself once and for all, like "the never-coming-to-rest" that Celan would ascribe to "the poetic."²⁵

Being may not be subject to the vacillating accidents of beings, such as "coming to be and perishing [γίγνεσθαί τε καὶ ὄλλυσθαι]" or "changing place [τόπον ἀλλάσσειν]" (Fr. 8),²⁶ but it is also not static in its motionlessness or indifferent in its sameness.²⁷ Hence, when the goddess addresses the same continuity of being in another fragment, it is just as imperative not to ball it all together as it is not to disperse it in one's mind:

> Gaze similarly upon absent things with your mind as steadily present. For it will not sever being from cleaving to being, as either scattering or congealing in every direction in every way in regular order.²⁸

> (λεῦσσε δ' ὅμως ἀπεόντα νόωι παρεόντα βεβαίως·
> οὐ γὰρ ἀποτμήξει τὸ ἐὸν τοῦ ἐόντος ἔχεσθαι
> οὔτε σκιδνάμενον πάντηι πάντως κατὰ κόσμον
> οὔτε συνιστάμενον.) (Fr. 4)

Or, as Wilhelm Capelle translates, placing a greater emphasis on spacing than on timing:

> See how even the distance is graspably near to your spirit; for it shall not separate being from being! Nowhere does it loosen itself in any way out of joint, nor does it ball itself back together.²⁹

> (Sieh, wie auch das Ferne deinem Geist greifbar nahe ist; denn er wird doch nicht das Seiende vom Seienden trennen! Es löst sich ja nirgends auch nur irgendwie aus seinem Gefüge noch ballt es sich wieder zusammen.)

What is key in these passages is the movement of difference that they articulate, and this holds true even if the goddess's assertion were to be taken for another way of affirming the oneness that Martin Heidegger would claim to be the be-all and end-all of things in *What Is Called Thinking*: "The unifying-singular-one that essences in its entirety, not divisible in pieces, and never first pieced together from that which is presencing and absencing awhile [Das Einende-Eine-Einzige, das als Gänze west, nicht zerstückbar und vollends nie erst zusammengestückt aus dem jeweils An- und Abwesenden]."[30] For the repetition that occurs from "being" to "being" (τὸ ἐὸν τοῦ ἐόντος) also says that its cleaving or holding (ἔχεσθαι) entails a minimal yet impassable gap, a limit of contiguity that keeps being back from itself (ἔχεσθαι) and that thus lends being a liminary character whose simple elimination simply could not be. Being cannot, that is, be said to form an uncut continuum without also saying that being is both leaving *and* cleaving to itself, which could not take place, if being were not also open through and through: if "there" were not a "gaping chasm [χάσμ' ἀχανὲς]" for this (transcendental) crossing, or "an open interval between one and the same [offenen Zwischenraum zwischen jenem einen Selben]."[31] However one might seek to affirm the oneness of being, it would therefore seem that its articulation cannot but break with any semblance of a continuum that would not be marked by rupture at every point. Being could no more be said than non-being,[32] then, but can solely be indicated through the differential movement of a language, which only ever broaches the threshold of "how it-is [ὡς ἔστιν]"[33] and which hinges upon its vanishing point.

By hedging or edging toward being in this way, Parmenides's lines thus allow being to appear not as the steady constant of all "absencing [ἀπεόντα]" and "presencing [παρεόντα]" but as that which is away from and beside itself: ἀπ-παρ-εόν. In so doing, however, they also indicate that being could not be seen in the way that the goddess enjoins her visitor to behold it: namely, via the light that shines through the commanding verb of her order, λεῦσσε ("gaze"), whose resonance reaches from λευκὸς ("white") to *lucet* ("it is light") and "lucid."[34] A cleft opens, in other words, between the goddess's word for sight and the threshold site to be seen, which should allow for both the "present" and the "absent" and, therefore too, both the "light" and the "night" that will later be said to compose all that is. As the goddess clarifies: "All is full of light and invisible night together [πᾶν πλεον ἐστὶν ὁμοῦ φάεος καὶ νυκτὸς ἀφάντου]" (Fr. 9),[35] recalling not only her previous words on the way "all is full of Being [πᾶν δ'ἔμπλεόν ἐστιν ἐόντος]" (Fr. 8)[36] but also the preliminary threshold of day and night, which had marked the juncture where "night rejoins day"[37] and where a chasm gapes in lieu of both. Nothing less than all of this is what the survey of being should reach, but the luminosity that the goddess privileges with her imperative translates to regarding the absent as present but not the presence of absence, to elucidating the night but not the dark in its obscurity, and to seeing through being but not the "through" of being as it cleaves to itself and cleaves open.[38]

By the goddess's own lights, however, these obscure aspects of being at the opposite end of the spectrum are no privileged knowledge of hers but the experience of privation that she acknowledges only to the dead, and presumably, soon abandons: "The corpse does not perceive light, heat, or sound on account of the ellipsis / leaving-out [ἔκλειψιν] of fire, but it does perceive cold and silence [τὸν νεκρὸν φωτὸς μὲν καὶ θερμοῦ καὶ φωνῆς οὐκ αἰσθάνεσθαι διὰ τὴν ἔκλειψιν τοῦ πυρός, ψυχροῦ δὲ καὶ σιωπῆς . . . αἰσθάνεσθαι]."[39] Yet if the discourse of the goddess does not and cannot illuminate these liminal dimensions of being—namely, its night and its "not"—what little is said of them here is not merely negative. Rather, it indicates that there could be no end to approaching the issues that will have opened through Parmenides's poem and that the truth at issue may have never had a home with the light-minded goddess but remains outstanding with the goddess at the gates of day and night and, more initially, with the threshold-language that will be carried on from there.

∽

The goddess who holds the keys at the gateway of Parmenides's poem is called Δίκη, whose name is most often rendered "Justice" but whose interpretations just as often diverge. Hermann Fränkel reads the word to signify not a primarily juridical notion but the "norm of correctness in essence and in thinking [Norm der Wesensrichtigkeit und der Denkrichtigkeit]," whence Dike's decisive role in permitting or refusing entry through the gates, according to the nature of the one who seeks passage.[40] And in his commentaries on both Parmenides and Anaximander, Heidegger similarly emphasizes the inadequacy of modern juridical concepts to the Greek thought of "justice" but circumvents all talk of norms in speaking of Δίκη as the "jointure" or "Fuge" within which beings come into their own by abiding for their times and letting one another be.[41] Along these lines, Dike would personify the function of the liminal area that she guards not only in Parmenides's poem but also in Hesiod's *Theogony*, where the limits of the earth had marked the junction where day and night alternate and where the Titans are cut off from the land of the living, each according to their essence. By contrast, in the translation of Parmenides's fragment from which Celan drew the title for "With a Changing Key," Dike is glossed as "the goddess of recompense [die Göttin der Vergeltung],"[42] evoking the very relations of repayment, exchange, and equivalence from which Fränkel and Heidegger take their distance.

In the poem that Celan names "With a Changing Key," however, what is translated is precisely this critical indecision over "Justice,"[43] as well as any other lines that could be drawn to order space, time, being, and language. Dike is not explicitly named or implicitly characterized in terms of veridical, ontological, or juridical economies, nor does any barred threshold appear to delineate a decisive crossing. Rather, whether it be a question of lucidity or obscurity, being or nonbeing, advantage or shortcoming, and so forth, no decisive judgment between alternatives could be imperative here, and no single passage, key—for all that is, is other than itself and underway to alteration from the outset.

WITH A CHANGING KEY

With a changing key
you unlock the house in
which the snow of the unsaid drifts.
Depending on the blood that spurts
from your eye or mouth or ear,
your key changes.

Your key changes, the word changes
that is allowed to drift with the flakes.
Depending on the wind that pushes you forth,
the snow balls around the word.[44]

(MIT WECHSELNDEM SCHLÜSSEL

Mit wechselndem Schlüssel
schließt du das Haus auf, darin
der Schnee des Verschwiegenen treibt.
Je nach dem Blut, das dir quillt

> aus Aug oder Mund oder Ohr,
> wechselt dein Schlüssel.
>
> Wechselt dein Schlüssel, wechselt das Wort,
> das treiben darf mit den Flocken.
> Je nach dem Wind, der dich fortstößt,
> ballt um das Wort sich der Schnee.)[45]

It is in keeping with the changing key of the title that no retributive or distributive justice but an anonymous other opens the house—namely, a "you," whose status as a pronominal "shifter" renders it alterable and distributable itself: "you" invokes another who is other with each instance of address and whose invocation may also reach no one at all, solicit no response, or remain without all correspondence. Hence, the house that "you" are said to "unlock" belongs to no one and nowhere: it is not the house of day and night, not the house of a goddess or the "house of being,"[46] and not the house of any addressee but merely "the house [das Haus]," whose situation remains utterly uncertain, there being no indication of its surroundings or any way it could be reached. If there were any determination outside the house here, it would be the empty space of the page that exposes it to be as much a placeless placeholder as the pronominal persona who opens it.

These lines may appear to be remote from Parmenides's poem, yet by leaving both the addressee and home address utterly open, Celan offers another version of the cosmic threshold that Parmenides had broached in drawing and departing from Hesiod's *Theogony*. And by drawing a blank in this way, Celan goes further in drawing out the resemblance of Parmenides's liminal area to the chasm of Hesiod's poem, which had similarly revealed nothing to be experienced, seen, or said but the abyss that was "there and there [ἔνθα καὶ ἔνθα]" all along (742). This thoroughly abyssal situation is not contradicted but becomes all the more pronounced when it changes, and snow is said to drift therein—"in / which the snow of the unsaid drifts [darin / der Schnee des Verschwiegenen treibt]"—and not only because this often-frequented topos in Celan's vocabulary marks a blank interval here and elsewhere.[47] For there is also no telling whether this snow ever entered from without before it began drifting within and therefore no telling whether there is any outside beyond these minimal elements of a setting, whose drifting exceeds and unsettles what little is said of them. Alone, even "Schnee" could hardly mean "snow" in any speakable sense of the word if it is precipitated from out of the "unsaid

[Verschwiegenen]," which estranges it from the crystalline formations that are otherwise known by that name—as well as any other referent, for that matter—and which thereby silences it as it speaks.

Yet the status of the "snow of the unsaid [Schnee des Verschwiegenen]" is not simply settled with silence, either; rather, its unspoken and opaque sense clears the way for its threshold-character to become more pronounced, through those sibilant, asemantic particles that not only render it at least as sonorous and porous as they are unvoiced but also carry forth the hissing static that had insisted from the "*Schlüssel*" ("key") onward, and that crosses through word-boundaries, at once bearing and interfering with all that the terms may otherwise convey.[48] In this muted way, the "snow of the unsaid" speaks at the limit of speech and silence, and it does so perhaps more radically than even Parmenides had done, when he touched upon the privative experience of "cold [ψυχρός]" and "silence [σιωπή]" that the corpse comes to sense in the absence of fire and the presence of night.[49] Either way, however, the many layers of the "snow of the unsaid" further indicate how the threshold-language of the poem voids and parts with itself to leave room for alternatives, leaving house and snow utterly without, in the most extreme sense of the word.

Within this "without"-language, the "h*ous*e" (*Haus*) thus barely differs from the *out* (*-aus*) that it can neither hold off nor keep in, but that instead turns it inside-out through the literal elements into which the "Haus" breaks down, while otherwise staying intact. Snow not only penetrates the interior and blurs its borders, as it is said in Celan's opening lines, for the house is itself ousted through a linguistic drift like that of the sibilant "snow of the unsaid [Schnee des Verschwiegenen]," which grows all the more apparent when the "Aug" or "eye" is drawn to resonate with "(H)aus" three lines later. These permutations of the "Haus" thus trouble the foundations of the establishment, as Parmenides's way had done when it continued past the goddess's home as if it were nothing. And beyond that, they also trace yet another version of the motionless movement that had characterized the reaching and cleaving of being to being. This time, however, the accent is placed not upon the continuity that holds together all that is but upon the ruptures and contingencies that cut across each word of substance, and that thus allow no decision over the ontological *or* verbal status of the house, its outside, or its contents. Hence, as the poem goes on, no further word will be given of that unsteady structure but only of the further alterations of key and word that should take place along with the draughts of wind and snow:

> Your key changes, the word changes
> that is allowed to drift with the flakes.
> Depending on the wind that pushes you forth,
> the snow balls around the word.[50]
>
> (Wechselt dein Schlüssel, wechselt das Wort,
> das treiben darf mit den Flocken.
> Je nach dem Wind, der dich fortstößt,
> ballt um das Wort sich der Schnee.)[51]

Far from any clear-cut departure, these lines make the initial situation still more explicit: there is only exile in this liminal space, whose thoroughly permeable "house" never could have stood for cover but stands in from the start as a cover name that may, as such, always be changed for another word—or none at all—as the poem goes on to snowball.

If no threshold is named—if no explicit entry to the home and no implicit exit to the winds takes place—then this can only be because there could be no limit to define the location of the liminary itself and because the liminary character of this language could not be limited by a single word. Thus, even when the poem comes closest to designating a threshold of sorts—even when, namely, the organs of perception are evoked as outlets for blood—these portals are not posited but are merely admitted as a series of alternative possibilities, marked off by disjunctive conjunctions that not only keep them apart—"from your eye *or* mouth *or* ear [aus Aug oder Mund oder Ohr]"—but also keep repeating, such that the drone of the "or" or the "oder" verges upon drowning out the "ear" or "Ohr" beside it. These iterations or variations are compounded, in turn, with the "aus" ("out") that sounds out through the "Aug" ("eye"), to say nothing of the "und" ("and") that is enclosed in the "Mund" ("mouth"), but that speaks through it nonetheless in this verse, where conjunctions and substantives alternately echo one another and thereby alter themselves in turn.[52] From the house at the poem's departure to the body parts "or" particles of grammar in its midst to the particles of snow and utterly unparticular "flakes [Flocken]" in the end, each term of "With a Changing Key" is a threshold-word that interminably opens to others beside itself. And in being beside itself in this way, each term *is* not so much as once—because it is at no time *one*—although it may be precisely "how it-is [ὡς ἔστιν]"[53] in the sense that Parmenides once broached, when he spoke of being as cleaving and thereby indicated the reach and the breach that are constitutive for its continuum—the "without"

without which it could not reach (for) itself. Once again, as Hamacher will have written, Celan's exposition of language occurs not in the "*House of Being*, but the '*out*' of being."⁵⁴

Because, however, the "'out' of being" could not be, without ceasing to be what it "is"—because it too would have to move out, as Hamacher also indicates in his analyses⁵⁵—its utterance can only be carried out in such a way that nothing is directly stated of it and nothing else that is stated stands firm. This is why the relatively conventional morphological and syntactic formations of Celan's verses are at once left as they *stand* and *left* as they stand through the elements that de-com-pose them, whose aleatory dispersion throughout the poem, more than any word or phrase, is what allows each word to be surrounded with the "snow of the unsaid." The fact that alliteration and consonance verge upon dissolving the very words that they nonetheless constitute only further indicates the nonpositive and therefore too nonoppositional character of the threshold-movements that Celan traces, and that is emphasized further with the line "allowed to drift with the flakes [das treiben darf mit dem Flocken]." This word of allowance ("dürfen") indicates a permissiveness for words, which may drift with the insubstantial flecks that (they also) are, and with all of the gaps that thereby open up within them. But it is also why this same coincidence of dispersion and condensation—both of which, according to Parmenides, cannot be: "Nowhere does it loosen itself in any way out of joint, nor does it ball itself back together [Es löst sich ja nirgends auch nur irgendwie aus seinem Gefüge noch ballt es sich wieder zusammen]"⁵⁶—cannot and does not rest with its implicit confirmation in these last lines of Celan's poem, either. As one of its permutations and near-homophones suggests, the "Wort" ("word") is already "fort" ("forth," "away") before it is said to be the nucleus around which the snow balls, while the balled snow itself could not but scatter to the wind that drives it forth. However close Celan's last verses may come to closure, then—however far they may go in drawing together the movement of words with the words for their movement—they also suggest that no attempt to catch the drift could catch up, and they thereby indicate yet again what Celan would later call in his letter to Jürgen Rausch the "infinite claim of every utterance in this area."⁵⁷

This claim against claims speaks from the threshold of Hesiod's *Theogony* to the threshold of Parmenides's proemium and beyond, but its insistence becomes still more pronounced through the poetic language of *From Threshold to Threshold* and, in particular, "With a Changing Key." It is a claim that delivers no judgment but that speaks for a movement of "transcending without transcendence" and thus remains as open-ended as it had been from the outset.[58] What seems to have opened close to the topoi of Parmenides's proemium thus appears to drift off ad infinitum, far from any supporting frame, let alone a steady "way" of being. But even as Celan parts ways with Parmenides, the poem also does not leave the threshold where, "with a changing key," Dike had disclosed a "gaping chasm [χάσμ' ἀχανὲς]" at the gates of day and night (Fr. 1).[59] Rather, it traces another approach to the abyss that Parmenides largely passes over in silence, and it does so through no discourse of divine revelation—and through no word that would break that silence—but through allowing each word to speak in such a way that it discloses its gaps and its muteness. Even in those formulations that remind of the decisions and distributions of Dike—"Je nach dem"—the poem echoes the sharp rupture, the "Jähe," that will have opened in her place, at an indefinite remove from every being, judgment, measure, or proportion.

Such is the alteration of key that traverses "With a Changing Key." Such is the threshold-language that precedes any being and that crosses through each and every one. Ever before every location, distribution, or attribution; ever before every transcendental structure or ontological substrate, "With a Changing Key" speaks, among others, for the liminal speech and silence that further and alter every speakable term. "From threshold to threshold," the poem speaks and alters, speaking: *a limine*.

## Notes

1. Hesiod, *Theogonia, Opera et dies, Sctutum*, eds. R. Merkelbach and M. L. West (Oxford: Clarendon Press, 1990), line 731. In the following, passages from this poem will be cited parenthetically by line number. Translations are provided, with occasional modifications, according to Eric A. Havelock, "The Cosmic Myths of Homer and Hesiod," *Oral Tradition* 2.1 (1987): 31–53, 45–49.

2. See Sigmund Freud, *Civilization and Its Discontents: The Standard Edition of the Complete Psychological Works of Sigmund Freud, Volume XXI (1927–1931): The Future of an Illusion, Civilization and its Discontents, and Other Works*, trans. James Strachey (London: Hogarth Press, 1968), 57–146, 69–71.

3. See Winfried Menninghaus, *Schwellenkunde: Walter Benjamins Passage des Mythos* (Frankfurt am Main: Suhrkamp, 1986), 29, 48, 55.

4. Havelock, "The Cosmic Myths," 52.

5. All references to the fragments of Parmenides are cited parenthetically by fragment number according to Hermann Diels and Walther Kranz's *Die Fragmente*

*der Vorsokratiker*, 3 vols. (Berlin: Weidmann, 1951). Unless otherwise noted, English translations of Parmenides's poem are adopted and modified on the basis of A. H. Coxon, *The Fragments of Parmenides: A Critical Text with Introduction and Translation, the Ancient Testimonia and a Commentary*, ed. Richard McKirahan (Las Vegas: Parmenides Publishing, 2009), 48–54.

6. This passage from Celan's letter from February 22, 1954, appears in Barbara Wiedemann's edition of Celan's poems, *Die Gedichte: Neue kommentierte Gesamtausgabe in einem Band*, ed. Barbara Wiedemann (Berlin: Suhrkamp, 2018), 705–6; my translation.

7. Werner Hamacher, "Die Sekunde der Inversion: Bewegungen einer Figur durch Celans Gedichte," in *Entferntes Verstehen: Studien zu Philosophie und Literatur von Kant bis Celan* (Frankfurt am Main: Suhrkamp, 1998), 323–68, 343; my translation.

8. Werner Hamacher, "95 Theses on Philology / *95 Thesen zur Philologie*," trans. Catherine Diehl, in *Give the Word: Responses to Werner Hamacher's 95 Theses on Philology*, eds. Gerhard Richter and Ann Smock (Lincoln: University of Nebraska Press, 2019), xi–lvi, xii.

9. Paul Celan, *Von Schwelle zu Schwelle: Vorstufen—Textgenese—Endfassung*, eds. Heino Schmull, Christiane Braun, and Markus Heilmann (Frankfurt am Main: Suhrkamp, 2002), 2. See also the editors' comments on the original manuscript in Celan, *Von Schwelle zu Schwelle*, ix.

10. As the editors of *Von Schwelle zu Schwelle* also note, Celan had written to his wife Gisèle Celan-Lestrange of this possible title on February 1, 1955. See *Paul Celan—Gisèle Celan-Lestrange: Correspondance (1951–1970)*, eds. Betrand Badiou and Eric Celan, 2 vols. (Paris: Seuil, 2001), 1:72; cf. Celan, *Von Schwelle zu Schwelle*, viii–ix.

11. To the extent that the formula, "Argumentum e silentio" gives word of the Greek ἀργός and ἄργυρος ("shining, glistening," "silver"), it indicates not only an elucidation *from out of* silence, but also the shining *of* silence. This possibility is emphasized in the poem, where the syntagma "between gold and forgetting [zwischen Gold und Vergessen]" similarly pairs the name for a bright metal with the evocation of that which is forgotten, obscure, and unspoken. What is said to lie between "gold and forgetting," however, is itself obscure: namely, "the night [die Nacht]," which allows for both ("Beide ließ sie gewähren."), and to which "you" are enjoined to add the word: "Lay, / you too now lay down what wants to a-/rise at dawn along with the days: / the word, star-overflown, ' sea over-poured [Lege, / lege auch du jetzt dorthin, was herauf- / dämmern will neben den Tagen: / das sternüberflogene Wort, das meerübergoßne]." Paul Celan, *Memory Rose into Threshold Speech*, trans. Pierre Joris (New York: Farrar, Straus, and Giroux, 2020), 154–55. When the poem goes on to dedicate to the night what is called "das erschwiegene Wort" or "the word silence won," this word likewise shines in its nocturnal silence, as it appears in lieu and in favor of another word that it itself is not.

12. In his copy of Wilhelm Capelle's translation of Parmenides's fragments, Celan had underscored the passage that reads: "There is the gate through which the paths of day and night go. Lintel and stone threshold encompass it. It itself—in the heights of the aether—is filled with the powerful wings of a door. To them Dike, the goddess of recompense, holds the changing keys. [Dort ist das Tor, durch das die Pfade von Tag und Nacht gehen. Türsturz und steinerne Schwelle umfassen es. Es selber—in Äthers Höhen—ist von mächtigen Türflügeln ausgefüllt. Zu ihnen hat Dike, die Göttin der Vergeltung, die wechselnden Schlüssel.]" Wilhelm Capelle, *Die Vorsokratiker* (Leipzig: Kröner, 1935), 162; my translation. Cf. *La Bibliothèque philosophique de Paul Celan*, eds. Alexandra Richter, Patrik Alac, and Betrand Badiou (Paris: Éditions Rue d'Ulm, 2004), 8. The copy that Celan owned dates from 1953, around the same time that he was composing the poems that would be collected in *Von Schwelle zu Schwelle* (1951–1955).

13. In addition to the dedication to Gisèle Celan-Lestrange that appears on the title page of the volume, the poem "Pursed at Night" ("Nächtlich geschürzt") is dedicated to Hannah and Hermann Lenz; "Argumentum e silentio," to René Char; and "The Vintagers" ("Die Winzer"), to Nani and Klaus Demus. See Celan, *Memory Rose*, 136–37, 154–55, 156–59.

14. See Celan, "Chanson einer Dame im Schatten," *Die Gedichte*, 41–42.

15. Celan, *Die Gedichte*, 706.

16. Werner Hamacher, "Tò autó, das Selbe, — —," in *Keinmaleins: Texte zu Celan* (Frankfurt am Main: Klostermann, 2019), 181–208, 183; my translation.

17. Celan, *Die Gedichte*, 706.

18. Coxon, *The Fragments*, 48–54. The last clause in the passage cited above differs especially from Coxon's version, which reads, "How it was necessary that the things that are believed to be should have their being in general acceptance, ranging through all things from end to end." As many commentators have pointed out, the translation of the adverb δοκίμως, which Coxon renders "in general acceptance," depends upon how one interprets the role of belief or opinion (δόξα) in Parmenides's thought; i.e., whether belief is merely illusory or a mode of appearance that has its foundation and legitimation in being. The latter interpretation is adopted here, on the basis of Hans Schwabl's arguments in "Sein und Doxa bei Parmenides," in *Um die Begriffswelt der Vorsokratiker*, ed. Hans-Georg Gadamer (Darmstadt: Wissenschaftliche Buchgesellschaft, 1968), 391–422, 402. In a translation and interpretation that is largely inspired by Heidegger's elucidations of semblance as implicated in being, Jean Beaufret similarly renders the verses in question: "Comment la diversité qui fait montre d'elle-même devait déployer une présence digne d'être reçue, étendant son règne à travers toutes choses." Jean Beaufret, *Le poème de Parménide* (Paris: Presses Universitaires de France, 1955), 79.

19. At the start of his study, Walther Kranz also emphasizes the abruptness of Parmenides's (ongoing) movement. Walther Kranz, "Über Aufbau und Bedeutung des

parmenideischen Gedichts," in *Studien zur antiken Literatur und ihrem Nachwirken* (Heidelberg: Winter, 1967), 128–43, 128.

20. Coxon's translation of the present participle ἱκάνων ("arriving at") does not come as close to emphasizing an ongoing reach as the translation that is offered in Kurt Riezler's version: "nearing our house [unserem Hause nahend]." See Coxon, *The Fragments*, 52; and Kurt Riezler, *Parmenides: Übersetzung, Einführung und Interpretation* (Frankfurt am Main: Klostermann, 2017), 25.

21. In his study, Kranz offers other arguments for reading the home that the maidens approach as the "House of Night." Kranz, "Über Aufbau und Bedeutung," 129–30. This possibility is elaborated at length in Raymond Prier's study, where he traces the similarities between Parmenides's verses and Hesiod's lines on the "House of Night" from the *Theogony*. Raymond Prier, *Archaic Logic: Symbol and Structure in Heraclitus, Parmenides, and Empedocles* (The Hague: Mouton, 1976), 99. In his meticulous reading of this passage, Jean Bollack draws the consequence: "The door does not give entry into a house . . . ; it opens upon an outside that transforms into an inside, the very same that one had left [La porte ne fait pas entrer dans une maison . . . ; elle s'ouvre sur un dehors, qui se transforme en un dedans, celui même que l'on quitte]." Jean Bollack, *Parménide: De l'étant au monde* (Paris: Verdier, 2006), 86; my translation.

22. The passage reads: "Only one myth of the way is still left: that / how it-is [μόνος δ'ἔτι μῦθος ὁδοῖο / λείπεται ὡς ἔστιν]." Coxon, *The Fragments*, 64.

23. Coxon, 78; my emphasis.

24. Coxon, 64.

25. Celan, *Die Gedichte*, 705.

26. Coxon, *The Fragments*, 78.

27. Bollack similarly observes: "L'Étant se mue en objet, dans les limites de ce mouvement qui l'habite dans l'immobilité et le soutient. Il s'y lie à lui-même, dans ses 'liens.'" Bollack, *Parménide*, 120. And later, he reiterates, albeit with regard to a different passage: "L'unité se fond sur le retour de quelque chose, la pression du semblable sur le semblable, à la place du dissemblable. Avec L'Étant qui se contient lui-même, Parménide pose les jalons de la dualité qui règle l'organisation du monde." Bollack, 163.

28. Coxon, *The Fragments*, 60.

29. Capelle, *Die Vorsokratiker*, 164; my translation.

30. Martin Heidegger, *Was heißt Denken?*, ed. Paola-Ludovika Coriando (Frankfurt am Main: Klostermann, 2002), 264; my translation. This portion of Heidegger's lecture course is available in the edition of the *Gesamtausgabe*, which Celan would not have read. See *La Bibliothèque philosophique*, 392.

31. Hamacher, "Tὸ αὐτό," 207.

32. As she addresses the alternative ways of being and not-being, the goddess says of the latter: "For you can neither know what is not (for it is impossible) nor

tell of it [οὔτε γὰρ ἂν γνοίης τό γε μὴ ἐόν, οὐ γὰρ ἀνυστόν, / οὔτε φράσεις]." Fr. 2; Coxon, *The Fragments*, 56.

33. Coxon, 64.

34. See Pierre Chantraine, *Dictionnaire étymologique de la langue grecque: Histoire des mots*, vol. 3 (Paris: Klincksieck, 1974), s.v. λεύσσω. Bollack also highlights this connection, writing: "The verb *leussein* evokes a vision pertaining to another order; the particular nature of this regard rests upon the light of the intellect [Le verbe leussein évoque une vision appartenant à un autre ordre; la nature particulière de ce regard s'appuie sur la lumière de l'intellect]." Bollack, *Parménide*, 308; my translation. Kranz also characterizes the voyage of the proemium, as well as the way of being that the goddess imparts, as the "way to light and truth [Weg zu Licht und Wahrheit]." Kranz, "Über Aufbau und Bedeutung," 134; my translation.

35. Coxon, *The Fragments*, 88.

36. Coxon, 70. This repetition has often been noted by commentators; see, for example, Coxon, *The Fragments*, 361; and Schwabl, "Sein und Doxa," 409–11.

37. Jean Bollack, *Parménide*, 80; my translation.

38. No mind could comprehend being at once and as one, since each "mind" (νόος) would have to be thought as inseverable from being as well, and therefore at variance with it and itself, as manifested in its varying degrees of lucidity. Hence, the goddess will explicitly state: "For as each holds a temper [of light and night] which it has of the vagrant limbs, so does the mind stand by for men [ὡς γὰρ ἕκαστος ἔχει κρᾶσιν μελέων πολυπλάγκτων / τὼς νόος ἀνθρώποισι παρίσταται]." Fr. 16; Coxon, *The Fragments*, 94. The blindness of any single-minded orientation toward light is perhaps most concisely addressed by Maurice Blanchot in *The Space of Literature*, however distant that space may otherwise seem to be from the journey of Parmenides. After introducing an "other" night than the night that we know by contrast with the day, he goes on to remark: "The first night is another of day's constructions. . . . The more [the day] expands, with the proud aim of becoming universal, the more the nocturnal element threatens to withdraw into the light itself: the more nocturnal is that which enlightens us, the more it is the uncertainty and immensity of the night." Maurice Blanchot, *The Space of Literature*, trans. Ann Smock (Lincoln: University of Nebraska Press, 1989), 166.

39. Coxon, *The Fragments*, 142.

40. Hermann Fränkel, "Parmenidesstudien," in *Wege und Formen frühgriechischen Denkens*, 2nd ed. (Munich: Beck, 1960), 157–97, 166, 169; my translation.

41. In "The Anaximander Fragment"—one of the essays that Celan had studied during the period from which "Mit wechselndem Schlüssel" dates—Heidegger writes of δίκη: "To presencing as such jointure must belong, thus creating the possibility of its being out of joint. What is present is that which lingers awhile. The while occurs essentially as the transitional arrival in departure: the while comes to presence between approach and withdrawal. . . . In this 'between' whatever lingers awhile is joined. This 'between' is the jointure in accordance with which whatever lingers is

joined, from its emergence here to its departure away from here." Martin Heidegger, "The Anaximander Fragment," trans. David Farrell Krell, in *Early Greek Thinking: The Dawn of Western Philosophy* (New York: Harper and Row, 1984), 13–58, 41; cf. *La Bibliothèque philosophique*, 356. In his lecture course on Parmenides from 1942 to 1943, Heidegger comments upon this word as an indication of jointure. See Martin Heidegger, *Parmenides* (Frankfurt am Main: Klostermann, 1982), 137.

42. Capelle, *Die Vorsokratiker*, 163; my translation; cf. *La Bibliothèque philosophique*, 8.

43. This is also no inessential trait of divine names in Parmenides, whose significance alters through his words. Bollack emphasizes the reinscriptions that divine names undergo in Parmenides in his commentary, on which, see, for example, Bollack, *Parménide*, 80–81. For an extensive study of the transformation that takes place with divine names through the thinking and writing of Heraclitus, Parmenides, and Empedocles, see Clémence Ramnoux, *Héraclite, ou l'homme entre les choses et les mots*, 2nd ed. (Paris: Belles Lettres, 1968).

44. Celan, *Memory Rose*, 119–21; trans. modified.

45. Celan, *Von Schwelle zu Schwelle*, 65.

46. This formulation appears in Heidegger's essay on Rilke. Martin Heidegger, "What Are Poets For?" in *Poetry, Language Thought*, trans. Albert Hofstadter (New York: Harper and Row, 1971), 87–139, 129. But the proemium of Parmenides may likewise be considered to characterize language as the house of being, with its echoes of an Odyssean journey from the errancy of mortal life to the home of a goddess who purports to speak the truth. Hence, Bollack summarizes the course that is traced as follows: "The return of the errant one is domiciled in the house of Being [Le retour de l'errant est domicilié dans la maison de l'État]." Bollack, *Parménide*, 18; my translation. This description only goes so far, however, in addressing the errancy that persists through all talk of "being," as well as the chasm that underlies and unsettles the home in question.

47. In his brief commentary on André du Bouchet's encounter with this poem in particular, Bernhard Böschenstein writes, for example, that Celan's evocation of the "snow of the unsaid" proceeds from out of an "Umgang mit der Pausensprache" that he had shared with other friends and poets such as du Bouchet. Bernhard Böschenstein, "Paul Celan im Gespräch mit deutschen und französischen Dichtern von Hölderlin bis zur Gegenwart," *Oxford German Studies* 34.1 (2005): 65–78, 77. In his essay on Celan titled "The Last to Speak," Blanchot also names "snow" among those "words that return with insistence" throughout Celan's oeuvre, commenting that "*Schnee, Ferne, Nacht, Asche* [snow, distance, night, ashes]" recur "as if to make us believe in a relationship with a reality or matter that is powdery, soft, light, perhaps welcoming, but such an impression is soon turned toward the aridity of *stone* (a word that is almost always there), of *chalk*, of *limestone* and *gravel* (*Kalk, Kiesel, Kreide*), snow whose sterile whiteness is always whiter white (crystal, crystal), without increase or growth: the white that is at the bottom of what is bottomless."

Maurice Blanchot, "The Last to Speak," in *A Voice from Elsewhere*, trans. Charlotte Mandell (Albany: State University of New York Press, 2007), 53–91, 69.

48. In his brilliant monograph devoted to Celan's poem, "Die Silbe Schmerz," Michael Levine explicates at length the divisibility of the minimal, literal elements of language that Celan's poetry exposes. See Michael Levine, *Atomzertrümmerung: Zu einem Gedicht von Paul Celan* (Vienna: Turia + Kant, 2018).

49. The outflow of blood that follows in "Mit wechselndem Schlüssel" only renders this possibility more plausible, and an earlier draft of Celan's poem even more emphatically suggests it, where the snow is said to be the fulfillment of the year that the night grants you, not unlike the night that is thought to fill the corpse in Parmenides: "Je nach dem Jahr, das die Nacht dir erfüllte / mit Schnee oder anderen Flocken." Celan, *Von Schwelle zu Schwelle*, 64.

50. Celan, *Memory Rose*, 121; trans. modified.

51. Celan, *Von Schwelle zu Schwelle*, 65.

52. Later, when the word for the porous formation called "Schnee" comes to alternate with "Flocken," its alternate similarly opens it to an indefinite range of divergent alternatives, from the flakes of snowfall to the dust of a fallout. Wolfgang Pfeifer traces "Flocke" to the Indo-European root "*pleuk-," which he glosses, "flake, feather, hair, fallout [Flocke, Feder, Haar, Abfall]." Wolfgang Pfeifer, *Etymologisches Wörterbuch*, s.v. "Flocke," accessed August 23, 2019, https://www.dwds.de/wb/Flocke). Celan suggests a similarly indefinite range of possibilities when he simply writes "Flocken," or, as he had put it in an earlier version of his poem: "snow or other flakes [Schnee oder anderen Flocken]." Celan, *Von Schwelle zu Schwelle*, 64; my translation.

53. Coxon, *The Fragments*, 64.

54. Hamacher, "Tò autó," 192; my translation.

55. Already the echoes and citational resonances of Hamacher's phrasing suggest this and thereby prevent the "Aus" that he names from assuming any settled status.

56. Capelle, *Die Vorsokratiker*, 164.

57. Celan, *Die Gedichte*, 706.

58. Hamacher, "95 Theses on Philology," xii.

59. Coxon, *The Fragments*, 50.

Chapter 8

# With—Paul Celan

Pasqual Solass

"With the hu, with the man, with the humans [Mit den Men, mit den Schen, mit den Menschen]," reads the tenth verse of Paul Celan's ". . . Plashes the Fountain."[1] Much has been written about the dialogic nature of Celan's poetry, about the encounter of the poem speaking to an other.[2] But what if, in fact, several encounters take place in the poem or *with* the poem? If the poem "itself" is not just the site of an encounter but encounters with . . . ? If a poem speaks with itself and with others within itself, and if a poem, due to such speaking, is a speaking with . . . or if a *con*versation (Mit*sprechen*) is itself always already situated within a *com*plex of "with-one-another" (*Miteinander*)? If the place (*Ort*) of an encounter can be found in the word (*Wort*)? "Where? / Spot the place, spot the word. / . . . Mismeasure, unmeasure, misplaced, unworded, / unwo [Wo? / Mach den Ort aus, machs Wort aus. / . . . Vermessen, entmessen, verortet, entwortet, / entwo]."[3] In the movement of spotting (*ausmachen*) the word(s), the place (*Ort*) turns toward its co-word (*Mitwort*) "word [Wort]"—just as *Wort* turns toward *Ort*—and thus they turn out to be co-words of a counterpart. Open for an encounter, the co-words of *Wort* give each other hope, an open door (*Tor*), an open ear (*Ohr*). And it is precisely this openness that points toward another overtone of the German *ausmachen*, "to turn off." What is turned off is the word insofar as it loses its isolating unity. By being co-words or open words, by having no fixed boundary, they are ecstatic. Co-words are in that specific sense no-words or unwording words, withdrawing from "themselves." Celan writes in another place: "The with-one-another of words in a poem: not only a with-one-another, but also an against-one-another. Also a towards-and from-one-another. Encounter, dispute and parting in one. [Das Miteinander der Worte im Gedicht: nicht nur ein Miteinander, auch ein Gegeneinander. Auch ein Zueinander und Voneinander. Begegnung, Widerstreit und Abschied in einem.]"[4] In the "nursery rhyme" of ". . . Plashes the Fountain," which is singing with the "hu," "man," and "human," "human" steps into a "with-one-another"[5] (*Miteinander*) with "hu" and "man," and it also enters into a dispute with its co-words, which—barely their "own" words, one might say, since they are elements of "human"—are the from-one-another (*Voneinander*) of "human." Then again, "hu" and "man" are *co-words* of a towards-one-another (*Zueinander*), heading for an interval within the co-word "hu-man." Nevertheless, "human" remains split, but *with* "hu" and "man," it parts from its elements and stands with them as co-words in a *lateral*, a col-lateral "with-one-another": "with the hu, with the man, with the human being."

The peculiarity that one might attest in such poetry gets complicated by what one could call the con-sonance (*Mitklingen*) of the "with." Not only because the "with" or "co-/con-/com-" within "word-intervals" renders them perceptible (*wahrnehmbar*), like the interval between "co-" and "-word"—and thus "always and again" points in the direction of an encounter—but also because it makes the question of such perceptibility (*Wahrnehmbarkeit*) co-speak with it. In another place, Celan notes that "an eye" walks "with the already seen to the single things—and with them further. For in a poem every single thing enters a happening, a happening that is co-determined by what is joining [mit dem bisher Gesehenen zu den einzelnen Dingen—und mit ihnen weiter. Denn im Gedicht tritt ein jedes in ein Geschehen, ein Geschehen, das vom Hinzutretenden mitbestimmt wird]."[6] Every single one (*ein jedes*) is being co-determined (*mitbestimmt*) by others, and, as it is joining them, each co-determines those others. Not determined in its entirety, an entirety or closure that the "with" suspends, a voice (*Stimme*) is given with what it is joining—by the eye, but also *to* the eye. It is such an eye for which the intervals in a poem become tangible.

With that however, the eye is also co-determined to see silence (*Schweigen*),[7] that is, to elevate the silence to visibility, to let it step into a "with." For what lets the "with-one-another" (*Miteinander*) of the co-words emerge, if not the "prayer-sharp knives / of my / silence [gebetscharfen Messer / meines / Schweigens]," as it goes in the first verses of ". . . Plashes the Fountain"?[8] As a caesura that the silence of an other cuts into the word, the word-interval steps in between the co-words "hu" and "man," where language pauses, takes a breath. Seeing such silence and letting it thereby speak with cut-up co-words becomes even more ocular where the interval is an empty space (*Leerstelle*), a blank space between words, like the blank line falling silent before our eyes between the stanzas of Celan's "On both Hands": "this meandering empty / hospitable middle [wandernde leere / gastliche Mitte]."[9]

Seeing silence, seeing speech: with that, Georg Büchner's Lucile is also evoked, the figure from *Danton's Death* whose eyes appear to be "talked into / blindness [zur Blindheit über- / redet],"[10] as it were, whose eyes are "blind to art [kunstblind]":[11] blind to that which, according to Celan's reading of Büchner, reappears, repeats itself mechanically, and is already known.[12] However, Lucile is thus blind to all that art-talk, to that which is "easy is to talk about"—"Von der Kunst ist gut Reden"—and thus to the art or *téchne* of talking, to *rhetoriké téchne*. Instead, she sees speech; she is open for language that has something "tangible [etwas Wahrnehmbares]" to it.[13] Lucile is open to that which intervenes (*was dazwischen kommt*) and thereby to intervening herself.[14] Around 1960, blindness and sight, silence and speech enter a "with-one-another," a constellation, and it will become clear that it gives direction toward the openness of language. In *The Meridian*, Celan's speech upon the occasion of receiving the Georg Büchner Prize, these co-words find with their constellation another co-word, which joins and at the same time wanders in the "ether,"[15] hospitable like that empty middle. "Together with him / the meridians wander [Mit ihm / wandern die Meridiane]."[16] Invisible, co-words find their encounter with *The Meridian*, "secret connections," "meridian-like," as Celan writes in a letter to his wife, Gisèle Celan-Lestrange. In that letter, written two years after his prize acceptance speech, he tells her about an autumn crocus or "Zeitlose" (literally "timeless") that crossed his way and that suddenly reminds him of a line from a poem with a *Zeitlose* in it but that also reminds him of a letter by Erich Eichhorn from Moscow, in which his friend writes that he is planning to stay in Colchis for vacation—Colchicum, another word for the *Zeitlose*.[17] As Michael Levine points out, these are loose, contingent connections—Celan calls them an "extra-human [außermenschlichen]" dialogue.[18]

How does poetry make such a "with-one-another" of co-words "visible," such an "invisible" (contingent) constellation, with an eye "blind to art"? And within what kind of "with-one-another" stand "the visible" character and the silence of the intervals, the blank spaces, but also the con-sonance of co-words in rhymes and assonances? How do the pauses—how does breath—join speech?

The editors of *The Meridian* for the *Tübinger Ausgabe* tell us that Celan worked between 1958 and 1960 on at least four projects, of which *The Meridian* speech was only one.[19] The notes that are collected in this volume bear traces of these projects and can be also conceived of as notes for, among others, "Conversation in the Mountains" (1959). It is precisely this text that can indicate a direction for investigating the constellation of silence and seeing further.

"They do not talk, they speak, and who speaks does not talk to anyone, cousin, he speaks because nobody hears him, nobody and Nobody [Er redet nicht, er spricht, und wer spricht, Geschwisterkind, der redet zu niemand, der spricht, weil niemand ihn hört, niemand und Niemand]."[20] One can barely decide whether they *talk* about the stone or already *speak*. A third figure comes along with the dialogue, and one could say that "he [er]" enters the conversation without being heard. The one who is heard by nobody, however, is not necessarily silent. Rather, it is said that the stone does not talk, or, to say it with the words of "Engführung," the stone, with its lapidary hospitality, does not lapse into words: "er / war gastlich, er / fiel nicht ins Wort."[21] And yet: "the silence [is] no silence at all. No word has come to an end and no phrase, it is nothing but a pause, an empty space between the words, a blank [das Schweigen ist kein Schweigen, kein Wort ist da verstummt und kein Satz, eine Pause ists bloß, eine Wortlücke ists, eine Leerstelle ists]."[22] Although the ones *talking* (*reden*) do not hear the stone, its silence *speaks* (*spricht*), speaks *with*. . . . It even appears itself to be a con-sonant (*Mitlaut*), a sonorous blank. And still, the consonant stays visible. For the stone is designated with the *s* that marks and truncates the impersonal pronoun *es*, and in a manner that does not just follow the verb *ist*, as in the more conventional *ist's*, but that converges with it in *ists*, with what one could call a "blank" that withdraws.

The poem "Streak" ("Schliere") speaks of a *Mitlaut* and enters a constellation with "Conversation in the Mountains" that con-sonates:

> Streak in the eye:
> so as to guard
> a sign carried through the dark,
> livened by the sand—or ice?—of
> an alien time for a more alien always
> and tuned as
> a mutely vibrating consonant.[23]

(Schliere im Aug:
daß bewahrt sei
ein durchs Dunkel getragenes Zeichen,
vom Sand (oder Eis?) einer fremden
Zeit für ein fremderes Immer
belebt und als stumm
vibrierender Mitlaut gestimmt.)

Silence, a "mutely vibrating consonant" or *Mitlaut*, is "tuned" or rather *voiced*, provided with a voice (*gestimmt*). And thus, the words "mute" (*stumm*)—as in: "mute vibrato [stummes Vibrato]"—and "voice" (*Stimme*) become co-words. The tuning or voicing (*Gestimmtheit*) makes the word "mute" (*stumm*) consonate (*mitlauten*) with the "-stimm-" in "gestimmt." This oscillation between *stumm-* and *-stimm*, between muteness and voice, is the vibrato that joins that which is mute *with* the audible voice. In his essay "The Poetry of Ossip Mandelstam" (1960), Celan writes: "This vibrato is everywhere: in the intervals between the words and the stanzas, in the 'yards / coronas,' in which the rhymes and assonances stand, in the inter-punctuation [Dieses Vibrato ist überall: in den Intervallen zwischen den Worten und den Strophen, in den 'Höfen,' in denen die Reime und die Assonanzen stehen, in der Interpunktion]."[24] The mute vibrato is consonant, sonorous in rhymes and assonances, and it is unheard of by the two speakers who meet in the mountains, this "with-one-another" (*Miteinander*) of the co-words that resonates. Already at this point, we notice how that which *speaks with* . . . is always already joining others: the openness of the "with-one-another" is exposed with an open series of co-words throughout Celan's texts: "pause" (*Pause*), "empty space between the words" (*Wortlücke*), "blank" (*Leerstelle*), "intervals" (*Intervalle*), "coronas" (*Höfe*), "rhymes" (*Reime*), "assonances" (*Assonanzen*), "inter-punctuation" (*Interpunktion*). All of these *syn*deta or *con*nections are symptoms of that very openness that the *with* introduces with *withdrawal*. And it is the withdrawal of the *w* that opens the word "word [Wort]" toward the co-word "place [Ort]": an open place that stays with the *w* insofar as it is *mutely* withdrawn while still being with the "*-Ort*."

∾

Another poem that speaks with a *Mitlaut* is "Muta." Here, the con-sonant is the letter *s*, which is cut off in the first word of the poem "Seul –": "Spoken to three [Zu dreien gesprochen]," the French word "seul," meaning "alone," remains singular, even when an *s* is joined with it in the third verse:

> Seul –: spoken to three, mute
> vibrato of the consonant.
> Seuls.²⁵

> (Seul –: zu dreien gesprochen, stummes
> Vibrato des Mitlauts.
> Seuls.)

In the plural form of "seul"—"seuls"—the second *s* is silent, *muta*, a mute vibrato. The con-sonant, the *Mit-* of the *Mitlaut*, makes the mute consonant *s* visible. The stone not only speaks in the pauses and blanks but also in mute letters, which nevertheless become "tangible" (*wahrnehmbar*), and thus can enter a "with-one-another" (*Miteinander*) both *alone* and still *with* one another. The silence of the letter *s*, which vibrates within "seuls," remains mute, but it becomes visible (*sichtbar*) in the plural form. There are two "seuls," as it were, and the second one is consonant with the first one, with "Seul –:." The consonant *s* in "Muta" is a "muta cum liquida" in reverse. Whereas in Latin metrics the liquid sound follows the "muta," like the *l* follows the *t* in the word *Mitlaut*, marking an interval between "Mit-" and "-laut," in the plural form "seuls," the muta *s* follows the liquid *l*. "Muta cum liquida" is being used in two senses here. First, it marks the "with-one-another" of words—"mit" with "laut"—and second, it makes the "muta" visible, that is, makes it striking to the eye.

"Muta cum Liquida" was the first title of the poem "Erratic" ("Erratisch"), which speaks of "lip- / picked syllables [Mit der Lippe auf- / gesammelte Silben]" that "help the creeping star / into their middle [helfen dem Kriechstern / in ihre Mitte]," and which goes on: "The stone, once / close to the temporal zones, now opens up: [Der Stein, / schläfennah einst, tut sich hier auf:]."²⁶ The "up [auf]" is followed by a colon and a blank space opening up "the mute middle of the poem [die stumme Mitte des Gedichts]," as Werner Hamacher writes.²⁷ The entire opening sequence of verses reads:

> The evenings dig themselves
> under your eye. With the lip ga-
> thered syllables—beautiful,
> soundless round—
> help the crawlstar
> in their midst. The stone,
> once temple-close, now opens here:

(Die Abende graben sich dir.
unters Aug. Mit der Lippe auf-
gesammelte Silben—schönes,
lautloses Rund—
helfen dem Kriechstern
in ihre Mitte. Der Stein,
schläfennah einst, tut sich hier auf:)

Later, after the "falling silent [of] thinking in the pause [verstummenden Denken in der Pause],"[28] the pause gets remembered. "In this 'later' [In diesem 'Später']," as Celan writes elsewhere in a note, "your word peaks [gipfelt dein Wort]."[29] In "Erratic," the blank middle peaks in the last word of the poem, "in the ether [im Äther]," and thus peaks up in the air, perhaps at a "breathturn."

∽

Consonance, silence that speaks with . . . , mute vibrato: in such paradoxical considerations, which we took up with the stone, "blind spots" co-appear *with* the "streak in the eye."[30] A "speaking with" can only occur when it is veiled in a web, in a speech-grille, in the inter-punctuation, the intervals, the "muta." This "speaking-with" is not being heard, and still it remains tangible, visible.

However, why is it the stone that opens to the "with" with which Celan's poems speak? Why is it not the "stick" from the "Conversation in the Mountains"? Why this *lapidary* (from the Latin *lapis*, "stone") accent? Celan writes in a note:

> The stone, the inorganic, the mineral, is the older, that which stands toward and opposite man from the deepest time-layer, from prehistory—that is also man's prehistory. The stone is the other, the extra-human [Außermenschliche], . . . with its silence it gives direction and space to the one who speaks.

> (Der Stein, das Anorganische, Mineralische, ist das ältere, das aus der tiefsten Zeitschicht, aus der Vorwelt—die auch des Menschen Vorwelt ist, dem Menschen Entgegen- und Gegenüberstehende. Der Stein ist das Andere, Außermenschliche, . . . mit seinem Schweigen gibt er dem Sprechenden Richtung und Raum.)[31]

The "extra-human [Außermenschliche]," "prehistorical [Vorweltliche]" (aspect of the) stone again leads to the poem "Streak" and to words of an "alien time [einer fremden / Zeit]."[32] Out of this "alien time," this "deepest time-layer," the stone stands toward and opposed to the human. The stone, which is invoked as a third figure of speech in Celan's "Conversation in the Mountains"—and as the one giving "direction" to the speaker(s)—*talks* to nobody. The stone is *with* the two speakers who meet in the mountains only due to its silence. And yet it is the one "who speaks, because nobody hears him [der spricht, weil niemand ihn hört]."[33] Speaking (*Sprechen*) seems to be a way of entering into a "with-one-another" that does not relate to an other in a rhetorical fashion (the German *Rede* designates "speech" in English, in the rhetorical sense of the word), and that, even more importantly, does not even relate to an other in terms of talking (*Reden*). The speaking of the stone does not relate *directly* to an addressee, but it has *direction*. This direction could be the direction of its silence, and it could be precisely the *direction* of its silence that makes silence speak. The stone speaks "with its silence," that is, it speaks through its silence and also speaks with it. Since it seems that speaking does not relate to a concrete someone, it is a silent, a mute kind of *with*. The stone is alone—*seul*, as in "Muta"—and yet its silence speaks with it, making it visible, just as the mute *con*sonant *s* in "seuls" becomes visible in writing: in that which is mute.[34]

∼

The second among the multiple beginnings that are marked in Celan's Büchner Prize speech opens the question of art:[35] "It is easy to talk about art [Von der Kunst ist gut reden]."[36] Shortly after this apodictic statement, which already draws our attention to the verb "talk [reden]," "someone" comes into view

> who hears and listens and looks . . . and then doesn't know what the talk was all about. But who hears the speaker, who "sees him speak," who perceives language and shape, and also . . . breath, that is, direction and destiny.
>
> (der hört und lauscht und schaut . . . und dann nicht weiß, wovon die Rede war. Der aber den Sprechenden hört, der ihn "sprechen sieht," der Sprache wahrgenommen hat und

Gestalt, und zugleich auch . . . Atem, das heißt Richtung und Schicksal.)[37]

Just as in "Conversation in the Mountains," "talking" and "speaking" are differentiated. Even more so, since with "seeing language" and seeing the one who is speaking, the visibility of language is being accentuated. Seeing speaking means perceiving a con-sonance (*Mitlauten*) of a mute vibrato. It is the visibility that we already encountered with the *s* in "ists" that marks a sonorous blank, and with the *s* in "seuls," the mute yet visible *s* that renders a "lone" word plural. In the latter case, it is the ability to see language that gives direction to punctuation, letters, words; a direction that lets them co-appear with one another as with their silence;[38] a direction that differs from the directness of talking, that even suspends this directness, and that thus opens eyes and ears for that which is "seuls."

This "someone [jemand]" who sees language, who perceives language—this "someone [jemand]" who resonates with the "no-one [niemand]" and "No-one [Niemand]" of the "Conversation in the Mountains"—is Büchner's Lucile, whom Celan also calls "one who is blind to art, the same Lucile for whom language is something person-like and tangible [die Kunstblinde, dieselbe Lucile, für die Sprache etwas Personhaftes und Wahrnehmbares hat]."[39] In a first draft of *The Meridian*, Celan still writes "visible [Sichtbares]" instead of the later "tangible [Wahrnehmbares]."[40] Both words—co-words with each other—introduce an interval that is marked off with the suffix that they both share: "-ible [-bares]." Visible, one could say, is that which *stays* visible, which remains to be seen, due to its "-ability." The visibility of language is not exhausted by bringing the visible into view—once and for all—but it is an -ability that stays as such only through a moment of *with*drawal, which is what yet another co-word of "-bar" points to, insofar as "bar" also signifies "without." One can "always and again [immer und wieder]" visit that which remains visible,[41] since something of it withdraws with its appearing. It is the "realm of the possible [Bereich des Möglichen]" that withdraws in language's visibility and that therefore accounts for a double movement of with . . . and also getting away with. . . .[42] Introducing an interval between the "vis-ibility" and the "tang-ibility" of language, the "-ible [-bares]"—the bare possibility—makes them co-words precisely through that which withdraws; or, put differently, both words stand with one another through that which is with them as withdrawing. This withdrawal of the possible in "visibility" and "tangibility" makes these words yet another figure of the "with." Even more than that, the withdrawal of the possible seems to belong to the complex structure of the "with," since it is precisely withdrawal as such that enters a "with-one-another" and thus speaks with. . . .

Language's inexhaustible visibility lets the possible "co-appear [miterscheinen]." Speaking with . . . and entering a "with-one-another" (*Miteinander*) means that within such a "with-one-another" of those that are other to each other the "with" withdraws and thus lets them remain other, lets them dwell within "the realm of the possible." Visibility of language in the poem is the possibility of remaining other while with one another. The "with" is always also the withdrawal from itself, however, a withdrawal that co-appears as such, precisely because it is *with* a "with-one-another." Therefore, the "with-one-another" is permeated with the possible. It remains open. One could also say that the moment of withdrawal within a "with-one-another," granted by the visibility and tangibility of language, gives direction toward openings. As we have already seen with the stone of "Conversation in the Mountains," that which speaks does not *talk* to someone or something directly but speaks with . . . , and with that, it also withdraws into the realm of the possible, which, by way of that very withdrawal, mutely co-appears. Through the withdrawal of that which speaks with . . . the *possibility of an encounter* with the other is held open. In that way, the visible *s* in "seuls" makes the "seul" "seuls," yet it also withdraws those who are "seuls" from any sort of audible gathering (e.g., from a group of talkers that would dissolve solitude). The withdrawal of the others who are "seuls" remains visible and thus retains the possibility of an encounter. "With-one-another" means standing with the withdrawal of one another.

In one poetological note, Celan writes:

> The poem is inscribed in the figure of the complete language; but language remains invisible . . . that which actualizes itself—language—takes steps, as soon as that has happened, back into the realm of the possible.
>
> (Das Gedicht ist als Figur der ganzen Sprache eingeschrieben; aber die Sprache bleibt unsichtbar . . . das sich Aktualisierende—die Sprache—. . . tritt, kaum ist das geschehen, in den Bereich des Möglichen zurück.)[43]

This note further complicates the undertaking of analyzing the possible and the "with." Here, language remains *invisible*, and it seems as if language, insofar as it is invisible, also dwells in the "realm of the possible" out of which it steps when it actualizes itself through the inscription of the poem. Reading this note with what was discussed before, one could say that what withdraws with the "with" of the poem is not so much language as an invisible whole but the invisibility and thus the possibility of language. And yet, with the inscription of the poem, the persistent invisibility of language, forever withdrawn, itself becomes visible as withdrawal in what is inscribed with the poem: in its pauses, in its "meandering empty / hospitable middle [wandernde leere / gastliche Mitte]."[44] What accounts for the inexhaustible possibility of seeing language (*Sprache*)—the visibility of language—is the fact that language itself (*die Sprache*) remains invisible. Language, the invisible, the possible, and one could very well add the open (*das Offene*) to that—possibly open—series, enter a "with-one-another" of a poem by withdrawing from that poem. That is to say, the aforementioned double movement of standing with . . . and getting away with . . . is a movement of *becoming* visible, that is, a movement of *appearance* or, to be more precise, of "co-appearance [Miterscheinen]."[45] The withdrawal of invisibility is the withdrawal of that which remains invisible, but also the withdrawal of invisibility, thus clearing sight for the visible. It makes language co-appear as that which is withdrawing.[46] In that sense, the possibility of seeing language via inscription is the possibility of a withdrawal of the withdrawal—or *with-drawal*—with which the invisible draws forth as invisible. The withdrawal of the invisible makes language visible as that which withdraws, which does not cease to withdraw itself. The ability of language to *remain* visible can thus also be understood as its way of staying true to an opening, maybe even to a "hospit-able" reserve of the possible, which grants the possibility to perceive language for and of "the eye." Just as one reads up on something, *etwas an-liest*, one can look at the visible, *es an-sehen*.[47] Thus, the visible comes into view only momentarily, for a blink of an eye (*Augenblick*), or as an *Eräugnis*, that is, "bringing into one's enowning" (*ereignen*), and "bringing into one's view, laying eyes on" (with "eye" being *Auge* in German, thus *Er-Äugnis*). Before the visible withdraws into "the realm of the possible," a singularity becomes actual with the "with."[43]

Thus, the poem, on the one hand, is the site of co-appearance, a *written* site. Where it becomes "lapidary" in the inscribed word, language co-appears with the poem, which has the "character [Charakter]" of an "inscription [Inschrift]"[49] or an "epigraph [Epigraphie]"[50] that is "waiting for a near or distant . . . eye [auf ein nahes oder fernes . . . Auge] "[51] With this epigraph, the "epiphany of language [Epiphanie der Sprache]" happens as that which enters a "with-one-another" in withdrawing from it.[52] On the other hand, however, the poem is not just a written, mute site, since this withdrawal or "epiphany" is the permanent, invisible co-word of every "with-one-another," as it were. The poem as co-appearance of language always lets what is not written shine through, which remains to be seen. Its co-appearing "background [Hintergrund]" is "the realm of the possible" or the openings of language. Hence, Celan lets the note on the co-appearance of language end with an equal sign followed by "a blank": "language as co-appearing . . . background = [die Sprache als miterscheinender . . . Hintergrund =]."[53]

Due to its visibility, the poem therefore oscillates between a lapidary inscription and the openings that traverse it. It is the oscillation between the possible and its actualization, not either-or but both-and, a site of with and withdrawal, the singular, momentary (*augenblickliches*) event (*Eräugnis*) of the oscillating *vibration* of a "with-one-another."

Being blind to art would mean being blind to that which is stable, fixated, to that which comes in handy, and thus is bare of the possible. Blind to the visual aspect of the image,[54] to that which too easily gets caught in the web of the veil within the eye, the person who is blind to art is *able* to perceive language as visible. And it is perhaps this ability of the "with" that makes co-words in the "Conversation in the Mountains" visible: there, too, word of an ocular web (*Gewebe*) comes with word of a "moveable [beweglichen]" veil, and with the veil (*Schleier*), the streak (*Schliere*).[55]

∽

If "language [Sprache]," as Celan writes, is the "encounter with the invisible [Begegnung mit dem Unsichtbarem],"[56] then the question arises as to how language is encountered within the poem, how co-appearance is an *encounter*. It is precisely this question that leads back to the blink of an eye (*Augenblick*) in which language co-appears (*miterscheint*) with the poem, that singular moment before language withdraws "into the realm of the possible."[57] In what way can we conceive of co-appearance (*Miterscheinen*) and encounter (*Begegnung*) as a "with-one-another" (*Miteinander*)? And is a "with-one-another" a way of encountering?

We are brought back to silence (*Schweigen*), which con-sonates (*mitlautet*), which vibrates, oscillating between *stumm* and *–stimm–*: if one only *sees* language like Lucile, as an inscription (*Inschrift*) or epigraph (*Epigraphie*), mute and yet speaking like stone. The poem, in turn, is a way of speaking [Sprechart]," which is made visible by "the written, i.e. the silent [Geschriebenen, also Stummen]."⁵⁸

"Stepping out of language," writes Celan, "the . . . poem steps <u>opposite</u> language. This opposition cannot be sublated. [Aus der Sprache hervortretend, tritt . . . das Gedicht der Sprache <u>gegenüber</u>. Dieses Gegenüber ist unaufhebbar.]"⁵⁹ The "gegen-" in this note—a co-word shared by "opposite" (*Gegenüber*), "counter" (*entgegnen*) and "encounter" (*Begegnung*)—gives a hint toward the "with-one-another" of co-appearance and encounter. The co-appearance of language within the poem is first and foremost the encounter with the invisible that is also a *Gegenüber*, which in German signifies not only "opposite" but also "counterpart," in the sense that a person can be your counterpart in a conversation, a dance, or some other relation of "with-one-another." The "encounter with the invisible" means that language introduces a persistent counterpart, a *Gegenüber* with the poem that is unsublat-able (*unaufhebbar*).

And yet it becomes visible, always and again, with the poem, the epiphany of language, just as the stone steps into the realm of speaking *with* the epigraph, *with* that which is mute. The co-appearance of language and the con-sonance of that which is mute are aligned with one another insofar as both can become "tangible" with the poem, with a singular moment (*Augenblick*). In that moment of co-appearance and con-sonance, the unsublatable gap between language and poem, between muteness and speaking, is held open by "the with," as it were. Appearing with . . . and speaking with . . . does not mean that this gap is bridged, or that the mute is sublated into the realm of speech, but that the interval between them, as with language or the stone, enters a "with-one-another." This gap or interval, which remains open—this hospitable middle—makes language a counterpart (*Gegenüber*).

Entering a "with-one-another" thus means to co-appear as a *Gegenüber*, that is, to encounter. The poem is the site of an encounter insofar as it is "keeping-silent-with-the-named [Mit-dem-Genannten-Mitschweigen gestimmt],"⁶⁰ insofar as the unsublatable counterpart, "something absent," comes "near" and steps up "<u>close to you,</u> someone even more absent," thereby in*scribing* itself *with* the named.⁶¹ Thus, the poem cannot enter the dialectical movement of the strange (*Fremdes*) and the proper (*Eigenes*). The unsublatable relation that a "with-one-another" introduces opens the possibility of an encounter with that which *remains* counter to one, a counterpart. It stays out of reach, out of control and fixation. A "with-one-another" always and again holds the possibility of getting away with being mute, strange, counter. In that sense, it means differentiating "between strange and strange [Zwischen Fremd und Fremd],"⁶² and it invites us to stay attuned to that which is "facing us with silence . . . as the other [schweigt es uns entgegen . . . als das Andere]."⁶³

The "with" is hospitable. It lets the silence of the stone vibrate, as it were, the silence of the other, a counterpart. These characteristics are congenital (*kongenital*) to it, however, in such a way that it does not constitute a relation that would allow one to grasp or enclose that which is extra-human, the other, strange.⁶⁴ A "with-one-another" is not keen on being with . . . ; it is not a relation that is instrumental or that could be used for any purpose that transcends any with. . . . The blank, the invisible, do not fall under the category of negativity. The empty middle is hospitable, which also means open. The "with," its hospitality, introduces openness; it is, always and again, an opening, and that might be what gives direction (*Richtung*) to "the one who speaks."

~

In a note on Martin Heidegger's *Introduction to Metaphysics*, Celan writes about the connivance (*Mitwisserschaft*) of the author, as the one who "elevates the poem into the realm of the visible [der das Gedicht ins Sichtbare hebt]."⁶⁵ However, the author "is put up with as confidant only for as long as the poem is emerging [nur so lange als 'Mitwisser' geduldet . . . , als das Gedicht im Entstehen begriffen ist]."⁶⁶ Here as well, Celan is thinking with the "with," which introduces an interval into the com-posites of "con-science" (*Mitwissen*) and "connivance" (*Mitwisserschaft*) and thus renders the other(s) to which conscience and connivance open tangible. The other remains an unsublatable counterpart, and the author, as a *Mit-Wisser* who is con-genital with the poem, loses her privileged status once the poem enters a "with-one-another" (*Miteinander*), once it opens up and bares itself as know-able (*wiss-bar*) to others. "Every poem," Celan writes, "necessarily raises the claim to singularity, unrepeatability [erhebt notwendig den Anspruch auf Einmaligkeit, Unwiederholbarkeit]."⁶⁷ Just as language momentarily co-appears with the poem and becomes a counterpart (*Gegenüber*), the poem also becomes a counterpart for the author. Now "an erratic language-block, it faces you with silence [ein erratischer Sprachblock, schweigt es dich an]."⁶⁸

In a movement of "radical Individuation [radikale Individuation]," language actualizes itself with the poem. This "self-realization [Sichrealisieren]" is a "singular, unrepeatable speaking of a single one [einmaliges, unwiederholbares Sprechen eines Einzelnen]," as Celan notes.[69] This singular speaking does not coincide with the voice or the experiences of the author. The "Mit-" in *Mitwisserschaft* rather shifts emphasis upon the falling apart of author and singular speaking; it becomes an erratic counterpart, and the author thus gets the chance to encounter herself as well.[70] The poem remains open for *Mitwisserschaft* and is, for the moment (*Augenblick*) of a "with," not only vis-ible, but repeat-ably vis-ible,[71] since, as Celan writes, "the word in the poem [is] only partly occupied by experience [Das Wort im Gedicht (ist) nur zum Teil erlebnisbesetzt]."[72] The poem gives the reader the chance to enter a "with-one-another" with the poem and to encounter its openness.[73] It gives direction, which is not *direct* or *definitive*—hence the hospitality of "the with." But the question which speaks with the poem as to the direction of "being-together [Beisammensein]"—the question as to the "where-from and where-to [Woher und Wohin]"—does not find an end but remains "pointing into the empty and free [ins Leere und Freie weisende]."[74]

~

In *The Meridian*, words enter a "with-one-another" as co-words that share the interval with "co-" or "con-." Already in the earliest convolute of the notes that Celan drew upon for this speech titled "On the Darkness of the Poetic [Von der Dunkelheit des Dichterischen]," one can read words on the "constitutive, congenital darkness [konstitutiven, kongenitalen Dunkelheit]" of the poem that would become part of Celan's final version.[75] These co-words—or in this case, com-posites—enter an even broader "with-one-another" (*Miteinander*) in *The Meridian*: they co-appear with the conservative "Conciergerie" of Büchner's *Dantons Tod*,[76] with Büchner's "aesthetic conception [ästhetische Konzeption],"[77] with the accommodating "Commode" of *Leonce und Lena*,[78] and with the "concentration [Konzentration]" of the poem, which is said to remain "mindful of all our dates [aller unserer Daten eingedenk]."[79]

The word "all" in "mindful of all our dates" is itself a co-word, however, with the "very own [allereigensten]" of the "own, very own behalf" on which the poem speaks, and with that, it marks the poem's hope "to speak . . . *on another's behalf* [in eines Anderen Sache zu sprechen]."[80] With the intensification of the own (*Eigenen*) in the "very own" (*Allereigensten*)—which "remains mindful of all our dates [aller unserer Daten eingedenk bleibt]"—the poem in fact hopes for an "encounter" with the other.[81] Celan describes the way from the *Eigenen* to the *Allereigensten*—that is, the way from the own to the ownmost of all, and thus the way toward the other and its behalf (*eines Anderen Sache*)—as a movement of remembrance (*Eingedenken*). He also finds another word for this movement: concentration (*Konzentration*). A co-word, "con-" with "-centration" stand with one another in "concentration." But what does this center or centering mean "in the light of u-topia [im Lichte der U-topie]" that Celan will soon evoke in his further elucidations of the poem and the human, among others?[82] With this word of a "center," those of a middle or midpoint (*Mittelpunkt*) come along, while the history of the word also suggests that "centering" would be a practice of inter-punctuation: "puncturing" the center of a circle with a compass.[83] In the context of this "with-one-another," the German phrase that speaks of speaking "on an entirely other's behalf" could also be understood to signify speaking "on an entirely other's matter / cause [in eines ganz Anderen Sache]," in the sense of puncturing, piercing, or centering the matter or thing that is *with* the other. *Con*-centration, in turn, would signify in-*com*-passing, puncturing a con-center: a practice that, by introducing the "with" or the co- / con-, suspends the center that might be the matter of the other in its very midst. Since the co-middle is shared / divided (*geteilt*),[84] the in-com-passing movement of con-centration would mean taking steps (*pas / Schritte*) with an other, divisive steps that always and again pass a divided middle.

If the middle is shared/divided (*geteilt*), it remains in between the margins of the divided middle, an "open wound," as Michael Levine writes with respect to *The Meridian*.[85] And if this divide (*Teilung*) of the middle is thus a movement not only of con-centration but also of *Mitteilung*, then the middle remains the vanishing point of con-centration and stays divisible, stays open. It is in this way that the middle, the center, emerges as a vanishing point and steps into the movement of in-com-passing, always and again being passed, always and again in passing, getting away with the "with-one-another" that con-centrates toward this vanishing point.[86] Only by the division of the middle through the con-centration of the "with-one-another"—a division that always and again lets an other middle "interfere" and thus keeps it open—the reach-able middle can itself co-appear. It becomes an other in a "with-one-another." The center of con-centration becomes a counterpart as well and stays with those who share / divide it, who impart it, and who thus enter a "with-one-another" as well. Concentration as in-com-passing stays open for all dates, open for a "with-one-another" of dates, even dates to come. Therefore it would be the movement that lets the "ownmost matter of all [allereigenste Sache]" con-cur with the matter of an altogether other, yet without coinciding with it; it would be a way of falling on the same date while falling away from one another, *einander entfallen*, "loosed from each other."⁸⁷ And this *Mitentfallen* would mean staying mindful (*eingedenk*). Of January 20 (*20. Jänner*), for instance: on that date, Lenz walks through the mountains, the same mountains where the concentration camp Natzweiler-Struthof was built in 1941. Or January 20, 1942: at the conference of Wannsee, Nazi officials organize the annihilation of the Jews in Europe. Or January 20: . . .⁸⁸

If the poem speaks "in" another's matter, "in" the ownmost matter of all, then the other, who con-curs with the matter, speaks with . . . in the concentrating speech of the poem. The poem's concentration is always and again faced with the silent hope of the open, an "empty," "hospitable middle" that hopes and opens for a coming other.

*With* the "with-one-another," words step into a "with-one-another" and are always and again co-words with silence, with the other's muteness, with the dead, with other voices, with confidants, with the "extra-human [Außer-menschliche]," with the "u-topia" that speaks with . . . with every "with."⁸⁹

∽

Only when with your most own pain you'll have been with the crooked-nosed and yiddy and goitery dead of Auschwitz and Treblinka and elsewhere, will you also meet the eye and the almond. And then you stand with your . . . falling silent thinking in the pause which reminds you of your heart, and don't speak of it. . . . And . . . speak, . . . later, of <u>yourself</u>. In this "later," in . . . there remembered pauses, in the cola and mora your word speaks; the poem today—it is a breathturn . . . that's how you recognize it.—be aware of it—.

(Erst wenn du mit deinem allereigensten Schmerz bei den krummnasigen und mauschelnden und kielkröpfigen Toten von Auschwitz und Treblinka und anderswo gewesen bist, dann begegnest du auch dem Aug und seiner Mandel. Und dann stehst du mit deinem . . . verstummenden Denken in der Pause, die dich an dein Herz erinnert, und sprichst nicht . . . davon. Und . . . sprichst, . . . später, von <u>dir</u>. . . . In diesem "Später," in . . . dort erinnerten Pausen, in den Kolen und Moren gipfelt dein Wort; Das Gedicht heute—es ist eine Atemwende . . . daran erkennst du's.—nimm es wahr—.)⁹⁰

## Notes

1. Paul Celan, *Poems of Paul Celan*, trans. Michael Hamburger (New York: Persea Books, 2002), 161; trans. modified; and Paul Celan, *Die Gedichte: Neue kommentierte Gesamtausgabe in einem Band*, ed. Barbara Wiedemann (Berlin: Suhrkamp, 2018), 143.

2. Gilda Encarnação, *Fremde Nähe: Das Dialogische als poetisches und poetologisches Prinzip bei Paul Celan* (Würzburg: Königshausen and Neumann, 2007).

3. Paul Celan, *Breathturn into Timestead: The Collected Later Poetry; A Bilingual Edition*, trans. Pierre Joris (New York: Farrar, Straus, and Giroux, 2014), 123; trans. modified; and Celan, *Die Gedichte*, 229–30.

4. Paul Celan, *Mikrolithen sinds, Steinchen: Die Prosa aus dem Nachlass*, eds. Barbara Wiedemann and Bertrand Badiou (Frankfurt am Main: Suhrkamp, 2005), 98. All translations from *Mikrolithen* are mine.

5. The noun "with-one-another" is my way of translating the compound noun "Miteinander," which consists of the morphemes "mit" (with), "ein" (one/a), and "ander" (other).

6. Celan, *Mikrolithen*, 142.

7. Note that the German *Schweigen* is translated with "silence" and that *Schweigen* is still closely related to "speaking" (*Sprechen*). It is not "silence" in the sense of *Stille*, which could also be translated into English as "silence," "stillness," or "quiet." *Schweigen* implies the falling silent and/or keeping silent of someone or something.

8. In those verses, Celan's correspondence with Hans Bender resonates. Celan's letter to Bender from May 18, 1960, was published in the second edition of the collection *Mein Gedicht ist mein Messer*. The letters to Bender speak of the singularity (*Einmaligkeit*) and unrepeatability of the poem. Celan links this complex to what he calls the connivance (*Mitwisserschaft*) of the poet. Cf. Volker Neuhaus, *Briefe an Hans Bender* (Munich: Hanser, 1984), 35, 48–49.

9. Celan, *Poems of Paul Celan*, 141.

10. Celan, "On Both Hands," in *Poems of Paul Celan*, 155; Cf. Celan, "Tübingen, Jänner," in *Die Gedichte*, 137.

11. Paul Celan, *The Meridian: Final Version—Drafts—Materials*, trans. Pierre Joris (Stanford: Stanford University Press, 2011), 3; Paul Celan, *Der Meridian: Endfassung—Entwürfe—Materialien*, eds. Bernhard Böschenstein et al. (Frankfurt am Main: Suhrkamp, 1999), 3. Since the page numbers of this English translation of *The Meridian* match those of the *Tübinger Ausgabe*, I will provide only one page reference for quotations from *The Meridian* throughout, unless otherwise indicated.

12. Celan, *Der Meridian*, 2.

13. Celan, 3.

14. Celan, 2.

15. Paul Celan, "Erratic," in *Memory Rose into Threshold Speech: The Collected Earlier Poetry*, trans. Pierre Joris (New York: Farrar, Straus, and Giroux), 279.

16. Celan, "In the Air," in *Poems of Paul Celan*, 201; Celan, *Die Gedichte*, 170.

17. Celan, *Mikrolithen*, 336.

18. Michael Levine, *Atomzertrümmerung: Zu einem Gedicht von Paul Celan* (Vienna: Turia + Kant, 2018), 86.

19. Celan, *Der Meridian*, xi.

20. Paul Celan, "Conversation in the Mountains," in *Collected Prose*, trans. Rosmarie Waldrop (Riverdale-on-Hudson, NY: Sheep Meadow Press, 1986), 17–22, 20; and Paul Celan, "Gespräch im Gebirg," in *Der Meridian und andere Prosa* (Frankfurt am Main: Suhrkamp, 1988), 26.

21. Celan, *Die Gedichte*, 119.

22. Celan, "Conversation in the Mountains," 19.

23. Paul Celan, "Streak," trans. John Felstiner, in *Paul Celan: Poet, Survivor, Jew* (New Haven, CT: Yale University Press, 1995), 97–98; Celan, *Die Gedichte*, 100.

24. Celan, *Die Gedichte*, 747; my translation.

25. Celan, 430; my translation.

26. Celan, "Erratic," in *Memory Rose*, 279; trans. modified; and Celan, *Die Gedichte*, 142.

27. Werner Hamacher, "HÄM: Ein Gedicht Celans mit Motiven Benjamins," in *Keinmaleins: Texte zu Celan* (Frankfurt am Main: Klostermann, 2019), 13–55, 20.

28. Celan, *Der Meridian*, 127.

29. Celan, 127; my translation.

30. See Celan, 138.

31. Celan, 98.

32. See Felstiner's translation in *Paul Celan*, 97–98; Celan, *Die Gedichte*, 100.

33. Celan, "Conversation in the Mountains," 20; Celan, "Gespräch im Gebirg," 26.

34. Celan writes of "the written, i.e. the silent [Geschriebenen, also Stummen]." Celan, *Der Meridian*, 107.

35. The recurring address to "Ladies and Gentlemen" throughout *The Meridian* suggests multiple moments of departure in the speech.

36. Celan, *Der Meridian*, 2.

37. Celan, 3.

38. Cf. Hamacher, "HÄM," 29, 32.

39. Celan, *Der Meridian*, 3.

40. Celan, 20. This change of words is not reflected in Joris's translation since he writes "tangible" in both places.

41. Celan, 8; my translation. Joris writes "again and again."

42. Celan, 104.

43. Celan, 104.

44. Celan, *Poems of Paul Celan*, 141.

45. Celan, *Der Meridian*, 105.

46. In his essay "The Origin of the Work of Art," Martin Heidegger develops the thought of what he calls *Lichtung* ("lighting" or "clearing"): "Only this clearing

grants and guarantees to us humans a passage to those beings that we ourselves are not, and access to the being that we ourselves are." Heidegger, "The Origin of the Work of Art," in *Poetry, Language, Thought*, trans. Albert Hofstadter (New York: Harper and Row, 1971), 17–87, 54. Heidegger then situates world and earth within a "primal conflict between clearing and concealing" and furthermore thinks of the happening of truth as the occurrence of this conflict (55–56). Perhaps in echo of this line of thought, Celan's idea of a co-appearance of language moves with and away from Heidegger, since he is not concerned with ontology and the question of being, but with language.

47. Celan notes: "Someone who is conducting experiments, makes observations.—The poet <u>looks, looks at</u> [Wer experimentiert, stellt Beobachtungen an.—Der Dichter <u>schaut, schaut an</u>]." Celan, *Mikrolithen*, 101.

48. Heidegger's thought on the event (*Ereignis*) reflects upon the "Eräugnis" and unfolds it as "im Blicken zu sich rufen, an-eignen," which could be rendered as an occurrence of "calling to oneself in viewing, appropriating." Heidegger, "The Principle of Identity," in *Identity and Difference*, trans. Joan Stambaugh (New York: Harper and Row, 1969), 21–41, 25. In the event, being (*Sein*) and man (*Mensch*) are each appropriated (*übereignet*) to one another (31, 36, 39). Whereas for Heidegger the essence of identity is the property (*Eigentum*) of the event (*Ereignis*), Celan seems to move with and away from Heidegger's idea of a "relation of with" that is essential for the synthetic self-sameness or identity that happens (*ereignet*) and appropriates (*übereignet*) man and being in the call into one's view. In the poem "Heute und Morgen," for example, it is precisely not a lighting (*Lichtung*) that is "eräugt," nor is it a matter of bringing anything into view, but an "Eräugtes / Dunkel" without eyes: "Washed out / of aeolian sand both / sockets at the lower forehead-seam. / En-eyed / darkness within [Von Flugsand / ausgewaschen die beiden / Höhlen am untern Stirnsaum. / Eräugtes / Dunkel darin]." Celan, *Die Gedichte*, 99; my translation. And so too can "language" not be enowned because it withdraws. The "with" that Celan envisions does not allow for appropriation because with the "with" always and again comes a withdrawal from it: a co-word—a word that speaks with . . . —is not even proper to itself.

49. Celan, *Der Meridian*, 98.

50. Celan, 98.

51. Celan, 98.

52. Celan, 105.

53. Celan, 105.

54. Celan also notes: "Vividness = not something visual, but something spiritual.— . . . <u>Sound-image</u> (something different from impressionistic tone-painting [Lautmalerei], timbre etc. = namely a way of speaking [Sprechart] / Visible from the language- or speechgrille [Bildhaftigkeit = nichts Visuelles, sondern etwas Geistiges.— . . . <u>Schallbild</u> (etwas anderes als impressionistische Lautmalerei, Klangfarbe usw. = nämlich Sprechart / Vom Sprach- oder Sprechgitter her sichtbar]." Celan, 101.

55. The passage reads: "But they, those cousins, have no eyes, alas. Or, more exactly: they have, even they have eyes, but with a veil hanging in front of them, no, not in front, behind them, a moveable veil. No sooner does an image enter than it gets caught in the web. [Aber sie, die Geschwisterkinder, sie haben, Gott sei's geklagt, keine Augen. Genauer: sie haben, auch sie, Augen, aber da hängt ein Schleier davor, nicht davor, nein, dahinter, ein beweglicher Schleier; kaum tritt ein Bild ein, so bleibts hängen im Geweb.]" Celan, "Conversation in the Mountains," 18; Celan, *Gespräch im Gebirg*, 24.

56. Celan, *Der Meridian*, 107.
57. Celan, 104.
58. Celan, 107.
59. Celan, 104–5.
60. Celan, 146.
61. Celan, 136. The passage reads in full: "Freud, Civilization and its Discontents p. 49: 'Writing is originally the language of the absent one' = in the poem something absent comes near, it steps up close to you, someone even more absent = [Freud, Unbehagen S. 49: 'Die Schrift ist urspr:üngl. die Sprache des Abwesenden' = im Gedicht wird ein abwesendes nahe, tritt es an dich einen noch Abwesenderen heran =]."
62. Celan, 7.
63. Celan, 98.
64. Celan, 84.
65. See Alexandra Richter, Patrik Alac, and Betrand Badiou, eds., *Paul Celan: La bibliothèque philosophique* (Paris: Éditions Rue d'Ulm, 2004), 352.
66. Richter et al., 352.
67. Celan, *Mikrolithen*, 10.
68. Celan, *Der Meridian*, 97.
69. Celan, *Mikrolithen*, 148.
70. Cf. Celan, 33.
71. Celan, 148.
72. Celan notes: "Another part is being occupied by the poem with experiences; another part stays free again, i.e. occupiable [ein anderer Teil wird vom Gedicht mit Erlebnissen besetzt; ein weiterer wieder bleibt frei, d.h. besetzbar]." Celan, 101.
73. Cf. Celan, 126.
74. Celan, 199.
75. Celan, *Der Meridian*, xi.
76. Celan, 2.
77. Celan, 4.
78. Celan, 12.
79. Celan, 9.
80. Celan, 8.
81. Celan, 8.

82. Celan, 10.

83. Wolfgang Pfeifer, "Zentrum," in *Etymologisches Wörterbuch des Deutschen* (Berlin: Akademie Verlag, 2013), 1601–2. "Center" probably derives from Greek κεντεῖν, meaning "pierce," "thrust," or "stitch."

84. Thomas Schestag points out that "Meridian" is a "gaping" or "*klaffendes*" word, insofar as it con-centrates the celestial and the geographic meridian. Schestag, *buk*: *Paul Celan* (Grafrath: Boer Verlag, 2015), 5.

85. Michael Levine, *A Weak Messianic Power: Figures of a Time to Come in Benjamin, Derrida, and Celan* (New York: Fordham University Press, 2013), 41.

86. The middle (*Mitte*) or center therefore is not equidistant from two extremes or ends, but gets away with an-other middle, a divided or shared middle. Werner Hamacher writes in "*Tò autó, das Selbe,——*": "Sie [die Mitte] bleibt die wandernde, sich er-andernde, bleibt die leere und darum die gastliche, die bei sich als anderer unterkommt und, was immer in sie eintreten mag, als Gast bei sich aufnimmt, weil sie diese Mitte auch dort bleibt, wo sie nie zuvor gewesen ist und niemals je sein wird." Hamacher, "*Tò autó, das Selbe,— —,*" in *Keinmaleins*, 181–208, 192.

87. Celan, *Poems of Paul Celan*, 161.

88. In his essay "Shibboleth," Jacques Derrida writes on the iterability of data or "gifts" in Celan's poetry: "Innumerable gifts, ciphered beyond counting by ever so many poems, we will not cite them." Derrida, "Shibboleth: For Paul Celan," in *Sovereignties in Question: The Poetics of Paul Celan* (New York: Fordham University Press, 2005), 1–64, 43.

89. Celan, *Der Meridian*, 10.

90. Celan, 127.

**Positions**

Chapter 9

# Occupiability

SARAH STOLL, TRANS. AIDA FENG

The Poem as an Interlinear Version:
"The poem is, in its own way, occupiable."

In a draft version of his acceptance speech for the Georg Büchner Prize in 1960, Paul Celan writes:

> The poem . . . wants to be understood, it offers itself up to an interlinear version . . . the poem carries, *as* poem, the possibility of the interlinear version, both real and virtual; in other words: the poem is in its own way *occupiable*.[1]

> (Das Gedicht will . . . verstanden sein, es bietet sich zur Interlinearversion dar . . . das Gedicht, *als* Gedicht, [bringt] die Möglichkeit der Interlinearversion mit, realiter und virtualiter; mit andern Worten: das Gedicht ist, auf eine ihm eigene Weise, *besetzbar*.)

The technicist term of an "interlinear version," which denotes a word-for-word translation standing between the lines of the source text that does not aim at a cohesive, grammatically correct text in the target language, but rather has to follow the structure of the source language and proposes corresponding equivalents for single words and often also multiple alternatives for one word as an aid to understanding the source text, is particularly noticeable and appears in the midst of Celan's literary language like a peculiar foreign body.[2] A similar relationship between the notion "interlinear version" and the language that surrounds it can be found at the end of Walter Benjamin's essay "The Task of the Translator," appearing as the introduction to his 1923 translations of Baudelaire, which develops the "great motif of integrating many tongues into one true language," and which perhaps allows for the juxtaposition of excerpts from both Celan and Benjamin that are centered around this term.[3] Benjamin writes:

> Hölderlin's translations from Sophocles were his last work; in them meaning plunges from abyss to abyss until it threatens to become lost in the bottomless depths of language. There is, however, a stop. It is vouchsafed in Holy Writ alone, in which meaning has ceased to be the watershed for the flow of language and the flow of revelation. Where the literal quality of the text takes part directly, without any mediating sense, in true language, in the Truth, or in doctrine, this text is unconditionally translatable. To be sure, such translation no longer serves the cause of the text, but rather works in the interest of languages. This case demands boundless confidence in the translation, so that just as language and revelation are joined without tension in the original, the translation must write literalness with freedom in the shape of an *interlinear version*. For to some degree, all great texts contain their potential translation between the lines; this is true above all of sacred writings. The *interlinear version* of the Scriptures is the prototype or ideal of all translation.[4]

Drawing from the biblical story of the Tower of Babel, Benjamin's philosophy of language considers the potential translation into all existing languages as a remembrance of the one forgotten language.[5] According to the story, all humans once spoke the same language up until the Babylonian confusion of tongues; following their dispersion, all languages remained incomplete, striving ever since for their complements, which Benjamin describes as a *supplementation (Ergänzung)* of languages—in the sense that "the way of meaning . . . is supplemented in its relation to what is meant"—in order to regain their original condition, which allowed for universal understanding among humans. The supplementation of languages in their "ways of meaning" does not concern an already given sense that is expressed in different ways in various languages, but rather a surplus of sense, or something other than sense that can only come to light in the mutual supplementation of different ways of meaning.⁵ The supplementation of languages, however, takes place in a negative way: translation opens up the target language to that of the so-called original, in a specifically inward motion, that is to say, as a movement aiming at the target language's very own disfiguration, in that the structure of the foreign language of the original is "displaced" ("versetzt," "verpflanzt") into the language of translation, penetrates it and thereby breaks open its "decayed barriers" from within.⁷ The specific shape of the *interlinear version* as a "virtual translation between the lines," which Benjamin comes to address only at the very end of his essay as an "ideal of all translation," denotes the vanishing point to which Benjamin's considerations are drawn. The interlinear version appears as the most radical form of translation in that it offers a view of the unique syntactic and semantic characteristics of the original, of its way of thinking language, while arriving at no closure or unity by itself. While an original text and its translation can be juxtaposed as two independent formations, since their respective semantic and syntactic unities are ensured, the interlinear version finds itself necessarily dependent on the original, having been placed in-between its lines. The interlinear version is revealed to be structurally different from the translation: rather than detaching itself from the source text and transferring it to a new location over the abyss that yawns between the languages, with the interlinear version, the times and places of reading in different languages do not stand apart from each other. The interlinear version does not even give the appearance of yielding a self-standing sense as it is demanded by a false conception of translation; every single word in it remains bound to a corresponding word in the source text. This structural disparity also affects the process of reading this hybrid formation: losing its linear temporality and becoming akin to studying, it tilts over vertically from word to word, from line to line.⁸

When Celan connects the term *interlinear version* with that of *occupiability* (*Besetzbarkeit*), however, he goes a step further than Benjamin in drawing the two places of reading together more narrowly. *Be*-setz*ung* (occupation) no longer takes place *between* the lines and words of the original but *on* and *in* the words of the original itself. The tilting from line to line, from word to word, becomes, for Celan, the tilting of the word itself. Occupiability is thus introduced as a new linguistic form that allows the poem itself to appear as translation, as an interlinear version, rendering unthinkable the subordination of the original and the translated text in the name of a theory of imitation whose impossibility Benjamin has already clarified.⁹ The possibility of occupying an already-occupied place, with the aim of holding it open, presupposes peculiar linguistic properties that Celan himself describes as "empty lines," not in a factual sense, but as a characteristic to be imagined "spatially" and "temporally."¹⁰

### The Poem as Conversation (*Gespräch*) and a Search for Reality: "unoccupiable // I and you, too . . ."

In his "Bremen Address," held two years before *The Meridian*, Celan highlights a particular aspect of conversation that, for him, always presents itself as one between languages:

> Poems . . . are underway: they are heading toward something.
>     Toward what? Toward something standing open, *occupiable*, perhaps toward an *addressable you*, toward *an addressable reality*. Such realities, I think, are at stake in a poem. . . . They are the efforts of someone who, overarced by stars that are human handiwork, and who, shelterless in this till now undreamt-of sense and thus most uncannily in the open, *goes with his very being to language*, stricken by and seeking reality.¹¹

> (Gedichte sind . . . unterwegs: sie halten auf etwas zu.
>     Worauf? Auf etwas Offenstehendes, *Besetzbares*, auf ein *ansprechbares Du* vielleicht, auf eine *ansprechbare Wirklichkeit*. Um solche Wirklichkeiten geht es, so denke ich, dem Gedicht. . . . Es sind die Bemühungen dessen, der, überflogen von Sternen, die Menschenwerk sind, der, zeltlos auch in diesem bisher ungeahnten Sinne und damit auf das unheimlichste im Freien, *mit seinem Dasein zur Sprache geht*, wirklichkeitswund und Wirklichkeit suchend.)

It is the reality-promising *addressability* of a "you" as a fundamental presupposition of dialogue, which appears in the form of *occupiability* in this quote. The inclusion of a "you," for the sake of whom the poet "goes with his very being to language [mit seinem Dasein zur Sprache geht]," distinguishes Celan's conception of translation from that of Benjamin's. Whereas Benjamin preliminarily leaves aside speakers and addressees—"since speakers and their audience occur only *because of* language, and *as* its functional extreme"¹²—Celan draws these "extremes" into his thinking of occupiability from the very beginning. Whereas the "you" for Benjamin takes on the position of the translated, as opposed to the translation, in view of a quasi-transcendental linguisticality (*Sprachlichkeit*), Celan does not simply abstract the "you," seeing it as a mere "position" in language, from language. It is precisely the "you" whose occupiability—both potential and factual—co-constitutes language. Whereas Benjamin, in his translation essay, stays his course for language alone, Celan holds course not only for this ("going with his very being to language") but also for a singular direction, a "you" that is not reducible to language, a move that shifts his poetics into a particular tension.

The demand for enabling "true understanding" in the interlinear version of the poem therefore deals not first and foremost with an understanding of the poem, but rather calls for the poem to be viewed as the locus of understanding in the form of a conversation whose positions are not yet occupied, but whose possibility of occupation is nevertheless sought after by the poem.¹³ A particular aspect from Celan's poetics of conversation is suggestive: the positions of "I" and "you" are not simply presented as analogous to those belonging to the original and translated text; they do not appear secured. Translation no longer shows up here as merely taking place between subjects and their speech, but instead as the extreme case of translation, a translation that emerges from not-speaking. The poem that is an address sets up a "you," in that it first presupposes something that is addressable, which only then allows the poem to constitute itself as address. The firmness of this direction, the "holding-course" (*Zuhalten*) is shown to be breached by the openness of the "for something" (*auf etwas*). The "you" as something occupiable seems entirely given over to the address, but the address in fact does not hold power over it and has not even reached it yet. The difficulty of "hold[ing] course for that occupiable distance" of a "you," only to arrive "close to something open and free," shows up in almost all of Celan's poems. Oftentimes, it is a "desperate conversation," a desperate "setting-course toward" the, as one of the lines in Celan's poem "Open Glottis" puts it, "uncathectable [unbesetzbar] // I and you, too."¹⁴

## *Häm*: Inhibition (*Hemmung*) and Placelessness (*Stellenlosigkeit*)

When Werner Hamacher reads Paul Celan's "Aus dem Moorboden" ("From the Moorfloor") in his text "HÄM," he sheds light particularly on the first aspect of Celan's radicalized idea of translation as occupiability and a tilting of the word itself as discussed above. Hamacher's reading concentrates on a "half-word" inside which an occupiable "empty line" of the sort Celan bespeaks is hidden:[15] "'Häm' is not one. It is not one word, not a nominal unit, but a 'multi-site' [vielstellige] complex of possible words and, moreover, a word in which each word is broken off . . . as an an-economic 'word,' as 'word' before any determinate historical or national language—be it Greek, Middle High German, Yiddish or Hebrew—before any political or linguistic-political community, before any community with its 'self,' its home or 'Häm.'"[16] The "word-stump" that exposes its "open- and halfness," which is closely tied to "Celan's use of the line-break," opens the language of the poem by functioning as an occupiable empty line: the language that inhabits the poem—the German language, Celan's mother-turned-murderer tongue—becomes inhibited by the broken-off word,[17] "Häm," which, for Hamacher, directly speaks its inhibition in that it transcribes the sound made by "clearing one's throat."[18] Yet, precisely in its withdrawal, disfiguration, and displacement, in its borderline dysfunctionality, this language can place itself in relation to other languages. It is the *circumcision of the word* (see Celan: "Einem der vor der Tür stand") that makes possible its "manifold semantic determinations," given that "Häm" can "speak in many tongues and idioms and take on many meanings."[19] Over the course of seven pages, Werner Hamacher collects meanings ranging from the "Greek, [h]aima" (αἷμα; blood) to the "Middle High German . . . *haem*," the "Yiddish 'Heym' [היים], the homeward bound," the Hebrew "'Em' [אם], signifying 'mother,'" and "once again [the] Greek *Hem*" (ἡμι-)—the prefix *half*—the French *aimée*, and the English *aim*, and so on.[20] In this way, Hamacher develops the translation-constellations set off by the half-word "Häm" as a communication or a dispute among the meanings that arise in the various languages evoked, meanings that "do not correspond with each other, but rather controvert one another."[21] And it is only in this most extreme tension that the poem seems to begin to speak.

More than the broken, inhibited word *Häm*, what enables Hamacher's reading is the inhibition of the German language in the poem that hinders any decision for *one* national language or for national languages *at all*. The fact that *Häm* can offer and bare itself as an "empty line" is, in the context of the poem, only possible through its grammatical (dis-)placement and (dis-)figuration, its occupiability on a syntactic level. With its mere infinitive constructions, all of which stand in connection to the infinitive "to climb" (*steigen*) in the second line, it is not only that the positions of "I" and "you" are not yet given in the poem; for the poem also sets up no clear position of subject or object, which is why, according to Hamacher, it carries the tone of a "memorial" or an "imperative":[22]

> FROM THE MOORFLOOR to
> climb into the sans-image,
> a Häm
> in the gun barrel hope,
> the aim, like impatience, mature,
> in it.
>
> Village air, rue Tournefort.[23]
>
> (AUS DEM MOORBODEN ins
> Ohnebild steigen,
> ein Häm
> im Flintenlauf Hoffnung,
> das Ziel, wie Ungeduld mündig,
> darin.
>
> Dorfluft, rue Tournefort.)

The ambiguity in syntax that is evoked through the infinitive constructions leaves open the question of whether the lines and the line pairs marked off by the first two commas each possess their own subject. In lines 1 and 2, the subject remains undetermined. It is possible, however, that the lines refer to the wish (*Wunsch*) for an "I" that is indicated in this way. In lines 3 and 4, the subject may appear to be "Häm"; in line 5, "das Ziel"; and in line 6, the "Dorfluft." Thus, it remains an open issue as to whether the lines are loosely juxtaposed, standing next to each other independently, nearly unconnected, and separated from one another, or whether all the above-mentioned possible subject positions are related to the "Häm" that is found in the third line in the middle of the poem's first part, which thus stands in connection with each of the five remaining lines (of the first verse) and forms their node or knot, marking a quasi-decentralized center of the poem. It is this very grammatical disfiguration and displacement that leads to a situation where *Häm*, as Hamacher reads it, can be both the "projectile" in the gun barrel *hope* as well as its "explosive" and "aim," in addition to—as I would like to add to Hamacher's reading—the remembered or conjured subject of "climbing." The fact that *Häm* does not exist as a word in any language, but merely as a syllable, a half-word, released from its wholeness by the line break that issues into emptiness (the Greek meaning of *hem*, half, designates, somewhat self-reflexively, this halfness), just underscores the uncertainty of its meaning and, consequently, the possibility of its manifold grammatical occupation. Both the semantic and syntactic aspects are interlocked, and they are not available separately from each other. Occupiability is therefore generated on the one hand semantically, through the inhibition of the German language, the word's syllabic character (*Silbigkeit*) and its opening up to other languages, and, on the other hand, syntactically through grammatical indetermination.

As an *unfinished* "intermediate being" with "blurred" semantic contours, *Häm*, for Hamacher, approaches "a shape again and again over deflected and fractured ways, and it does so only partially and inchoately with each reading attempt."[24] *Häm* arises, following Hamacher, like Kafka's female figures, from what Benjamin, in his Kafka essay, calls the "Moorboden" of a pre-world, and with it, the poem arises as well—for the *Häm* binds to itself not only the previous lines ("Aus dem Moorboden ins / Ohnebild steigen" [lines 1–2]) but also the ones that follow ("im Flintenlauf Hoffnung" [line 4] and "das Ziel . . . / darin" [lines 5–6]).[25] Climbing "into the sans-image" of "an image without image," and thus as an "image of an unimageability," *Häm*, for Hamacher, partakes in both the image-apt as well as in the image-less.[26] He can thereupon read the moorfloor as a language decomposed into its smallest syllabic elements, which, in facing its grammatical and semantic constitution as a sort of prelinguisticality, appears as the basis for every language, but as a language that appears before every decision for *one* (national) language. With these *linguistic particles*, the poem climbs out from the moorfloor.[27]

Werner Hamacher reads Celan's poem "Aus dem Moorboden" as a poem on hope, which presents itself "as a weapon, as a protective and combative device that is launched in a political and linguistic struggle, a struggle over language and politics, over the politics of language and the language of political history."[28] Although Hamacher writes that the hope "possesses the aggressivity of a handgun," a hoping or firing subject is not (yet) constituted.[29] Instead of a subject, the "Häm" in Hamacher's reading becomes a "gesture of impatience," an instance of speaking, as it were, in the poem that configures the poem's language as a temporal structure of intention.

The supplementation of the subject position by the word *Ziel* in line 5 is especially accentuated in Hamacher's reading, given that the *Ziel* is already contained in *häm* in its English form (*aim*) and therefore appears as doubled (line 3 and line 5). Lines 3 to 5 could therefore be read as follows: "ein Ziel / im Flintenlauf Hoffnung, / das Ziel, wie Ungeduld mündig, darin." The node, "Häm," that up until now has connected the lines and pairs of lines of the poem, becomes, at this juncture, knotted in itself. In reading *Häm* as *aim*, the *Häm* appears not only as the target and goal due to the double-meaning of *Ziel*; the *Ziel itself*, since it is now a target inside a target, appears as separated from itself and inhibited then and there: "The aim 'therein,' in the *Häm* of hope, would still be an aim *against* the aim, an aim on the way to something other than the one that is presented, and therefore an aim without an aim, an aim-less one, which follows the movement of the Häm,' the movement of de-distantiation (*Ent-fernung*). Therefore, in Celan's poem, *Ziel* does not signify a telos that defines the horizon of experience and language."[30] Viewing the *Ziel* as a target or aim, argues Hamacher, renders it "first an aim toward the aim" and thus indicates that there is not yet a target.[31] Only as a true, that is, not yet anticipated, target, as a "turn toward what is missing" does it become independent and consequently "mature" enough to speak. It finds its language only when released from itself.[32] The target's capacity for language and self, to which the word "mündig" (mature) refers, replaces any "target-language" in which the poem could arrive.[33] A target language no longer has to be "targeted" in the conventional conception of translation as bearing over the abyss and reaching a new shore "because it is [the target-language] itself that speaks," and in which the non- and multilingualism, the being-between-the-languages of the poem speaks.[34] The arrival at the *one* target language is hindered by way of the target (*Ziel*) wedged in its way. The focus shifts toward the target wedged in front of the *Ziel*, the temporary target-language of each reading. As Hamacher's reading shows, the poem thus speaks not only structurally but also thematically on occupiability as a radicalization of Benjamin's concept of translation.

What Hamacher does not talk about is the constitution of "I" and "you" in the poem. While an "I," as addressed above, is first evoked through the ways in which the grammatical indetermination of the poem allow it to be read as the wish of an "I," a "you" is to be found solely in the in-between stages of reading, which appear to correspond with certain languages, with levels of translation and occupation; it disappears, however, in other linguistic occupations. The wish of the "I" therefore consists not only in letting a poem, and with it, languages, climb up; the wish of the "I" consists in the constitution of a place through the language of the poem, of a home, an "at home," and this "at home" arises solely through its occupation by Yiddish. Only with this place, which the poem wants to let rise, can a "you" acquire a nebulous, albeit only temporary shape. As the "you," the subject of the climb along with the place, the Yiddish "Heym," emerges also the mother who appears solely in the occupation of *Häm* through the Hebrew (אם). The mother is attributively and affectively occupied, in turn, by the French occupation *aim*e ([I] love) or *aimée* (beloved). She even attains corporeal form if one adds to Hamacher's collection of meanings—his *Häm* lexicon—the English term *hem* (*Kleidersaum*). The hem thus comes into view as the *pars pro toto* for the mother. The German idiom *jemandem am Rockzipfel hängen* (to ride on someone's coattails) establishes the "I" of the wish as someone childlike and commemorative. The seam is also that which the half-word *Häm* has lost, namely, its limitation. A stripped shred of a word, it is constantly in danger of disintegrating, and of losing its place in the text, or becoming a mere thread (of remembrance). Only through the occupations that occur in reading is the thread of *Häm* recaptured and a textual weave produced.

Memories arise with *Häm*. It is Celan's murdered mother who is remembered as the one who arises in the poem. And, as seen above, *Häm* can lose its way of ascent in the poem and fall before the gun barrel as its *Ziel*. Both the mother and her murder are thus restaged in the poem. Yet another possible occupation of *Häm*, of which Hamacher does not speak, appears here, again through Hebrew, although now through the Hebrew *chaim* [חיים], life, whose pharyngeal [ח] (chet) disappears in the German transcription. Home, mother, life—the poem should offer all a place according to the wish of the "I," yet the memory stands in contradiction to this wish. Repressed, it breaks into the wish's reality when *Häm* loses its way of ascent and falls before the gun barrel as the target (*Ziel*). The poem appears thus as a *flip-flop image* of the contradicting modes of wish and memory, a *flip-flop image* of the constitution and loss of a "you" and its place, the poem. *Häm* falls with the mother, the hem, and life, and with it, the poem—through which alone a remembered "you" could emerge—falls before the gun barrel.

The Parisian street *Rue Tournefort*, which signifies a "forceful turning point," is the street to which Celan moved in 1968, during the era of the student revolts and two years before his suicide. The "Dorfluft" (village air) that is foregrounded in the last line and stands antithetical to the metropolis of Paris not only recalls the "moorfloor" from the first line.[35] The words contained within it (*dort* and *fort*, with *fort* redoubled in *rue Tournefort*) appear to echo the motion of Celan's finger that, in his *Meridian* speech, is said to search on a map for an inhibited homeland, a so-called "Herkunft" (place of origin), but does so unsuccessfully:

> I am . . . searching for the place of my origin . . . with a . . . fidgety finger . . . on a child's map. . . .
> None of these places can be found, they do not exist, but I know where, especially now, they should be, and . . . I find something![36]

> ([D]en Ort meiner eigenen Herkunft . . . suche [ich] . . . mit . . . unruhigem Finger . . . auf einer Kinder-Landkarte. . . .
> Keiner dieser Orte ist zu finden, es gibt sie nicht, aber ich weiß, wo es sie, zumal jetzt, geben müßte, und . . . ich finde etwas!)[37]

In the ensuing sentences, the place of origin is not just turned into multiple places, which already points to the biographical story of Celan's exodus and his homelessness; these places are, at the same time, also the places that all have a say in the poem, with their own languages, cultures and contexts, people, and historical dates. However abstract, complex, or deconstructed it may be, the poem's detours tell a life story. The languages of these places of origin carve out the poem's errant pathways—its cartography.

Celan's poem "Aus dem Moorboden" makes one thing clear in an exemplary way: like Benjamin's philosophy of translation, Celan's poems consider translation to be a displacement and disfiguration of language. Indeed, his poem "Aus dem Moorboden" seems to have lost the "decayed barriers" of the German language. The syntactic and semantic indeterminacy, in constellation with the syllabic word-stumps, opens up the language of the poem, although not in any way that would invite vague and arbitrary interpretations. On the contrary, the occupiability of Celan's poems appears, as Adorno would say, as an acutely "determinate indeterminacy" (*bestimmte Unbestimmtheit*), through which conventional readings are obstructed and opened anew.[38] Appearing as *determinate indeterminacy*, the structures of the poem sketch out entirely precise ways of reading while excluding others, first and foremost, that of a monolingual reading. The German word for occupiability, *Besetzbarkeit*, already embodies, to a certain extent, the concept that it names, for it carries in its midst a "spatial" and "temporal" vacancy akin to the "empty line" Celan addresses in his *Meridian* speech: in German, the syllable *bar* means empty, unoccupied. At the same time, the suffix *-bar* (corresponding to the English *-able*), suggests that something can be done and consequently points to the "structural possibility" of occupiability.[39] Occupiability, even in its ostensible gesture toward occupation, thus appears as dis-occupation, as a mode of holding open for as long as possible, as a conversation between conflicting meanings, as in- and ex-scription, as an *Er-* and *Entschreiben*.[40] The wounds of the poem and its language cannot be closed through one reading, one translation or occupation, for with the closing of its wounds, the poem falls mute. A closure of the wound would correspond with the decision for *one* language to the exclusion of all others and their affinities; a language that would be left behind, maimed and fixed in meaning. Historical places and times wander through Celan's poems with plural languages. They are languages biographically connected to Celan.

## Three Stories of Occupiability from 1967/1968

Next to *The Meridian* and the Bremen speech, three poems from the years 1967 and 1968 circle around the concept of occupiability: ". . . auch keinerlei" from the volume *Fadensonnen*, produced on May 7, 1967, at the university psychiatric hospital; "Ein Leseast," an unpublished poem from the period of *Schneepart* written August 21–22, 1968, in Paris, Rue Tournefort; and "Offene Glottis," also an unpublished poem from the *Schneepart*-period, written at Rue Tournefort in Paris on the same day as "Aus dem Moorboden." According to the commentary by Barbara Wiedemann in her new annotated edition, Celan had already planned a cyclical title for the *Sprachgitter* volume: "Unbesetzt, Frei, Besetzbar."[41] In these "occupiability"-poems, the concepts of "I" and "you" as occupiable are made particularly clear. That said, two of the three poems deal with unoccupiability. In *The Meridian* and in Celan's Bremen speech, occupiability is unequivocally positively connoted. It is tied there with the addressability of a "you" and with its reachability. Along this line of reasoning, however counterintuitive it may be according to everyday usage, unoccupiability seems to be negatively connoted for Celan. The terms are less an allusion to military operations and rather recall Sigmund Freud's theories of energy and drives.[42] An object, a "you," would consequently be unoccupiable or uncathectable (*unbesetzbar*) if it can no longer be loaded up with energies and affect and thus goes lost (*verläuft*) in its unreachability.

Anything that is occupied in Celan's poems can only ever appear as a stopover that is overtaken by other realities and thereby deconstructed; that is, it can only ever be a half, something broken or injured. This concept is shown in an exemplary way in the poem ". . . auch keinerlei":

> . . . THOUGH NO KIND OF
> peace.
>
> Graynights, preconscious-cool.
> Stimuli quanta, otterlike,
> over consciousness-gravel
> on the way to
> memory-vesicles.
>
> The grisaille of matter.
>
> A halfpain, a second, without
> permanent trace, halfway
> here. A halfpleasure.
> The moved. The occupied.
>
> Repetition-compulsion-
> Camaïeu.[43]
>
> (. . . AUCH KEINERLEI
> Friede.
>
> Graunächte, vorbewußt-kühl.
> Reizmengen, otterhaft,
> auf Bewußtseinsschotter
> unterwegs zu
> Erinnerungsbläschen
>
> Grau-in-Grau der Substanz.
>
> Ein Halbschmerz, ein zweiter, ohne
> Dauerspur, halbwegs
> hier. Eine Halblust.
> Bewegtes, Besetztes.
>
> Wiederholungszwangs-
> Camaïeu.)

"The occupied" (line 12), which simultaneously appears as that which is moved and thus as something that is in the process of occupations from within the framing concept of occupiability, is accompanied by a series of half-measures (*Halbheiten*): "Eine Halblust" (line 11), followed by "Ein Halbschmerz," which is immediately doubled ("ein zweiter" [line 9]) but has also only arrived "halfway here" ("halbwegs / hier" [lines 10–11]) in the poem. That the occupation, and with it the occupied, cannot last long is explicitly pronounced in lines 9–10. It is "without / permanent trace" ("ohne / Dauerspur" [lines 9–10]). This unsteadiness in its constitution is already named by the title itself, with ". . . auch keinerlei / Friede" (lines 1–2). In the transient place of the language of the poem, what is "occupied" only receives the status of "Erinnerungsbläschen" (line 7) that can easily burst and disintegrate. The "Bläschen" appear as an echo of the "Häm" rising from the moorfloor. In its communication with the poem ". . . auch keinerlei," "Häm" itself shows up as a memory-vesicle, as the smallest part of an injured memory of greatest fragility. Even the memory landscape (*Gedächtnislandschaft*) surrounding the memory-vesicle points to injury: "consciousness-gravel" ("Bewußtseinsschotter" [line 5]), "Graynight, preconscious-cool" ("Graunächte, vorbewußt-kühl [line 3]), and "Stimuli quanta, otterlike" ("Reizmengen, otterhaft" [line 4]) reveal a semantic field of injured memory. The way in which injured memory becomes thematic here has an autobiographical aspect. Celan drafted the poem ". . . auch keinerlei" on May 7, 1967, in the university psychiatric hospital. He struggled with memory problems, of which he later wrote in a letter from April 6, 1970, to his childhood friend from Czernowitz, Ilana Shmueli, who was then living in Israel.[44] The preconscious coolness, as well as the otterlike character of the stimuli, once again point to the moorfloor as a pre-world of a pre-language decomposed into its smallest pieces, out of which, once again, the poem can rise only in memory-vesicles. Even the *Schotter* (gravel) of the next line, related to *Schutt* (debris) and *Schütten* (dumping), points to this prelinguistic character, to something not-yet-established. The synonyms *Kiesel* or *Kieselstein* (pebble), which often come up in Celan's poems together with the attempt at constituting a "you," suggest, along with the allusion to ballasted train tracks, that the *Bewußtseinsschotter* or "consciousness-gravel" contain a "you" of stone that is no longer and not yet constituted, while simultaneously paving the way to memory in the poem. This way to the memory-vesicles and to the "you" keeps breaking off, it is "ohne / Dauerspur" (lines 9–10). The breaking itself, however, does not give up, in spite of the displeasure of defeat. *Wiederholungszwang* changes its meaning in the context of the poem from the Freudian term ("repetition compulsion") to the compulsion to repeat, that is, to remember.

With this necessity comes pain, which, however, can itself only half-appear, over and over, due to the injured memory that is offered through the vesicles. "Graynights" ("Graunächte" [line 3]), the "grisaille" ("Grau-in-Grau" [line 8]) of the remembered substance, its undifferentiated and shapeless quality, its "Camaïeu" (line 14), all point to the loss of color in that which is remembered. The gray tones and the colorlessness indicate the incompleteness, the deficiency, the bleaching of memories, which now only appear faintly vesicular (*bläßchenhaft*). Furthermore, gray is the color of the stone and the gravel from line 5, as well as that of the "you" that is reiterated with the stone. Yet, night, darkness, and distant memory are somewhat opposed in the last line with "Camaïeu." Camaïeu-style painting only ever uses one color, which then appears in varying nuances. This special form of monochromatic painting, however, excludes the color gray. Monochromatic works prepared in gray tones are designated as Grisaille, after the "gris," the French word for gray. In this way, the last line of the poem imposes a chromatic, if only monochromatic, accent. The constitution of the poem therefore appears as a way out of the preconscious, the night, and the gray, toward a (mono)chromatic memory-vesicle, which can be read as a correlate to the retrieved memory, to the simple occupation. The "I" thus appears in the poem as one that is remembering. On account of the "stimuli quanta," it finds no peace in the night, but in the poem it succeeds in rendering these stimuli quanta productive. Passing through the halfpains, the "I" of the poem turns from *Grau-in-Grau* to monochromaticity, to the memory-vesicles, in which even the "you" that is hidden in the consciousness-gravel has hope of constitution. The yet to be established place of the poem merges here with the memory that is to be reestablished. Writing appears as remembrance of a "you," and therefore as something passive. Although the poem appears to describe the condition of the writing "I," the germs of a "you" can nevertheless be traced.

## "Ein Leseast": Unoccupiable Capital

The notion that the constitution of a "you" in the poem accompanies the constitution of a place is also demonstrated in Celan's second occupiability-poem, "Ein Leseast":

> One reading branch, one,
> feeding the forehead skin,

one light source, by you
sleepily swallowed,
passes the hungry
host-tissue,

visual-aid, striated,
over moon scouring
backscatter-probes. On a large: on a small scale.

Earths, still and always, earths.
Cornea-covered
basalt,
rocket-kissed:
cosmic
orbital-show, and yet:
landlocked horizons.

Terrestrial, terrestrial.

One reading branch, one,
feeding the forehead skin—as if you wrote
poems—,
it comes to the postcard greeting—
back then, before
the bloodclotplace, on the lung-
threshold, yearward, from Pilsen,
yearover,
time-wild from so much
quiet unfurling:

*Bon vent, bonne mer,*

a flickering
brainlobe, a
seapiece,
is hoisting, where you live,
its capital, the un-
occupiable.[45]

(EIN LESEAST, einer,
die Stirnhaut versorgend,

eine Lichtquelle, von dir
schläfrig geschluckt,
passiert das hungrige
Wirtsgewebe,

Sehhilfe, streifig,
über mondbefahrene
Rückstreu-Sonden. Im großen: im kleinen.

Erden, immer noch, Erden.
Hornhautüber-
zogner Basalt,
raketengeküßt:
kosmisches
Umlauf-Geschau, und doch:
Binnenland-Horizonte.

Terrestrisch, terrestrisch.

Ein Leseast, einer,
die Stirnhaut versorgend – als schriebst du
Gedichte –,
er trifft auf den Kartengruß auf,
damals, vorm
Blutklumpenort, auf der Lungen-
schwelle, jahrhin, aus Pilsen,
jahrüber,
zeitwild von soviel
Leisegepreßtem:

*Bon vent bonne mer,*

ein flackernder
Hirnlappen, ein
Meerstück,

hißt, wo du lebst,
seine Hauptstadt, die
unbesetzbare.)

Here, too, the writing of the poem appears to be passive, though now explicitly so in comparison to the writing in ". . . auch keinerlei." The constitution of a "you" appears here as the occasion and motivation to write a poem at all. This reason is offered for the development of the poem: "as if you wrote / poems—" ("als schriebst du / Gedichte –" [lines 19–20]). The "reading branch" ("Leseast"), whose repetition in lines 18–19 marks the second half of the poem ("One reading branch, one, / feeding the forehead skin" ["ein Leseast, einer, / die Stirnhaut versorgend"]; lines 1–2 and 18–19) and lends the poem the momentum of a song, at the same time recalls the compulsion to repeat observed in ". . . auch keinerlei." Behind the "Leseast," which could intuitively be interpreted as a reading guide, a doubly passive concept of writing emerges. The writing of the poem first appears as a gleaning (*Auflesen*), indeed as a gleaning of the "light source, by you" ("Lichtquelle, von dir" [line 3]). Still, this gleaning does not occur actively but rather "sleepily swallowed" ("schläfrig geschluckt" [line 4]), which is underscored by the line break after "by you" ("von dir" [lines 3–4]). The direction of reception is shown to go from the "you" to the "I." The gleaning, which also seems to be a swallowing, occurs in a sort of preconscious mode between dreaming and waking, only half alive, or hardly alive. The words are administered to the poeticizing "I" the way medicine is administered to a patient. The writing "I" is hungry for it (line 5). In the poem, it presents itself not as a person but as "hungry / host-tissue" ("hungrige[s] / Wirtsgewebe" [lines 5–6]) that is dependent on the source-input given through the "you" in order to come into existence. At the same time, it presents itself—and this is yet a further step in the passive direction—as the literal recipient of that which is given to it through the "you." For it is not only a recipient in the sense of capturing the "light source" that comes from the "you" and is brought onto paper when gleaned by the "I." It also presents itself as the recipient of what they have written in this way, that is, as the reader of the text that lies before us. The "as if" ("als ob" [line 19]) simultaneously makes clear that the "you" itself is not (any longer) in the position to write poems. The "I" "writes" for—that is to say, in place of—the "you" and this way transforms itself from writer to reader.

The "you" therefore functions as a "visual-aid" ("Sehhilfe [line 7]), albeit "striated" ("streifig"), that is, a damaged or dirtied one, which enables the "I" that has been catapulted into the darkness of the universe and lost all possible orientation to attain a view of the earth appearing from various distances, and thus in the plural. This reading is supported by the designation of the visual aid as "backscatter-probes" ("'Rückstreu-Sonden" [line 9]) that measure reflected light just as passively as the "I" of the poem writes by receiving "one light source, by you" ("eine Lichtquelle, von dir"). Through its contribution, the "you" alone makes it possible for the "I" to get a visual hold upon—multiplied—"horizons" ("Horizonte" [line 16]) that indicate the terrestrial, the solid ground split into "Binnenland-Horizonte. // Terrestrisch, terrestrisch" (lines 16–17). Standing on its own, the repetition of the word "terrestrisch" in the middle of the poem initially accentuates uncertainty and incredulity as well as the subsequent confirmation of the discovery of secure inner territory, removed from water and sea. The "Cornea-covered / basalt" ("Hornhautüber- / zogener Basalt" [lines 11–12]), a hybrid of organic and inorganic nature, lets appear the terrestrial area as a region of lost, petrified, unconstituted or no longer to be constituted, *yous*. The attribution "rocket-kissed" ("raketengeküsst" [line 13]) also allows both spaces, terrestrial and cosmic, to merge.

A change in place occurs in the second half of the poem from the cosmic realm to an injured body, when the "reading branch" "back then" encounters the "postcard greeting" ("Kartengruß" [line 21]), and the memory shows itself to the "you" as a memory of its writing, its written greeting from Pilsen. The clash between the writing of the "you" and that of the "I," which is only made possible with the 'you" as its source, happens (in the present) "before / the bloodclotplace, on the lung- / threshold" ("vorm / Blutklumpenort, auf der Lungen- / schwelle" [lines 22–24]). With a disturbance of spatiality comes a disturbance of temporality: the temporal indices "yearward" ("jahrhin") and "yearover" ("jahrüber") appear as "time-wild" ("zeitwild" [lines 24–26]).

"*Bon vent, bonne mer*" (line 28) stands on its own, like "Terrestrisch, terrestrisch" (line 17, middle of the poem), and is further accentuated through its italicization. "Pressed quiet" ("[l]eisegepreßt[]" [line 27]), a concentrated matter that speaks no more, while nevertheless speaking through the poet, speaks here of travel at sea. The "flickering / brainlobe" ("flackernder / Hirnlappen" [line 29]), as the "I" of the poem designates itself, again refers to impaired memory. Like a broken, flickering lamp, the brainlobe stands in contrast to the light source of the "you." Instead of applying its impaired memory, it uses itself as a flag, which it immediately hoists to mark its place, the place "where you live" ("wo du lebst" [line 32]), as the "capital" ("Hauptstadt" [line 33]). The insertion of "a / seapiece" ("ein / Meerstück" [line 31]) reinforces the notion that this city can no longer actually be a city but instead must become a site, a site of remembrance, a site of the writing of the "I" and, with it, the "you." The mainland ("Binnenland," line

16) from the first half of the poem has not just disappeared again—at sea there can be no land seizure, no occupation via the hoisting of a flag. The flag that is hoisted in the "Meerstück" either floats in unbounded water or goes under. Only when the seapiece is read as a piece of the sea of remembrance can it go from an unoccupiable place to a place of occupiability, of remembrance, where the lost "you" ("wo du lebst," line 32) can live on.

Memory, which is injured, does not itself appear throughout the poem in the form of a story of a past time in Pilsen or in Celan's home in Czernowitz, the capital city of Bucovina that was occupied in 1941 by Romania. Under the regime of military dictator Ion Antonescu Romania had switched from an ally of France and Britain to one of Nazi Germany.[46] Memory takes place only suggestively, as a gesture toward the mode of remembering and its presupposition, the reception of a "you." The unoccupiable capital city is accompanied by an unoccupiable "you." It is unreachable but its reflections nevertheless serve the writing "I" as a source for the poem that lies before us. The "Lichtquelle, von dir" from line 3, the phrase "als schriebst du / Gedichte –," from lines 19 to 20, and consequently the poetry-writing itself all seem belatedly to come from the place "wo du lebst" (line 32), that is, from the "you," from the unoccupiable capital city of the brainlobe, from the seapiece of memory. Whereas the "you" in "Ein Leseast" only becomes unoccupiable by way of the unoccupiable capital city, the "I" and the "you" in "Offene Glottis" are directly marked as unoccupiable.

### "Offene Glottis": "unoccupiable / I and you, too . . ."

OPEN GLOTTIS, airstream,
the
vowel, effective
with the one
formant,

consonant-thrusts, filtered
by clarity clear
from afar,

protection shield: consciousness

uncathectable
I and you, too,

overtruth-
ed
the eye-,
the memory-greedy rolling
commodity-
sign,

the temporal lobe intact,
like the visionstem.[47]

(OFFENE GLOTTIS, Luftstrom,
der
Vokal, wirksam,
mit dem einen
Formanten,

Mitlautstöße, gefiltert
von weithin
Ersichtlichem,

Reizschutz: Bewußtsein,

unbesetzbar
ich und auch du,

überwahr-
heitet
das augen-,
das gedächtnisgierige rollende
Waren-
zeichen,

der Schläfenlappen intakt,
wie der Sehstamm.)

The poem's first strophe describes the physical production of a glottal stop, the inaudible sound that opens the body's pharyngeal cavity in preparation for speaking. The filtered consonant thrusts leave only this silent sound to sound off the poem. In place of the "Stimuli quanta" ("Reizmengen" [line

4]) from ". . . auch keinerlei," there is a "protection shield: consciousness" ("Reizschutz: Bewußtsein" [line 9]). It appears in place of the preconscious (see ". . . auch keinerlei," line 3) and the "Bewußtseinsschotter" (see ". . . auch keinerlei," line 5). Contrary to "Ein Leseast," the "temporal lobe" ("Schläfenlappen") and the "vision stem" ("Sehstamm" [lines 18–19]) appear intact here; a "visual aid" offered by the "you" is not required. The poem paints a largely undamaged picture of memory. The line toward which the poem seems to be moving, "Unbesetzbar / ich und auch du," lets the "I" and the "you" appear as intact as well, as lives that can be told in a linear way. Yet, nothing is told. What remains is the mere affirmation of their unoccupiability.

The fifth strophe is wholly set under the sign of the hypervisibility of a "commodity- / sign" ("Waren- / zeichen"). The strophe therefore stands in opposition to the surrounding ones that are haunted by inaudibility. Truth and commodity are at stake, landmark (*Wahrzeichen*) and brandmark (*Brandmarkung*). The "eye-, / the memory-greedy rolling / commodity- / sign" ("augen-, / das gedächtnisgierige rollende / Waren- / zeichen" [lines 14–17]) draws all attention toward itself due to its catchiness as a memorable corporate brand whose rolling can be understood as its circulation in the context of a marketing concept. When read in communication with "Ein Leseast," however, the trademark can also appear as a landmark of the unoccupiable capital city and can therefore be traced back to a concept of memory that urges a displacement from the automated, unavoidable, manipulative memory recording (*Im-Gedächtnis-Bleiben*) of the advertising logo toward the internalized recall (*In-Erinnerung-Rufen*) of the branded, toward an entirely different mode of remembrance.

In this mode, the inaudible glottal stop moves again to the center of attention—away from the visible, away from the audible. The initial sound that opens the pharyngeal cavity for speaking and thus prepares for the production of words is written in the Hebrew. As a transcription of this glottal stop, aleph (א) functions as a graphic indication with no phonetic value and therefore remains mute. Elsewhere within the word, though also at the beginning of the word, aleph can also function as a vowel. Aleph (א) is also the first letter of the Hebrew words "ani" (אני), meaning "I," and "at" (את), meaning "you" (female), or ata (אתה), "you" (male). The poem, with a Hebraic "occupation," therefore appears as an attempt to express an "I" and a "you." These attempts to utter consonants in addition to the mute initial sound nevertheless appear filtered, inhibited. That which is filtered is "clear" (see line 8), that is, it belongs to the realm of the trademark, the manipulated mode of remembrance. The "I" of the poem, which seems here to describe its own (memory) condition, knows what is responsible for the fact that "I" and "you" cannot be spoken. The words already get stuck with the glottal stop in preparation for speaking, that is, even before any sound or stuttering. The description of arrested speech as a phonetic description of the production of a glottal stop attests to a clear rationality. In place of the Hebraic "I" and "you," a German poem emerges; it intervenes in the constitution of "I" and "you." Thus, "I" and "you" indeed appear to be unoccupiable and intact but also untranslatable since the intrusion of other languages is hindered by the intactness of the poem's language. Differently than in "Aus dem Moorboden," where the German language of the poem is inhibited, and "you" and "I" are thus made occupiable, "you" and "I" are not addressable or reachable here. The only thing that remains is the affirmation of the unoccupiability of "I" and "you."

The constitution of a "you" in Celan's poems seems possible only in passing through an injured memory that is only able to stand the pain through its being injured, and only with the help of the injured, and that means occupiable, language of the poem, a language of halfpains. Occupiability therefore does not appear to be a fundamentally positive term. Only for the condition of the poet and poetry after the Holocaust does it appear as a possibility for remembering. The only thing in the poem that is open, that is, occupiable, is the glottis through which the air flows, the breath that can generate the sounds that form words like ani (אני) and "at/ata" (את / אתא).

## The Poem Has Shape: Lucile, the Occupiable

> Twice, with Lucile's "Long live the king," and when the sky opened as an abyss beneath Lenz, the *Atemwende*, the breathturn seemed to happen. Perhaps also when I tried to set course toward that inhabitable distance which finally becomes visible only in the figure of Lucile. And once, due to the attention given to things and beings, we also came close to something open and free. And finally, close to utopia.[48]

> (Zweimal, bei Luciles "Es lebe der König," und als sich unter Lenz der Himmel als Abgrund auftat, schien die Atemwende da zu sein. Vielleicht auch, als ich auf jenes Ferne und Besetzbare zuzuhalten versuchte, das schließlich ja doch nur in der Gestalt Luciles sichtbar wurde. Und einmal waren wir auch, von der

den Dingen und der Kreatur gewidmeten Aufmerksamkeit her, in die Nähe eines Offenen und Freien gelangt. Und zuletzt in die Nähe der Utopie.)

A third aspect of Celan's understanding of occupiability becomes apparent in *The Meridian*. Occupiability for Celan there becomes visible "in the figure of Lucile."[49] It appears as "jenes Ferne und Besetzbare" toward which the poem, but also Celan's speech, tries to set course ("zuzuhalten versucht[]").[50] The figure, who only appears two times in Georg Büchner's four-act drama *Dantons Tod* and whose second appearance concludes the play, marks another fissure in Celan's concept of occupiability, which has thus far been reconstructed in terms of the inhibition of language and its opening to multilingualism, as well as the constitution of "I" and "you."[51] The piece stages Robespierre's decision to execute former leaders of the French Revolution as counterrevolutionaries. Among them was Lucile's husband, Camille Desmoulins, who allowed himself the liberty of criticizing the ongoing *terreur*, the public mass executions by guillotine of those who were suspected of opposing the revolution.

While all three pieces by Büchner that Celan summons to the place of his speech make a mockery of art, each does so in different figurations: the trained ape in *Woyzeck*, the automaton in *Leonce und Lena*, and the marionette in *Dantons Tod*. Because anything that is artificial and runs smoothly seems predictable and dehumanized, Celan finds in Lucile the alternative projection for a creatureliness (*Kreatürlichkeit*) in art that his poetry also seeks. She can only come into appearance when the systematic nature of art goes wrong, when the automatons "break down—for this single short moment [versagen . . . für diesen einmaligen kurzen Augenblick]."[52] In her first appearance, Lucile is the one who shifts her attention. She does not listen when Camille speaks about art. Camille criticizes art for being an ideal reproduction, which comes to be the only thing of consequence in contrast to the events of the "erbärmliche[n] Wirklichkeit" because solely the copy, being an idealistic stylization, is still capable of drawing forth emotion. Due to the drastic nature of art, people risk losing their sense for the real, which would appear too ordinary for them thereafter. The exclamation "oh, art! [ach, die Kunst!]" that appears so prominently in Celan's speech finds its counterpart in the exclamation that Camille likewise makes: "Oh, wretched reality! [ach, die erbärmliche Wirklichkeit!]."[53] Lucile is not interested in art—in something so overtly drawing attention to itself, something overly visible, comparable to the trademark, the "Waren- / zeichen," from "Offene

Glottis." As someone "blind to art" ("[k]unstblind[]"), she shifts her attention to the speaking of her husband, whom she "love[s] to watch . . . talk," to the materiality and corporeality of his language, to his "shape," to his "breath, that is, direction und destiny," to the "human," to the "you."[34] She sees, not in the sense of a conspicuous marketing logo but through a change of media that she has carried out: she shifts her awareness from the content of the communication to the materiality of communicating, and still more, to the person who speaks.

In her second and last appearance, with which the play concludes, the situation switches from the initial, relaxed private conversation, at the end of which Lucile senses Camille's impending death when Danton delivers news of his own arrest, to the moment of the execution of Camille Desmoulins and his fellow convicted companions at the *Place de la Révolution*. The execution of Danton, Camille, Lacroix, Phillipeau, Fabre, and Hérault becomes a theatrical play for curious spectators of the public. As they climb up to the guillotine one after another, taking leave and commenting upon the execution directly before them, "some voices" in the audience react with disappointment to the play presented to them ("That's been said before. What a bore. [Das war schon einmal da! Wie langweilig!])."[55] The execution itself, Camille's death, is not performed; we learn of it, as Celan says, "two scenes later through a word foreign—yet so near—to him [zwei Szenen später, von einem fremden—einem ihm so nahen—Wort her]," through Lucile.[56]

*A street.*

LUCILE. . . . The river of life would stop if a single drop were spilled. That blow would give the whole earth a wound.—Everything moves. Clocks tick, bells peal, people walk, water trickles, everything—except in that one place. No! It can't be allowed to happen. I shall sit on the ground and scream until everything stops in fright and nothing moves any more. [*Sits down, puts her hands over her eyes and screams. Pause. She gets up.*] It's no good. Everything is just as before: the houses, the street, the wind blowing, the clouds passing. We shall just have to bear it.

. . .

LUCILE. Camille! Where shall I look for you now?[57]

Lucile cannot understand how the world could simply resume its course after the life of her beloved was taken, together with the "countless hundreds of thousands" others who had fallen under the sickle.[58] When her repeated cries of "no!" and her closed-eye scream—which shows that she has lost language—fail to alter anything, she replaces both with an "absurde[s] Wort," an absurd word that pays homage to the "majesty of the absurd as witness for the presence of the human [für die Gegenwart des Menschlichen zeugenden Majestät des Absurden]."[59] She cries: "Es lebe der König!," the penultimate word in Büchner's piece:

*Place de la Révolution.*

. . .

[LUCILE *enters and sits on the steps of the guillotine.*]

LUCILE. You silent angel of death, let me sit in your lap.

[*Sings*] Behold the reaper, death by name,
    His power from highest heaven came.
    You cradle, who rocked my Camille asleep and stifled him among your roses. You passing bell whose sweet tongue sang him to his grave.

[*Sings*] Souls beyond number, one and all,
    Under his mighty sickle fall.

[*Enter a patrol.*]

CITIZEN. Qui va là?

LUCILE [*reflects a moment, then suddenly decides*]. Long live the King!

CITIZEN. In the name of the republic!

[*The watch surround her and take her away.*][60]

In no way a "declaration of loyalty to the *ancien régime*," the formulaic phrase for confirming the old power becomes, in Lucile's mouth, a counterword (*Gegenwort*), which "cuts the 'string'" and appears even as an "act of freedom," as a "turning of the breath" (*Atemwende*).[61] Because Lucile follows neither the old ideology nor the new one and thereby places herself, singular and isolated, outside of both systems, Celan perceives her as an open position that is, according to him, occupiable. Like the poet in "Ein Leseast," she receives a "you," one through which she first speaks, with which she empathizes and dies (*mitfühlt und mitstirbt*). Dietmer Goltschnigg compares Lucile's self-sacrifice to Celan's writing of poetry when he writes: "If nothing, neither nature nor society, comes to a standstill in the face of the barbaric events of world history, then art stalls, the commemorating poem, by marking its formal aesthetics with an unmistakable caesura."[62] This caesura appears in *The Meridian* in connection with Lucile's self-sacrifice in the form of the breath turn (*Atemwende*):

> The poem tarries and tests the wind—a word related to the creaturely—through such thoughts.
> Nobody can tell how long the breath pause—the testing and the thought—will last. The "swift," which has always been "outside," has gained speed; the poem knows this, but heads straight for that "other," that it considers reachable, able to be set free, perhaps vacant, and thus turned—let's say: like Lucile—turned toward it, the poem.[63]

> (Das Gedicht verweilt oder verhofft—ein auf die Kreatur zu beziehendes Wort—bei solchen Gedanken.
> Niemand kann sagen, wie lange die Atempause—das Verhoffen und der Gedanke—noch fortwährt. Das "Geschwinde," das schon immer "draußen" war, hat an Geschwindigkeit gewonnen; das Gedicht weiß das; aber es hält unentwegt auf jenes "Andere" zu, das es sich als erreichbar, als freizusetzen, als vakant vielleicht, und dabei ihm, dem Gedicht—sagen wir: wie Lucile—zugewandt denkt.)

Celan says, "das Gedicht verhofft . . . bei Gedanken." Through the verb *verhoffen*, the poem is implicitly compared with a wild animal standing before the hunter's rifle, who, already sensing mortal danger, stands still to listen intently. The Middle High German meaning of *verhoffen* (to hope intensely and to give up hope) connects utmost hope and despair, the two modes that describe the risky moment of Lucile's *Gegenwort* as well as the *Atempause* in Celan's poems. Just as Lucile "tests the wind" in searching for the lost "you," so too does the poem. Along with "Häm," the *pars pro toto* of the poem "Aus dem Moorboden," this poem too appears in view of the barrel of the gun, like a hunted doe, as its *Erinnerungsbläschen (memory-vesicles)* rise and take personal shape. *Verhoffen*, "wie lange . . . noch"—"how much longer?" The suspension of breath, the resumption of breathing, is itself mirrored by the movement of occupation (*Besetzen*) and de-occupation (*Ent-setzen*).

## Notes

1. Paul Celan, *Der Meridian* (Frankfurt am Main: Suhrkamp, 1999), 140; Paul Celan, *The Meridian*, trans. Pierre Joris (Stanford: Stanford University Press, 2011), 140; emphasis in the original. For the remainder of this chapter, I will be citing the English translation; the pagination in both the English and German publications of the text is the same.

2. See German Wikipedia, "Interlinearversion," accessed September 21, 2018, https://de.wikipedia.org/wiki/Interlinearversion.

3. Walter Benjamin, "The Task of the Translator," trans. Harry Zohn, in *Selected Writings*, vol. 1, 1913–1926 (Cambridge, MA: Harvard University Press, 1999), 253–63, 259.

4. Benjamin, "The Task of the Translator," 262–63; my emphasis. Against the advice of Benjamin and his thesis of the untranslatability of a translation, Hölderlin's translation of Sophocles was translated into both English and French.

5. The Babylonic Talmud (Sanhedrin 109a) contains the saga of Rabbi Yochanan, in which the tower is destroyed in three steps: the first part was burned, the second sunk into the earth, and the third remained as a ruin. The surrounding air has enveloped the ruins in oblivion ever since. The ones who survived the punishment live in the ruins, but they have forgotten the event of the destruction. With reference to the Talmudic saga, Benjamin conceives of translation as an act of remembrance. Compare his concept of the "unforgettable." Benjamin, "The Task of the Translator," 16. See also Daniel Heller-Roazen, *Echolalias: On the Forgetting of Language* (New York: Zone Books, 2005), 230.

6. Benjamin, "The Task of the Translator," 257.

7. Benjamin, 258, 261. For the term *original*, see Werner Hamacher, "Intensive Languages," trans. Ira Allen and Steven Tester, in *Modern Language Notes* 127.3 (2012): 485–541, 493: "The essence of a language lies in its translatability—in this, it imparts not its contents but rather its impartibility to another language. Only with

respect to its translation, its status as translatable, does a text become an original; and only with respect to the language of the translation does the language of the original become language. The linguisticality of a language is defined not by what that language means, but by the other language toward which it points the way."

8. The tilting from line to line is also the literal translation of *interlinear version*. *Version* means in fact *translation*, but it is derived from the Latin *vertere*, what means *to tilt/to turn*, and this meaning has only survived in the compound *interlinear version*.

9. Benjamin, "The Task of the Translator," 256.

10. Celan, *The Meridian*, 140. Employing the term *interlinear version* as a mere "auxiliary word," Celan asks his reader to imagine "these empty lines as spatial, as spatial {–} and—temporal."

11. Paul Celan, "Ansprache anlässlich der Entgegennahme des Literaturpreises der freien Hansestadt Bremen," in *Gesammelte Werke*, vol. 3, eds. Beda Allemann and Stefan Reichert (Frankfurt am Main: Suhrkamp, 1992), 185–86, 186; Paul Celan, "Speech on the Occasion of Receiving the Literature Prize of the Free Hanseatic City of Bremen," trans. John Felstiner, in *Selected Poems and Prose of Paul Celan* (New York: Norton, 2001), 395–96, 396; my emphasis.

12. Hamacher, "Intensive Languages," 487.

13. Celan, *The Meridian*, 140.

14. Celan, 11, 9. Paul Celan, "Open Glottis," in *Breathturn into Timestead*, trans. Pierre Joris (New York: Farrar, Straus, and Giroux: 2014), 370–71. Translator's note: *Unbesetzbar* is also widely translated in Joris's renditions as "uncathectable," a Freudian concept that Stoll elaborates at a later point in this text.

15. Werner Hamacher, "HÄM: Ein Gedicht Celans mit Motiven Benjamins," in *Jüdisches Denken in einer Zeit ohne Gott: Festschrift für Stéphane Mosès*, eds. Jens Mattern, Gabriel Motzkin, and Shimon Sandbank (Berlin: Vorwek 8, 2001), 173–97, 185; trans. Feng.

16. Hamacher, 179–80.

17. Hamacher, 197.

18. Hamacher, 181.

19. Hamacher, 184–85.

20. Hamacher, 179–85.

21. Hamacher, 185.

22. Hamacher, 179.

23. Paul Celan, "From the Moorfloor," in *Breathturn into Timestead*, 373. Here, "ein Häm" is translated as "a hemo," and "mündig" is translated by "of age."

24. Hamacher, "HÄM," 175–76.

25. Hamacher, 174–75. See also Walter Benjamin, "Franz Kafka. Zur 10. Wiederkehr seines Todestages,'" in *Gesammelte Schriften* II.2, eds. Rolf Tiedemann and Hermann Schweppenhäuser (Frankfurt am Main: Suhrkamp, 1977), 409–38.

26. Hamacher, "HÄM," 178.

27. See Michael G. Levine, *Atomzertrümmerung: Zu einem Gedicht von Paul Celan* (Vienna: Turia + Kant, 2018).

28. Hamacher, "HÄM," 179.

29. Hamacher, 179.

30. Hamacher, 187.

31. Hamacher, 188.

32. Hamacher, 196.

33. Hamacher, 188.

34. Hamacher, 188.

35. Hamacher, 192.

36. Paul Celan, "The Meridian: Speech on the Occasion of Receiving the Georg Buchner Prize, Darmstadt, 22 October 1960," in *Collected Prose*, trans. Rosemary Waldrop (New York: Routledge, 2003), 54.

37. Paul Celan, "Der Meridian," in *Gesammelte Werke in fünf Bänden*, vol. 3 (Frankfurt am Main: Suhrkamp 1986), 202.

38. Theodor W. Adorno, *Ästhetische Theorie* (Frankfurt am Main: Suhrkamp, 1970), 265.

39. See Samuel Weber, *Benjamin's -abilities* (Cambridge, MA: Harvard University Press, 2010), 6.

40. I would like to thank Thomas Schestag for his suggestions on this point.

41. Paul Celan, *Die Gedichte: Neue kommentierte Gesamtausgabe in einem Band*, ed. Barbara Wiedemann (Berlin: Suhrkamp, 2018), 1158.

42. Jean Laplanche and Jean-Bertrand Pontalis, "Besetzung," in *Das Vokabular der Psychoanalyse*, trans. Emma Moersch (Frankfurt am Main: Suhramp, 1972), 92–96.

43. Paul Celan, ". . . though no kind of," in *Breathturn into Timestead*, 198. Here, "Besetztes" is translated as "the cathexed"; "Camaïeu" is translated as "monochrome."

44. Ilana Shmueli, *Sag, daß Jerusalem ist: Über Paul Celan. Oktober 1969–April 1970* (Aachen: Rimbaud, 2010), 75.

45. Paul Celan, "One Reading Branch," in *Breathturn into Timestead*, 386–89. Translator's note: I applied a few modifications to the translation so it better resonates with the author's analysis. The lines "von dir / schläfrig geschluckt" are translated here as "sleepily / swallowed by you"; I have rearranged the English words in order to retain the emphasis placed by the author on "von dir"; "Umlauf-Geschau" is translated as "circulation-gawking" (I chose "orbital-show," as rendered by Popov and McHugh, to continue the cosmic vocabulary from the previous lines); "zeitwild" is translated as "ensavaged" (my more literal translation puts emphasis on the temporal indices conveyed by "jahrhin" and "jahrüber"); "Leisegepreßtem" is translated as "pressed into muteness"; in the line "hißt, wo du lebst," I omitted the word "there" that appears in the English translation.

46. In August 1941, Antonescu ordered the establishment of a ghetto in the city, where fifty thousand Bukovina Jews were deported, two-thirds of whom would be deported in October 1941 and early 1942 to Transnistria, where the majority was murdered.

47. Celan, "Open Glottis," in *Breathturn into Timestead*, 370–71.
48. Celan, *The Meridian*, 11.
49. Celan, 11.
50. Celan, 11.
51. Georg Büchner, "Danton's Death," in *Danton's Death, Leonce and Lena, and Woyzeck*, trans. Victor Price (Oxford: Oxford University Press, 1971), 1–71, 33–35, 64–65, 70–71.
52. Celan, *The Meridian*, 7.
53. Celan, 4–5. "Oh, wretched reality!" from the Büchner quote is Feng's translation; elsewhere it is translated as "oh . . . . how pitiful reality is!" See Büchner, *Danton's Death*, 33.
54. Büchner, 45, 39. Celan, *The Meridian*, 3.
55. Büchner, *Danton's Death*, 69.
56. Celan, *The Meridian*, 3.
57. Büchner, *Danton's Death*, 70.
58. Büchner, 71. "Viel hunderttausend ungezählt," trans. modified.
59. Celan, *The Meridian*, 3. See Büchner, *Danton's Death*, 70. On the "absurd word," see also Sieghild Bogumil-Notz, "Zeitgehöft," in *Celan-Handbuch: Leben—Werk—Wirkung*, eds. Markus May, Peter Großens, and Jürgen Lehmann (Stuttgart: Metzler, 2012), 131.
60. Büchner, *Danton's Death*, 71.
61. Celan, *The Meridian*, 40.
62. Dietmar Goltschnigg, "Das 'Gegenwort'—Georg Büchner," in *Celan Handbuch*, 306–7 (trans. Feng).
63. Celan, *The Meridian*, 8.

Chapter 10

# For Shame of Language

DOMINIK ZECHNER

### Limits of Experience

In the paralipomena to his *Aesthetic Theory*, Theodor W. Adorno included a couple of pages dedicated to the fate of the hermetic poem at the end of which he addresses the poetry of Paul Celan. The concept he uses to characterize Celan's work is that of *shame*:

> His poetry is permeated by the shame of art in the face of suffering that escapes both experience and sublimation. Celan's poems want to speak of the most extreme horror through silence. Their truth content itself becomes negative.[1]
>
> (Diese Lyrik ist durchdrungen von der Scham der Kunst angesichts des wie der Erfahrung so der Sublimierung sich entziehenden Leids. Celans Gedichte wollen das äußerste Entsetzen durch Verschweigen sagen. Ihr Wahrheitsgehalt selbst wird etwas Negatives.)

This qualification of Celan's poetry invites further contemplation. To begin, it is striking how Adorno links the "permeation" ("Durchdringung") of language and shame to a movement of withdrawal: something cannot be grasped, fails to be experienced, and blocks even the route of sublimation that some would argue provides the very precondition of art. It is the withdrawal of suffering from experience and sublimation whose confrontation ensconces art in shame. By including the preposition "angesichts" to designate this very confrontation, however, Adorno seems to suggest that the withdrawal of pain from suffering does not necessarily entail the total loss of experience. If art is ashamed when "facing" the withdrawal of suffering from experience and sublimation, the very destitution thus acknowledged is still experienced *somehow*, otherwise there would be no reason for shame to arise in the first place.

A marker of corrosive self-reflexivity, shame sets in when the failure or insufficiency of experience itself is experienced. And since the very object of this insufficiency is suffering, the experience of experience's limits is not conceived as something per se painful, but "merely" shameful. As though functioning as a placeholder for pain or suffering ("Leid"), shame names the almost-pain that sets in when the withdrawal of pain from experience can no longer be experienced as something painful, as it's the very absence of suffering that causes this final suffering. Shame signals the pain about the inability to experience pain—more than that, it signals the pain experienced about this very inability to experience. This, however, means that experience is not entirely lost. As a matter of fact, experience restores itself in the shame that arises from the failure to grasp the vanishing object. At the very point where experience collapses, shame is recovered as its ultimate chance, as though in shame experience were to survive in the medium of painlessness. A transformation, perhaps even a translation, takes place here, as the inability to experience suffering morphs into the quasi-painful experience of shame. And would it be too far-fetched to call this transformation a process of sublimation?

What remains once experience witnesses its own limit as it loses access to suffering is the shame that occupies the very spot from where pain was dislodged. A first, provisional definition of shame, then, would locate in it the inaccessibility of pain: shame arises from a privation. It is the deprivation of suffering, the feeling that arises when the only remaining suffering is the loss of the ability to experience suffering. Yet shame accomplishes more than passively registering the doubling of experience in reaching its own limit. There is a certain linguistic "will" that inscribes itself in shame: "Celans Gedichte *wollen* das äußerste Entsetzen durch Verschweigen sagen." The emphasis on facing, gazing, and visuality marked in the preposition "angesichts" by which Adorno designates the confrontation of experience with its own collapse, thus moves toward the verbal—as shame does not remain locked in the state of merely *beholding* the diremption of experience but realizes a certain will-to-language: "das äußerste Entsetzen durch

Verschweigen *sagen*." The term "Verschweigen" here is confusing, perhaps even misleading, as it seems to imply a certain agency on the part of the poem. Not to be confused with a mere *analogon* to the aforementioned *withdrawal* ("Entziehen"), "Verschweigen" belongs to the register of a willful *withholding*: something is kept a secret, purposefully concealed, which implies the possibility of disclosing what is suppressed, articulating what has hitherto remained hidden and inaccessible. The willfulness implied by the *Sagenwollen* that Adorno ascribes to Celan's poems appears exaggerated, even doubled, in the use of "Verschweigen," which combines an initial desire to speak with the suppression of this very speech so that the will-to-language becomes the *will-to-language-as-will-to-withhold-language*, which, for Adorno, is the only remaining way in which Celan's poems can express themselves.

But at what object does this complex will aim? It would be a mistake simply to assume that the very suffering whose loss for experience is initially stated would subsequently become translated into the content of Celan's poems, articulated through concealment ("Verschweigen"). The object or intention of Celan's *Sagenwollen* is not the suffering in withdrawal whose witnessing infuses art with shame; rather, what these poems attempt to keep in language is what Adorno terms "äußerstes Entsetzen." Almost impossible to render in English, *Entsetzen* seems, at first glance at least, to circumscribe a particular affect: the sensation of being appalled, horrified by something. What gives cause to this horror? Is it the experience of suffering—or its sheer withdrawal? Or must *Entsetzen* prove to be irreducible to the registers of experience? At first glance, the "horrifiedness" introduced by Adorno seems to settle on the side of witnessing ("angesichts"), and thus on the side of art.[2] What the poem *wants to say* through the willful suppression of saying seems to be the very horror not of suffering as such but of what ensues when experience splits from experience as it experiences its own inability to experience, suffering the loss of suffering itself.

Beyond this horror-inducing sensation, however, the term "Entsetzen" structurally bears upon the very language for which Celan's *Sagenwollen* supposedly reaches. If his poems suppress speech for the sake of articulating "äußerstes Entsetzen," as Adorno holds, one may wonder if there can be any other way for *Entsetzen* to be articulated than through the sheer loss of speech. If we, provisionally, view language as a grammatically organized structure that logically presents a referential truth about objective reality, the elements of this language occupy designated positions within its structure. Logically cognizable and grammatically organized languages may thus be called posited or positive languages. In German, this register of positivity and positionality revolves around the verb *setzen* ("to posit"; the English "to posit" derives from the Latin *ponere* for "to put," "to lay," "to place"). If we keep the word's semantics in mind, Adorno's term *Entsetzen*, far from merely denominating an experienceable affect (e.g., horror), names the sheer corrosion or de-posing of the very language through which it seeks expression. The will linguistically to express *Entsetzen* thus discloses a peculiar wish: for *Entsetzen* is never reducible to a linguistic content, it always affects—it will always have affected—the very structure of the language that seeks to express it. Hence, the question arises: How could any language possibly "say" *Entsetzen* if the very possibility of saying anything relies on language's not being *entsetzt* (i.e., de-posed, undone)? If *Entsetzen* is indeed more than a mere sensation to be represented through poem's language, yes, if *Entsetzen* afflicts, affects, and vexes the poem's very language, thus ceasing to be its object, instead determining its very movement and reality, if *Entsetzen* marks the very condition of possibility of Celan's poetry—then the suppression of language ("Verschweigen"), as Adorno has it, cannot function as its vehicle of expression. A language dislodged or de-posed—*ent-setzt*—is contentless and grammarless, phenomenally unanchored and without reference, less simply illogical than ana-logical—a language that cannot possibly be repressed or concealed (*verschwiegen*) because it has effectively ceased to *be* a language (or has *not yet* become a language in any [re-]cognizable sense). *Entsetzen* is no longer a language or not yet one. In any event, it offers or contains nothing that could be the object of a willful act of withholding. If it is indeed the case that Celan's poems seek to say *Entsetzen*, that is so because *Entsetzen* marks their very own linguistic de-posing, the profound un-settling of speech affecting all the structural and formal elements that recognizably define a finite and positive language, a language used to transmit a given experiential content and *say something*.

If it is true that the ana-logic of *Entsetzen* besets its medium in such a way that it can never become the object of an expression without effectively un-doing its very possibility of expression, there remains no reliable way of saying *Entsetzen* other than through the very de-posing, un-settling, and un-doing of language itself. And this undoing includes the operation or action of deliberate *Verschweigen*—which under the conditions of *Entsetzen* becomes a mode of *Zerschweigen* (i.e., destruction through silence), marking a silence devoid of any content or possibility of retention and retrieval, detached from any controlling will. If *Entsetzen* is expressed in silence, this silence does not reflect a subjectively determined will; rather, it's the silence that accompanies language's radical self-deconstitution and decomposition. Even the phrase "under the conditions of" proves fallacious in this respect, however, for the movement of *Entsetzen* does not establish new conditions, as would be the case with "lawmaking violence" in the Benjaminian sense—it does not intervene to usher in a new kind of positive order.[3] *Entsetzen entsetzt.* In that it speaks the sheer undoing of linguistic structure, the occurrence of *Entsetzen* discloses the very condition of conditionality, but it cannot itself adhere to or offer any type of reliable condition.[4] A paradox arises thus, which Schiller, in *Die Braut von Messina,* elegantly captured by stating, "Entsetzt vernehm' ich das Entsetzliche."[5] There is no way of perceiving, let alone cognizing, *Entsetzen* other than through the very affliction by dint of which it corrodes one's ability clearly to perceive and logically to cognize.

"Celans Gedichte wollen das äußerste Entsetzen durch Verschweigen sagen." If Adorno detects in Celan's poems a certain kind of *Sagenwollen* or will-to-language, and if this will, as stated above, is in fact double because Celan's will-to-language expresses itself in Adorno's appraisal through a will-to-conceal ("Verschweigen"), effectively amplifying its striving into the will-to-language-as-will-to-withhold-language, we now observe that what is withheld, or "expressed" through withholding, is not anything that could actually be *spoken*. It's the very undoing of expression. "Entsetzen durch Verschweigen sagen" entails bringing to language language's very annihilation, the de-posing of its positionality. *Entsetzen* (dis-)articulates the moment when language itself breaks off from language, altering itself from within. In order to save Adorno's assessment from drowning in its own inherent and unsolvable contradictions, salvaging, perhaps, its one genuine meaning, it must be read not as a *philosophical* appraisal but as the articulation of a *philological* truth. Rather than reading the *Wollen* and the hidden agency behind the term *Verschweigen* as subjective functions, they ought to be understood as attributes of the very language at work in the poem. If the occurrence of *Entsetzen* were fully and entirely unfolded, there would be no factual poem to speak of—or any token of positive, readable language for that matter. This means that the de-constitution and de-posing, the un-doing of linguistic reality, is something that itself occurs as a process in concealment. Behind or beneath or within every linguistic entity; every phrase, clause, word; every syllable; every particle, there lingers the silent and silently destructive occurrence of its *Entsetzen,* essentially threatening, but through this threat also determining, its positive form. Otherwise put, in all expression there is a kind of un-settling un-doing at work that is concealed by the expression's own positive form—a form that effectively corrodes through the very process it attempts to conceal.

The problem now presents itself as to whether the concept of shame with which Adorno starts his assessment has become superfluous in the face of ("angesichts") an occurrence of *Entsetzen* that affects both medium and message to the same immeasurable degree. If shame arises from a privation, if it signals, as stated before, the deprivation of suffering that permeates the poem's very language, then what exactly is the relation between the poem's *Sagenwollen* that is determined by its *Entsetzen* and the "shame of art" that emerges as the phantom pain of an experience that experiences nothing but the inexperiencibility of pain itself? Arguably, "shame" is the name of the very language that remains when the positive linguistic order falters, ridding language of its experiential directedness and phenomenal, cognizable content (what Adorno calls "suffering"), thus forcing it to fold back upon itself, as it experiences, through the collapse of experience, the painless pain of pain's withdrawal. In shame, there pulsates a kind of *Sprachschmerz* (a language-pain) that mourns precisely the loss of world that language suffers, without, however, being able to continue to classify this suffering as "suffering," that is, as a pain that could still be experienced.[6] Shame names a language that experiences only itself, that is, its inability to experience. Yet even in its solipsism, it remains split asunder through the occurrence of *Entsetzen* by which it is inherently marked but which it can say only through the *failure to say* as its undoing force silently accompanies every element of speech. Exposed as utterly inadequate, the language that remains—for Celan's poems, but perhaps also for us—fails to correspond to the object of its withdrawal and the occurrence of its undoing. In other words, for the object of *Entzug* and the occurrence of *Entsetzen*, there remains no *Entsprechung*. The adequacy and correspondence of *Entsprechung* is already fragmented into the hyphenated *Ent-sprechung* (un-speaking), the unsaying of saying that persists as saying's last and only possibility, ever so precariously.[7]

## proto and para

Shame is what envelops and afflicts all elements of a language that remains unable to say its own *Entsetzen* except through a self-inflicted silence. Linguistic shame or *Sprachscham* arises from the very chasm through which language is dislodged from itself.[8] To the degree that language falls short of grasping the world's suffering (i.e., suffering as experienceable phenomenon—one could call it "history"), it may, thus thrown back at itself, only experience a quasi-suffering and almost-pain over the loss of the experience of suffering itself. This self-reflection reveals a process of *Entsetzen* at the core of linguistic being—a core that coheres or "is" only through a permanent dislodging, unsayable in any positive or cognizable fashion but silently reverberating in all effable elements. To the degree that language is thrown back at, but in this very solipsism also split away from, itself, there remains an irreducible distance between language's expression and that which unsayably reverberates in it. This distance turns out to be unbridgeable, nothing the use of language could manage to overcome. It inherently determines any possible utterance, immanently threatening while at the same time remaining inconceivable.

In a recently published essay from 2008, dedicated to the missed (discursive) encounter between Adorno and Celan, Werner Hamacher finds a concise formulation to thematize this distance: "Wie die Scham ist die Dichtung wesentlich Sprach-Ferne" ("Like shame, poetry, in its essence, is distance from language").[9] The distance thus named includes both the distance *from* as well as the distance *within* language, which is to say the distance that precisely marks the gap between what is said and that which *in* and *through* this very saying must remain silent. What reverberates in every expression without being actualized is language's dislodging and de-posing, the *Entsetzen* whose medium is the silence accompanying every concrete linguistic form. Hamacher assumes an equality between shame and the linguistic distance of "Sprach-Ferne." The analogy driving his formulation proves deceptive, however: "*Wie* die Scham ist die Dichtung." If the essence of shame, *like* that of poetry, lies in language's dislodging (or in the distance *to* language), one could be led to assume a distance even between shame and poetry. Not exactly identical, they would only be alike.[10] As though one could conceive of a poem devoid of shame, not actually shame*less* but perfectly innocent, a poem unpressed to account for the *Entzug* of its experience and the *Entsetzen* of its very linguistic being.

In order to avoid this phantasm of linguistic innocence, it is imperative to understand the likeness—and thus difference—between shame and poetry as rooting in the same essence of "Sprach-Ferne." Already degraded in Hamacher's formulation to a mere adjective ("wesentlich"), this essence is itself afflicted by the very dislodging it serves to name. If the essence of shame and poetry is a certain linguistic distance, the alienation inherent in such *Ferne* must also afflict its very own concept. If *Sprach-Ferne* is the essential trait of poetry, this essence names the displacing excision of essence from essence itself so that the essential quality denominated by language's distancing indicates merely a non-essence: the disintegration of all essential quality into the vast expanses of an unmeasured remoteness ("Ferne"). Only due to this disintegration can shame and poetry be distinct and through this distinction share the same essence (and, to recall Adorno's formulation, *permeate one another* ["Lyrik . . . durchdrungen von der Scham"]). Hence, the analogy structuring Hamacher's formulation signals an entangling co-implication according to which *poetry as shame* would mark language's dislodgment. It is through a shameful residue of language, not more than an echo, decoupled from any referential object or phenomenal experience, that the poem may speak. Shame is poetry's mode of evoking a language essentially distanced.

Hamacher proceeds to characterize this language as:

> the pre-language of every language and therefore the language of language. No meta-language in which the rules of speech could be registered in order to be displaced, but a proto- and para-language that speaks with every language as a silent reservation against speaking, as the unspeaking denial of speech.[11]

> (die Vor-Sprache jeder Sprache und deshalb die Sprache der Sprache. Keine Metasprache, in der die Regeln des Sprechens nur verzeichnet werden könnten, um verschoben zu werden, sondern eine Proto- und Para-Sprache, die in allem Sprechen als stummer Vorbehalt gegen das Sprechen, in jeder Sprache als Sprach-Versagen mitspricht.)

The breakdown of language inscribed in the term "Versagen" runs parallel to the *Ent-sprechung* of language in the face of ("angesichts") the withdrawal ("Entzug") of experience and the *Entsetzen* of language's inherent structure. "Sprach-Versagen" renames exactly this *Ent-sprechung* or un-wording with which language responds to that for which no adequate response can be found as all adequation, correspondence, and equivalence ("Entsprechung") have been nullified. For Hamacher, this *Versagen*, an unspeaking denial of speech, operates according to the structure of "speaking-with," what he calls *Mitsprechen*. Such speaking-with occurs as an inaudible echo, a reverberation of *Entzug* and *Entsetzen* in every uttered word (contrary to Adorno, he uses the term "stumm" ["silent"] and, a page prior to the section just cited, speaks of "Verstummen" and even "ent-sprechen," thus dispelling any kind of residual investment in agency or subjective willfulness).[12] The "with" of "speaking-with" ("Mitsprechen"), however, does not indicate the relay between two equally solidified and identifiable parts of speech. What *speaks-with*, accompanying the language of the poem as the echo of "Entzug" and "Entsetzen," is what Hamacher calls a 'proto- and para-language." Contrary to a transcendental meta-language through which the poem's positive order would become transparent and theoretically accessible, the proto- and para-language that speaks *with* every language as its un-speaking denial ("Versagen") is marked by a temporal gap as well as a spatial vicinage. While the "proto" carries a sense of "beforeness," temporal priority, and even originality, the prefix "para" spatializes this dimension and endows this language with a certain side- or by-presence so that it appears as an *adjacent language of apposition*, neighboring to the very degree that it is temporally removed, echoing from linguistic pre-history.[13] Both these dimensions are brought together in the German preposition "vor," which Hamacher uses as a prefix to qualify the language of every language, "Vor-Sprache jeder Sprache."

The shame of language occurs as the shame about the sheer unmasterability of language's *Vor*. Both prior and adjacent, the *Vor* of "Vor-Sprache" condenses language's *para-* and *proto-* thus naming the distance that marks and drives apart every positive linguistic element from within. Yet insofar as this para- and proto- language co-articulates itself to the elements of every positive language—namely as their unspeaking denial and breakdown ("Versagen")—it is neither temporally nor spatially removed but echoing *with* the expression as that which *in* saying withdraws *from* saying. Hamacher speaks of a "Vorbehalt gegen das Sprechen," which can mean both *reservation against* but also, literally, a *pre-retaining* of language ("vor-behalten"), which co-speaks in every finite and posited linguistic element. This sense of keeping and retaining ("behalten") is pivotal, for it helps to disperse the originary myth of a primordial language, irretrievably lost and object of a lasting nostalgia, situated "before" the speech that is accessible to us. On the contrary, "Vor-Sprache" is remote and removed from speech only to the degree that this very removal signals the intimacy of apposition and adjacency, silently co-speaking in the very finite language from which it withdraws and which it undoes from within. The remoteness, distance, removal, and dislodging ("Ferne") marking the *Vor* of "Vor-Sprache" does not point to a forgotten linguistic prehistory that we might somehow strive to recover but is kept and retained ("behalten") in all that is sayable. "Vor" marks the unsayable dimension of all saying that nonetheless accompanies all that is said.

Every positive language, every formed and posited linguistic entity, every concrete element of an expressive reality is determined by the very "Vor" that it is unable to grasp. To the extent that every positive linguistic entity is undone precisely by the silent retaining reservation against speech ("stummer Vorbehalt gegen das Sprechen"), it is itself transformed into some kind of *Vorsprechen*, especially if one keeps in mind that this term, in German, may also mean "to audition for something." There is a kind of irreducible imperfection inherent to positive speech so that any kind of saying becomes a mere *audition for language*: it's not quite there yet, essentially removed from becoming language through the *proto-* and *para-* of language's *Vor* that necessarily co-speaks as the un-speaking denial and breakdown of speech. Thus, even in posited and formed speech, there remains a certain linguistic openness that connects positive language to the proto- and para-language that is as-of-yet-unformed and in fact announces the sheer undoing of form.

"Wie die Scham ist die Dichtung wesentlich Sprach-Ferne." Arguably, Hamacher's early encounter with Hegel offers a critical hint regarding the essential relation between shame and the dislodgment (be it temporal, spatial; a-temporal, a-spatial) of language's *Vor*. In his fragment on love, penned in the fall of 1797, which Hamacher discusses in *Pleroma*, Hegel attempts to develop a concept of shame from the perspective of perishability and offers the following definition: "Shame . . . is not the fear *for* the mortal, the proper, but the fear *of* it [Die Scham . . . ist nicht eine Furcht *für* das Sterbliche, Eigene, sondern *vor* demselben]."[14] The prepositional switch from "für" to "vor" responds to the problem of finitude that haunts the possibility of shame on a fundamental level. Shame, Hegel seems to suggest, is the very response, if a fearful one, to life's mortality. If there is a future inherent to the language of shame, however, we need to assume that its movement does not exhaust itself in the "fear of mortality." Rather, in shame there gapes an opening through which the transgression of finitude's boundary can be dared. If shame is not afraid *for* the lovers' mortal life and lives, but as a matter of fact suspends the very threat of perishability, its fear *of* finitude indicates the precarious possibility of negating death: "In shame, love turns against the possibility of death which is immanent to love itself [Gegen die ihr immanente Möglichkeit des Todes kehrt sich die Liebe in der Scham]," as Hamacher comments on Hegel's definition.[15]

The movement of shame, as Hamacher's formulation makes clear, is not simply one of death's overcoming, as a kind of anticipation of an infinite beyond "after finitude." On the contrary, the possibility of turning-against ("sich kehren gegen") that realizes itself in love's turning-upon-death is not one that would simply transcend death, for it has to recover the possibility of its resistance from within the very finitude against which it revolts: "die *ihr immanente Möglichkeit* des Todes." It therefore becomes possible to argue that in shame love turns against *itself* as its own finite being. The resistance to death thus discovered cannot fall on either side of the distinction between finitude and infinitude, for it marks the very possibility of outlasting death from within the space of the finite.

Rather than the outright abolition of death, shame's resistance against finitude signals a movement of survival. It is thus more than an intertextual inside joke when Hamacher concludes his commentary on shame in Hegel with an allusion to Kafka: "The life of dialectic pulses through the closures of shame. But even in this process it is no different; it is as though shame should survive it [Durch die Schlüsse der Scham pulsiert das Leben der Dialektik. Aber auch in diesem Prozeß ist es nicht anders, als sollte die Scham ihn überleben]."[16] A similar gesture is repeated in the essay on Adorno and Celan, when he writes: "History only survives as the shame that history existed, and only the shame that falls silent before it is uttered by poetry [Von der Geschichte überlebt nur die Scham, daß es sie gegeben hat, und nur die Scham, die vor ihr verstummt, wird von der Dichtung ausgesprochen]."[17] Shame is the language of poetry, and this language occurs as a movement of survival that defies the distinction between death and immortality.[18] If the actuality of language is inevitably marked by its phenomenal/referential deprivation ("Entzug") as well as its internal de-posing ("Entsetzen"), this implies that any possibility of speaking is enacted as a kind speaking-on in the face of ("angesichts") the immanent threat of finitude. The *Vor-Sprache* that co-speaks in every language precisely indicates the limit where effable speech becomes finite, but as such it endows a will-to-language ("Sagenwollen") that speaks on through and beyond this very finitude.[19] In every utterable linguistic element, then, there is something that responds to the threat of finitude, and in responding defies it. This defiance is exposed in poetry. And it is exposed *as* shame. What survives in poetry's shame is precisely language's *Vor*—the *para-* and *proto-* contracted in the *Vor* as the dislodgment that keeps language apart from itself. Poetry traces this movement of survival. It is the survival of the para- and proto- of language's *Vor* that co-speaks, as un-speaking denial ("Versagen"), in every posited linguistic entity. Language survives in the silent echo of what it is unable to say. One name for this inability is shame. Shame names the surviving speaking-with of language's de-posing in a poem that suffers the withdrawal of experience.

## *Vor Scham* (of Language)

Shame rarely becomes thematic in Celan's poems. On March 26, 1966, however, he wrote the following verses dedicated to his wife, directly addressing some of the questions discussed above:

> For shame, for despair,
> for self-
> loathing you insert yourself,
>
> dislodged from language,
> the unearthly comes, pivots
> back into itself,
>
> By the earthly resi-
> due, by
> the elm roots
> it digs out a new chamber
> without dreams,
>
> once, always[20]
>
> (VOR SCHAM, vor Verzweiflung,
> vor Selbst-
> ekel fügst du dich ein,
>
> sprachfern,
> kommt das Unirdische, kippt
> in sich zurück,
>
> beim erdig Umher-
> liegenden, bei
> den Ulmenwurzeln
> hebt es ein neues Gelaß aus,
> ohne Geträum,
>
> einmal, immer)

Structurally, the short poem consists of four strophes, with the concluding one only comprising two adverbs and a comma: "einmal, immer." The rest of the text is organized around other parts of speech, in particular compound nouns, verbs, and prepositions. Hence, the first three strophes morphologically mirror each other in their actions of "in-serting," "pivoting back," and "digging out" ("fügst ein," "kippt zurück," "hebt aus"); as well as in their use of prepositions: "bei" in the third strophe, "in" in the second one, and, of course, "vor" in the first: "Vor Scham, vor Verzweiflung, / vor Selbst- / ekel fügst du dich ein."

At first glance, the use of the preposition "vor" in Celan's poem seems to run counter to some of what has been argued so far. This is due to the fact that his formulation corresponds to an idiomatic use of the word according to which it can name a causal relation. The poem seems to stage shame the same way in which a variety of physical or mental reactions may, in German, be linked back to their causal agent through the preposition "vor." Recall expressions like "vor Neugierde platzen" ("to burst with curiosity"), "vor Schmerz schreien" ("to squall in pain"), or the proverbial "gelb vor Neid" ("green with envy"). In all these cases, "vor" functions as the relay connecting an effect with a cause and could therefore each time be translated with "due to.'

Were we to align Celan's "Vor Scham" with this usage, we would concede that the phenomenal occurrence of shame would be the logically determinable reason behind the gesture of fitting in, self-insertion, submission ("fügst du dich ein"). This causal logic would defy what Adorno and Hamacher have argued with regard to shame and offer an alternative to the vision of a language internally unsettled and de-posed, deprived of experience ("entsetzt," "entzogen"). It would conceive a language based on a firm referentiality that would ensure the existence of propositions capable of communicating a given experience. "Vor Scham . . . fügst du dich ein" would thus become readable as a causal statement in which the dislodgment of language from language ("Sprach-Ferne") were restored to full unity, and the essential exposure to *Entzug* and *Entsetzen* would have transformed itself into a secure, grammatically stable, logically sound, and referentially anchored relation to the world.

This supposed proposition, however, does not come to a conclusion as the strophe ends. As a matter of fact, the poem runs on as a long-winded multi-clause sentence, without, however, reaching a definitive point of termination—as the last strophe ("einmal, immer") is not followed or ended by a period, leaving the comma as the only punctuation mark whose usage can be observed throughout. If we take into account how this non-sentence, its propositional fiction, moves into the second strophe, it is precisely the one-word clause that starts it off and functions as the link between the poem's first two parts that debunks its phantasm of linguistic coherency: "Vor Scham, vor Verzweiflung, / vor Selbst- / ekel fügst du dich ein, // *sprachfern*, / kommt das Unirdische, kippt / in sich zurück." Introducing the second strophe, the composite "sprachfern" ("dislodged from language") appears to be a supplement to the poem's opening: chiasmically mirroring the opening phrase's sound and shape—"Vor Scham," "sprachfern"—it apparently serves to qualify the entire cluster of opening lines. Clamped in-between the frame of two commas, the adjective "sprachfern," a clause in itself, seems attributively to belong to the poem's first stanza from which it is, however, cut off through a line-break. Were "sprachfern" merely to open the second strophe, there would be no necessity to set it apart from what follows through the use of another comma: "sprachfern [comma] kommt das Unirdische." If the adjective were simply to qualify the arrival of the unearthly, the comma would be superfluous; hence, its use and place irritates and disrupts the poem's progress, referring us back to the beginning rather than securing the text's continuation. "Vor Scham . . . fügst du dich ein, // sprachfern."

The poem's linguistic stability, its referential anchorage and reliable report on experience and lived emotion, are thus disturbed precisely by linking this phenomenal experience to a distancing in language (recall Hamacher: "Wie die Scham ist die Dichtung wesentlich Sprach-Ferne"). The initial phrase, "Vor Scham," therefore remains irreducible to its causal meaning. As a matter of fact, this fiction of causality is only possible through the simultaneous acknowledgment of language's distancing. But if the report on a phenomenal event (i.e., the experience of shame) is only possible if this report signals its linguistic dislodgement, its phenomenal content and the causality it indicates become questionable. In other words, any report on the experience of shame is already marked by the shame about the very incommunicability of experience that essentially ("wesentlich") characterizes the structure of linguistic mediation. Again, language is haunted by the experience of its very inability to experience—yet this haunting remains inexpressibly, silently retained (as "stummer Vorbehalt") in the poem's positive appearance. "For shame, you insert yourself" is a statement aiming at the poem's folding and unfolding, prior to the possibility of attempting to transmit subjective emotions or experiences. The report on the experience of shame is disturbed by the shame about experience's unreportability. Beyond the experiential phenomenon it purportedly describes, the poem's very language is subject to the "Sprach-Ferne" that, for Celan, accompanies an immersion in shame ("fügst du dich ein").

The poem's opening thus describes its very own verses as they *insert* themselves: for shame, the poem inserts itself, dislodged from its language. The causality implied by the preposition "vor," feigning the restoration of a logic through which subjective experience would become reportable, turns out to be haunted by the dislodging thrust of language's *para-* and *proto-*, spatially and temporally corroding the possibility of communicating a phenomenal content or subjective experience. If the language of poetry is one of shame, the phrase "Vor Scham" translates into the *Vor-Sprache* that Hamacher calls "the language of language," co-speaking in every positive linguistic entity as the un-speaking denial of speech ('Versagen"), entangling the loss of experience ("Entzug") with the inherent de-posing of linguistic reality ("Entsetzen"). The shame of language names the inability to speak the immemorial *Vor-Sprache* that never becomes effable but silently accompanies—like the death drive—the shapes of effability. Shame is the survival of *Vor-Sprache* in the gap of *Sprach-Ferne*.

One could easily interject, however, that the analytic emphasis on shame is unfounded, as the poem does not open by invoking only one affect. In addition, it names the dispositions of despair ("Verzweiflung") and disgust ("Ekel"), which raises the question as to how these latter two affects correspond to the stated primacy of shame. As a preliminary response to this concern, let me point out that each of the three terms invoked in the first stanza confirm and corroborate the sense of immanent dislodging and displacement ("Ferne") that have been established as traits of shame. In the case of "despair," the signifier itself exposes its own movement of dislodging as the German "Verzweiflung," a derivative of *Zweifel* (doubt), roots in the Middle High German *zwifel* and the Germanic *twifla* for "twofold." As with the syllable "-pair" in English, the German "-zwei-" insists on a moment of doubling and thus disintegration, the coming apart of unity, a dislodging and distancing between one and one. "Disgust," in turn, accomplishes something similar, especially to the extent that Celan invokes the composite "Selbstekel" ("self-loathing" or "self-disgust"), yet only to split it up again by inserting a hyphen, followed by a line-break: "vor Selbst- / ekel." One can speak of a "self" here only to the extent that it is a self hyphenated into a break with it-self. The self's hyphen overextends the self, compelling it to trespass the boundary of its unity—not, however, with the goal of restoring it but to expose the self to sheer disgust with itself. To the degree that "-ekel" makes the compositum complete, one may argue that the "self" envisioned here exists only in as much as it is a self filled with disgust for itself. It is a self split from itself in the very moment it recognizes itself as a "creep" (*Ekel*), disintegrated in a gesture of self-reflexive self-loathing: a fragmented self that is already more (and less) than one.[21] It's precisely its inability to be a self that disgusts the self with itself.

The disintegration of the self, performed throughout the first strophe, raises the question concerning the status of the subsequent address. Who is the "you" summoned here? "Vor Selbst- / ekel fügst *du* dich ein . . ." Does the self's decomposition proceed to corrode the unity of the second person in question? Celan's idiomatic use of the term "vor" allows for two possibilities. As stated, "vor" can either indicate a state of being enwrapped with something or signal a spatial or temporal difference. Hence, the action of insertion ("einfügen") could either describe something that takes place *before* disgust sets in, or it transpires *because* self-disgust makes itself felt. Even though an ear sensitive to German idiomaticity might readily declare the latter possibility to be most plausible, Celan nonetheless presents us with a structurally undecidable ambivalence. This means that the "you" invoked in his poem must sustain the aporia of all colliding possibilities pertaining to the preposition "vor." And as the preposition is reiterated, this aporetic structure affects the entire first strophe. "Vor Scham" means both "through" *and* "before" shame; "vor Verzweiflung" means prior to despair *and* because of it, and so forth.

## vor; fors

This structural undecidability that states that the subject of shame is at the same time enwrapped *by* shame and spatiotemporally distanced *from* it does not halt before the affective state itself. Which is to say that the aporia Celan introduces through his multilayered usage of the preposition "vor" not only disturbs the presumed subjective carrier(s) of the affects educed ("self"; "you"), the *pre*-position also (and perhaps especially) affects the very position it precedes so that "Vor Scham" becomes readable as "Vorscham" ("pre-shame"), "vor Verzweiflung" as "Vorverzweiflung" (and, due to the line-break in the second line, "Selbst" as "Vorselbst"). Otherwise put, to the degree that something happening "vor Scham" always means it happens *because of* but also *distanced from* (prior to, before, in front of) shame, the affect's very capacity to qualify its subject's experience falls flat.[22] Another way of phrasing this would be to say: there is no immediacy of affect. If the very experience of shame implies an unbridgeable distance between experience and shame, the shame in question ceases to be shame "proper" and becomes a kind of pre-shame ("Vorscham"); the affect always anticipates itself without ever fully coming to fruition. It is always not yet (and therefore never) fully what it is meant to be. Arguably, if what predicates the subject is shame, the entire process of predication is bound to collapse, for shame introduces an inevitable distance that corrodes all elements involved. It divides self from affect, but also self from self as well as affect from affect.

Still, the question remains as to why the linguistic vertigo induced by this permanent distancing should be reducible to the problem of shame. Celan's own reading practice and the sources he considered as he composed the poem might be of service as we attempt a coherent response to this quandary. As indicated in the *Kommentierte Gesamtausgabe*, the creation of Celan's poem was profoundly informed by an encounter with the 1935 novel *Of Time and the River*, written by North Carolina novelist Thomas Wolfe, who passed away of miliary tuberculosis in 1938 at the age of thirty-seven. The German translation of the novel appeared in 1937, not long after its original publication, under the title *Von Zeit und Strom*, translated by Hans Schiebelhuth. The first version of Celan's poem was penned in a notebook that also features various passages copied from Wolfe's novel. At the time, Celan was staying at the Sainte-Anne Hospital Center; as with all the poems written during this period, he refrained from adding a place to the original version. The poem was written immediately following rounds by Celan's attending physician.[23]

How seamlessly the scene of reading (Wolfe) transitions into the scene of writing (the poem) can be observed already in the first strophe, which in large parts appears to be directly lifted from Schiebelhuth's translation. Writes Celan: "Vor Scham, vor Verzweiflung, / vor Selbst- / ekel fügst du dich ein." The corresponding sentence in Schibelhuth reads: "Und Eugen saß da, krank vor Scham, vor Selbstekel und Verzweiflung, außerstande, ihr zu erwidern."[24] The character named in this sentence is Eugene Gant, the novel's protagonist (and, to the extent that the text presents an exercise in autofiction, Wolfe's alter-ego). Celan directly adopted the three affects Wolfe offers to account for Eugene's condition: *Scham, Selbstekel, Verzweiflung*. But he does so not without applying a few significant changes such as breaking up the pair "Selbstekel und Verzweiflung" and switching their positions. Most importantly, however, the emphasis on externality signaled by Schiebelhuth's use of "außerstande" is turned inward, becoming a movement of insertion ("fügst du dich ein"). It is noteworthy that, detached from the spatial marker "ein," the German reflexive verb "sich fügen" means as much as "to acquiesce," "to comply," and also "to resign." This liminal resignation mirrors the incapacitation stated in Schiebelhuth's translation, which renders Eugene unable to give a response: "außerstande, ihr zu erwidern." This lack of response, in turn, anticipates the strange adjective "sprachfern" that Celan uses to disturb the transition between the first and second strophes of his poem, as discussed above. "Sprachfern," Eugene is unable to give response.

Though the poet apparently worked with Schiebelhuth's German rather than Wolfe's American English, it is still worth exploring how the passage plays out in the original. A first striking interlinguistic difference one can observe is that, congruent with Celan's poem, Thomas Wolfe's sentence does without the mention of proper names: "And he sat there, sick with shame, self-loathing, and despair."[25] The scene takes place at a turning point in the novel, just before the character decides to leave his hometown in order to start over in New York City. Following an uncontrolled bender culminating in his arrest, the sequence tells of Eugene's remorseful way home to confess to his mother. Having silently listened to his resolution to expiate his crimes, the mother then speaks at length of her disappointment in all her children, but especially in Eugene—the youngest, the one with the brightest future, proud Harvard graduate yet ultimately nothing but a drunk troublemaker. Her monologue ends: "'Too much to ask of me!' she whispered huskily and suddenly drew the sleeve of the old frayed sweater across her weak wet eyes, with the pathetic gesture of a child—a gesture that tore him with a rending anguish of pity, shame, and inexpiable regret. 'Too hard . . . too hard,' she whispered. 'Surely there's a curse of God upon us if after all the pain and sorrow all are lost.' And he sat there, sick with shame, self-loathing and despair, unable to reply."[26] The passage shows that Eugene's ultimate inability to respond is already preempted by his mother's exasperated outcry "too much to ask of me!"—as though *she* and not her son were the one called upon to account for herself. This reversal of call and response, sender and addressee, is further corroborated when the mother herself, before the very eyes of her child, turns into an infant: "with a pathetic gesture of a child" she covers her crying eyes with a sweater, and it is this "sudden" gesture that fills Eugene with a profusion of affect, "a rending anguish of pity, shame, and inexpiable regret." Note that it is the *wordless* regression of the mother into a child that triggers these emotions. "*Sprachfern*, you cover your eyes with your sweater," one could paraphrase.

As the context of the passage shows, the triad of substantives that Celan chooses to include in his poem ("shame, self-loathing, and despair") is preceded by yet another triad according to which Eugene's character is overcome by "pity, shame, and . . . regret."[27] Both affective chains unfold in almost the same instant. And in both cases, it is the narrator who reports on Eugene's condition. The mediating relay (thus also the distance) between the two affective clusters, and thus the condition of one's transformation into the other, appears to be the state of shame. Shame is the only substantive subject to iteration, the sole element taking part in both affective chains, thus the link between the two (pity—*shame*—regret; *shame*—self-loathing—despair). If the second series displays a rewriting and rearrangement of the first, it is the state of shame that connects the two and allows for the change to happen without risking a complete rift in Eugene's affective disposition.[28] The doubling of shame signals that in both instances a certain breakdown of language is at stake; both instances are determined by a lack of responsiveness, the inability to give account. Just like the mother's "too much to ask!" is reflected in Eugene's being "unable to reply," the doubling of shame arises from a twofold communicative collapse, each time a dislodgment of language from language.

If Hamacher states that shame is essentially *Sprach-Ferne* and as such a dislodging and distancing of language from language, the *Ferne* indicated in Wolfe has to do with the collapse of schemas of communication to the extent that they require information to be sent, received, processed, and responded to. Shame, then, serves to name language's very own loss of language. Shame is *sprachfern* because in shame language is dissociated from language, forfeiting its ability to respond according to a concrete communicative reality.[29] If "vor Scham" (as in Schiebelhuths "krank vor Scham") implies both the meaning of being displaced *from* shame and of being enwrapped *by* it, then to experience the shame of language means being in language in the sense of dwelling in language's sheer loss of itself. For shame, language does not allow us to communicate. For shame, language does not respond. For shame, one sits there, unable to reply.

The rest of the poem, too, is very much informed by some of the translation choices Celan observed in Schiebelhuth's rendition of Wolfe's novel. The invocation of tropes that engender a certain phantasy of death in the third strophe ("Ulmenwurzeln"; "Gelaß . . . ohne Geträum") also purloins its signifiers from Wolfe. Of particular note in this regard is the rare German noun "Gelaß," which Schiebelhuth frequently uses to render a multiplicity of English terms. The same chapter that includes the passage on Eugene's encounter with his mother tells of his arrest during his drunken escapades. Wolfe describes the confined space of the jail cell as follows: "The cell Eugene sat in was a little cubicle of space, perhaps eight feet deep, and four or five feet wide." Schiebelhuth translates: "Die Zelle, in der er saß, war ein kleines, niedriges Gelaß. . . ."[30] The choice of "Gelaß" for "cubicle" might seem antiquated and even counterintuitive, yet it captures an important dimension of the word's original's meaning: while the term "cubicle," now most often used with reference to small (work) spaces, used to mean bedroom (*cubare*: to lie down), "Gelaß" originally denominates a cozy place.[31] The word's more recent usage, however, clouds this meaning such that the official *Duden* definition reads: "kleiner, enger, dürftig eingerichteter [Keller]raum" ("small, narrow, scarcely furnished [basement] room").[32] Not only does this latter definition ostensibly shift away from any implication of coziness, it adds, more importantly, a topological index: apparently, this type of space is usually found beneath the ground, in the basement. Hence, Celan can establish a connection between "Gelaß" and earth or soil ("beim erdig Umher- / liegenden"), and furthermore insinuate that "Gelaß" is something to be "dug out" ("hebt . . . aus"), reminiscent of a dungeon or trench. Or a crypt or grave.

As discussed above, the adjective "sprachfern" can be read as both an attribute that refers back to the poem's opening ("you insert yourself, dislodged from language") and one that points ahead, introducing the second strophe ("dislodged from language, / the unearthly comes, pivots / back into itself").[33] The lines speak of a certain if unannounced advent, the "coming" of something unearthly, in which Celan recognizes the very force that reaches into the earth to dig out a hollow space that becomes identifiable as the realm of death: "Gelaß ohne Geträum," dreamless bedstead, cubicle of death, recessed into the ground, among the elm roots. Perhaps it is this quasi-gravesite that the compound verb of the first strophe anticipates: while it initially remains unclear what type of space the action of "sich einfügen" ("to insert oneself"; "to fit oneself in") anticipates, the possibility now becomes concrete that the space invoked by the action of "insertion" is precisely the narrow grave ("Gelaß") dug out in the penultimate strophe. It is critical, however, that the poem refrains from declaring, let alone representing (a) death. If the final line invokes a process that takes place "once, always" ("einmal, immer"), this signals both the event's uniqueness as well as the possibility of its infinite iteration, rather than a conclusive endpoint of sorts. Something that happens "once, always" does not happen *once and for all*. But it may happen once *and* always, thus establishing an unresolved tension between the singularity of a one-time occurrence and its iteration throughout eternity.

In a peculiar way, then, Celan's use of the German preposition "vor" also echoes the French "fors," yet another preposition, prominently featured in the title of Jacques Derrida's introduction to Abraham and Torok's *The Wolf Man's Magic Word: A Cryptonymy*.[34] *Fors*, too, is the name for a strange space, a type of "Gelaß," if you will: Derrida uses it to talk about the formation of what Torok and Abraham call "crypts," that is, spaces in which something dead is kept alive through a process of failed mourning resulting in acts of what they term "incorporation." Incorporation poses a challenge to finitude that transpires in a similar fashion as the poetic self's insertion into its dreamless crypt. And it, too, operates "dislodged from language," as Derrida explains: "Incorporation keeps still, speaks only to silence or to ward off intruders from its secret place," and he proceeds to claim that "language . . . inhabits the crypt in the form of 'words buried alive.'"[35] Thus, there is an echo of *fors* in *vor* that refines our sense of a death that fails to constitute a proper endpoint. It's a death through which the dead are kept alive, in this ever new chamber, dug out by the elm roots. Every *Vor-Sprache* is a *fors-Sprache*, a crypt-language that survives, in and as shame, all boundaries of finitude.

Derrida talks at length about the type of "preservation," another form of survival, that happens in the crypt: "The inhabitant of the crypt is always a living dead, a dead entity we are perfectly willing to keep alive, but *as* dead, one we are willing to keep, as long as we keep it, within us, intact in any way save as living."[36] In his aforementioned reading of Hegel, Hamacher argues that such resistance to finitude happens through love, in particular through that moment in love that we call "shame."[37] The kind of shame with which we are confronted in Celan's poem, in turn, occurs detached from any type of subjective affect. Rather than a psychological state, it describes a philological movement, an occurrence in language. Hence, the odd vitality that dwells in the "Gelaß" or crypt, indicating a form-of-survival no longer alive but still persisting, bears on the attribute "sprachfern" that determines both moments of this oscillating movement: the advent of the force that will dig out this grave and the self's insertion into it. Language is the medium—the distance, the remoteness—through which this oscillation takes place and becomes possible. For shame, the self, divided from and disgusted by itself, inserts itself, dislodged from language, into the dreamless chamber of death—where it survives.

Once and always.

## Notes

1. Theodor W. Adorno, *Ästhetische Theorie*, eds. Gretel Adorno and Rolf Tiedemann (Frankfurt am Main: Suhrkamp, 1973), 477. See Theodor W. Adorno, *Aesthetic Theory*, trans. Robert Hullot-Kentor (London: Continuum, 1997), 322. As my argument heavily bears upon the semantics of the German original, I will, in what follows, for the most part disregard the translation and base my observations solely on the German.

2. On the problematic relationship between *Entsetzen* and aesthetic affectivity, see my brief discussion in "De-posing the Uncanny," *OLR* 42.2 (Winter 2020), 314–18. See also my essay "Ausstellen, Entsetzen: Thomas Bernhards Museumsroman *Alte Meister*," *Museales Erzählen: Dinge, Räume, Narrative*, eds. Johanna Stapelfeldt, Ulrike Vedder, and Klaus Wiehl (Munich: Fink, 2020), 203–22; this essay owes much of its conceptual insight to Werner Hamacher's "Ausstellungen der Mutter: Kurzer Gang durch verschiedene Museen," in *"geteilte Aufmerksamkeit": Zur Frage des Lesens*, ed. Thomas Schestag (Frankfurt am Main: Peter Lang, 1997), 53–90.

3. Walter Benjamin, *Toward the Critique of Violence*, eds. Peter Fenves and Julia Ng (Stanford: Stanford University Press, 2021).

4. See Werner Hamacher's seminal reading of Benjamin's "Toward the Critique of Violence" in "Afformative, Strike," *Cardozo Law Review* 13.4 (1991): 1133–57.

5. "De-posed I experience that which de-poses"; my translation. Friedrich Schiller, *Die Braut von Messina oder Die feindlichen Brüder* (II.6).

6. See Werner Hamacher, "Other Pains," trans. Ian Alexander Moore, *Philosophy Today* 61.4 (2017): 963–89. The connection between shame and mourning is emphasized in a short piece of linguistic criticism that Adorno wrote in 1967. There, he bemoans the use of the term "Uromi" ("great-granny") in an obituary, which he views as a linguistic fetish that feigns intimacy while desecrating its object. He declares this an instance of the shameless use of language and concludes: "Weil die Sprache die Scham verlernt hat, versagt sie sich die Trauer." Again, Adorno seems to insinuate a certain agency behind the term "verlernen" ("unlearning"), as though shame were something that could willfully be expunged, yet his insight furthermore corroborates the idea of an essential tie between a shame that occurs solely in language and the possibility of mourning. See Theodor W. Adorno, "Uromi," in *Gesammelte Schriften* 20.2 (Frankfurt am Main: Suhrkamp, 1986), 571.

7. Celan's neologism to capture this movement is "ent-worten." See, for instance, his poem, "Und wie die Gewalt": "Hier, es entwortet im Für"; in *Die Gedichte: Kommentierte Gesamtausgabe*, ed. Barbara Wiedemann (Frankfurt am Main: Suhrkamp, 2012), 521. See also Werner Hamacher, "*Für*—die Philologie," in *Was zu sagen bleibt* (Schupfart: Engeler, 2019), 7–49, 35–46. Here, Hamacher explicitly discusses the relationship between "entsprechen" and "entworten"; for instance: "'entsprechend' kann seinerseits, durch die Umdeutung eines Präfix, in ein 'ent-sprechend' und weiterhin, wie es bei Celan geschieht, in ein 'entwortet' ver-

wandelt werden" (42); see Werner Hamacher, "For—Philology," trans. Jason Groves, in *Minima Philologica* (New York: Fordham University Press, 2015), 107–56, 148.

8. The term "Sprachscham" is borrowed from Walter Benjamin who coined it in the context of discussing Robert Walser. See Walter Benjamin, "Robert Walser," in *Gesammelte Schriften* II.2, eds. Rolf Tiedemann and Hermann Schweppenhäuser (Frankfurt am Main: Suhrkamp, 1991), 324–28.

9. Werner Hamacher, "Versäumnisse," in *Keinmaleins: Texte zu Celan* (Frankfurt am Main: Klostermann, 2019), 57–91, 85; my translation. As a preliminary conclusion drawn from this claim, one can hold that poetry introduces a kind of language that breaks with any pretense of immediacy. Adorno says as much in the above-mentioned note on the word "Uromi," when lamenting that communicative language denigrates all distance. "Der Geist einer kommunikativen Sprache, die . . . alle Distanzen herabsetzt" (571).

10. A major contribution to the thinking of likeness was recently delivered by Paul North in his *Bizarre-Privileged Items of the Universe: The Logic of Likeness* (New York: Zone, 2021). Though his study can hardly be called a philological one, North does take on the problem of likeness in language, in particular in order to restore an understanding of language that would rely on resemblance rather than difference: "Language looks like a differential system, a semiotic system, because the homeotic affinities among its parts have been carved away by history" (242). It remains to be seen how much of this claim's argumentative edge too will have been carved away by history.

11. Hamacher, "Versäumnisse," 85; my translation.

12. "Was in ihr [der Dichtung, D.Z.] spricht, ist ihr *Verstummen* davor, daß sie noch nicht spricht. *Wahr* ist sie nur deshalb, weil sie sich gegen jede geschichtliche Korrespondenz *ent-spricht* und in eine andere hineinspricht." Hamacher, *Keinmaleins*, 84; my emphases (except "wahr").

13. One thinks of a moment in Benjamin's essay on Kafka where forgetting is at stake. In Kafka's stories, Benjamin holds, "everything forgotten mingles with what has been forgotten of the prehistoric world [Vorwelt]." Walter Benjamin: "Franz Kafka: On the Tenth Anniversary of His Death," in *Illuminations: Essays and Reflections*, trans. Harry Zohn (New York: Schocken Books, 1968), 111–40, 131. The term "Vorwelt," in this context, could also be translated as "proto- or para-world" as it indicates a realm akin to the "Vor-Sprache" Hamacher finds in Celan. On the connection between Celan, Benjamin, and Kafka, see also Hamacher's "HÄM: Ein Gedicht Celans mit Motiven Benjamins," in *Keinmaleins: Texte zu Celan* (Frankfurt am Main: Klostermann, 2019), 13–55.

14. Georg Wilhelm Friedrich Hegel, *"Der Geist des Christentums": Schriften 1796–1800*, ed. Werner Hamacher (Frankfurt am Main: Ullstein, 1978); my translation.

15. Werner Hamacher, "Pleroma—zur Genesis und Struktur einer dialektischen Hermeneutik bei Hegel," in *"Der Geist des Christentums,"* 7–333, 98. See

Hamacher, *Pleroma: Reading in Hegel*, trans. Nicholas Walker and Simon Jarvis (Stanford: Stanford University Press, 1998), 83; trans. modified.

16. Hamacher, "Pleroma," 102; see *Pleroma*, 87; trans. modified. See also Franz Kafka, *Der Proceß*, ed. Malcolm Pasley (Frankfurt am Main: Fischer, 2002), 312: "'Wie ein Hund!' sagte er, was war, als sollte die Scham ihn überleben."

17. Hamacher, "Versäumnisse," 84; my translation.

18. One thinks of Auden's famous line: "For poetry makes nothing happen: it survives." "In Memory of W. B. Yeats," in *Selected Poems*, ed. Edward Mendelson (New York: Vintage, 1979), 80–83, 82.

19. See Hamacher's remarks on what he terms "Endlichkeit der Sprache" in *Was zu sagen bleibt* (Schupfart: Engeler, 2019), 117. See "What Remains to Be Said," trans. Kristina Mendicino, in *Give the Word: Responses to Werner Hamacher's 95 Theses on Philology*, eds. Gerhard Richter and Ann Smock (Lincoln: University of Nebraska Press, 2019), 217–354, 255: "Endlichkeit besagt hier: apriorische Selbst-Entfernung der Sprache in ihrem Geben."

20. Paul Celan, "Vor Scham," *Die Gedichte*, 488; translation mine.

21. Recall Hamacher's pun on Hegel's name in "Pleroma": "Von Ekel ist die Rede. Von Hegel" (301).

22. One could argue that the preposition "vor," in this poem, displays what Celan calls "Vielstelligkeit des Ausdrucks." The aporias and undecidabilities unfolded by an expression that occupies multiple linguistic places do not, however, serve the purpose of making things more opaque; on the contrary, the multiplicity of places nonetheless guarantees something like poetic precision. In a short text written in response to a prompt asking philosophers and poets briefly to report on their current endeavors, Celan offers a short characterization of German literature and poetry (as opposed to their French counterparts), arguing that due to its historical responsibility the German poetic tradition has grown "grey" and "distrustful of beauty" and euphony. He explains that German constitutes a factual language, and adds: "Dieser Sprache geht es, bei aller unabdingbaren Vielstelligkeit des Ausdrucks, um Präzision." Paul Celan, "Antwort auf eine Umfrage der Librairie Finkler, Paris (1958)," in *Gesammelte Werke*, vol. 3 (Frankfurt am Main: Suhrkamp 1983), 167–68, 167. See "Reply to a Questionnaire from the Flinker Bookstore, Paris, 1958," in *Collected Prose*, trans. Rosemarie Waldrop (Manchester: Carcanet, 2003), 15–16. See also Peter Szondi's reading of Celan's poem "Engführung," where he claims that ambiguity of meaning yields precision: "Ambiguity, which has become a means of knowledge, . . . serves the cause of precision." Peter Szondi, "Reading 'Engführung,'" in *Celan Studies*, trans. Susan Bernofsky with Harvey Mendelsohn (Stanford: Stanford University Press, 2003), 27–82, 82, see also 65.

23. See Paul Celan, *Die Gedichte*, 940: "Entstehung: Samstag, 26.3.1966. . . . Der Datierung ist hinzugefügt: 'nach der Visite von Dr. Oshnneski.'" See also 792.

24. Thomas Wolfe, *Von Zeit und Strom*, trans. Hans Schiebenhuth (Berlin: Hofenberg, 2016), 417.

25. Thomas Wolfe, *Of Time and the River: A Legend of Man's Hunger in His Youth* (New York: Scribner, 1999), 409.

26. Wolfe, 409.

27. Schiebelhuth translates the passage as "und dies war die rührende Gebärde eines Kinds, eine Gebärde, die ihm in der Seele weh tat und an ihm riß mit den Krallen des Mitleids, der Scham und untilgbarer Reue." Wolfe, *Von Zeit und Strom*, 417.

28. Taking up Hamacher's above-mentioned Kafka pun, it is worth noting that Kafka, too, when composing the end of his second novel, *Der Proceß*, revised the novel's final sentence multiple times, yet each time keeping the substantive "shame" as the constant element connecting all the variants, ultimately resulting in the famous line: "es war, als sollte die Scham ihn überleben" ("It was as though the shame should survive him"). See above, endnote 16; see also my discussion in "Precarious Futures: Kafka's Prose of Survival," *Yearbook of Comparative Literature* 63 (2017), 113–37, esp. 122–26.

29. In *Was zu sagen bleibt*, Hamacher states the following: "Ob in ihrer Bedeutungs- oder ihrer Setzungsfunktion, Sprache ist sie 'selbst' nur, wo sie ihrem Nicht-Selbst, ihrer Unsprachlichkeit, also ihrem Setzungs- und Bedeutungs-Unvermögen ausgesetzt ist," 110. See "What Remains to Be Said," 246. The term "Unsprachlichkeit" (or "non-linguistic character," as Mendicino suggests translating) in this context might surprise, but what Hamacher is getting at here is nothing that lies *outside* of language, be it an ungraspable reality, a "referent in itself," or the like. On the contrary, his argument emphasizes precisely the essential remoteness of language *from* itself, *within* itself. The moment language forfeits its positive and effable form, the moment it therefore ceases to *mean* and indicate *reference*, it de facto becomes exposed to its own nothingness, the formless occurrence whence positing and meaning become possible in the first place. Hamacher calls this formlessness "unsprachlich" because it does not possess the traits of any positive, finite language. It is indiscernible, nothing speaks (in any concrete and cognizable sense, at least). "Unsprachlichkeit" and "Vor-Sprache" and "Sprach-Ferne" are therefore related terms in that they all mark a critical distance to language's positive and formalized character. Part of what my article has tried to demonstrate is that 'shame" is connected to this "nonlinguistic" dimension of language. If we think of shame as a philological problem rather than a psychological phenomenon, the passages analyzed in Adorno, Celan, and Wolfe testify to the kind of breakdown of communication that is proper to the very essence of language. Language: sick with shame.

30. Wolfe, *Of Time and the River*, 387 (*Von Zeit und Strom*, 391). At an earlier point in the text, Schiebenhuth already translated "cubicle" with "Gelaß" (157; German 133); at other times, he chooses "Gelaß" as the translation of terms like "cell" (297; German 294) and "small room" (453; German 464). A reference to "Ulmen" can be found on page 196 (German 176).

31. This is the opening definition in Grimm's dictionary: "bequemer raum." Formed from the verb "lassen" ("to let"), the noun "Gelaß," the Grimms add, generally

means a space in which things can be left behind: "der begriff ist ganz allgemein 'der raum wo man dinge lassen kann.'" Jacob and Wilhelm Grimm, "GELASZ," in *Deutsches Wörterbuch*, vol. 5 (Leipzig, 1854), column 2871.

32. "Gelass, das," *Duden online*, accessed January 23, 2023, https://www.duden.de/rechtschreibung/Gelass.

33. It is noteworthy that the only thing we know about this disembodied "unearthly" force is that it "pivots back into itself." Thus, a contrast arises between this nameless force able to fold in on itself and the "self" invoked in the first strophe that appears as disintegrated and torn by self-loathing.

34. As Barbara Johnson explains in a footnote to her English translation: "The word *fors* in French, derived from the Latin *foris* ('outside, outdoors'), is an archaic preposition meaning 'except for, barring, save.' In addition, *fors* is the plural of the word *for*, which, in the French expression *le for intérieur*, designates the inner heart, 'the tribunal of conscience,' subjective interiority." Jacques Derrida, "Fors: The Anglish Words of Nicolas Abraham and Maria Torok," trans. Barbara Johnson, in *The Wolf Man's Magic Word: A Cryptonymy*, by Nicolas Abraham and Maria Torok (Minneapolis: University of Minnesota Press, 1986), xi–xlviii, xi–xii. Coincidentally, the translation of Derrida's essay into the German language was done by Werner Hamacher: Jacques Derrida, "FORS: Die Winkelwörter von Nicolas Abraham und Maria Torok," in *Kryptonymie: Das Verbarium des Wolfsmanns*, by Nicolas Abraham and Maria Torok, trans. Werner Hamacher (Frankfurt am Main: Ullstein, 1979), 5–58.

35. Derrida, "Fors," xvii, xxxv.

36. Derrida, xxi.

37. "Gegen die ihr immanente Möglichkeit des Todes kehrt sich die Liebe in der Scham"; see above, endnote 15.

# Translations

Chapter 11

# Poetic Approach

## Celan's Radio Essay "Die Dichtung Ossip Mandelstamms"

IRINA KOGAN

On July 8, 1959, during his stay in the mountainous Swiss region Sils, Paul Celan received a request from journalist and literary scholar Werner Weber to send some poetry from up there, where Celan was staying, down to where he, Weber, was: "And could you be lured to donate something to me down here, lyric poetry or so . . . ? [Und könnte es Sie locken, mir etwas herunter zu spenden, Lyrik oder so . . . ?]."[1] Celan, without sending the requested originals, promises, instead, an attempt at translation:

> On my table is lying the Jeune Parque: perhaps I can translate the missing fifty lines here, perhaps. (Translations: approach attempts, sometimes, rarely, the other and the other's language meets one a little halfway: God created languages hardly in view of their translatability . . .).
>
> (Auf meinem Tisch liegt die Jeune Parque: vielleicht kann ich hier die fehlenden fünfzig Verse übersetzen, vielleicht. [Übersetzungen: Annäherungsversuche, manchmal, selten, kommt einem auch der andere und des anderen Sprache ein wenig entgegen: Gott hat die Sprachen kaum im Hinblick auf ihre Übertragbarkeit geschaffen . . .]).[2]

In his parenthetic reflection on the act of translating, Celan refers to it in the plural (*Übersetzungen*) and interrupts its path with several punctuation marks, thereby calling into question an overarching concept of translation that could function as an exemplary placeholder for this always singular and precarious act of reaching out. Rather than conceiving of translations as accomplishable acts of decoding and substituting, the poet highlights their doubly tentative nature—evident in the notion of both "approach" (*Annäherung*) and "trial" or "attempt" (*Versuch*). Significantly, too, Celan envisions translation not as an active enterprise on the part of the translator but as a passive experience: a rare occurrence of—hesitant even in its rarity ("manchmal, selten")—being approached and faced with or accommodated by (*entgegenkommen*) the other and the other's language. What Celan says here about translations anticipates what he will have to say about poems.

## In Search of a Poetics

Paul Celan's poetological statements have been so firmly etched into the discourse on his poetry that one almost takes their granular exactitude for granted.[3] However, as is evident from his refusal in November 1954 to contribute to writer and editor Hans Bender's anthology on the poetic craft (*Handwerk*), the poet did not always have a well-articulated poetics at his disposal: "—and yet: the How and the Why of that qualitative change, which the word experiences in order to become the word in the poem, I still cannot determine more closely today [—und doch: das Wie und Warum jenes qualitativen Wechsels, den das Wort erfährt, um zum Wort im Gedicht zu werden, weiß ich auch heute nicht näher zu bestimmen]."[4] At stake in Celan's admission to Bender is a definitional question for the field of poetics: the question of the essential quality of the poetic word, the question of what a poem is. Notably, as he reports a certain difficulty in approaching (*näher bestimmen*, "determining more closely") this question, Celan articulates it in terms of change (*Wechsel*) and thus a transformation or translation. Celan's use of the definite article points to the fundamental nature of the border in question: if only, that is, one could pinpoint this essential and yet so elusive transition through which *the* word (das *Wort*)—and thus, metonymically, language, sense, thought—has to pass in order to turn into *the* word in *the* poem (das *Wort* im *Gedicht*).[5] And yet, directly preceding Celan's admission of definitional hesitancy is a note about that which is circumstantial: "Life circumstances, life in a foreign linguistic space have made it so that I treat my language much more consciously than earlier—and yet: the How and the Why . . . [Die Lebensumstände, das Leben in fremdem Sprachbereich haben es mit sich gebracht, daß ich mit meiner Sprache viel bewußter umgehe als früher—und doch: das Wie und Warum . . .]."[6] The circumstances of daily life in a foreign tongue have led the poet to a much more conscious attitude toward language—yet, not exactly toward language as such (i.e., the word) or even the poet's native language more narrowly. Rather, the possessive pronoun in Celan's formulation "with my language [mit meiner Sprache]" would perhaps be more accurately interpreted as the poet's singular relation to this language.

It is also noteworthy that Celan's reflections on the nature of poetry emerge increasingly at a crossroads of circumstances.[7] These circumstances involve steps to approach the other and the other's language. Among them, for instance, is Celan's renewed interest in philosopher Martin Heidegger's thought on language and poetry,[8] as well as his encounter—as reader, as translator—with fellow poet Osip Mandelstam.[9] Short of discovering a compass toward definitional poetological truths, these circumstances—the how and the why, as it were—allow for the tracing of a practice, if not a theory, of that transition, which the word might have to pass through, or perhaps be derailed by, in order to become a word in a poem.

The occasion that allows some of these paths to intersect is Celan's introduction of a foreign poet to German-speaking audiences by way of a radio essay titled "Die Dichtung Ossip Mandelstamms." Commissioned by the North German radio, it was broadcast in March of 1960 under a title borrowed from Celan's translation of a poem by the Russian-speaking poet: "The Freedom That Is Dawning There. Poems by Osip Mandelstam, translated from Russian and introduced by Paul Celan [Die Freiheit, die da dämmert. Gedichte von Ossip Mandelstamm, aus dem Russischen übertragen und eingeleitet von Paul Celan]."[10] A clear border is drawn: the poems, as the program's title announces, are Mandelstam's; their introduction and translation—Celan's. Having reviewed the script, the program's editor, Wilhelm Asche, assures the poet of the reliability of his essay's transmission: "This text, together with the poems, will surely give an exact picture [Dieser Text wird zusammen mit den Gedichten sicherlich ein genaues Bild geben]."[11] Tasked with introducing and familiarizing,[12] Celan's radio essay appears at first glance as a particularly familiar version of translation: compensation for distances—between languages, cultures, and physical spaces.

Preceding the news of Celan's recognition with the Georg Büchner Prize by a couple of months, this radio essay acquires further significance as an inadvertent precursor to what has come to be regarded as Celan's main poetological statement, namely, his address *Der Meridian*, recited by the poet on October 22, 1960, in Darmstadt, Germany, on the occasion of accepting the aforesaid prize and recognition.[13] Crucial passages from the radio essay reappear in the acceptance speech. Woven into the fabric of this acceptance (*Entgegennahme*) is the coming-toward, meeting-halfway (*entgegenkommen*) by the other and the other's language. In this way, Celan's introduction of a foreign poet and his poems reemerges in an account of his own poems and, ultimately, a reflection on poetry.[14] From this angle, "Die Dichtung Ossip Mandelstamms" seems crucial for the emergence of Celan's poetics: at stake is, to be sure, this *Dichtung* itself, but also, and perhaps more significantly, the act of its introduction and transmission.

For all of its apparent accidentality and instrumentality, this radio essay nonetheless goes beyond a transparent reproduction of a foreign poetry into a familiar language. Foregrounding his introduction of Mandelstam with an increasingly dense meditation on the nature of the poem (*das Gedicht*), Celan intersperses it with six poems by the to-be-introduced poet.[15] Yet, for all of Celan's emphasis in this text on the specifically Mandelstammian poem ("Gedicht Ossip Mandelstamms"/ "das Mandelstammsche Gedicht"),[16] no mention is made within the essay's text of the fact that the poems recited in it are precisely not the originals of the to-be-introduced Mandelstam, but rather the introducer's—Celan's—translations. Given the degree to which Celan's translations do not simply reproduce their originals in German,[17] this minimization of the translator is not self-evident, even if it thereby follows the conventions of cultural dissemination and popularization. At the same time, however, this circumstance would perhaps be erroneously characterized as a failure on the mediator's, Celan's, part.[18] It leads, rather, to a foregrounding of the liminal space between the language of the introducer and that of the to-be-introduced poet.[19] As though struggling to achieve a proper balance and border between the to-be-introduced poetry and his own introduction, Celan admits to the program's editor: "The text had grown over my head; it was harder to cut it than to write it [Mir war der Text über den Kopf gewachsen, ihn zu kürzen war schwerer als ihn zu schreiben]."[20] Significantly, then, in its theorization of the singular language of poetry (*Dichtung*) as the poem (*das Gedicht*), "Die Dichtung Ossip Mandelstamms" has poems-in-translation stand in for poems *as* poems. Moreover, Celan's effort to transmit Mandelstam's *Dichtung*—translatable as "poetry" but perhaps also as the activity or process whereby "poetry" takes shape—critically references and revises Martin Heidegger's idiom. In my reading of

Celan's radio essay, I want to draw attention away from its arguable merit as an accurate transmission of Mandelstam's theory and practice of poetry in order to highlight, rather, the peculiar coincidence in it of circumstances and translations. In this intersection of languages and poetries, Celan begins to articulate a poetics that, in lieu of the word's qualitative change from non-poetic to poetic, comes up against an inextricable boundedness to the other and the other's language.

## One Literary Emigrant Introduces Another

While the circumstance that Celan's "Die Dichtung Ossip Mandelstamms" takes the form of a radio essay is perhaps quite accidental, it can nonetheless be situated within a larger logic of cultural production and a renewed, albeit questionable, energy this cultural production experienced in Germany in the 1960s.[21] Speaking publicly in postwar Germany is not a self-evident matter, and the uneasy gesture on the part of exiled intellectuals of stepping out and addressing an audience whose members may well have contributed to the addressers' exclusion and expulsion—and therefore to their inability to speak and address in the first place—has been rigorously explored.[22] The texts usually considered under this angle are public speeches: in Celan's case, his Bremen and Darmstadt prize acceptance addresses.

I would like to suggest that Celan's radio essay on Mandelstam's poetry can also be considered in this light. Here, however, the act of public speaking acquires added complexity due to its marked indirection. In this essay of advocacy and remembrance, Celan speaks not for himself, but rather for someone else—and, moreover, for someone who is no longer able to speak. Furthermore, Celan steps into the background as speaker and as the essay's univocal authorial origin: not only by using gestures of report and hearsay but also by distributing the essay's script between two alternating voices (first speaker and second speaker).[23] Finally, insofar as his introduction of the foreign poet is transmitted by way of radio waves, Celan is not addressing an audience directly in front of him. Qua radio listeners, this essay's recipients cannot be exactly predetermined or located with certainty.

Indeed, Celan's introduction of Mandelstam acquires added resonance as a radio broadcast: even as it stands in tension with the tradition of radio as a centralizing instrument of culturalization, as a radio broadcast (*Rundfunkübertragung*), whose generic function consists in centralizing and unifying by way of informing—from a single origin—as many listeners at once as possible, about something that concerns all of them.[24] Here, one may recall a particularly blatant instance of this consolidating practice, pervasively deployed in the essay's very recent past for the purpose of mass propaganda: physician and poet Gottfried Benn's open letter titled "Answer to the Literary Emigrants" ("Antwort an die literarischen Emigranten")—a public response to a private letter from writer Klaus Mann that was broadcast by the Berlin radio on May 24, 1933, as well as published in the *Deutsche Allgemeine Zeitung*, a month after the broadcast of Benn's dogmatic address to the German nation, "The New State and the Intellectuals" ("Der neue Staat und die Intellektuellen"). In his wall-building address, Benn dictates a patronizing call for homogeneous experience within national borders as a prerequisite for the shareability of political discourse:[25]

> Only those who went through the tensions of the last months, who witnessed all of this continuously, from immediate proximity—hour to hour, newspaper to newspaper, radio broadcast to radio broadcast—wrestled with it night and day, even those who did not greet all of this jubilantly but rather suffered it, with all of them one can speak, but with the fugitives who traveled abroad one cannot.
>
> (Nur die, die durch die Spannungen der letzten Monate hindurchgegangen sind, die von Stunde zu Stunde, von Zeitung zu Zeitung, von Umzug zu Umzug, von Rundfunkübertragung zu Rundfunkübertragung alles dies fortlaufend aus unmittelbarer Nähe miterlebten, Tag und Nacht mit ihm rangen, selbst die, die das alles nicht jubelnd begrüßten, sondern es mehr erlitten, mit diesen allen kann man reden, aber mit den Flüchtlingen, die ins Ausland reisten, kann man es nicht.)[26]

Most flagrant in this unabashedly verbose and widely transmitted address is its denial to the other of the bare minimum: the ability to speak. To be sure, the refugees may certainly speak, but their speech will be utterly futile, sent into thin air and not received by what Benn understands to be authentic speakers—speakers bound to their homeland with an immediate bond ("aus unmittelbarer Nähe") of direct experience. One's capacity to transmit to the other is confiscated once one steps outside of the threshold of the national borders, whose radius is circumscribed by the national radio.

The ominous shadow of Benn's nationally broadcast demand for a common tongue of an immediately shared experience sets Celan's radio essay and its gesture of transmission into sharp relief. Whereas Benn appeals to a first-person plural standpoint easily translatable into the ubiquitous third-person "one" (*man*), the very possibility of such a shareable, transmittable perspective poses a profound problem in Celan's introduction of Mandelstam. To be sure, Celan too uses the pronoun *man*—yet not as a transparent substitute for an all-encompassing "we" (*wir*) but, rather, as a defamiliarizing indication of its indirect provenance: of an elsewhere from which this report about Mandelstam originates: "In 1913, a slender volume of poems appears in St. Petersburg: *Stone*. These poems have—one recognizes this—weight; one would like . . . to have written them oneself [1913 erscheint in Petersburg ein schmaler Gedichtband: 'Der Stein.' Diese Gedichte haben, das erkennt man, Gewicht, man möchte sie . . . selbst geschrieben haben]" (215; my emphasis). Indeed, written a year before the construction of the Berlin Wall, Celan's radio essay on Mandelstam is marked by circumstances of separation and exclusion. Here, one poet, living away not only from his no longer existent homeland but also from places where his native German is spoken, is trying to bring something closer to speakers of German in Germany—most of whom may nominally share a language with the poet, but likely from a vastly different angle.[27] To be brought closer is the poetry of another poet: one whose poetic language—that is, whose singular relationship to his native Russian—earned him not only expulsion from the literary profession but also exile, albeit within the borders of Russian-speaking territory.[28] Persecuted by the totalitarian Soviet state for failing to conform to the parameters of language and thought prescribed by it, Mandelstam and his poems were posthumously erased from the state-sanctioned cultural discourse.[29] Notably, too, Celan's radio essay on Mandelstam and his poetry coincides with his own experience of persecution: by slanderous accusations of plagiarism and thus by attempts to erase the accused poet's singular relationship to language, his singular poetic idiom.[30] Written in the wake of the unspeakable consequences of the national—linguistic, cultural, intellectual—totalization hailed by Benn, Celan's "Die Dichtung Ossip Mandelstamms" reads as a particularly poignant missive from one literary emigrant about another, directed toward the speakers of the German language, in Germany—a defiant gesture of poetry against exclusionary borders, categories, and idioms. In this light, then, even as it appears at first glance as a helpful mediator between an unknown poet and an unknowing audience, Celan's radio essay "Die Dichtung Ossip Mandelstamms" emerges as a complex intersection between an encounter, a confrontation, and a dissemination.

## A Defamiliarizing Introduction

Indeed, given these circumstances of exclusion and foreignness, one would expect Celan's essay of introduction to serve as a path toward familiarization and reconciliation. However, from the outset, Celan oddly insists on a certain estranging quality of the to-be-introduced poet and his poems: "One would like, as the poets Georgij Iwanow and Nikolaj Gumiljow admit, to have written them oneself, but—these poems *appear strange/alienate* [Man möchte sie, wie die Dichter Georgij Iwanow und Nikolaj Gumiljow bekennen, selbst geschrieben haben, aber—diese Gedichte *befremden*]" (215). Introduced with an adversative "but" (*aber*) and a dash, the word *befremden* cannot be assimilated easily into its surroundings and yet insistently intervenes three more times in the course of the essay's introductory pages.[31] This word, however, does not lend itself easily to translation. Most idiomatically rendered as "disconcert," it also contains an echo of its components—the transitive prefix *be-* and the adjective *fremd*—suggesting not only that a certain foreignness is contained in the subject being introduced but also that the quality thus verbalized could affect the recipients of this introduction as well. The to-be-introduced poems take by surprise, appear strange, alienate but perhaps also distance, render foreign—a veritable predicament for an essay of introduction.

Despite the reportedly estranging character of Mandelstam's poems, Celan rejects a series of three composite nouns—seemingly fitting translators of strangeness—as these poems' characterizations: they are neither "word-music [Wortmusik]" nor "tone-colors [Klangfarben]" nor "mood-poetry [Stimmungspoesie]" (215). All three of them in some way synesthetic, these terms seek to unite two disparate semantic elements in order to cross a certain boundary by poetic means, as it were[32]—a possible solution, to be sure, to the puzzle about the qualitative transition that the word has to go through in order to become the word in the poem.[33] Celan further contrasts Mandelstam's poems with the poetic practice of spatiotemporal overreach—futurism: "In contrast to the futurism that is simultaneously gaining more ground, these verses are free from word-creations, word-agglomerations, word-fragmentations; they are no new 'art of expression' [Diese Verse sind, im Gegensatz zu dem sich gleichzeitig Raum greifenden Futurismus, frei von Wortschöpfungen, Wortballungen, Wortzertrümmerungen; sie sind keine neue 'Ausdruckskunst']" (215).[34] It is not, then, from an imagined future, colonized for the purposes of the present, that Mandelstam's poetry imports its strangeness. Nor does the constitutively estranging characteristic of his poems proceed from an unfamiliar technique or art (*Kunst*) of putting together a novel means of expression—this, after all, would allow for a gradual domestication of that which is newly expressed. Rather, foreignness is constitutive of these poems *as* poems.

With his largely negatively formulated introductory report, Celan sets Mandelstam's attitude toward language apart from the more familiar one: language as a posterior translator and instrument of familiarization with something essentially prior to and separate from it. Rather than lying outside as an object importable *into* poetry, the estranging factor identified by Celan in Mandelstam's poetic language is inextricably bound up with this language itself. It seems, then, these to-be-introduced poems estrange, *befremden*, in a strange manner.

## Seeking Refuge in Philosophy

Celan's vocabulary of wonder-causing estrangement is reminiscent of Martin Heidegger's invocation of the Greek verb *thaumazein*,[35] which the philosopher translates into German as "Erstaunen" ("to wonder") and interprets as the authentically philosophical predisposition in his essay from 1955, "Was ist das—die Philosophie?"[36] In this address, delivered on foreign ground (Cerisy-la-Salle, Normandy) but on a fundamental topic, Heidegger, not unlike Celan in his radio essay, takes on the role of mediator, translator, and introducer. Under the shield of the familiar first-person plural pronoun "we" (*wir*), the German-speaking thinker transmits to speakers of French essential missives about philosophy, which he mines from its original language: "Through the word, heard in the Greek way, we are directly by the matter at hand, not just by a mere word-meaning [Wir sind durch das griechisch gehörte Wort unmittelbar bei der vorliegenden Sache selbst, nicht zunächst bei einer bloßen Wortbedeutung]."[37] By reaching over for *the* properly heard Greek *word*, Heidegger wants to bypass the obstacle of mere words in order to gain immediate access to the thing itself: the fundamental question of what philosophy is.[38] Similar to Celan's wonder about the qualitative change necessary for the word to become the word *in* the poem, Heidegger is in search of a path toward the entrance *into* philosophy: "But the goal of our question is to walk into philosophy, to stay in it, to comport ourselves according to its way, i.e., to 'philosophize' [Aber das Ziel unserer Frage ist, in die Philosophie hineinzukommen, in ihr uns aufzuhalten, nach ihrer Weise uns zu verhalten, d.h. zu 'philosophieren']."[39] The philosopher-guide is concerned with identifying the qualitative change necessary for the word—the thought—to become the word and the thought in philosophy (*die Philosophie*).

Even as Heidegger seems to acknowledge the wondrous nature of his inquiry's subject matter by interrupting the flow between the question ("Was ist das") and its object ("die Philosophie"), he wants to balance this situation out:

> Our speaking must cor-respond to that by which the philosophers are addressed. If we succeed in this cor-responding, then we an-swer in the genuine sense the question: What is it—philosophy? The German word "antworten" actually means as much as cor-respond.
>
> (Unser Sprechen muß dem, wovon die Philosophen angesprochen sind, ent-sprechen. Wenn uns dieses Ent-sprechen glückt, dann ant-worten wir im echten Sinne auf die Frage: Was ist das—die Philosophie? Das deutsche Wort "antworten" bedeutet eigentlich soviel wie ent-sprechen.)[40]

The philosopher lends an attentive ear to a speech (*Sprechen*) that is authentic enough to be a cor-respondence ("Ent-sprechen"), and one that could be translated with no leftovers ("as much as," "soviel wie") as the German word ("das deutsche Wort") "ant-worten." With this origin-seeking equation, Heidegger pinpoints the notion of "correspondence" (*Entsprechen*), which, starting from his essay from 1936, "Der Ursprung des Kunstwerkes," frequently resurfaces in the philosopher's later theories about language and poetry.[41] Most readily rendered in English as the verb "to correspond," the word *entsprechen* may appear to go against Heidegger's signature critique of truth as correspondence, although, to be sure, the philosopher's elusive use of the term resists this apparent contradiction.[42]

Yet in a preparatory note to his radio essay on Mandelstam, Celan, who owned and likely read Heidegger's essay about the essence of philosophy,[43] seems to refuse to lend an ear precisely to the idiosyncratic subtlety of Heidegger's terminology of correspondence. The poet insists on an irreducible foreignness that cannot be canceled out:

> The poem is here the place where that which is beheld and perceived through language—that which is named—comes, with its <u>time</u>, into a relationship of <u>tension</u> with the beholding and the speaking one. *That which is foreign remains foreign, it does not "correspond" <u>entirely, it retains its opacity [which lends it relief and appearing (phenomenality)]</u>.
>
> (Das Gedicht ist hier der Ort, wo das Angeschaute und sprachlich Wahrgenommene—das Genannte—mit seiner <u>Zeit</u> in ein <u>Spannungs</u>verhältnis tritt zum Anschauenden und Sprechenden. *Das Fremde bleibt fremd, es "entspricht" [und antwortet] nicht <u>ganz</u>, es behält seine [ihm Relief und Erscheinen (Phänomenalität) verleihende] Opazität.) (71)

Shortly, we will encounter the final version of these notes, but in this incipient articulation they attest to a peculiar borrowing from Heidegger, which, rather than outright reject the philosopher's vocabulary, interjects into its wholesome linguistic equation a number of diacritic correctives that call into question the possibility of uncompromised transmission from the ostensibly originary language of thinking. Instead, Celan envisions the poem as a place of confrontation and tension *within* and *through* language: "that which is beheld and perceived through language—that which is named [das Angeschaute und sprachlich Wahrgenommene—das Genannte]." In this linguistically hesitant note about (poetic) language there emerges the gesture of approaching, reminiscent of Celan's aforementioned note to Werner Weber from July 1959. There, trying to approach translation, Celan attributed, counterintuitively, the gesture of coming closer, half-way, against (*entgegenkommen*), not to the translator but to the to-be-translated other and this other's language. Here, in this slightly later preparatory note, Celan locates the gesture of moving toward (*tritt zum*), not in the one who is speaking but in that which is spoken, perceived through language.

Whereas Heidegger imagines philosophy as a coveted destination, into which one finds entrance through appropriate hearing and transmission ("heard in a Greek way," "griechisch gehört") and in which one finds refuge through appropriate conduct ("to comport ourselves according to its way [nach ihrer Weise uns zu verhalten]"), Celan sees the poem as the space *in* and *through which* something takes place—and not just a univocal something but rather a relation and, moreover, a relation of tension. This way, the moment of approach, tension, and non-identity intervenes into Celan's reflections on the question that, perhaps only seemingly corresponding to Heidegger's formulation, could be formulated as "What is it—a poem?" Different from the ultimately harmonious state of wonder in Heidegger, the tension of foreignness and strangeness envisioned by Celan in the space that is a poem precludes the possibility of definitional, qualitative borders.

## Being or Poem

Whereas Heidegger wants to carry out a smooth transmission from the philosopher-guide to his keen listeners, Celan's vision of the poem is much more indirect. Instead of filling in the gaps left by the negatively formulated opening remarks about the strangeness of the to-be-introduced poet and poems, Celan proceeds to an exceedingly circuitous definition of the poem, one that, several months later and in a slightly altered form, will reemerge in the poet's *Meridian* speech:[44]

> The poem is here the poem of someone who knows that he speaks under the angle of inclination of his existence, that the language of his poem is neither "correspondence" nor language as such, but rather *actualized* language, voiced and voiceless at the same time, set free in the sign of an individuation that, while radical, is at the same time remaining mindful of the limits set to it by language, of the possibilities opened up to it by language.
>
> (Das Gedicht ist hier das Gedicht dessen, der weiß, daß er unter dem Neigungswinkel seiner Existenz spricht, daß die Sprache seines Gedichts weder "Entsprechung" noch Sprache schlechthin ist, sondern *aktualisierte* Sprache, stimmhaft und stimmlos zugleich, freigesetzt im Zeichen einer zwar radikalen, aber gleichzeitig auch der ihr von der Sprache gesetzten Grenzen, der ihr von der Sprache erschlossenen Möglichkeiten eingedenk bleibenden Individuation.) (215, Celan's italics)

Once again rejecting Heidegger's notion of correspondence (*Entsprechen*), which Celan here inflects slightly as *Entsprechung*,[45] the poet borrows, and decisively edits, another word from the philosopher's vocabulary: *Individuation*.⁴⁶ At a crucial definitional locus in his magnum opus *Being and Time*,⁴⁷ Heidegger stakes out his vision of philosophy in the following manner:

> Being and the structure of Being lie beyond every entity and every possible character which an entity may possess. *Being is the transcendens pure and simple.* And the transcendence of Dasein's Being is distinctive in that it implies the possibility and the necessity of the most radical *individuation.* Every disclosure of being as the transcendens is *transcendental* knowledge. *Phenomenological truth (the disclosedness of Being) is veritas transcendentalis.*⁴⁸

> (Sein und Seinsstruktur liegen über jedes Seiende und jede mögliche seiende Bestimmtheit eines Seienden hinaus. *Sein ist das transcendens schlechthin.* Die Transzendenz des Seins des Daseins ist eine ausgezeichnete, sofern in ihr die Möglichkeit und Notwendigkeit der radikalsten *Individuation* liegt. Jede Erschließung von Sein als des transcendens ist *transzendentale* Erkenntnis. *Phänomenologische Wahrheit (Erschlossenheit von Sein) ist veritas transcendentalis.*)⁴⁹

Curiously, it is also in this paragraph that the philosopher will preemptively apologize for the imminent awkwardness of his diction, citing as an excuse the peculiarity of the subject matter—Being (*Sein*) as opposed to mere entities (*Seiendes*)—and an absence of adequate linguistic tools to capture it.⁵⁰ At this definitional juncture, however, Heidegger writes not only quite clearly but also with the authority of canonical Latin philosophical terminology. It is noteworthy, then, that in a passage appearing to correspond to Heidegger's vocabulary, Celan unapologetically puts forward an emphatically convoluted reflection and does so in an effort to introduce and transmit someone else's (Mandelstam's) poetic language.

Heidegger's definitional consideration subordinates everything to a transcendent beyond—albeit structurally and not literally: Being (*Sein*). Celan's, in contrast, foregrounds that which is most concrete bound to its here and now: the poem (*das Gedicht*). Likewise, differently from Heidegger's declaratively articulated statements in which individuation is mentioned merely as a distinct moment within the ontological hierarchy envisioned by him, Celan weaves his reflection on individuation from a tightly interconnected series of past and present participles—"set free [freigesetzt]," "set [gesetzt]," "opened up [erschlossen]," "remaining mindful [eingedenk bleibend]." Beginning with "the poem" (*das Gedicht*), this participial chain does not arrive at "individuation" until the very end of the sentence. The link between "the poem" and "individuation" lies in the possessive pronoun *dessen* ("whose" or "of someone who"): "The poem is here the poem of someone who . . . [Das Gedicht ist hier das Gedicht dessen, der . . .]"). Both emphatically bound and open at once, this pronoun allows Celan's essay to step beyond a narrowly biographical report and to venture instead into a meditation on poetry tout court. However, rather than offer a generic-poetological definition, Celan envisions poetry in terms of a single, concrete poem whose singularity lies in its inextricable tie to a someone who . . . (*dessen*). That is, the poem *as* poem is *of* someone: of someone, more precisely, who is aware of his or her singular moment of speaking—what Celan here and elsewhere calls "angle of inclination of one's existence [Neigungswinkel seiner Existenz]."[51]

"Existence" is, of course, likewise a technical Heideggerian term used by Heidegger to characterize the specifically human mode of being, which he calls *Dasein*. For Heidegger, *Existenz* harbors the sense of being-outside of oneself, which he sees as a definitive characteristic of *Dasein* and which he relates to the problem of ecstatic temporality more generally.[52] This sense of being turned toward something outside of itself is legible in Celan's characterization of Mandelstam's poems:

> These poems are the poems of a perceiving and attentive one, of one who is turned toward that which appears, one who questions and addresses that which appears; they are *conversation*. In the space of this conversation, that which is being addressed constitutes itself, becomes present, gathers itself around the I that is addressing and naming it. But that which is being addressed and, as it were, becomes a you through the act of naming brings with it its otherness and foreignness.
>
> (Diese Gedichte sind die Gedichte eines Wahrnehmenden und Aufmerksamen, dem Erscheinenden Zugewandten, das Erscheinende Befragenden und Ansprechenden; sie sind *Gespräch*. Im Raum dieses Gesprächs konstituiert sich das Angesprochene, vergegenwärtigt es sich, versammelt es sich um das es ansprechende und nennende Ich. Aber in diese Gegenwart bringt das Angesprochene und durch Nennung gleichsam zum Du Gewordene sein Anders- und Fremdsein mit.) (216)

Here, once again, Celan characterizes Mandelstam's poems by specifying *whose* poems they are. And again, in lieu of a biographical portrayal, Celan defines this genitive in terms of a relation, but rather than presenting the relata as preexisting entities that can enter into relations with one another within time,[53] he emphasizes their irreducible boundedness to, and constitution through, the moment of encounter. Here too, constructed around a series of nominalized participles, Celan's characterization of "these poems" shifts the substantive meaning away from its usual carrier: away from nouns that are a posteriori capable of performing certain actions (finite conjugated verbs). That is, these poems are someone's not in the sense of being the product of this someone's autonomous genius, but rather in the sense of registering this someone's irreducible relation to another. The participle, then, allows Celan's characterization of the poem to evade the border between the speaking and the spoken and to remain rather in the liminal space between them.

As much as Celan's diction in this passage resembles Heidegger's, the poet nonetheless complicates the philosopher's analysis of the human mode of being as *Ek-sistenz* by probing an in-between, a space of tension:

> It is this tension relationship of the times, of one's own and a foreign one, that lends to the Mandelstammian poem that painful-mute vibrato through which we recognize it. (This vibrato is everywhere: in the intervals between the words and the stanzas, in the "courtyards" in which the rhymes and the assonances are standing, in the punctuation. All of this has *semantic* relevance.) Things step toward each other, but even in this being-by-each-other speaks the question about their Wherefrom and Whereto—a question that "remains open," "comes to no end," points into the open and the occupiable, into the empty and the free.
>
> (Es ist dieses Spannungsverhältnis der Zeiten, der eigenen und der fremden, das dem mandelstamm'schen Gedicht jenes schmerzlich-stumme Vibrato verleiht, an dem wir es erkennen. (Dieses Vibrato ist überall: in den Intervallen zwischen den Worten und den Strophen, in den "Höfen," in denen die Reime und die Assonanzen stehen, in der Interpunktion. All das hat *semantische* Relevanz.) Die Dinge treten zueinander, aber noch in diesem Beisammensein spricht die Frage nach ihrem Woher und Wohin mit—eine "offenbleibende," "zu keinem Ende

kommende," ins Offene und Besetzbare, ins Leere und Freie weisende Frage.) (216)

Somewhat counterintuitively identifying the positively unrecognizable characteristic of tension (*Spannungsverhältnis*) as a mark of recognition ("an dem wir es erkennen"), Celan insists on alterity as a constitutive feature of Mandelstam's poems.[54] We have already encountered this relation of tension between times ("Spannungsverhältnis der Zeiten") in Celan's preparatory notes, where he corrected Heidegger's synchronizing verbs "to correspond" (*entsprechen*) and "to answer" (*antworten*) with the verdict "The foreign remains foreign [Das Fremde bleibt fremd]." Here, in the broadcast version of that remark, Celan insists that the strangeness of these to-be-introduced poems lies not in their self-contained essence but, rather, in their constitutive transcendence of themselves: in their relatedness. Resonating in Celan's notion of individuation is perhaps something like *dividuation*: relation, tension.

In his reflections on the role of time and language in Mandelstam's poetry, Celan singles out the non-finite verb form as a definitive aspect of Mandelstam's own poetic language:

> This question [about their Wherefrom and Whereto] realizes itself not only in the "thematics" of the poems; it also takes shape in language—and precisely thereby becomes a "theme": the word—the Name!—shows an inclination towards the nominal, the adjective wanes, the "infinite," the *nominal forms* of the verb prevail: the poem remains *time-open*, time can step up, time *participates.*
>
> (Diese Frage [nach ihrem Woher und Wohin] realisiert sich nicht nur in der "Thematik" der Gedichte; sie nimmt auch—und eben dadurch wird sie zum "Thema"—in der Sprache Gestalt an: das Wort—der Name!—zeigt eine Neigung zum Substantivischen, das Beiwort schwindet, die "infiniten," die *Nominalformen* des Zeitworts herrschen vor: das Gedicht bleibt *zeitoffen*, Zeit kann hinzutreten, Zeit *partizipiert*.) (216, Celan's italics)

In a double move of translation, Celan renders the familiar Latin-derived word "verb" as its much less familiar German equivalent "Zeitwort," while at the same time opting for a rare Latinized rendering (*partizipieren*) to articulate the peculiar role of time in Mandelstam's poems: "Time *participates* [Zeit *partizipiert*]." Entangling merely grammatical categories with their concrete implications, this peculiar word choice does not so much correspond to Mandelstam's original Russian as it recalls Celan's own prominent use of participial constructions—that is, "infinite" verb forms—in his description of Mandelstam's poems. Why, one might ask, does Celan attribute to Mandelstam's poetic idiom a linguistic idiosyncrasy much more characteristic of his own diction?[55] This entanglement of idioms is complicated further by the circumstance that non-finite verb forms, and participles in particular, are prevalent in Heidegger's German—the present participle *Seiendes* and the nominalized infinitive *Dasein* are just two crucial examples. It is certainly noteworthy that, in an attempt to familiarize radio listeners with someone's (Mandelstam's) poetry, Celan critically engages with the language of another (Heidegger). In this way, in lieu of an adequately corresponding transmission, an insistent interference can be traced in Celan's radio introduction of Mandelstam.[56]

## *Leideform der Zukunft*

Celan concludes his essay of introduction with a note on Mandelstam's self-reported affinity for a grammatical category from the past, the Latin gerundive:

> In one of his last publications, the Armenian Diary published in 1932 in the Leningrad journal "Zwezda," we also find some notes on questions of poetry. In one of these notes Mandelstam remembers his preference for the Latin *gerundive*.
> 
> The gerundive—that is the participle of the passive form of the future.
> 
> (In einer seiner letzten Veröffentlichungen, dem 1932 in der Leningrader Zeitschrift "Swesda" erschienenen Armenischen Tagebuch, finden wir auch einige Aufzeichnungen zu Fragen der Dichtung. In einer dieser Notizen erinnert sich Mandelstamm an seine Vorliebe für das lateinische *Gerundiv*.
> 
> Das Gerundiv—das ist das Mittelwort der Leideform der Zukunft.) (221; Celan's italics)

Here, Celan is referring to Mandelstam's prose piece *Journey to Armenia*, in whose penultimate chapter Mandelstam writes: "—What tense would you like to live in?—I would like to live in the imperative future participle, in the passive voice—in the having-to-be."[57] Having rejected a series of composite nouns as possible designations for Mandelstam's poetry in the beginning of his essay, Celan closes it by invoking a concept composed of not one but three composite nouns: "the participle of the passive voice of the future" (literally, "the middle-word of the passive-form of the to-come" [das Mittelwort der Leideform der Zukunft]). As Bernhard Böschenstein has pointed out, this formulation is a bizarre substitution for the familiar Latin grammatical designations: *Partizip, Passiv, Futurum*.[58] In contrast to Heidegger's appeal to Latin philosophical terms (e.g., *veritas transcendentalis*) at the beginning of his proper introduction to philosophy proper, Celan concludes his own introductory text and its apparent task of familiarization by defamiliarizing the most perfunctory tools of language and thought: grammatical concepts that, qua invisible infrastructure, would seem to transcend the necessity of translation in the first place. Peculiarly tangible and concrete, these grammatical terms superfluously translated into German—*Mittelwort, Leideform, Zukunft*—stick out as irreducibly foreign, belying the apparent neutrality of linguistic terminology and its promise of translation as correspondence and equivalence, without remainder.

Somewhat abruptly concluding his sketch of Mandelstam's poetry with the word "future" (*Zukunft*), Celan reaches out beyond this introductory text's borders, as though pointing to a dimension of the to-be-introduced poet and poetry that cannot be congealed into an individual image, contained within a familiar frame, and preserved in a transmissible, introducible past. To be sure, Celan's reference to something that is yet to come (*Zukunft*) is peculiarly ecstatic, oriented beyond itself and toward something or someone else. Yet, differently from a neutrally structural-Heideggerian sense, it is also bound up with a foreshadowing of something irreducibly concrete and ontic, as it were: namely, the sense of "suffering" latently legible in the word *Leideform*.[59] Notably, too, these final remarks, meant to close an essay of introduction, are cited from the to-be-introduced poet's own reflections on questions of poetry (*Dichtung*). In this manner, Celan's essay ends with a peculiar intertwining of a concrete existence and poetry, insisting on a notion of the latter that does not lend itself to a generically atemporal definition: a poetry, that is, that always takes place as singular poems, inextricably bound to concrete moments in, and relations to, time.

In light of the unmistakable traces of Heidegger's language in Celan's essay on Mandelstam, it is notable that Celan, in the preface to his translations of forty poems by Mandelstam from 1959, uses a word—"availability" (*Vorhandensein*)—that will strike anyone familiar with Heidegger's terminology as decidedly unexpected in a discussion of something as elevated as poetry: "To the selection, provided to the German-speaking reader with this book . . . should, first of all, be given the chance, which remains the first among many of every poetry: the chance of merely being available [Der mit diesem Buch dem deutschsprachigen Leser vorgelegten Auswahl . . . soll zunächst die Chance gegeben sein, die unter den vielen die erste jeder Dichtung bleibt: die des bloßen Vorhandenseins]."[60] Representing one of the modes of being in Heidegger's ontological hierarchy, the term *vorhanden* (literally, "available") has been translated as "present-at-hand" to render the sense of a merely inner-temporal mode of being.[61] And yet, it is precisely this mere availability that Celan identifies as indispensable to poems. Different from Heidegger's hierarchization of modes of being from more to less deficient, Celan points to the irreducible vulnerability and precarity of poems, against which no fundamental-phenomenological analysis can offer a safeguard. Rather, as Celan seems to insist, poems inevitably rely on the precarious gestures of translation and transmission.

## *Geschiedensein* of Languages

On March 26, 1960, a week after the transmission of Celan's essay about Mandelstam by the North German radio, Celan sends some reflections on translation to the aforementioned journalist and literary scholar Werner Weber, on the occasion of Celan's recently completed translation of Paul Valéry's "La Jeune Parque"—a fragment of which the poet had promised the critic in place of the originally requested lyric poetry (*Lyrik*):

> For languages, as much as they appear to correspond to one another, are different—separated by abysses. . . . Yes, the poem, the translated poem must remain mindful of this otherness and difference, of this separateness, if it wants to be there one more time in the second language. . . . But how many of those are there today who perceive such aspects of the poetic at all? Those who perceive the poem as a human presence—and therefore

accompanied by the mystery of singularity? How many are there of those who know how to be silent with the word, to remain with it when it is standing in the interval, in its "courtyards," in its—key-distant—openness, felling the voiced from the voiceless, clarifying the diastole in the systole, avid for the world and infinity at the same time.

(Denn die Sprachen, so sehr sie einander zu entsprechen scheinen, sind verschieden—geschieden durch Abgründe. . . . Ja, das Gedicht, das übertragene Gedicht muß, wenn es in der zweiten Sprache noch einmal dasein will, dieses Anders- und Verschiedenseins, dieses Geschiedenseins eingedenk bleiben. . . . Aber wieviele sind es heute, die solche Aspekte des Dichterischen überhaupt wahrnehmen? Das Gedicht wahrnehmen als menschliche—und mithin einmalige und vom Geheimnis der Einmaligkeit begleitete—Präsenz? Wieviele sind es wohl, die mit dem Wort zu schweigen wissen, bei ihm bleiben, wenn es im Intervall steht, in seinen "Höfen," in seiner—schlüsselfernen—Offenheit, das Stimmhafte aus dem Stimmlosen fällend, in der Systole die Diastole verdeutlichend, welt- und unendlichkeitssüchtig zugleich.)[62]

At points unmistakably echoing the radio essay,[63] this passage situates Celan's reflections on Mandelstam's poems—and what it means to write poems—within his contemporaneous reflections on what it means to translate poems.[64] Once again departing from Heidegger's focus on language as such (*Sprache*), Celan writes of languages in the plural (*Sprachen*). In this way, the poet envisions language from the perspective of its a priori difference, thereby subverting the familiar notion of translation as a posterior correspondence between an original and a copy. For Celan, the seeming correspondence (*entsprechen*) of languages to one another—insofar as they are thought to be uniform tools of communication—is destabilized by the unbridgeable distinctions between them ("separated through abysses [geschieden durch Abgründe]"). Here, moreover, the notion of correspondence and adequation (*entsprechen*), repeatedly invoked and revised by Celan in his radio essay, acquires a double meaning. While the word *entsprechen* could be read datively in its familiar meaning "to correspond," its proximity to the word "Sprachen" in Celan's formulation—"Denn die Sprachen, so sehr sie einander zu entsprechen scheinen, sind verschieden"—brings out the verb's admittedly nonidiomatic, accusatively negative resonance: *ent-sprechen* ("de-language"). That is, languages in the plural, *Sprachen*, cannot de-language one another into a zero-sum aggregate of a self-same single language and can never cancel one another out. No perfectly fitting translation could ever conceal the poem's a priori translatedness. In this light, what seems like a merely appositive specification—"the poem, the translated poem [das Gedicht, das übertragene Gedicht]"—suggests, more emphatically, that a poetic text, for Celan, is by definition a translated one, oriented beyond itself. The mode of being of the poem—and not just of the translated poem but of every poem *as* translated—is then not so much *Sein*, Being, as *Geschiedensein*: being-separated or being-divided. Through a practice of translation and transmission, Celan's poetological concern seems to have undergone a transformation: the poet's poetological hesitancy in 1954 about translating the word into the word in the poem has, by 1960, transformed into a question of "the poem, the translated poem."

In his letter to Weber, Celan inscribes "poems" into his remarks on translation, tersely stating, "poems are gifts [Gedichte sind Geschenke]."[65] As at several other points in his letter, Celan implicitly references Heidegger's vocabulary—here, specifically, the philosopher's understanding of a poem (*Gedicht*) as a gift (*Geschenk*).[66] Yet, here too Celan revises the philosopher's neutrally accretive equation, punctuating it with several stumbles and correctives: "Poems—yes, poems are gifts; gifts—from whose hand? [Gedichte—ja, Gedichte sind Geschenke; Geschenke—aus wessen Hand?]."[67] Celan's revision is further legible as he downplays the poet-translator's feat of handling the untranslatable,[68] foregrounding instead the irreducible question of the poem's provenance: "—from whose hand? [aus wessen Hand?]." For Celan, then, the poet does not so much dispense (*schenken*) a poem but finds themselves on the receiving end of this donation. In an odd abdication of authority, Celan registers his wonder at having been approached by his German translation, "Die junge Parze": "To this day, it appears wonderful to me that this poem came to me [Mir erscheint es noch heute wunderbar, daß dieses Gedicht zu mir kam]."[69] Instead of penning down the poem in full mastery of its composition and meaning, the poet assumes a passive role, is visited, and is approached by the poem. Notably, too, the poem, which Celan recalls came toward him, is the German translation "Die junge Parze," and not the French original, "La Jeune Parque."

Two months later, in May of 1960, once again declining Hans Bender's request for collectible poetological insight, Celan will take up this figure of the hand and its insistence on the inextricable boundedness of the poem to a moment of encounter: "Only true hands write true poems. I see no fundamental difference between a handshake and a poem [Nur wahre Hände schreiben wahre Gedichte. Ich sehe keinen prinzipiellen Unterschied zwischen Händedruck und Gedicht]."[70] This remark also comments on the poet's attempt to introduce and translate the foreign poet Osip Mandelstam and his strange poems as inextricably bound up with the gesture at the core of letting a poem emerge: the gesture of stepping out and being affected by the other and the other's language.[71]

## Notes

1. Werner Weber, *Werner Weber: Briefwechsel des Literaturkritikers aus sechs Jahrzehnten* (Zurich: Verlag Neue Zürcher Zeitung, 2009), 146. Unless specified otherwise, translations from German are my own.

2. Weber, 146.

3. For a critique of Celan scholars' overreliance on Celan's poetological texts written around 1960, see Thomas C. Connolly, *Paul Celan's Unfinished Poetics: Readings in the Sous-Oeuvre* (Cambridge: Legenda, 2018), 30–41.

4. Paul Celan to Hans Bender 18 November 1954, *Briefe an Hans Bender*, eds. Ute Heimbüchel and Volker Neuhaus (Munich: Hanser Verlag, 1984), 34–35.

5. I thank Paul North for pointing out the possible implications of Celan's vocabulary of "Wort" in this passage.

6. Paul Celan to Hans Bender 18 November 1954, *Briefe an Hans Bender*, 35.

7. Around the time of working on his radio essay on Osip Mandelstam, Celan was contemplating an essay on his translation of Paul Valéry's poem "La Jeune Parque" as well as an essay on Mandelstam. See Paul Celan, *Der Meridian: Endfassung—Vorstufen—Materialien*, eds. Bernhard Böschenstein and Heino Schmull (Frankfurt am Main: Suhrkamp, 1999), xi.

8. On the traces of Heidegger's language in Celan's reflections on poetry, see Amir Eshel, "Paul Celan's Other: History, Poetics, and Ethics," *New German Critique* 91 (2004): 57–77; James Lyon, *Paul Celan and Martin Heidegger: An Unresolved Conversation, 1951–1970* (Baltimore, MD: Johns Hopkins University Press, 2006), 81–91; Joachim Seng, *Auf den Kreis-Wegen der Dichtung: Zyklische Komposition bei Paul Celan am Beispiel der Gedichtbände bis "Sprachgitter"* (Heidelberg: Universitätsverlag C. Winter, 1998), 154–60.

9. For an account of Celan's encounter with Mandelstam's poetry, see Victor Terras and Karl Weimar, "Mandelstam and Celan: A Postscript," *Germano-Slavica* 2.5 (1978): 353–70, 354–56.

10. Paul Celan, *Mikrolithen sinds, Steinchen: Die Prosa aus dem Nachlass*, eds. Barbara Wiedemann and Bertrand Badiou (Frankfurt am Main: Suhrkamp, 2005), 884.

11. Celan, 835.

12. This task is succinctly outlined in the inquiry sent to Celan by Wilhelm Asche: "On the 19th of March we have programmed a 20-minute broadcast with poems by Osip Mandelstam. Of course, half of it should be a biographical-analytical commentary about the author [Am 19. März haben wir eine 20 Minuten-Sendung mit Gedichten von Ossip Mandelstamm im Programm. Freilich soll die knappe Hälfte davon ein biographisch-analytischer Kommentar über den Autor sein]." *"Fremde Nähe" Celan als Übersetzer: eine Ausstellung des Deutschen Literaturarchivs in Verbindung mit dem Präsidialdepartement der Stadt Zürich im Schiller-Nationalmuseum Marbach am Neckar und im Stadthaus Zürich*, eds. Axel Gellhaus et al. (Marbach am Necker: Deutsche Schillergesellschaft, 1997), 362.

13. For an argument against reading *The Meridian* as a purely poetological text, see Kristina Mendicino, "An Other Rhetoric: Paul Celan's *Meridian*," *Modern Language Notes* 126.3 (2011): 630–50, 630–35.

14. On this radio essay's significance for Celan's *Meridian*, see Bernhard Böschenstein, "Celan und Mandelstamm: Beobachtungen zu ihrem Verhältnis," *Celan-Jahrbuch* 2 (1988): 155–68, 156–59; Asche, "*Fremde Nähe*," 364; Christine Ivanovic, *Das Gedicht im Geheimnis der Begegnung* (Tübingen: Max Niemeyer Verlag, 1996), 321–25; Lehmann, "Die Dichtung Ossip Mandelstamms," in *Celan Handbuch: Leben—Werk—Wirkung*, eds. Peter Gossens, Jürgen Lehmann, and Markus May (Stuttgart: Verlag J.B. Metzler, 2012), 164–67.

15. The scope of this paper does not permit an analysis of Celan's translations of Mandelstam's poems or their placement within the radio essay. For a reading of Celan's translations of Mandelstam's poems in this essay, see Anna Glazova, "The Poetry of Bringing about Presence," *Modern Language Notes* 123.5 (2008): 1108–26, 1114–23.

16. Celan, *Der Meridian*, 215. Henceforth, I will cite this source parenthetically in the text of my paper.

17. For a discussion of the contemporaneous reception of Mandelstam's translations with respect to the problematic of translation adequacy, see Barbara Wiedemann, "'Gezeitigte Sprache': Paul Celan's Mandelstamm-Übertragungen aus dem Mai 1958," in *Zwischentexte: literarisches Übersetzen in Theorie und Praxis*, eds. Claudia Dathe, Renata Makarska, and Schamma Schahadat (Leipzig: Frank and Timme Verlag, 2013), 165–96, 165–70.

18. On this essay's apparent failure to fulfill its function of introduction and familiarization, see Lehmann, "Die Dichtung Ossip Mandelstamms," 167. On this essay's eminent inefficacy as an introduction proper, see Ivanovic, *Das Gedicht im Geheimnis der Begegnung*, 343–44.

19. On the role of translation in Celan's poetics, see Leonard Olschner, "Grenzgänge und Gegenwart: Notizen zu Celans Poetik der Übertragung," in *Unverloren. Trotz allem: Paul Celan Symposium Wien 2000*, eds. Hubert Gaisbauer, Bernard Hain, and Erika Schuster (Vienna: Mandelbaum Verlag, 2000), 244–64.

20. Asche, '*Fremde Nähe*," 366.

21. On the attempts in West Germany during the 1960s at rehabilitation and reconciliation, see Amir Eshel, *Zeit der Zäsur: Jüdische Dichter im Angesicht der Shoah* (Heidelberg: Universitätsverlag C. Winter, 1999), 83–85; Wolfgang Emmerich, "'Ich bin der, den es nicht gibt': Der Plagiatsvorwurf gegen Paul Celan und die Folgen," *Unverloren*, 178–204, 183.

22. On the difficulty experienced by exiled Jewish and German intellectuals of speaking publicly after the Shoah, see Sonja Boos, *Speaking the Unspeakable in Postwar Germany* (Ithaca, NY: Cornell University Press, 2014), 3–23.

23. Cf. Glazova, "The Poetry of Bringing about Presence," 1124.

24. On early German radio's political function of centralization, see Solveig Ottmann, *Im Anfang war das Experiment: Das Weimarer Radio bei Hans Flesch und Ernst Schoen* (Berlin: Kulturverlag Kadmos, 2013), 156–63.

25. On the diminishing estrangement and ensuing potential for propaganda in Benn's open letter, see Olga Solovieva, "'Bizarre Epik des Augenblicks': Gottfried Benn's 'Answer to the Literary Emigrants' in the Context of his Early Prose," *German Studies Review* 33.1 (2010): 119–40, 137.

26. Gottfried Benn, "Antwort an die literarischen Emigranten," in *Sämtliche Werke*, ed. Gerhard Schuster, 7 vols. (Stuttgart: Klett-Cotta, 1986), 4:24–25.

27. See Celan's poignant remarks in his Bremen speech from 1958: Paul Celan, "Ansprache anlässlich der Entgegennahme des Literaturpreises der Freien Hansestadt Bremen," in *Gesammelte Werke in fünf Bänden*, eds. Beda Allemann and Stefan Reichert, 5 vols. (Frankfurt am Main: Suhrkamp, 1983), 3:185–86, 186. Celan immigrated to France in 1948. On Celan's anxiety when crossing the German border, see Emmerich, "'Ich bin der, den es nicht gibt,'" 182.

28. On the state-induced barriers to Mandelstam's literary career, see Clare Cavanagh, *Osip Mandelstam and the Modernist Creation of Tradition* (Princeton, NJ: Princeton University Press, 1994), 193–212.

29. As Celan mentions in the preface to the volume of his translations of forty poems by Mandelstam from 1959, the latter's name was just as unavailable to contemporary speakers of Russian: "In Russia, the homeland of this poetry, Osip Mandelstam's poetry volumes still belong to that which has been hushed up, that which has gone missing, that which is mentioned in passing at best [In Rußland, der Heimat dieser Dichtung, zählen die Gedichtbände Ossip Mandelstamms . . . noch immer zum Totgeschwiegenen, Verschollenen, allenfalls am Rande Erwähnten]." Celan, *Gesammelte Werke*, 5:623.

30. On this defamation campaign and its relation to the repressed anti-Semitism of postwar German cultural institutions, see Emmerich, "'Ich bin der, den es nicht gibt,'" 178–85.

31. After three insistent iterations, *befremden* comes up once more—this time without italics: "The twenty poems from this volume of poetry estrange [Die zwanzig Gedichte aus dem Gedichtband 'Der Stein' befremden]" (215).

32. I thank Kirk Wetters for calling my attention to the synesthetic character of these three nouns as well as to Celan's rejection of a poetics of synesthesia.

33. Celan's rejection of these terms is also an allusion to his rejection of similar vocabulary used by the contemporaneous press reviews of his own poetry. Celan, *Mikrolithen*, 874.

34. Celan's term *Ausdruckskunst* is also his translation of "expressionism." Celan, *Mikrolithen*, 874.

35. Similarly by way of introduction, Celan mentions that one knows of Mandelstam "among other things . . . that he has studied philosophy in Heidelberg and presently raves about the Greek language [unter anderem . . . , daß er in Heidelberg Philosophie studiert hat und gegenwärtig für das Griechische schwärmt]" (215). To be sure, Celan's insistence on the estranging quality of Mandelstam's poems could be borrowing from the philologist Gleb Struve's biographical-critical preface to the two-volume edition from 1955 of Mandelstam's writings, which Celan was working with. However, whereas Struve uses the neutral, or even positively charged, verb *udivlyat'* ("to surprise," "to cause wonder") and the related adjective *udivitel'nyj* ("wondrous" or "wonderful") to characterize the effect of Mandelstam's poems, Celan not only intensifies it with the word "disconcert/estrange' (*befremden*)—connoting alienation, strangeness, repulsion—but also insists on it four times in the compact opening remarks of the essay. Cf. Gleb Struve, "Opyt biografii i kriticheskogo kommentariya," in *Collected Works*, by Osip Mandelstam (New York: Chekhov Publishing House, 1955), 8.

36. Hanging on to the Greek words for fear of spilling some of their original authority via translation, Heidegger writes, "The wonder is as πάθος the ἀρχή of philosophy [Das Erstaunen ist als παθος die ἀρχή der Philosophie]." Martin Heidegger, "Was ist das—die Philosophie?" in *Gesamtausgabe*, ed. Friedrich-Wilhelm von Herrmann, 102 vols. (Frankfurt am Main: Vittorio Klostermann Verlag, 1975–), 11:3–26, 22.

37. Heidegger, 13.

38. On the links between Heidegger's thought and Nazi ideology, see Adam Knowles, *Heidegger's Fascist Affinities: A Politics of Silence* (Stanford: Stanford University Press, 2019), 7–35.

39. Heidegger, "Was ist das—die Philosophie?" 7; Heidegger's italics.

40. Heidegger, 19.

41. On Celan's critique of Heidegger's notion of *Entsprechen*, see David Brierley, *"Der Meridian": ein Versuch zur Dichtung und Poetik Paul Celans* (Frankfurt am Main: Peter Lang, 1984), 203–4; Lyon, *Paul Celan and Martin Heidegger*, 118–19, 130–32; Seng, *Auf den Kreiswegen der Dichtung*, 157.

42. On Heidegger's ambiguous concept of correspondence, see Susan Bernstein, "Correspondances—Between Baudelaire and Heidegger," *Modern Language Notes* 130.3 (2015): 607–22, especially 614–21.

43. Lyon, *Paul Celan and Martin Heidegger*, 220.

44. Here is a closely related passage from Celan's *Meridian* speech, discussed by Seng, *Auf den Kreiswegen der Dichtung*, 157:

> This Still can only be a speaking. That is, not language as such and presumably not, on the basis of the word, "correspondence." But rather actualized language, set free under the sign of an individuation that, while radical, is at the same time remaining mindful of the limits drawn to it by language, of the possibilities opened up to it by language. / This Still of the poem can surely be found only in the poem of someone who does not forget that he speaks under the angle of inclination of his existence, the angle of inclination of his creatureliness. [Dieses Immer-noch kann doch wohl nur ein Sprechen sein. Also nicht Sprache schlechthin und vermutlich auch nicht erst vom Wort her "Entsprechung." Sondern aktualisierte Sprache, freigesetzt unter dem Zeichen einer zwar radikalen, aber gleichzeitig auch der ihr von der Sprache gezogenen Grenzen, der ihr von der Sprache erschlossenen Möglichkeiten eingedenk bleibenden Individuation. / Dieses Immer-noch des Gedichts kann ja wohl nur in dem Gedicht dessen zu finden sein, der nicht vergißt, daß er unter dem Neigungswinkel seines Daseins, dem Neigungswinkel seiner Kreatürlichkeit spricht]." (Celan, *Gesammelte Werke*, 3:197)

45. Brierley, *"Der Meridian,"* 203.

46. See Lyon, *Paul Celan and Martin Heidegger*, 120; Seng, *Auf den Kreiswegen der Dichtung*, 157.

47. On Celan's reading of Heidegger's *Being and Time*, see Seng, *Auf den Kreiswegen der Dichtung*, 154.

48. Martin Heidegger, *Being and Time*, trans. John Macquarrie and Edward Robinson (New York: Harper and Row, 1962), 62.

49. Martin Heidegger, *Sein und Zeit* (Tübingen: Max Niemeyer Verlag, 2006), 38; Heidegger's italics.

50. Heidegger writes: "With regard to the awkwardness and 'inelegance' of expression in the analysis to come, we may remark that it is one thing to give a report in which we tell about *entities*, but another to grasp entities in their *Being*. For the latter task we lack not only most of the words but, above all, the 'grammar.' [Mit Rücksicht auf das Ungefüge und das 'Unschöne' des Ausdrucks innerhalb der folgenden Analysen darf die Bemerkung angefügt werden: ein anderes ist es über Seiendes erzählend zu berichten, ein anderes, Seiendes in seinem Sein zu fassen. Für die letztgenannte Aufgabe fehlen nicht nur meist die Worte, sondern vor allem die 'Grammatik']." Heidegger, *Being and Time*, 63; Heidegger, *Sein und Zeit*, 38–39; Heidegger's emphasis.

51. See Celan's response to a questionnaire from 1958 by the Librairie Flinker in Celan, *Gesammelte Werke*, 3:167–68, 168.

52. Heidegger, *Die Metaphysik des deutschen Idealismus, Gesamtausgabe*, 49:53–54.

53. On temporalization in Celan's radio essay, see Glazova, "The Poetry of Bringing about Presence," 111–13.

54. On the role of alterity in Celan's poetics, see Ivanovic, *Das Gedicht im Geheimnis der Begegnung*, 323, 346–50.

55. On this point, see Tatiana Baskakova's commentary on Celan's radio essay in Paul Celan, *Poems. Prose. Letters*, eds. Tatiana Baskakova and Mark Belorusets (Moscow: Ad marginem, 2008), 409.

56. I thank Kirk Wetters for suggesting the notion of interference to characterize what is at work in Celan's radio essay.

57. Osip Mandelstam, *Sobranie Sochinenij*, vol. 2 (Moscow: Progress-Plejada, 2010), 338.

58. Böschenstein, "Celan und Mandelstamm," 158.

59. I thank Alexandra Richter for pointing out this sense of the word "Leideform" and its possible anticipation of suffering to come.

60. Celan, *Gesammelte Werke*, 5:623.

61. Heidegger, *Being and Time*, 100.

62. Paul Celan to Werner Weber 26 March 1960, *Weber: Briefwechsel*, 148–49; my italics.

63. In the closely related passage from the radio essay, Celan highlights the significance of punctuation (*Interpunktion*) in Mandelstam's poems: "(This vibrato is everywhere: in the intervals between the words and the stanzas, in the 'courtyards,' in which the rhymes and the assonances are standing, in the punctuation. All of this has *semantic relevance*.) [(Dieses Vibrato ist überall: in den Intervallen zwischen den Worten und den Strophen, in den 'Höfen,' in denen die Reime und die Assonanzen stehen, in der Interpunktion. All das hat *semantische Relevanz*.)]" (216; Celan's italics).

64. On the poetological significance of this letter, see Werner Hamacher, "HÄM: Ein Gedicht Celans mit Motiven Benjamins," in *Jüdisches Denken in einer Welt ohne Gott—Festschrift für Stéphane Mosès*, eds. Jens Mattern, Gabriel Motzkin, and Shimon Sandbank (Berlin: Vorwerk 8, 2000), 173–97, 184; Olschner, "Grenzgänge und Gegenwart," 250.

65. Paul Celan to Werner Weber 26 March 1960, *Weber: Briefwechsel*, 148.

66. On Celan's borrowing from Heidegger of the notion of the poem as a gift, see Lyon, *Paul Celan and Martin Heidegger*, 113; Olschner, "Grenzgänge und Gegenwart," 252.

67. Paul Celan to Werner Weber 26 March 1960, *Weber: Briefwechsel*, 148.

68. On Rilke, an avid translator of Valéry, considering "La Jeune Parque" untranslatable, see Ute Harbusch, *Gegenübersetzungen: Paul Celans Übertragungen französischer Symbolisten* (Göttingen: Wallstein Verlag, 2005), 370.

69. Paul Celan to Werner Weber 26 March 1960, *Weber: Briefwechsel*, 14.
70. Celan, *Gesammelte Werke*, 3:177.
71. I thank Kirk Wetters, Paul North, and Katrin Trüstedt for their invaluable comments at various stages of this paper. Any flaws are my own.

Chapter 12

# The Mimetic Desire of Translation
## Reading Celan and Derrida with Girard

CHRISTINE FRANK

The cultural theory of René Girard is based in a paradigmatic analysis of European novels, mostly texts from nineteenth-century realism. Girard developed his theories over the span of more than five decades, from an initial concept of triangular desire via the discovery of the scapegoat mechanism to a general theory of violence, ultimately culminating in a critical apology of Christianity.

Unlike Erich Auerbach in his seminal study *Mimesis* (1946), Girard did not understand mimesis to be a method of representing reality in literary imagery, but instead recognized within it a more fundamental motivation, a form of appropriation, which according to him is the basis of all human relationships and all cultural developments. As he expands the conclusions he drew from his analysis of the "mimetic desire" of novel characters into a more fundamental model of inter-individual behaviors in social reality, Girard presupposes that the novels he examines are themselves of a representative character.

Girard's concept of mimetic desire, as he developed it in his first book *Deceit, Desire, and The Novel* (1961),[1] relies on three basic preconditions:

1. Girard assumes that desire is not original but is the result of imitation: only what is already desired by others appears worthy of desire. This results in a triangular relation between subject (self), mediator (other), and object.

2. Through their desire, or rather because of their desire, the Other is elevated to a model of action and being for the Self. While the Self seeks definition through desiring the Other, the actual object of desire can fade into the background. By definition, mimetic desire exceeds orientation toward the object; unlike erotic desire or hunger, it also mostly eludes any concrete way of being satisfied. Because the desired object is occupied by the Other, the desire becomes only all the more precious. Desire itself becomes a reason for being, a fundamental driving force, the very essence of motivation: Girard also calls this "metaphysical desire."

3. Through desire, the Self imitates the Other. It aligns itself with it, appropriates it, usurps it. The question of how the difference between Self and Other can be dissolved (*effacé, relevé*) becomes the actual subject matter of the protagonists' actions, of the literary texts, and of Girard's cultural theory itself.

It is at this juncture that Girard's concept is expanded into a general cultural theory. In the real world, shared desire of the same Object turns Subject (self) and Other (mediator, according to the perception of the Subject) into rivals; structurally speaking, they become antagonists. According to Girard, this relation can culminate in a forceful elimination of one or both antagonists. He states that desire is highly "contagious": desire is not just imitated by one subject but by many, which results in an accumulation of rivalry and antagonism that can discharge into a so-called *scapegoat mechanism*, that is, the vicarious killing of a (sacralized) sacrifice. Girard describes a pattern that he recognizes as a model of social behavior in the real world but which is represented through fictional characters. Going beyond literary analysis in his general cultural theory, he then determines this to be a fundamental schematism that he claims can be verified throughout all of cultural history. Of particular interest to him are mechanisms that were used to confront mimetic desire, and therefore the escalation of violence. This includes concepts of the sacred, concepts of religion, and also language itself.

Considering the role that Girard would later play as a theorist of violence in the history of cultural development, people often tend to overlook his relation to French structuralism at the beginning of his work on the theory of mimetic desire and the credo guiding his efforts in literary analysis. I would like to expand briefly on this with a remarkable quote from *Deceit, Desire, and the Novel* in which Girard formulates explicit perspectives for literary analysis. It is remarkable because it is only contained in the English version of his book, published in 1966, five years after the French first edition. Comparing that edition to the French original titled *Mensonge romantique et vérité romanesque* (1961), there are various differences that stand out, one of them being the title as it indicates a shift of focus in Girard's examinations of "mensonge romantique" (romantic lie) and "vérité romanesque" (romanesque truth), which very noticeably determine his argument in the French original. In addition, the French edition contains an epigraph originating with Max Scheler ("L'homme possède ou un Dieu ou une idole") that is omitted from the English version. Originally, Girard had been prompted by Leo Spitzer to add the epigraph. Spitzer was a colleague in Romance studies at Johns Hopkins to whom he had given the manuscript for proofreading. Spitzer also inspired passages in the book in which Girard refers to Scheler's *Das Ressentiment im Aufbau der Moralen* (1912).[2] The parallels between his own argument and Scheler's approach—whose study he had indeed read—completely eluded him, as Girard explains in a later interview; he later added the passages "in a way because of the mimetic influence of Leo Spitzer," but without explicitly mentioning his name.[3] This side note is an indication of how "mimetic desire" connects to other scholarly authors. It is possible that relationship troubles between colleagues are also the reason for certain remarks inserted into the first chapter of *Deceit, Desire, and the Novel*, which I would like to quote here in their entirety. The fact that they begin with one negation after the other is already indicative of their character:

> The triangle is no *Gestalt*. The real structures are inter-subjective. They cannot be localized anywhere; the triangle has no reality whatever; it is a systematic metaphor, systematically pursued. Because changes in size and shape do not destroy the identity of this figure, as we will see later, the diversity as well as the unity of the works can be simultaneously illustrated. The purpose and limitations of this structural geometry may become clearer through a reference to "structural models." The triangle is a model of a sort, or rather a whole family of models. But these models are not "mechanical" like those of Claude Lévi-Strauss. They always allude to the mystery, transparent yet opaque, of human relations. All types of structural thinking assume that human reality is intelligible; it is a logos and, as such, it is an incipient logic,

> or it degrades itself into a logic. It can thus be systematized, at least up to a point, however unsystematic, irrational, and chaotic it may appear even to those, or rather especially to those who operate the system. A basic contention of this essay is that the great writers apprehend intuitively and concretely, through the medium of their art, if not formally, the system in which they were first imprisoned together with their contemporaries. Literary interpretation must be systematic because it is the continuation of literature. It should formalize implicit or already half-explicit systems. To maintain that criticism will never be systematic is to maintain that it will never be real knowledge. The value of a critical thought depends not on how cleverly it manages to disguise its own systematic nature or on how many fundamental issues it manages to shirk or to dissolve but on how much literary substance it really embraces, comprehends, and makes articulate. The goal may be too ambitious but it is not outside the scope of literary criticism. It is the very essence of literary criticism. Failure to reach it should be condemned but not the attempt. Everything else has already been done.[4]

These remarks read like Girard's legacy for literary criticism. I quoted the passage at length also because it serves as a bridge—historically as well as in terms of my argument—to the subsequent considerations based on Derrida. The quoted remarks sound noticeably uncertain or irritated whenever they talk about, on the one hand, the term structure ("structure," "structural geometry," "structural model"), and, on the other, the terms "system" or "literary substance." I would posit that this points to the historical moment of a theoretical paradigm shift initiated by French literature and theory, in the wake of which Girard then formulated his concept while he was in the United States.

The same year the English translation of his book was published, a generous grant of the Ford Foundation allowed René Girard and his younger colleague Eugenio Donato as well as the director of the recently founded Humanities Center at Johns Hopkins University, Richard A. Macksey, to organize a large international conference. This conference, titled "The Language of Criticism and the Sciences of Man" (October 18 to 21, 1966), was to be of historic importance for the impact of French structuralism and the then-nascent movement of post-structuralism, a process later dubbed "the French Invasion." All the leading structuralists from France had been invited to the conference, and most of them also came. Among them were Jacques Lacan and Jacques Derrida, whose meeting in Baltimore was their first. Even though he had been cautioned against it, Lacan insisted on holding his lecture in English because he considered it essential for the "linguistic message" he sought to transmit: "Of Structure as the Inmixing of an Otherness Prerequisite to Any Subject Whatever." The last speaker of the conference was Derrida, whose international career was still in its early stages. His lecture, "La structure, le signe et le jeu dans le discours des sciences humaines." was published a year later in *L'écriture et la différence*. An English version was first published in 1970 as part of the conference proceedings.[5] Derrida's closing lecture marked the end of structuralism and the beginning of post-structuralism in the United States, while also serving as the first document of his deconstructivist methods.

For my attempt at reading Celan and Derrida with Girard, I want to look at the use of language by Derrida and Celan in terms of a mimetic desire directed at language itself: language occupied (by the Self) as one's "own" language but one that is necessarily always already occupied by the Other. Both the prohibition against one's "own" language as with Derrida and the loss of the originary language space as Celan experienced it motivate their desire for language in specific ways. Both react with ways of speaking and writing that seek to make visible that experience as difference. I would posit that translation plays a central role in this process, in a particular sense that is yet to be specified. Let me therefore return to Girard's concept of mimetic desire before it was expanded into a general cultural theory and consider whether the general model of mimetic desire Girard discovered based on his reading of European novels could also be used as a model to describe desire of/for language. For Celan, I will first focus on his Bremen address (1958) and then on his poem "Schibboleth" (1954).[6] This will lead me to Derrida and his study *Schibboleth: For Paul Celan* (1986), which explores questions of multilingualism and translation.[7]

## Mimetic Desire, the Scapegoat Mechanism, and Celan's Bremen Address

To begin, I would like to read Celan's Bremen address against the backdrop of Girard's theoretical model. In his acceptance speech, Celan defines his position on postwar German society in a programmatic way. He does this not by delivering a formal speech but by explicitly and performatively *addressing* his audience as speakers of the German language. He addresses them as a community of German speakers—a community to which he naturally belongs. It was precisely this belonging, however, that was disputed. The desire for the German language united Celan with his listeners—and yet radically separated him from them. At the same time, as we now know, there were already signs of the plagiarism accusations that would end up being fatal for Celan—a form of the cycle of "scapegoating" and violence Girard describes. The accusations were specifically directed against Celan as a speaking person, as a person who used German as the language of his poems, and against his poems' ways of speaking.

Allow me briefly to recapitulate the events. In December 1957, Celan was awarded the Bremen Literature Prize. Two years prior, he had published *Von Schwelle zu Schwelle* (*From Threshold to Threshold*, 1955), and six years prior, his first volume of poetry in Germany, *Mohn und Gedächtnis* (*Poppy and Memory*, 1952), appeared. The award was not only a sign of public recognition of his work, but it was also an important signal of solidarity; Celan was very aware of that. To this day, the Bremen Literature Prize is still being awarded annually, ever since it was first bestowed by the Free Hanseatic City of Bremen on the occasion of the seventy-fifth birthday of Bremen author Rudolf Alexander Schröder in 1953. It was at the time considered one of the most important literary awards in the Federal Republic. Celan had already been considered by the award committee in 1955; however, R. A. Schröder himself objected and the nomination was discarded. Schröder could not bring himself to see the award go to a Jew. Celan had already visited Bremen one year before (on February 2, 1957) to give a reading, but he ended up fleeing the city abruptly when allusions to the plagiarism affair were made. While traveling to Bremen once more for the award ceremony at the end of January 1958, Celan first stopped for two days in Cologne to confer with his friends at the time, Heinrich Böll and Paul Schallück, regarding the affair as well as other anti-Semitic incidents (January 23 to 25, 1958). Böll and Schallück both were instrumental in founding the Germania Judaica one year later, the largest special library on the history and culture of German-speaking Judaism in Europe. It was intended as an answer to the rapid rise of anti-Semitism in Germany at the end of the 1950s, which was in no way simply a fantasy of Celan's. I mention all of these dates because I consider them essential for a better understanding of the rhetorical strategy behind Celan's address in Bremen. It is a sort of confession, his own binding explanation about his relationship with the German language. Also included were intertextual references to poetological and philosophical positions of several of his contemporaries (from Mandelstam to Benn and Eich, from Adorno and Horkheimer to Heidegger). Celan probably composed the first notes for his brief address after his discussion with his friends in Cologne, during his train ride to Bremen on January 25, 1958. The speech itself was written in his Bremen hotel room only shortly before the ceremony on January 26.[8]

In his address, Celan leaves no doubt about the fundamental significance of the persecution and annihilation of European Jews by the National Socialists for his destiny as a survivor and as a German-language poet. However, he markedly avoids any talk of victimization or assigning of guilt. He gives names and dates but refuses explicitly to spell out the things that happened. He also avoids the plagiarism accusations that had been raised against him since 1952 (the so-called Goll-affair was only half public at the time of the award ceremony and escalated only later when he was awarded the Büchner Prize). However, the intentions of his address become very clear: Celan understands poems to be, by definition, *intentional* speech (poems "aim towards something"), and this conviction is expressed also in the way his address is structured and how its language is performed. "Racked by reality and in search of it," he writes, circumscribing his own damaged state of being and providing a conscious alternative to the categorical (and religiously connoted) imperative, "Zahor!"[9]

My argument is that the center of this intention is not an identification with the *inclusive* religious practice of remembrance, but instead an insistence on the inviolable demand of recognizing the Other. Refusal of that recognition was at the core of Nazi ideology, and Celan's claim that it is inviolable seeks to restore it. For Celan, the only way to achieve this is to recognize the Other as a speaker, and thus also to recognize their desire for the German language. But this was exactly what later became the point of contention in the "Celan Incident." In the words of Girard's terminology, Celan's desire was aimed at something already occupied by the desire of Others, the Germans (i.e., the German language). At the same time, however, that language was for him the only way to process the total loss of the region where he grew up, where he acquired language, where he had been at home, and where he had lived with parents, relatives, and friends: "Only one thing remained reachable, close and secure amid all losses: language" [Erreichbar, nah und unverloren blieb inmitten der Verluste dies eine: die Sprache].[10] When the war ended, Celan left the Bukovina forever, and since 1949 he lived in France. He married a French woman in 1952 and became a French citizen in 1955. For him, the German language was a necessity, the only adequate form of expression that could allow him to process the unimaginable, unspeakable losses he had suffered—losses that would forever remain inseparable from the German language. Celan's use of this language became a major stumbling block for his listeners even before his poems were printed. He traveled to Germany for the first time in 1952. He had been invited as a representative of the Austrian delegation to the spring meeting of Gruppe 47, a loose association of authors, critics, and publishers that had been constituted under the leadership of Hans Werner Richter in 1947 and that decisively shaped the West German literary scene until its last meeting in 1967. Celan's reading at the Gruppe's 1952 spring meeting in Niendorf by the Baltic Sea was met with negative reactions, in particular to the way he read and the way he pronounced the German language. The responses ranged from associating his delivery with Talmudic recitations to drawing a comparison with Goebbels's way of speaking. Richter's wife asked Celan, the poet who had fled Romania and arrived from France, where he had learned German so well. Among the group members, Celan was clearly perceived as a stranger, a Jew whose mother tongue could not be German. From his first appearance in Germany, Celan was viewed with suspicion by many, and his competence in German was often publicly questioned, sometimes even denied. Moreover, fueled by Claire Goll's accusation of plagiarism, the authenticity of his poetry was also questioned. This suspicion not only included the (unjustified and manipulative) accusation of intellectual theft; by accusing Celan of linguistic esoterism, critics also questioned which realities his poems were speaking about.[11]

These claims are proof of nothing except that they are defensive reflexes evoked in parts of the German-speaking public by Celan's impertinence of using the German language to engage in a process of collective mourning. Can these defensive reflexes caused by Celan's poetry and his position within the German literary world be read in terms of Girard's scapegoat theory? My thesis is that Celan did in fact recognize the mechanism behind the opposition he was facing—and that he sought to react to it in his Bremen address as well as in his poems and translations.

It seems to be quite fruitful to immerse oneself in the historical moment of Celan's actual speech, with all his pauses and emphases. The address opens with the following lines:

> The words "denken" and "danken," to think and to thank, have the same root in our language [Worte ein und desselben Ursprungs]. If we follow it to "gedenken," "eingedenk sein," "Andenken" and

"Andacht" we enter the semantic field of memory and devotion. Allow me to thank you from there.

The region from which I come to you—with what detours [Umwegen]! But then, is there such a thing as a detour?—will be unfamiliar to most of you. It is the home of many of the Hassidic stories which Martin Buber has retold in German [uns allen auf deutsch wiedererzählt hat]. It was—if I may flesh out this topographical sketch with a few details which are coming back to me from a great distance—it was a landscape where both people and books lived. There, in this former province of the Habsburg monarchy, now dropped from history, I first encountered the name [kam . . . auf mich zu] of Rudolf Alexander Schröder while reading Rudolf Borchardt's "Ode with Pomegranate." There, the word Bremen took shape [Umriß] for me: in the publications [in der Gestalt der Veröffentlichungen] of the "Bremer Presse."

But though Bremen was brought closer through books, through the names of writers and publishers of books, it still had the sound of the unreachable.[12]

"Ursprung," "(Um)Wege,' encountering a name, "Umriß" and "Gestalt"—Celan endows all of these terms with great importance during these years in poetological reflections that finally culminate in his Büchner Prize speech. In this first address to a representative audience, he uses them to sketch an outline of his language origins and his present condition, blending words and names and thus places, people, and literature. Celan tries to phrase things politely and personally, but despite the ornate rhetoric, his address has clear moments of sharp emphasis.

It should be noted that Celan himself never declared his address to be an acceptance speech or a thank-you note. It has been titled and published in a rather roundabout manner as his "Address on the Occasion of Accepting the Literature Prize of the Free Hanseatic City of Bremen." Celan speaks with self-confidence and directly addresses the audience on several occasions. When his first lines consider the etymological relation between "denken" and "danken" and then evoke their various composite words ("gedenken," "eingedenk sein,' "Andenken," "Andacht"), he is not simply making a linguistic observation—he is sending a performative signal: Celan announces his intention to do the work of remembrance, reaching all the way to the religious immersion inherent in "Andacht" (devotion).[13] "From here," Celan says, he would like to give his thanks. Gratitude thus becomes a *consequence* of the thoughts experienced collectively in this moment: *giving* thanks. In doing so, Celan mimetically imitates the argumentative *mode* of Heidegger, without explicitly *using his name*; therefore, he also invokes the implications of Heidegger's argument.

As it is well known, after the end of the war, Heidegger was suspended from university service because of his support for the National Socialists, and he was barred from any public appearances or participation in university functions. It was only after his early retirement in 1951 that he could return to the university and thus to the public stage. The first lecture that he gave upon his return was titled "Was heißt Denken?" ("What Is Called Thinking?"), in which he examines the relation between thinking and thanking. Heidegger had already equated thinking and thanking in his 1929 inaugural address, "Was ist Metaphysik?" ("What Is Metaphysics?"), and he brought both concepts into a genuine connection with poetry. Celan was of course familiar with these deliberations and their historical contexts. His interest in Heidegger's philosophy is evident from the contents of his library all the way back to 1950, though they possibly go back much further. Ingeborg Bachmann, who defended her doctoral dissertation on the reception of Heidegger's philosophy of existence, might have played crucial role. Unlike the assertions Celan makes in the introductory passages of his Bremen address, Heidegger's lecture is dominated by questions:

> What is it that is named with the words "think," "think-ing," "thought"? Toward what sphere of the spoken word do they direct us? . . . Is thinking a giving of thanks? What do thanks mean here? Or do thanks consist in thinking? What does thinking mean here? Is memory no more than a container for the thoughts of thinking, or does thinking itself reside in memory?[14]

> (Was ist mit den Worten "Denken," "Gedachtes," "Gedanke" gemeint? In welchen Spielraum des Gesprochenen weisen sie? . . . Ist das Denken ein Danken? Was meint hier Danken? Oder beruht der Dank im Denken? Was meint hier Denken? Ist das Gedächtnis nur ein Behälter für das Gedachte des Denkens, oder beruht das Denken selber im Gedächtnis? Wie verhält sich der Dank zum Gedächtnis?)

Gerhard Richter suggests "that Heidegger here implicitly echoes Hegel's distinction between *Gedächtnis* and *Erinnerung*, that is, between memory as a kind of reflective thinking (encrypted in the aspect of *Gedächtnis* that relates to *Gedanke* and *Denken*) and memory as a nonthinking interiorization (*Erinnerung* as the mnemonic act of the one who interiorizes, *er innert*."[15] Richter further explains that Heidegger interprets thanking as the "gift" of thinking and that he sees a connection between such a gift and the recognition of the Other.[16] It is this recognition for which Celan expressed gratitude when he accepted the Bremen Literature Prize. But in the same breath Celan demanded understanding and recognition in a much deeper sense: the recognition of the speaker as speaker—as he becomes manifest within his poem. Celan repeatedly sought to explain the intention of speech in his poem in this sense, as an act of speaking intentionally directed toward the Other. This also explains why he insists on calling his speech an *address*: intentionally directed at someone and informed as much as irritated by Heidegger's thinking. Ostensibly, Celan takes Heidegger by his word when he not only imitates his speaking style but also *mimetically* reproduces the desire inherent in it. Celan's relation to Heidegger was one of both closeness and ambivalence, and I think that the concept of mimetic desire can be useful to describe it more precisely.

"The words 'denken' and 'danken,' to think and to thank, have the same root in our language. . . . Allow me to thank you from there [Denken und Danken sind in unserer Sprache Worte ein und desselben Ursprungs. . . . Erlauben Sie mir, Ihnen von hier aus zu danken]."[17] He who speaks here knows to whom he speaks. His language "had to go through its own lack of answers, through terrifying silence, through the thousand darknesses of murderous speech [durch die tausend Finsternisse todbringender Rede]."[18] He who speaks is aware of the reservations of R. A. Schröder and the rekindling of anti-Semitism in the Federal Republic. And so he begins his address with a sentence in which he deliberately refers to words of "our language" that "have the same root in our language [Worte ein und desselben Ursprungs]." The same origin and a common language, however, are exactly what the anti-Semites sought to deny Celan and other Jews. To speak "our language" is the unerring and unquestioned desire Celan expressed in his poems, a desire that he would never relinquish. He is well aware of the differences between him and his audience: "Allow me to thank you from here," that is, from the demand of a common language. It is precisely that difference between Celan and his audience that speaks here in person and that otherwise speaks within his poems, as Celan sharply details in the second paragraph of his address. In not exactly polite terms, Celan emphasizes a radical asymmetry when he points out that the Bremen audience is probably unaware of the region of his origin, while on the other hand he himself was familiar with those "publications of the 'Bremer Presse'" while he lived in the Bukovina, a "former province of the Habsburg monarchy, now dropped from history." The distance between them is so vast that the people and landscapes could hardly ever have had personal encounters. But they could come in contact with one another through literature: stories, a poem, a series of publications, texts that were published in their common language, including those "Hassidic stories which Martin Buber has retold in German." Once again Celan utilizes the common German language—a language that itself creates commonality, here with a reference to translation—in order to make an appeal. The region where Celan grew up was a multilingual space, a space in which many languages and cultures were at home, a space that was distant but could nevertheless be transmitted through the German language, a common language that creates a connection between all the people gathered in the audience that day: authors as diverse as Celan, Schröder, Borchardt (a poet and translator of Jewish origin living *outside* of Germany), and Martin Buber, who managed to retrieve that which was inaccessible and lost by way of translation *for us all* ("uns allen wiedererzählt hat") into German. Among the things that Buber presented "for us all in German," as the audience at the time must have been aware, were not only Franz Rosenzweig's *Die Schrift* (1926–1938) but also the German translation of the Hebrew Bible; the last volume of the first edition of that translation had only just been published in Germany in 1955.

As in his Bremen address, Celan insists in his poems on the German language as the only possible language that could express the things that happened. In a "Reply to a Questionnaire from the Flinker Bookstore, Paris, 1961," which inquired "into language, into thinking, into poetry" ("nach der Sprache, nach dem Denken, nach der Dichtung"), Celan makes a very clear statement: "I do not believe there is such a thing as bilingual poetry. . . . Poetry is by necessity a unique instance of language [An Zweisprachigkeit in der Dichtung glaube ich nicht. . . . Dichtung—das ist das schicksalhaft Einmalige der Sprache]."[19] In his Bremen address, Celan stages (the German) language as though it was an autonomous personal subject to whom the testimony of historical events would be attached, silently or vocally. Celan's own desire for the German language is inseparable from his desire to survive. To try and "write poems in this language [In dieser Sprache . . . Gedichte zu schreiben]" was his only chance to fulfill the "demand" of expressing what happened in the sense of what he later calls "chart[ing] my reality [Wirklichkeit zu entwerfen]."[20] It seems as though this radical demand for the recognition of a common origin and his resolve to mourn in "our" language—the German language common to him and the others—have made Celan the *scapegoat* of German postwar society. Meanwhile, this recognition of the other that Celan is so insistent on is primarily decided through belonging to language. This is the explicit theme of another of Celan's texts, his poem "Schibboleth." Reading this poem with Girard in mind, I argue that it becomes more readily apparent how mimetic desire applies to the question of difference between Self and Other, between one's own desire and the desire of that which the Other, in turn, desires. By spelling out the differentiating word, the eponymous shibboleth, the inherent violence is transcended by the poem when it confidently emphasizes the act of speaking itself, anticipating the word as counter-word. By speaking *repeatedly*, the poem *dissolves* the violent situation by way of *remembrance*—it becomes both memory and an instrument of liberation.

## "Schibboleth" and Monolingualism of the Other

In his deliberations, "Zu einer neuen Verdeutschung der Schrift" [Regarding a new German translation of the Holy Writings], Martin Buber remarks: "But what was created in speaking can only live and live again in speaking, and only be perceived and received through it . . . even the original Hebrew word for 'reading' means 'shouting out' [Was aber im Sprechen entstanden ist, kann nur im Sprechen je und je wieder leben, ja nur durch es rein wahr- und aufgenommen werden . . . schon die hebräische Bezeichnung für 'lesen' bedeutet 'ausrufen']."[21] A number of Celan's poems engage with this situation. They posit reading as speaking out loud, an act of performance with the inherent existential risk of "being recognized" through the disclosure of one's language and way of speaking. Already one of Celan's early poems, "Ein Krieger" from 1943, ends with the words: "Ich steh. Ich bekenne. Ich ruf [I stand. I confess. I shout]."[22] Similarly, his last poem, "Rebleute," formulates an ambivalent relation among reading, confession, and being recognized: "du liest: // die Offenen tragen / den Stein hinterm Aug, / der erkennt dich, / am Sabbath [you read, // the Open ones carry / the stone behind their eye, / it knows you, / come the Sabbath]."[23] This final word itself functions, within Celan's poetry, as a kind of shibboleth. "Sabbath" is perhaps a word of utmost distinction not only in form but also in meaning. In this poem, the initial "du liest" (occurring twice in the poem) is followed by a long pause, a thoughtful break. This "reading" is no longer the "shouting" that is demanded in the poem "Schibboleth."

"Schibboleth" is explicitly about memory, perhaps also evoking Hölderlin's "Mnemosyne," which is in fact directly addressed at the end of the first half of the poem.[24] Before that, the first two stanzas *remember* a personal experience of violence; the attack includes the lyrical "I" and the testaments of their sorrow—"stone" and "crying" appear as stereotypical signifiers in Celan's poem for the marker of a grave. The following two stanzas call for remembrance of two historical events: one is the quashing of the last resistance against fascism in Europe during the second half of the 1930s in Vienna and Madrid. Memory creates a visible, enduring ("for today and forever") mark of sorrow that functions as identification ("your flag"). The confession demanded in the subsequent fifth stanza articulates itself both personally ("heart") and publicly ("in the middle of the market") through a sign, the "shibboleth." Here the shibboleth is not merely a more or less arbitrary and semantically irrelevant word functioning "only" as a test of pronunciation, but it is a semantically over-coded two-part password composed of a date and a quotation: "February. No pasarán." The second part of the phrase absurdly repeats a popular watchword of Spanish freedom fighters that had functioned as a *mot de passe*, quite literally the opposite of what it says ("they shall not pass"). Meanwhile, this same phrase was also used during World War I by French soldiers at Verdun. Such a doubling is a notorious instrument of this poem: "flag," "middle of the market," "half-mast," "twin flutes," and "twin redness" systematically point to a double content within the scene, within memory, within signs and signifiers, and within remembrance and recognition. But it is not simply a watchword that is uttered and recognized here. The situation in which this occurs is itself perceived as a contradiction: "in the foreign of the home" (line 22). Such contradictions can be observed in other places as well, such as in the different receptions of the "flag." The name called out at the end ("Einhorn") similarly contains a double meaning: the mythical animal of the unicorn (that often has a Christian connotation) and a real person, Celan's childhood friend from Czernowitz Erich Einhorn, with whom he had been part of a resistance movement. While he never explicitly explained this reference, Celan once mentioned in a letter that "the unicorn [Einhorn] is—also—poetry."[25] Thus the "unicorn" (the name Einhorn) stands alongside other terms Celan used metonymically for what poetry meant to him, such as "stone" or "tear." With a knowledge of such "stones" and "water," the lyrical "I" in the poem ultimately promises the addressed "you" to "guide [you] forth" (lines 27–30) to the "voices of Estremadura." What is happening here? What is the intention of speech in this poem—who is it talking to and to whom is it directed?

As mentioned above, Celan's poem shows a basic structure of doubling, sometimes used antagonistically. One could say that speech is mimetically encoded, that anything that is said serves consistently *to repeat* what has already been spoken and thus imitates it in terms of its intention (i.e., its desire). It remembers, it repeats, it works through. It is only through this repeated redoubling that the difference between the doubles and their imitation can be recognized. But despite the doubling, each instance represents a unique act of speaking, marked by the specific situation of time and place that is inherent in that act (dated, signed, as Derrida has demonstrated). It is the term "shibboleth" that turns the scene of violence evoked by the poem into a recurring scene of history—but it nevertheless remains a unique event, uttered through the tension between "I" and "you" as a personal memory. According to the Bible, the pronunciation of the Hebrew word "shibboleth" was a means of establishing belonging and granting passage. In Celan's poem, it seems as though another word—the noun *and* name Einhorn—functioned *as* a shibboleth: an agreed-upon identifier whose wording does not have to match its function and can indeed be understood as its exact opposite by both the initiated and the uninitiated. This "shibboleth" prefigures Lucile's "counter-word" from Celan's Büchner Prize speech: it is meant to allow what is nominally forbidden.

Unlike the ghastly consequences from the Bible story, getting the shibboleth wrong in the poem opens up a surprising prospect of liberation that reads like a promise. It seems that there could be a possibility of awakening from the nightmare of history. That promise is poetry. It also appears in the figure of the unicorn: in the moment in which the demand to exclaim "the shibboleth" is *uttered*, the name Einhorn turns into something to talk to, to address—a name the poem can now *speak to*. Remembering this name, the scene of the violence immanent in the shibboleth turns into an intention to speak in a double sense: the performance of an enacted promise, and an "abduction"—in the sense of a liberation—to the "voices / of Estremadura." It is the promise of a transgression into an ever imaginary, faraway, remembered region carrying a Spanish name. It is the first time that Celan speaks of "voices" in one of his poems, that he lets "voices" speak. This would blossom into a central meaning just a few years later in his volume *Sprachgitter* (*Speech-Grille*).[26] It is a liberation in and through the act of speaking in the poem, but also a liberation in another language space in the sense of another form of *speaking* (the space of political resistance, the space of poetry).

Can Celan's poem "Schibboleth" therefore be read in the sense of the mimetic desire that Girard details at the beginning of his study using the example of the novel hero Don Quixote? In both his actions and his manner of speaking, Don Quixote imitates the knightly desires of his great idol Amadis de Gaula. The novel is not, however, simply an *undifferentiated* imitation of the Amadis novel. The protagonist's behavior in Cervantes's novel is more differentiated compared to its role model. Cervantes questions his hero's behaviors in terms of their value for allowing Don Quixote to establish a connection to reality and for transmitting patterns of action with various consequences for the creation of (social) reality. The reflective repetition of such patterns in language and through language contains a moment of difference. Something similar—albeit under very different historical conditions—occurs in Celan's poem "Schibboleth" as well. The difference lies in the experience of violence that forms the basic motivation for Celan's speech and the necessity of remembrance that results as a consequence of it. They ultimately lead to a poetics of difference, a translation but also a liberation and a dissolution.

In an interview with Évelyne Grossmann in the summer of 2000, Jacques Derrida summarizes his views on Celan by elaborating on two characteristics of his poetic language:

> I believe Celan tried to leave a mark, a singular signature that would be a counter-signature to the German language and, at the same time, something that happens to the German language—that comes to pass in both senses of the term: something that approaches the language, that reaches it, without appropriating it, without surrendering to it, without delivering itself to it; but also something that enables poetic writing to occur, that is to say, to be an event that marks language.[27]

Derrida already expanded this view in his study *Schibboleth: Pour Paul Celan* in greater detail. Based on the poem "Schibboleth," its resonances throughout the works of Celan, and the often multilingual character of his poems, Derrida also talks about translation as a primary characteristic of Celan's poetry. In the later interview, Derrida explains that it is the task of the translator-poet "to explain, to teach, that one can cultivate and invent an idiom, because it is not a matter of cultivating a given idiom but of producing the idiom. *Celan produced an idiom*; he produced it from a matrix, from a heritage, without, for obvious reasons, yielding in the least to nationalism. In my opinion, today such poets have a political lesson to teach to those who need it about the question of language and nation."[28]

According to Derrida, instead of appropriating language, Celan is able to *produce* a specific idiom thanks to his desire for language and his linguistic skill. As Celan puts it in his Büchner Prize speech: "This 'still-here' can only mean speaking. Not language as such, but responding and—not just verbally—'corresponding' to something. In other words: language actualized, set free under the sign of a radical individuation which, however, remains as aware of the limits drawn by language as of the possibilities it opens."[29]

## Notes

1. René Girard, *Mensonge romantique et vérité romanesque* [*Romantic Lie and Romanesque Truth*] (Paris: Grasset, 1961); *Deceit, Desire, and the Novel: Self and Other in Literary Structure*, trans. Yvonne Freccero (Baltimore, MD: Johns Hopkins University Press, 1966).

2. See Max Scheler, *Ressentiment*, trans. William W. Holdheim (New York: Free Press of Glencoe, 1961).

3. René Girard, *Evolution and Conversion: Dialogues on the Origins of Culture* (London: Continuum, 2008), 22.

4. Girard, *Deceit, Desire, and the Novel*, 2–3.

5. Jacques Derrida, "Structure, Sign, and Play in the Discourse of the Human Sciences," in *The Languages of Criticism & the Sciences of Man*, eds. Richard Macksey and Eugenio Donato (Baltimore, MD: Johns Hopkins University Press, 1970), 247–65 (new edition pub. under the title *The Structuralist Controversy*, 2007).

6. Paul Celan, "Ansprache anlässlich der Entgegennahme des Literaturpreises der Freien Hansestadt Bremen," in *Werke: Historisch-kritische Ausgabe*, eds. Andreas Lohr and Heino Schmull, vol. 15.1 (Frankfurt am Main: Suhrkamp, 2014), 23–25; see "Speech on the Occasion of Receiving the Literature Prize of the Free Hanseatic City of Bremen," in *Collected Prose*, trans. Rosemarie Waldrop (Riverdale-on-Hudson, NY: Sheep Meadow Press, 1986), 33–35. Paul Celan, "Schibboleth," in *Die Gedichte: Neue kommentierte Gesamtausgabe*, ed. Barbara Wiedemann (Berlin: Suhrkamp, 2018), 87–88.

7. Jacques Derrida, *Schibboleth: Pour Paul Celan* (Paris: Galilée, 1986); "Shibboleth: For Paul Celan," in *Sovereignties in Question: The Poetics of Paul Celan*, trans. Thomas Dutoit (New York: Fordham University Press, 2005), 1–64.

8. See the genesis of the speech as documented in Paul Celan, *Werke* 15.2:43–60, especially 45, 60.

9. Celan, "Speech on the Occasion," 35.

10. Celan, 34; Paul Celan, "Ansprache anlässlich der Entgegennahme des Literaturpreises der Freien Hansestadt Bremen" (1958), *Werke* 15.1:23

11. See Barbara Wiedemann, ed., *Paul Celan: Die Goll-Affäre. Dokumente zu einer 'Infamie'* (Frankfurt: Suhrkamp, 2000); Klaus Briegleb, *Missachtung und Tabu: Eine Streitschrift über die Frage: "Wie antisemitisch war die Gruppe 47?"* (Berlin: Philo, 2003).

12. Celan, "Speech on the Occasion," 33–34; Celan, "Ansprache anlässlich der Entgegennahme des Literaturpreises der Freien Hansestadt Bremen (1958)," *Werke* 15.1:23

13. According Grimm's Dictionary, "Denken" originates "von dem verlornen dinke danc dunken (Gramm. 2, 60), zu welchem auch die verba danken, dünken gehören und bezeichnet wie diese eine bewuszte thätigkeit des geistes, entgegengesetzt einer unwillkürlichen empfindung, ein schweigendes reden; etwas nachdrücklicher ist gedenken und hat noch eigene bedeutungen" (t. 2, col. 927). *Deutsches Wörterbuch von Jakob und Wilhelm Grimm*, accessed July 15, 2021, http://woerterbuchnetz.de/cgi-bin/WBNetz/wbgui_py?sigle=DWB&mode=Vernetzung&lemid=GD01555#XGD01555.

14. Martin Heidegger, *Was heißt Denken?* (Tübingen: Max Niemeyer, 1954), 91; Martin Heidegger, *What Is Called Thinking?* trans. Fred D. Wieck and J. Glenn Gray (New York: Harper and Row, 1968), 138–39.

15. Gerhard Richter, *Thought-Images: Frankfurt School Writers' Reflections from Damaged Life* (Stanford: Stanford University Press, 2007), 162.

16. Richter, 162–63.

17. Celan, "Speech on the Occasion," 33; Celan, *Werke*, 15.1:23.

18. Celan, "Speech on the Occasion," 34. Note that Celan neither says "my" nor "the German" language.

19. Paul Celan, "Antwort auf eine Umfrage der Librairie Flinker" (1961), *Werke* 15.1:81; see Paul Celan, "Reply to a Questionnaire from the Flinker Bookstore, Paris, 1961," in *Collected Prose*, 23–24, 23.

20. Paul Celan, "Ansprache anlässlich der Entgegennahme des Literaturpreises der Freien Hansestadt Bremen" (1958), *Werke* 15.1:24; see Paul Celan, "Speech on the Occasion," 34.

21. Martin Buber, "*Zu einer neuen Verdeutschung der Schrift* (Beilage zum ersten Band: Die fünf Bücher der Weisung)," in *Die Schrift: Verdeutscht von Martin Buber gemeinsam mit Franz Rosenzweig* (Stuttgart: Deutsche Bibelgesellschaft, 1992), 35.

22. Celan, *Die Gedichte*, 15; translation mine.

23. Celan, 577. See John Felstiner, *Selected Poems and Prose of Paul Celan* (New York: Norton, 2001), 377.

24. See Felstiner, *Selected Poems and Prose*, 75.

25. Celan, *Die Gedichte*, 728.

26. This title also invokes a connection to the line "behind the grate [hinter den Gittern]"; see "Schibboleth," line 3.

27. Évelyne Grossmann and Jacques Derrida, "Language Is Never Owned: An Interview," trans. Thomas Dutoit and Philippe Romanski, in *Sovereignties in*

*Question: The Poetics of Paul Celan*, eds. Thomas Dutoit and Outi Pasanen (New York: Fordham University Press, 2005), 97–107, 99.
    28. Grossmann and Derrida, 103; emphasis mine.
    29. Paul Celan, "The Meridian," in *Collected Prose*, 37–55, 49.

# List of Contributors

**Michael Auer** is professor of modern German literature at the University of Vienna.

**Christine Frank** is professor of Modern German Literature at the Freie Universität Berlin.

**Irina Kogan** is visiting assistant professor of German at Lafayette College.

**Michael Levine** is professor of comparative literature and German, Russian, and East European languages and literatures at Rutgers University.

**Natalie Lozinski-Veach** is assistant professor of German and comparative cultural studies at Arizona State University.

**Kristina Mendicino** is professor of German studies at Brown University.

**Jan Mieszkowski** is the Reginald F. Arragon professor of German and humanities at Reed College.

**Pasqual Solass** is a PhD candidate in German studies at Brown University.

**Simone Stirner** is assistant professor of German, Russian, and East European studies at Vanderbilt University.

**Sarah Stoll** is a fellow at the Franz Rosenzweig Minerva Research Center at the Hebrew University of Jerusalem.

**Naomi Waltham-Smith** is associate professor at the Centre for Interdisciplinary Methodologies at the University of Warwick.

**Dominik Zechner** is assistant professor of German language and literature at Rutgers University.

# Index

Adorno, Theodor, 1, 3–4, 6–9, 10n7, 11n13, 11nn15–16, 84–100, 101n4, 101n7, 102n18, 103n40, 103–104n52, 113–116, 118, 121, 122n2, 123–124n22, 124n27, 124n30, 209, 231–238, 241, 243, 252n6, 253n9, 293

aesthetics, 36–37, 43, 63, 84–100, 101n3, 105n76, 189, 225, 252n2

Agamben, Giorgio, 129

alliteration, 7, 113, 120, 167

allophony, 7, 112–113, 117–122, 125n42

art (*Kunst/Ausdruckskunst/Dichtkunst*), 43, 65, 84–88, 90–92, 96, 98, 100, 118, 177, 182–183, 186, 222–223, 225, 231–233, 236, 266–267, 283n34, 290

Artaud, Antonin, 130, 142

assonance, 7, 46–47, 55n55, 112–113, 117, 177, 179, 273

aurality, 5, 7, 129, 136

Bachelard, Gaston, 46, 48

Bachmann, Ingeborg, 296

being, 8, 50, 88–91, 141, 154, 157–163, 165–168, 170n18, 171–172n32, 172n38, 173n46, 193–194n46, 194n48, 202–203, 237, 270–273, 277–279, 284n50

Benjamin, Walter, 1, 10n3, 70, 200–203, 206–207, 209, 226n5, 235, 253n8, 253n13

Benn, Gottfried, 263–265, 293

Blanchot, Maurice, 30, 31n14, 172n38, 173–174n47

Böll, Heinrich, 292

Borchardt, Rudolf, 295, 298

breath, 36, 38, 41–52, 54nn42–44, 54n46, 54–55nn48–49, 56n55, 57n63, 113, 118, 120–121, 129, 131–132, 134–136, 139–142, 144–145, 177, 181–183, 221, 225–226

Buber, Martin, 45, 48, 55n43, 55n46, 57n63, 295, 298–299. *See also* Buber-Rosenzweig Bible

Buber-Rosenzweig Bible, 45, 48, 55n43, 55n46, 57n63, 298–299

Büchner, Georg, 5–6, 18–19, 28, 85, 177, 183, 186, 189, 191, 221–226; *Dantons Tod*, 32n27, 177, 183, 186, 189, 221–226; *Lenz*, 191, 221–222; *Leonce und Lena*, 189, 222; *Woyzeck*, 18–19, 222

Carson, Anne, 6, 36, 53n9

Celan, Paul, "Abzählreime," 125–126n49; "Argumentum e silentio," 156–157, 169n11, 170n13; *Atemwende*, 131, 134, 136, 142–

Celan, Paul *(continued)*
143; "... auch keinerlei," 210–213, 216, 220; "Aus dem Moorboden," 203–210, 212, 221, 226; "Blume," 6, 70–77, 81n40; Bremen address, 26–27, 32n27, 95–96, 118, 202, 210, 263, 291–299; "Cello-Einsatz," 7, 134–137, 140–141, 143; "Chanson einer Dame im Schatten," 170n14; "Deine Augen im Arm," 175; "Der Tauben weißeste," 66–67, 79n16; "Die Dichtung Ossip Mandelstamms," 261–263, 265–278, 280n7, 281n12, 283n35, 285n63; "Die Winzer," 170n13; "Ein Leseast," 210, 213–218, 220, 225; "Einem, der vor der Tür stand," 204; "Eis, Eden," 110–111, 120, 123n15; "Engführung," 6, 35–52, 52n4, 52–53n7, 53n16, 55n49, 56n55, 57n65, 110, 124n30, 178; "Erratisch," 180–181; *Fadensonnen*, 210; "Gespräch im Gebirg," 7, 84, 95–98, 101n3, 124n27, 178, 181–184, 186, 195n55; "Grabschrift für François," 156; "Große, glühende Wölbung," 144; "Heute und Morgen," 194n48; "In der Luft," 110–111, 177; "In Eins," 121–122; "In Memoriam Paul Eluard," 156; "Inselhin," 156–157; "Kenotaph," 156; "Kermorvan," 110, 118, 120; "Ein Krieger," 299; "Mit wechselndem Schlüssel," 7–8, 156–157, 163–168, 173–174nn47–52; *Der Meridian*, 8, 16, 18–23, 29, 32n27, 38, 42–46, 48–49, 54n46, 83–85, 88, 91–94, 96–99, 117–118, 123n13, 177–178, 181–191, 194–195n54, 195n61, 199, 202, 209–210, 221–226, 227n10, 262–263, 270, 272, 284n44, 295, 301, 303; *Mikrolithen sinds, Steinchen*, 176, 188–189, 194n47, 195n72; *Mohn und Gedächtnis*, 22, 66, 156, 292; "Muta," 179–180; "Nachmittag mit Zirkus und Zitadelle," 110–111, 118–121; "Nächtlich geschürzt," 170n13; "Niedrigwasser," 76; *Die Niemandsrose*, 7, 67–70, 110–122; "Offene Glottis," 203, 210, 218–221, 223; "Psalm," 67–68, 73, 76, 80n22, 123n15; "... rauscht der Brunnen," 111, 175–176; "Rebleute," 299; "Reply to a Questionnaire from the Flinker Bookstore," 103–104n52, 105n76, 109, 254n22, 298; "Schibboleth," 291, 299–302, 304n26; "Schliere," 178–179, 182, 186; *Schneepart*, 210; "Selbdritt, Selbviert," 110, 115–118, 121, 125–126n49; "Die Silbe Schmerz," 68–70; "Singbarer Rest," 110, 141–143; "Sprachgitter," 7, 98–100, 134; *Sprachgitter*, 70, 73, 83, 109–110, 210, 301; "Sprich auch du," 5–6, 15–30, 31n14; "Todesfuge," 27, 36–37, 109–110; "Tübingen, Jänner," 18, 177; "Und wie die Gewalt," 252–253n7; *Von Schwelle zu Schwelle*, 7–8, 154–157, 169n10, 292; "Vor Scham," 8–9, 241–251; "Was geschah," 110–113, 118, 120; "Zu beiden Händen," 157, 177, 185, 191

Char, René, 156, 170n13

Cixous, Hélène, 7, 130–131, 135–141, 143–145, 148n36; *Insister: à Jacques Derrida*, 138, 144–145; *Jours de l'an*, 7, 130–131, 135–141, 143, 148n36

consonance 47, 72, 112, 167, 178–183, 186–187, 219–220

creature/creatureliness, 44, 85, 98–99, 222, 225, 284
date, 16–19, 32n27, 42, 44, 47, 141–142, 189–191, 209, 300–301

Daive, Jean, 36, 44
deconstruction/deconstructive/desconstructed/deconstructivist, 7, 127, 130–134, 136, 139, 209–210, 291
de Man, Paul, 81n38
Derrida, Jacques, 5–6, 7, 16–22, 25–26, 28–29, 31n7, 31n12, 62, 78n1, 125n48, 127–133, 136–145, 251, 256n34, 290–291, 301–303; *The Beast and the Sovereign*, 131, 144; *Béliers*, 131, 143–144, 148n36, 196n88; "Fors," 251, 256n34; *Genèses*, 137; *Glas*, 62, 78n1; *H. C. pour la vie*, 131, 139, 143–144; *Of Grammatology*, 130; "L'Oreille de Heidegger," 131, 144; *La peine de mort*, 137; "La pharmacie de Platon," 148n36; *Psyche*, 143; *Shibboleth*, 5, 16–22, 25–26, 28–29, 31n7, 31n12, 128–129, 131, 141–142, 196n88, 291, 302; *Théorie et pratique*, 127–128; "Tympan," 132–133; "Le ver à soie," 138; *La voix et le phénomène*, 132, 139; "White Mythology," 62, 73n1
difference/differences, 62, 66–67, 85, 87, 90–91, 96–99, 113, 121, 159, 161, 237, 246, 253n10, 277–278, 280, 288–289, 291, 297, 299, 301–302
dissonance, 67, 86, 117

encounter, 5, 8, 29, 38, 42–44, 85, 90, 92, 175–176, 184, 186–187, 189, 237, 247, 261, 266, 273, 280, 298
*Entsetzen*, 4, 8, 231–239, 241, 243, 245, 252n2
experience, 3–4, 8, 36, 38, 44, 48–49, 51, 84, 92, 94, 97, 127–129, 189, 207, 231–238, 241, 243–247, 264–265

Freud, Sigmund, 154, 168n2, 195n61, 210, 212
flower, 6, 61–77, 78n1, 78n3, 78n5, 79n18, 81n35

Gadamer, Hans-Georg, 3, 72, 142
George, Stefan, 114–118, 125n42
Girard, René, 9, 287–294, 299, 301–302

Hamacher, Werner, 1–5, 8, 10, 11n14, 124n26, 130, 155, 157, 161, 167–168, 169n8, 170n16, 171n31, 174nn54–55, 174n58, 179n17, 180, 196n86, 203–208, 237–241, 243–244, 249, 251, 252n6, 252–253n7, 253nn12–13, 255n29, 285n64; "Bogengebete," 54n31; "For–Philology," 3, 10nn 4–6, 252–253n7, 253n9; "HÄM," 180, 203–208, 253n13, 285n64; "Intensive Languages," 226–227n7; *Keinmaleins*, 10n1, 11n10, 157, 161, 167, 170n16, 171n31, 174nn54–55, 180, 196n86, 237–241, 253n9, 253nn12–13, 255n29; *95 Theses on Philology*, 2–3, 5, 10nn2–3, 11n17, 155, 168, 169n8, 174n58; "Other Pains," 252n6; *Pleroma*, 240–241, 251; "Die Sekunde der Inversion," 79n17, 124n26, 169n7

heart, 75–76, 112–113, 199, 121, 139, 143, 158, 191, 256, 300; heartbeat, 50; heartwall, 71
Hegel, G. W. F., 240–241, 251, 296–297
Heidegger, Martin, 1, 3–4, 9, 11n9, 93, 144, 156, 161–164, 170n18, 171n30, 172–173n41, 173n46, 188, 193–194n46, 194n48, 261–262, 267–279, 283n36, 284n50, 296–297; "The Anaximander Fragment," 172–173n41; *Being and Time*, 271–273, 276, 284n50; *Introduction to Metaphysics*, 188; "The Origin of the Work of Art," 193–194n46, 268; "The Principle of Identity," 194n48; "Was ist das–die Philosophie?," 267–270, 283n36; "What Are Poets For?," 173n46; *What Is Called Thinking?*, 161, 171n30, 296–297; "What Is Metaphysics?," 296
hermeneutics, 4, 36, 53n8, 142–143
Hesiod, 153–155, 158, 163–164, 167–168, 168n1, 171n21
history, 5, 35–38, 42–44, 47, 49–52, 84–89, 91–93, 95–100, 103n40, 103–104n52, 105n76, 209–210, 225, 236, 239, 241, 253n10, 254n22, 290, 294, 296, 298–299, 301–302
Hölderlin, Friedrich, 62, 114, 124n26, 200, 300
Husserl, Edmund, 4, 11n10, 48–50, 56n56, 57n65

imagination, 62–65, 69, 72, 76, 78n5, 81n35

Jewish, 22, 27, 54n43, 54n46, 84, 95–98, 101n3, 191, 228n45, 282n22, 292–294, 297–298

justice, 93, 131, 162–164, 168, 170n12, 172–173n41

Kafka, Franz, 103–104n52, 206, 241, 253n13, 255n28
Kant, Immanuel, 6, 62–63, 65

Lacan, Jacques, 291
Lacoue-Labarthe, Philippe, 1
Levinas, Emmanuel, 4, 57n60

Mandelstam, Ossip, 9, 49–50, 116, 119–120, 125n45, 179, 261–263, 265–268, 272–278, 280, 280n7, 281n12, 281n15, 282n29, 283n35, 293
memory/remembrance, 36–38, 47, 49, 51, 54n33, 55n43, 55n46, 55–56n48, 56n55, 64, 84, 88–89, 91–94, 105n76, 111, 134–135, 140–141, 181, 190–191, 200, 205–206, 208, 212–213, 217–218, 220–221, 225–226, 226n5, 245, 263, 293, 295–296, 299–302
meridian, 6, 16–23, 25–26, 28–29, 33n29, 100, 177, 196n84
Merleau-Ponty, Maurice, 50, 57n69
mimesis, 7, 9, 37, 65, 84, 89–93, 96–98, 100, 138, 287–297, 299, 301–302; mimetic desire, 287–297, 299, 301–302
music, 5, 48–49, 57n65, 85, 109–121, 122n6, 124n25, 124n27, 124n30, 131, 134–136, 139, 141–144. *See also* song

Nancy, Jean-Luc, 7, 129
nature, 3, 5–7, 61–77, 84–100, 101n3, 217, 225. *See also* flower

nothing/nothingness, 26–27, 62–65, 67–68, 77, 79n18, 158–159, 165–165, 167, 225n26, 254n18, 298

occupiability (*Besetzbarkeit*), 8, 189, 199, 201–210, 212–213, 217–218, 220–222, 225–226, 273–274, 288, 293

paronomasia, 7, 91, 112–113, 118
Parmenides, 1, 7–8, 154, 156–168, 168–169n5, 170n12, 170–171nn18–22, 171n27, 171–172n32, 172n34, 172n38, 173n43
perception, 36, 38, 41–42, 49–51, 62–63, 176–177, 180, 182–186, 225, 235, 269, 272, 277, 299
phenomenology, 38, 48–50, 56n56, 57n63, 57m69, 277
philology/philological, 1–5, 10, 235, 251, 253n10, 255n29
position/positionality, 4–5, 8–9, 167, 203–205, 207, 233–235, 237, 239–241, 244, 255n29

radio, 261–266, 274–275, 278, 281n12
reference/referentiality, 6, 61, 65, 67, 72–73, 83, 233–234, 238, 241, 243–244, 255n29
Resnais, Alain (*Night and Fog*), 35, 43, 51–52, 52n2
Rousseau, Jean-Jacques, 6, 62, 63–65, 69, 81n38

Sachs, Nelly, 116, 125n42
Scarry, Elaine, 62–57, 69, 76–77, 78n3, 81n35
Scheler, Max, 289
Schiller, Friedrich, 53, 235
Schönberg, Arnold, 114–116, 118, 125n42

Schröder, Rudolf Alexander, 292, 295, 297–298
shame, 8–9, 231–233, 236–238, 240–251, 252n6, 253n8, 255n28, 255n29
shibboleth, 121, 299–301
Shoah, 31n14, 35, 37, 43–44, 47, 49, 51–52, 87, 92, 101n3, 103n40, 103–104n52, 134–135, 140, 221, 228n45, 282nn21–22, 293
silence (*Schweigen/Verschweigen*), 4, 8, 36, 55n46, 56n48, 85, 93, 95, 97–98, 100, 115–116, 118, 121, 130, 132, 134, 136–137, 140–142, 156, 162, 165, 168, 169n11, 176–183, 186, 188, 191, 192n7, 231–237, 278, 297
Solla, Gianluca, 22–23, 32n20
song (*Lied*), 7, 110–121, 123–124n22, 141–143. *See also* music
Spitzer, Leo, 289
stone, 6–7, 73–77, 85–86, 89–93, 97–98, 100, 178, 180–182, 184–188, 212–213, 299–300
survival/*survivre*, 132, 134, 140, 142–144, 232, 226n5, 241, 245, 251, 254n13, 255n28
Szondi, Peter, 1, 5–6, 37, 42–43, 52n4, 54n33, 72, 74–75, 101n4, 122n6, 254n22

threshold, 1, 7–8, 127–129, 131–132, 134, 153–174, 264–266
translation, 5, 9, 30, 52n2, 57n63, 125n45, 137, 199–204, 207, 209–210, 221, 226n5, 226–227nn7–8, 232, 247–251, 255n30, 259–263, 266–269, 274–280, 280n7, 281n15, 282n31, 291, 294, 302; and Babel, 200–201, 226n5

Valéry, Paul, 259, 277–279, 280n7

Wills, David, 7, 136–137, 140–141
with/withness, 6, 8, 29–30, 35–52, 175–191, 238–239

witness, 22–23, 31n14, 36–38
Wolfe, Thomas, 247–251, 255n27, 255n30

www.ingramcontent.com/pod-product-compliance
Lightning Source LLC
Chambersburg PA
CBHW031706230426
43668CB00006B/124